IFIP Advances in Information and Communication Technology 778

IFIP Advances in Information and Communication Technology

The IFIP AICT series publishes state-of-the-art results in the sciences and technologies of information and communication. The scope of the series includes: foundations of computer science; software theory and practice; education; computer applications in technology; communication systems; systems modeling and optimization; information systems; ICT and society; computer systems technology; security and protection in information processing systems; artificial intelligence; and human-computer interaction.

Edited volumes and proceedings of refereed international conferences in computer science and interdisciplinary fields are featured. These results often precede journal publication and represent the most current research.

The principal aim of the IFIP AICT series is to encourage education and the dissemination and exchange of information about all aspects of computing.

Amany Elbanna · Marijn Janssen ·
Yogesh K. Dwivedi · Mohammad Hossain ·
Anna Sigridur Islind
Editors

Digital Adoption, Diffusion and Innovation in the Augmented and Digital Society

23rd IFIP WG 8.6 International Working Conference on Transfer and Diffusion of IT, TDIT 2025
Jakarta, Indonesia, September 2–4, 2025
Proceedings, Part I

Springer

Editors
Amany Elbanna
University of Sussex
Brighton, UK

Marijn Janssen
Delft University of Technology
Delft, The Netherlands

Yogesh K. Dwivedi
King Fahd University of Petroleum
and Minerals
Dhahran, Saudi Arabia

Mohammad Hossain
RMIT University
Melbourne, VIC, Australia

Anna Sigridur Islind
Reykjavik University
Reykjavik, Iceland

ISSN 1868-4238 ISSN 1868-422X (electronic)
IFIP Advances in Information and Communication Technology
ISBN 978-3-032-16774-3 ISBN 978-3-032-16775-0 (eBook)
https://doi.org/10.1007/978-3-032-16775-0

This Springer imprint is published by the registered company Springer Nature Switzerland AG
The registered company address is: Gewerbestrasse 11, 6330 Cham, Switzerland

Preface

The boundaries between physical and digital worlds are becoming increasingly porous, as advanced technologies continually augment, simulate, and transform our lived experiences. This convergence is not simply a technical evolution but a profound socio-technical shift. With digital infrastructures becoming more interconnected and data-driven, they now enable unprecedented levels of data collection, integration, processing, and application across diverse contexts-spanning commerce, governance, education, health care, transportation, and personal life.

These advancements open vast opportunities for innovation, efficiency gains, and new forms of value creation, yet they also introduce significant complexities and risks. Organizations of all types are under pressure to adapt their strategies, infrastructures, and cultures to leverage emerging technologies while safeguarding against operational, ethical, and societal harms. This technological momentum is reshaping organizational dynamics, disrupting established hierarchies and workflows, altering management and decision-making practices, and redefining professional domains. It raises many research problems, including understanding the drivers and barriers to adoption, identifying effective pathways for technology transfer, and examining the interplay between innovation, regulation, and societal trust.

In shaping an augmented and digital society, it is critical that technological innovation is guided by societal, organizational, and individual priorities and values rather than purely market-driven imperatives. Research plays a key role not only in diagnosing emerging tensions and opportunities but also in providing conceptual, methodological, and evidence-based frameworks to steer the diffusion of digital innovations toward resilient, ethical, and sustainable outcomes.

Aligned with these challenges and priorities, this book presents papers that have been presented and discussed in the 2025 conference of the International Federation of Information Processing Working Group 8.6 (IFIP WG8.6). The IFIP Working Group 8.6 aims to foster understanding and enhance research on the adoption, transfer, and diffusion of information and communication technology—spanning practices, methods, and techniques used during and after technology development through to implementation and use. Since its inception, IFIP WG8.6 has focused on IT transfer, diffusion, and implementation at individual, organizational, and societal levels, welcoming contributions from all research paradigms and methods. The conference was held online and was hosted by Binus University in Jakarta, Indonesia. We are grateful to Binus University and the local organising team for their commitment and effort in organising the conference. The conference followed a virtuous double-blind reviewing process to develop papers and direct authors to other types of submissions when the criteria of full-papers were not met. This volume comprises 44 full-length and short papers representing 93 authors from 14 countries. The conference received 187 papers, and the acceptance rate was close to 24%. The book is a post-conference publication where authors had the opportunity to develop their papers based on the discussion during the conference.

Best paper awards were introduced for both short and full papers, with six papers nominated in total. The committee selected one winner in each category. The **Short Best Paper Award** was presented to *"From Strategy to Oversight: Navigating AI Accounting and Governance in FinTech"* by **Ahmad Juma'H**. The **Best Paper Award** went to *"Beyond the Visible: Harnessing Dark Data Ethically for Strategic Advantage"* by **Hanlie Smuts, Danielle Badenhorst, Nicolle Abrahams, and Eugene van der Merwe**. Congratulations to all authors for their outstanding contributions!

The 2025 IFIP conference featured the distinguished keynote speaker, Prof. H. Raghav Rao. His keynote lectures offered deep theoretical insights and practical implications on prompt design for Large Language Models. A brief abstract of the lecture is included in this volume.

This book is organised into seven parts to reflect the themes of the conference and papers. Part One includes papers that examine digital government, public services and society. Part Two includes papers that address digital entrepreneurship and innovation. Part Three presents papers that discuss the adoption of intelligent systems and technologies in different contexts. Part Four includes papers that examine the recent developments in data and digital transformations. Part Five includes papers that investigate the AI ethics in different context including health care. Part Six presents papers on digital security and safety while the final Part includes papers on AI in Marketing and consumer behaviour.

Events like these cannot be staged without collaboration and support. Thank you to the contributing authors, peer reviewers, presenters, and track chairs, program co-chairs, and IFIP 8.6 Executive Committee. Our meeting would not have been possible without the support of Prof. Kevin Deniswara and the hard work of Dr. Darusalam Darusalam and all members of the local organising team. A special thanks must also be given to the IFIP 8.6 members and authors for their resilience and rising to the different challenges of making this conference a success despite the global circumstances. It is remarkable to experience the continued growth and development of this international conference. We hope that our meeting and the collection of papers included in these proceedings progress our understanding of the diverse, complex, and uncertain context of the adoption and diffusion of technology and inspire further research.

October 2025

Amany Elbanna
Marijn Janssen
Yogesh K. Dwivedi
Mohammad Hossain
Anna Sigridur Islind

Organization

General Chairs

Deborah Bunker	University of Sydney, Australia
Kevin Deniswara	Binus University, Indonesia
Jamaliah Said	Universiti Teknologi MARA, Malaysia
David Wastell	University of Nottingham, UK

Conference Chairs

Marijn Janssen	Delft University of Technology, The Netherlands
Amany Elbanna	The University of Sussex, UK
Yogesh K. Dwivedi	King Fahd University of Petroleum and Minerals, KSA

Programme Chairs

Amany Elbanna	The University of Sussex, UK
Anna Sigridur Islind	Reykjavik University, Iceland
Mohammad Alamgir Hossain	RMIT University, Australia

Local Organising Chairs

Darusalam Darusalam	Binus University, Indonesia
Tommy Andrian	Binus University, Indonesia
Michael Angelus S. E.	Binus University, Indonesia
Archie Nathanael Mulyawan	Binus University, Indonesia

Program Committee

Alvedi Sabani	RMIT University, Australia
Amany Elbanna	University of Sussex, UK
Amjad, Fayoumi	Lancaster University, UK
Anthon Manfreda	University of Ljubljana, Slovenia

Arpan Kar	Indian Institute of Technology Delhi, India
Ayomikun Idowu	University of Sussex, UK
Brian Donnellan	Maynooth University, Ireland
Brian Fitzgerald	University of Limerick, Ireland
Darusalam Darusalam	Binus University, Indonesia
David Wastell	University of Nottingham, UK
Debora Bunker	University of Sydney, Australia
Denis Dennehy	Swansea University, UK
Emmanuel Ayaburi	Baylor University, USA
Gaurav Gupta	NEOMA Business School, France
Helena Vallo Hult	University West, Sweden
Helle Zinner Henriksen	Copenhagen Business School, Denmark
John Oredo	University of Nairobi, Kenya
Jun Zhang	The University of Sheffield, UK
Kamranv Mahroof	University of Bradford, UK
Karlheinz Kautz	RMIT University, Australia
Lorraine Morgan	University of Galway, Ireland
Marijn Janssen	Technology University of Delft, Netherland
Markus Nuettgens	University Hamburg, Germany
Maryam Shahbazi	The University of Sydney, Australia
Mohammad Hossain	RMIT University, Australia
Panos Panagiotopoulos	Queen Mary University of London, UK
Peter Bednar	University of Portsmouth, UK
Sachithra Lokuge	University of Southern Queensland, Australia
Savvas Papagiannidis	Newcastle University, UK
Steven Alter	University of San Francisco, USA
Sujeet Kumar Sharma	Indian Institute of Management Nagpur, India
Ulrika Lundh Snis	University West, Sweden
Yogesh K. Dwivedi	King Fahd University of Petroleum and Minerals, KSA
Zainah Qasem	The University of Jordan, Jordan

Contents

Digital Government, Public Services and Society

Decoding Digital Adoption in India's Data Exchange DPI: A Framework-Based Adoption Study of DigiLocker

Shahrish Khan[1](✉), Gayatri Doctor[1], Ameya A. Naik[2], and Mathews P. Joseph[3]

[1] CEPT University, Ahmedabad, India
shahrishkhan21@gmail.com, gayatri.doctor@cept.ac.in
[2] ODI Global, London, UK
[3] Egov Foundation, Bangalore, India
mathews.p@egovernments.org

Abstract. Building digital infrastructure is no longer the challenge, ensuring its meaningful use is. In the age of digital transformation, the true test of digital public services lies not in their technical deployment, but in their societal adoption. This paper investigates India's DigiLocker, an ambitious data exchange Digital Public Infrastructure (DPI) that allows citizens to access, store, and share verified documents seamlessly. Despite its robust architecture, DigiLocker's potential hinges on public trust, behavioural intent to use, and actual usage.

To decode these adoption dynamics, this study introduces an adapted assessment framework inspired by the Unified Theory of Acceptance and Use of Technology (UTAUT), reimagined for data exchange platforms. Through a survey-based analysis of key stakeholders, the research evaluates the influence of factors like social norms, performance expectations, privacy concerns, and voluntariness on user behaviour.

Findings reveal that while ease of use and institutional mandates support adoption, voluntary engagement and user confidence remain limited. Issuers, meanwhile, report technical and administrative constraints that hinder proactive participation. By applying the UTAUT model to both user and institutional perspectives, this research offers a holistic understanding of adoption barriers and enablers in the context of DigiLocker. The research contributes to the growing discourse on inclusive digital transformation and provides a framework for evaluating DPI adoption in emerging and advanced digital societies alike.

Keywords: Digital Public Infrastructure (DPI) · Data Exchange DPI · Digital Trust and Adoption

1 Introduction

In today's increasingly interconnected and data-driven world, Digital Public Infrastructure (DPI) has emerged as a crucial enabler of inclusive, transparent, and efficient digital societies [1]. DPI refers to foundational digital systems that are open, interoperable, and

Published by Springer Nature Switzerland AG 2026
A. Elbanna et al. (Eds.): TDIT 2025, IFIP AICT 778, pp. 3–21, 2026.
https://doi.org/10.1007/978-3-032-16775-0_1

secure, designed to support essential public services at scale [2]. These infrastructures empower governments and institutions to deliver digital services that enhance financial accessibility, governance efficiency, and data security while placing citizens at the centre of service design and delivery [3]. Among countries leading this transformation, India has positioned itself as a global pioneer in DPI, achieving remarkable progress by implementing world-class infrastructure for digital identity (Aadhaar), financial transactions (Unified Payments Interface, UPI), and data sharing (DigiLocker). Together, these systems have not only revolutionized service accessibility and economic participation but have also established a global benchmark for scalable digital transformation [2].

While the rapid and widespread adoption of digital identity and payment infrastructures has transformed the way citizens access public and financial services, the third critical layer of consent-based data exchange is now emerging as a strategic priority in the global digital landscape [4]. Data exchange infrastructures play a pivotal role in breaking down information silos, promoting interoperability across government and private entities, and ensuring secure, citizen-controlled data sharing. In an era where concerns around data privacy, security, and surveillance are intensifying, ensuring that individuals retain control over their personal information while navigating increasingly complex digital ecosystems has become imperative [5].

In India, the Consent-Based Data Exchange Layer is facilitated by DigiLocker, a national platform that enables citizens to securely store and share digitally verified documents with service providers in a transparent, efficient, and tamper-proof manner [6]. As a key component of India's DPI architecture, DigiLocker has the potential to streamline public services, reduce reliance on paper-based processes, and empower individuals with greater agency over their personal data [7]. While DigiLocker has achieved significant operational milestones, its adoption growth seems to have followed a steadier pace relative to the rapid scaling observed in platforms like Aadhaar and UPI.

Even more than a decade after its introduction, large portions of document authentication and data exchange in India continue to rely on traditional methods such as physical paperwork, attested photocopies, and unverified scanned documents. This adoption lag underscores a crucial challenge in India's digital journey while infrastructure has been built and technological readiness exists, societal acceptance and behavioural adoption of data exchange platforms like DigiLocker remain uneven.

This research paper responds to this challenge by examining the adoption dynamics of DigiLocker as India's Data Exchange DPI. Recognizing the need for a nuanced, citizen-centric perspective on platform adoption the study proposes a framework-based adoption assessment adapted from the Unified Theory of Acceptance and Use of Technology (UTAUT). Through a user survey and analytical assessment, the research investigates how factors such as performance expectancy, social influence, voluntariness, and privacy concerns shape adoption behaviour in the context of DigiLocker. In doing so, the paper aims to contribute to a deeper understanding of the social, behavioural, and institutional drivers that enable or hinder the diffusion of data exchange infrastructures, offering insights that are both nationally significant and globally transferable in an era of rapid digital transformation.

2 DigiLocker: India's Consent-Based Data Exchange Platform

2.1 Introduction to DigiLocker

DigiLocker is a flagship initiative by the Government of India aimed at fostering a paperless, digitally empowered society by enabling the storage and exchange of authenticated digital documents. Operated under the Digital India program by the Ministry of Electronics and Information Technology (MeitY), DigiLocker serves as a secure, cloud-based platform where citizens can store, access, and share digital versions of critical documents such as Aadhaar cards, driving licenses, academic certificates, insurance policies, and more [6]. The platform is legally recognized under the Information Technology (Preservation and Retention of Information by Intermediaries Providing Digital Locker Facilities) Rules, 2016, which grants digital documents the same legal validity as physical ones [8] (Fig. 1).

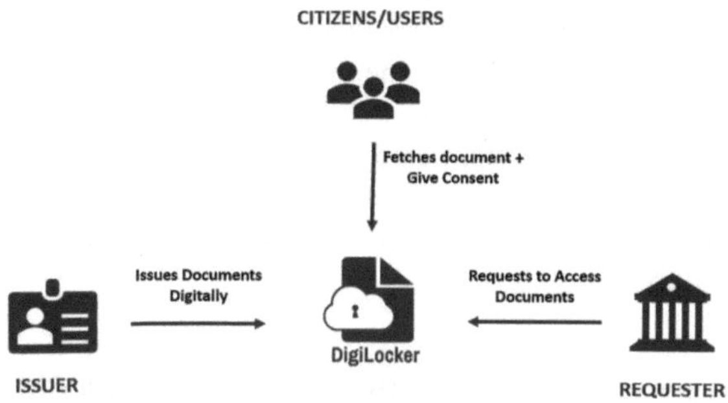

Fig. 1. DigiLocker ecosystem; Source: [6]

DigiLocker not only facilitates direct issuance of documents by partner institutions but also enables secure sharing through an embedded consent mechanism. Integrated with India's Digital Public Infrastructure (DPI) and aligned with the principles of the Data Empowerment and Protection Architecture (DEPA), it embodies a citizen-centric model of data exchange [9]. Through APIs and authentication layers, it connects with government agencies, financial institutions, and educational bodies, ensuring a seamless, efficient, and secure document verification process. With more than 448 million registered users and over 9.25 billion documents issued as of February 2025, DigiLocker is a cornerstone in India's journey toward inclusive and trusted digital governance [6].

DigiLocker operates on a secure, structured framework focused on ease of use, data privacy, and document authenticity. Users register through Aadhaar-linked OTP verification to access their digital locker, where they can either manually upload documents or receive them directly from integrated issuing authorities.

The platform supports a dual document system officially issued documents from bodies like Central Board of Secondary Education (CBSE), Unique Identification Authority of India (UIDAI), Regional Transport Offices (RTOs), and the Income Tax Department ensure legal validity and tamper-proof records, while manual uploads allow storage of personal scanned files, expanding its utility.

Verification is enabled through an API-based system, allowing organizations to instantly verify documents without physical paperwork, thereby reducing fraud and simplifying processes like admissions and job applications. Importantly, DigiLocker follows a consent-based model, where users control access. Documents are shared only upon user approval, and in encrypted form ensuring data security and compliance with privacy standards.

2.2 Framing the Adoption Challenge

While DigiLocker has evolved into a critical component of India's Digital Public Infrastructure, its impact ultimately hinges on sustained and meaningful user adoption. Despite operational maturity and a robust legal-technological foundation, the platform's integration into everyday citizen use remains uneven. A significant proportion of document verification and data exchange processes in India still rely on traditional methods, revealing a persistent behavioural and institutional gap.

To understand what enables or hinders the adoption of DigiLocker, it is essential to move beyond technical design and examine the socio-psychological and infrastructural factors that shape user engagement. This calls for a structured analytical framework capable of capturing both individual perceptions and broader contextual influences. In response to this need, the following section adopts the Unified Theory of Acceptance and Use of Technology (UTAUT) as a guiding model to systematically assess adoption behaviour in the context of DigiLocker.

3 Theoretical Framework: Unified Theory of Acceptance and Use of Technology (UTAUT)

To investigate the adoption dynamics of DigiLocker, this study applies the Unified Theory of Acceptance and Use of Technology (UTAUT) model as the foundational analytical framework. The UTAUT model synthesizes and integrates key constructs from eight prominent models in the field of information systems and behavioural sciences, including the Technology Acceptance Model (TAM), Theory of Reasoned Action (TRA), Theory of Planned Behaviour (TPB), Innovation Diffusion Theory (IDT), and Social Cognitive Theory (SCT) [10]. Its purpose is to provide a comprehensive explanation of user intentions and actual usage behaviour of technology systems.

The original UTAUT model identifies four core determinants of intention and usage:

- **Performance Expectancy**: The degree to which an individual believes that using the system will help them attain gains in job or task performance.
- **Effort Expectancy**: The perceived ease of use associated with the system.
- **Social Influence**: The degree to which individuals perceive that important other (e.g., family, peers, colleagues, institutions) believe they should use the new system.
- **Facilitating Conditions**: The degree to which users perceive that an adequate organizational and technical infrastructure exists to support system usage [10].

These core constructs are moderated by four individual difference variables: gender, age, experience, and voluntariness of use. The UTAUT model is widely recognized for its empirical robustness, having demonstrated significantly higher explanatory power for user intention and behaviour compared to earlier individual models (Fig. 2).

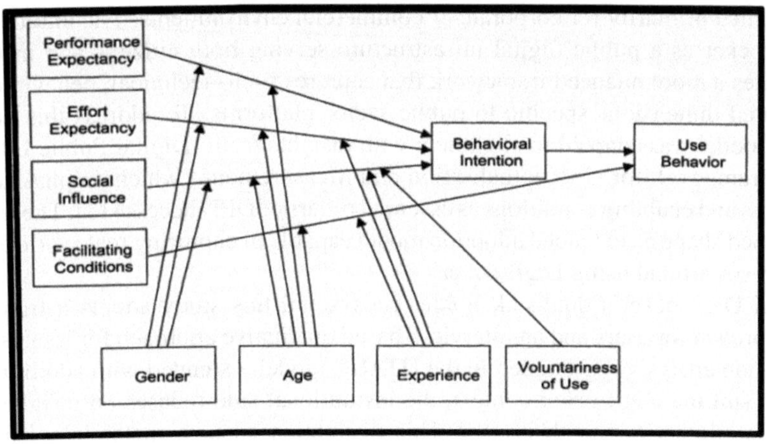

Fig. 2. Unified theory of acceptance and use of technology (UTAUT) model; Source: [10]

3.1 Why UTAUT for Assessing DigiLocker Adoption?

The choice of UTAUT as the theoretical lens for this study is both strategic and contextually appropriate. DigiLocker, as a public-facing data exchange platform, exists in a complex socio-technical environment where user perception, institutional influence, and regulatory mandates converge. UTAUT is particularly suitable for this context for several reasons:

Comprehensive Integration of Behavioural Drivers: Unlike simpler models that rely on one or two behavioural predictors (e.g., perceived usefulness in TAM), UTAUT captures a more nuanced landscape of technology adoption by integrating multiple psychological, organizational, and contextual factors. This holistic perspective aligns with the multifaceted nature of digital public services like DigiLocker, where usability, social norms, data privacy, and infrastructural support all play interdependent roles.

Adaptability to Public Sector and Voluntary-Mandatory Contexts: DigiLocker operates in both voluntary and quasi-mandatory use environments e.g., when academic institutions or government portals require its use for document submission. UTAUT accounts for voluntariness as a moderating factor, making it well-suited to examine user adoption in such hybrid settings, unlike earlier models which were primarily developed for private-sector contexts.

Empirical Strength and Validation: UTAUT has been widely validated across domains, including government services, education, healthcare, and e-governance platforms. Its consistent ability to explain a high percentage of variance in behavioural intention and usage lends it a robust empirical foundation, making it a reliable tool for assessing national-level platforms like DigiLocker.

3.2 Modified Framework for DigiLocker Adoption

While the original Unified Theory of Acceptance and Use of Technology (UTAUT) provides a robust foundation for understanding user behaviour toward new technologies, it was designed primarily for corporate or commercial environments. The unique context of DigiLocker as a public digital infrastructure serving both citizens and institutions necessitates a more nuanced framework that captures socio-technical, behavioural, and trust-related dimensions specific to public sector platforms. To address this need, the UTAUT model was adapted in alignment with insights from 'Digital Public Infrastructure: A Framework for Conceptualisation and Measurement,' which emphasizes trust, inclusivity, and enabling conditions as essential pillars of DPI success [11]. These dimensions helped shape an extended adoption model capable of capturing real-world attitudes and concerns around using DigiLocker.

Given DigiLocker's dual-stakeholder ecosystem, this study adopts a framework-based approach for users and an interview-based qualitative approach for issuers. While the user-side analysis is grounded in the UTAUT model, extended with additional constructs to suit the DigiLocker context, the institutional side focuses on insights drawn from expert interviews with issuers. This distinction ensures methodological alignment with the available data, enabling deeper behavioural analysis for users and richer contextual understanding of institutional adoption dynamics.

3.3 Users' Adoption Model

For citizens, the adoption of DigiLocker goes beyond functional convenience; it also involves digital trust, perceived security, and individual confidence with technology. The user-specific model retains the four foundational UTAUT constructs of Performance Expectancy (perceived usefulness), Effort Expectancy (ease of use), Social Influence (peer and institutional encouragement), and Facilitating Conditions (technical and institutional support).

However, several key modifications were made to better reflect users' realities:

Self-Efficacy replaces the demographic variable "Gender" as a more meaningful moderator. In the context of digital public services, the user's confidence in navigating digital platforms (e.g., managing documents, responding to consent requests) is a stronger predictor of behavioural intent than demographic attributes. This construct is especially relevant in a country like India, where digital literacy levels vary significantly.

Data Security is added as a new construct, reflecting increasing public concern about digital privacy, surveillance, and data misuse. For DigiLocker to be meaningfully adopted, users must trust that their sensitive documents are safe from unauthorized access. This construct influences both Social Influence and Facilitating Conditions.

Anxiety is introduced as another key construct to capture psychological barriers. Even when users perceive DigiLocker to be useful, anxiety related to navigating digital interfaces or the fear of "something wrong" can significantly hinder adoption. This construct indirectly affects both effort expectancy and self-efficacy.

Voluntariness of Use is maintained as a moderator, reflecting the spectrum of experiences from optional use (personal storage) to mandated use (submission of credentials

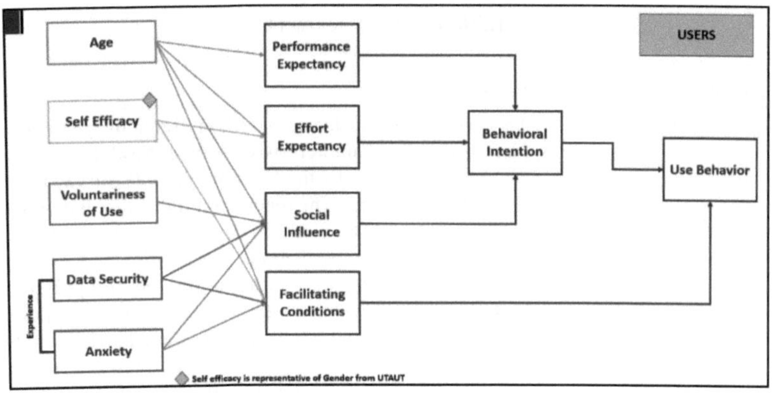

Fig. 3. Adapted framework to study DigiLocker adoption

for admissions or employment). Along with Age, these moderators help account for variability in adoption across demographic groups and usage contexts (Fig. 3).

By integrating these constructs, the user model provides a more holistic view of the cognitive, emotional, and infrastructural factors influencing DigiLocker adoption among the general population.

This combined approach allows for a comprehensive understanding of DigiLocker adoption across its ecosystem, capturing individual behavioural drivers through the adapted user-side UTAUT model and uncovering organizational and systemic enablers through qualitative insights from institutional stakeholders. Together, these methods offer a more holistic perspective on adoption dynamics and extend the applicability of the UTAUT framework to the context of public digital infrastructures like DigiLocker.

4 Research Methodology

To examine the factors influencing DigiLocker adoption, this study adopted a mixed-method research design, combining quantitative surveys with qualitative interviews. This dual approach enabled a comprehensive understanding of both measurable trends and contextual insights, particularly relevant in the evaluation of Digital Public Infrastructure (DPI).

4.1 Target Segments

In alignment with DigiLocker's dual-stakeholder structure, the research focused on three distinct user segments: individual users (citizens), institutional stakeholders (issuers/requesters) and the DigiLocker Team. Each group plays a critical role in the adoption ecosystem of DigiLocker and faces unique motivational and infrastructural challenges (Table 1).

Table 1. Target segment

Target segment	Reasoning
Users (Ages 18–30 years)	This segment was selected based on digital usage trends identified in the Comprehensive Annual Modular Survey (CAMS) conducted by the National Sample Survey Office (NSSO) in 2022–23. The report highlights that individuals between the ages of 18 and 30 demonstrate the highest levels of digital engagement, particularly in activities such as data sharing, document management, and digital transactions [12]. Given their high digital literacy, this group was considered best positioned to provide insights into both the enablers and barriers of DigiLocker adoption. Targeting this segment also allowed the study to assess behavioural responses from digitally fluent users who might be expected to engage more easily with platforms like DigiLocker. The findings from this demographic provide important clues for improving user experience design and policy targeting
Issuers/Requesters (Universities)	Universities were selected as the institutional segment due to their strategic importance within the DigiLocker ecosystem. Following government mandates requiring all higher education institutions to issue digital academic records via the National Academic Depository (NAD) integrated with DigiLocker, the education sector has witnessed a substantial rise in participation. This makes universities ideal candidates for analysing institutional adoption behaviour, policy compliance dynamics, and technology integration at scale. Furthermore, with 90 Crore documents issued, the education sector currently represents the largest category of verified issuers on the platform, contributing significantly to both document volume and outreach. Thus, this segment provides both relevance and richness for institutional analysis. Instead of using a detailed UTAUT-based survey for issuers, interviews were conducted with university representatives. However, the interview questions were designed around key factors from the UTAUT model, ensuring that insights into performance expectancy, effort expectancy, social influence, and facilitating conditions were systematically captured
DigiLocker Team	The third important stakeholder considered in this research was the DigiLocker team itself. To incorporate the service provider's perspective, we conducted interviews with key representatives from the DigiLocker team. These interviews provided valuable insights into the platform's operational challenges, ongoing initiatives, and future plans for enhancing user experience and expanding adoption. Understanding the views of the DigiLocker team helped bridge the gap between user experiences, issuer/requester adoption, and the platform's strategic priorities. Their inputs were crucial in building a comprehensive understanding of the factors influencing the usage and growth of DigiLocker as a Digital Public Infrastructure

4.2 Survey Design and Data Collection

The user survey was structured using the modified UTAUT framework, adapted specifically for the DigiLocker context. It incorporated both the original UTAUT constructs, Performance Expectancy, Effort Expectancy, Social Influence, and Facilitating Conditions and extended constructs reflecting the platform's public and secure nature: Self-Efficacy, Data Security, Anxiety, and Voluntariness of Use.

Each construct was operationalized through multiple Likert-scale statements. Participants were asked to rate their agreement on a 5-point scale ranging from "Strongly Disagree" (1) to "Strongly Agree" (5).

The survey was administered digitally using Google Forms, leveraging its accessibility and ease of distribution through educational networks, social platforms, and email lists. A total of 250 valid responses were utilised for user surveys assessment. Responses were screened for completeness and consistency, with invalid or duplicate entries removed to ensure data quality.

4.3 Data Analysis Methodology

Survey responses were converted into numerical scores and aggregated to calculate average values for each construct. Based on these averages, adoption factors were classified into:

- **Supportive (≥ 3.5)**
- **Neutral (2.5 - 3.4)**
- **Barriers (< 2.5)**

This enabled a structured interpretation of drivers and inhibitors of adoption. Results were visualized through comparative bar charts.

4.4 Qualitative Interviews and Contextual Insights

To complement the quantitative findings, semi-structured interviews were conducted with representatives from universities registered on the NAD-DigiLocker system. These interviews aimed to uncover the institutional perspective on DigiLocker adoption capturing motivations, challenges, operational experiences, and policy alignment. Each interview was conducted either in person or via telephonic call.

The interview protocol was aligned with the modified UTAUT model for institutions, exploring constructs such as institutional Self-Efficacy (e.g., IT readiness, resource availability), Data Security (e.g., concerns around student records and access), Voluntariness (e.g., compliance versus choice), and Performance Expectancy (e.g., impact on academic administration). These discussions provided nuanced insights into regulatory, infrastructural, and cultural factors shaping institutional behaviours.

By combining structured survey data with expert interviews, this research employed a holistic approach to understand DigiLocker's adoption dynamics. The quantitative strand captured broad trends and statistically significant patterns, while the qualitative strand provided depth, context, and interpretive richness. Together, they enabled the formulation of grounded insights that reflect the realities of users and institutions operating within a DPI ecosystem.

5 Adoption Insights from Users

5.1 User Survey Insights: Patterns, Preferences, and Barriers

The user survey conducted for this study offers a multifaceted view of DigiLocker adoption. While awareness of DigiLocker is high, deeper analysis reveals key gaps between registration, use, and long-term engagement (Fig. 4).

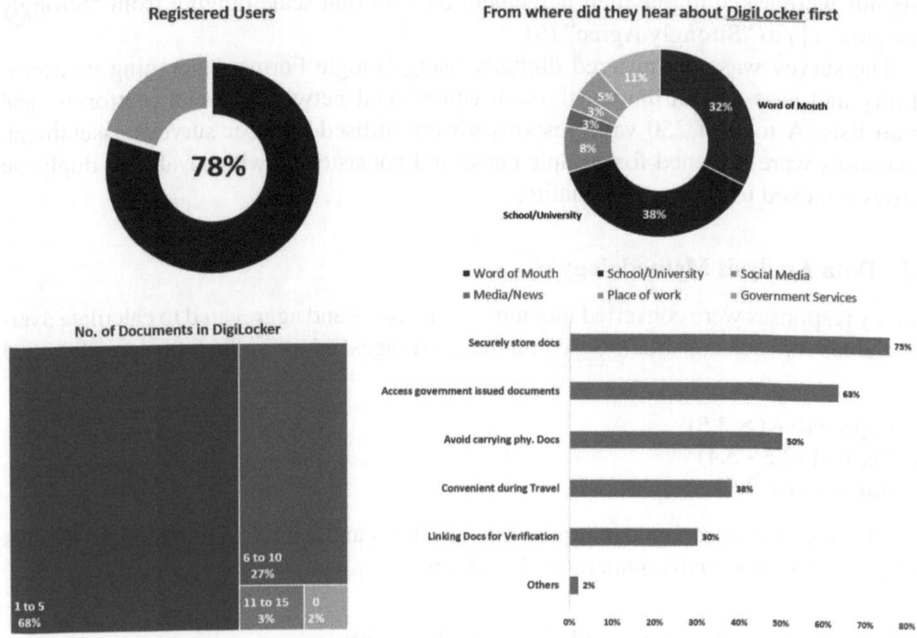

Fig. 4. Adoption insights from user survey

Awareness and Use: Awareness of DigiLocker is nearly universal among respondents, with schools (38%) and word-of-mouth via family and friends (32%) being the most cited sources. However, only 78% had registered on the platform, indicating that recognition doesn't always translate to onboarding. This discrepancy points to the importance of demand-side motivators, such as institutional requests or service linkages.

Usage Patterns and Document Storage: Among registered users, 68% store between 1 to 5 documents, and 27% store between 6 to 10, suggesting limited but specific use cases. Fetch rates reflect this pattern: Aadhaar is the most fetched document (95%), followed by PAN (68%), Class X/XII certificates (79%), and Driving Licenses and Academic Bank of Credits ID (43% each). This implies that DigiLocker is currently used primarily for identity and academic documentation.

Feature Use and Platform Perception: The core document storage feature is widely used (85%), but advanced functionalities like My Consent (20%), DigiLocker Drive (28%), and QR Scanner (15%) see limited engagement. Nominee and Activity Log features are almost unused. This pattern indicates that while DigiLocker has successfully positioned itself as a digital document repository, its potential as an interoperable data-sharing platform remains underutilized. This also reflects limited awareness and perceived necessity among users for engaging with these broader functionalities.

Purposes of Use: The most common use case (75%) is secure document storage, followed by accessing government-issued documents (63%) and avoiding carrying physical documents (50%). Lower usage for verification (30%) and travel (38%) suggests underutilization of the platform's broader capabilities.

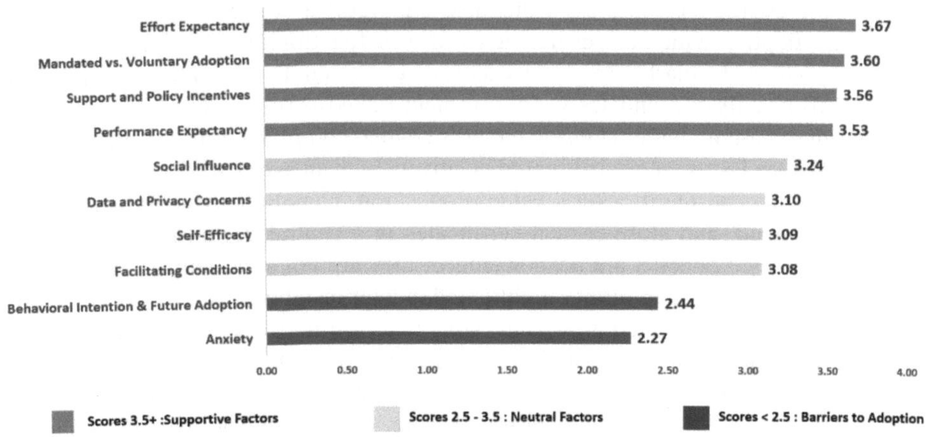

Fig. 5. Adoption drivers and barriers-DigiLocker

5.2 Adoption Drivers and Barriers

The visual summary of adoption assessment in Fig. 5 provides a clear lens into how different factors are influencing the usage and perception of DigiLocker among surveyed users. The coloured bars group the factors into three broad categories: supportive(green), neutral(yellow), and barriers to adoption(red), helping distil which dimensions are aiding or hindering uptake of the platform.

Effort Expectancy received the highest average score of 3.67, classifying it as a strong supportive factor. This suggests that users overwhelmingly find the DigiLocker platform intuitive and easy to use, and users experienced minimal friction. High ease-of-use perception often translates into greater satisfaction and willingness to reuse a digital service, however when looked collectively with other factors, the ground reality remains different with citizens unwilling to use the platform.

Despite high ratings for ease of use (Effort Expectancy- 3.67) and perceived usefulness (Performance Expectancy - 3.53), actual user preference for DigiLocker over traditional physical documents remains moderate (3.09). This points to a behavioural gap where technological friendliness does not necessarily translate into consistent usage suggesting that users may still lean towards the tangibility and perceived security of physical documents.

Mandated vs. Voluntary Adoption with an average of 3.60 reinforces the observation that much of DigiLocker's current adoption is driven by external mandates such as institutional requirements or government policies. While this might boost numbers, it raises important questions about long-term engagement, especially in the absence of compulsion. Importantly, the data underscores that mandating usage has a significant influence on adoption (Mandated Use- 3.60 compared to Voluntary Use- 3.15). This indicates that adoption rates are likely to increase when institutions such as universities or employers require DigiLocker use, rather than leaving it as an optional tool.

Another influential driver is Support and Policy Incentives (3.56), which indicates that users recognize and respond positively to structural nudges provided by institutions. This factor reflects the effectiveness of top-down policy in scaling digital public infrastructure like DigiLocker. However, this also highlights a concerning gap in organic, bottom-up adoption which is a critical tenet of well-functioning DPI [2]. While DPI is ideally expected to be market-responsive and citizen-driven, DigiLocker's adoption continues to rely heavily on mandates and government-linked use cases. This signals the need to foster more natural, habitual usage patterns beyond compliance-driven interactions.

Performance Expectancy also scored positively with an average of 3.53. This shows that users appreciate DigiLocker's value proposition, namely, access authentic documents on demand, and store critical certificates in a central digital space. However, while the expected benefits are acknowledged, they are not sufficient on their own to drive repeated usage, a gap further highlighted in later insights.

Social Influence averaged 3.24, suggesting that peer networks and family referrals have a modest impact on adoption. Users may learn about DigiLocker from others but do not necessarily feel social pressure to engage with the platform. This indicates that while social channels contribute to awareness (Fig. 4), they may not strongly influence decision-making.

Data and Privacy Concerns (3.10) reflect a balanced sentiment. Users neither strongly distrust nor fully trust the system. While DigiLocker is built on a secure framework, transparency about data usage, encryption, and recourse mechanisms needs strengthening to build greater user confidence and awareness. Concerns related to data security and privacy emerged as significant deterrents. Although not alarmingly high, Privacy Concerns and Third-party access to data without consent (3.10), Fear of Losing Documents (2.05), and Technical Issues (2.20) indicate a trust deficit in the digital medium. These concerns potentially override the functional benefits of DigiLocker for a segment of users.

Self-Efficacy and Facilitating Conditions scored 3.09 and 3.08, respectively. This indicates that while users feel moderately confident in their ability to use DigiLocker it is not yet a strong enough enabler. More guidance, real-time assistance, and integration with offline touchpoints (like helpdesks in colleges or CSCs) could help convert these into stronger supporting factors.

Behavioural Intention & Future Adoption stands at a low 2.44 classifying it as a barrier to adoption. Despite finding the platform useful and easy, users show a lack of willingness to engage with it proactively unless required. This may be due to limited real-life use cases, fragmented service linkages, or lack of compelling reason for regular use. It suggests that current engagement is largely reactive, not habitual, or voluntary. While users may recognize the benefits of DigiLocker, this low intent highlights a need for sustained engagement strategies and stronger value articulation.

Anxiety scored the lowest at 2.27, reinforcing that a segment of users feels uneasy or overwhelmed when interacting with the platform. This may stem from fear of making errors, unfamiliarity with digital verification processes, or concern about potential data misuse. Reducing this digital anxiety through handholding, video walkthroughs, and assurance mechanisms will be key to making the platform more inclusive.

5.3 Summary

Overall, this assessment chart offers a hazy picture: while foundational aspects like ease of use, utility, and policy support are strong, the platform's voluntary engagement levels and user confidence remain weak. While DigiLocker is gradually gaining traction, users remain unconvinced about its long-term utility, revealing a gap between adoption and genuine acceptance. A major bottleneck lies in the lack of proactive involvement from requesters and issuers. Without regular prompts from institutions or seamless document issuance, users have limited motivation to return to the platform (Table 2).

Table 2. Insights from users adoption assessment of DigiLocker

Data result	Inferences
High Ease of Use but Moderate Adoption (Effort & Performance Expectancy)	Effort Expectancy (3.67) and Performance Expectancy (3.53) are among the highest-rated factors, yet the preference for DigiLocker over physical documents is lower (3.09). While DigiLocker is perceived as useful and user-friendly, users may still feel more comfortable with physical document handling
Security & Privacy Concerns Exist	Privacy Concerns- Data used by third-party, (3.10), Fear of losing documents due to technical issues (2.20) are key deterrents
Social Influence (3.24) & Facilitating Conditions (3.08) Are Moderate	Adoption is not heavily influenced by peer pressure or external promotions. Instead, institutional integration and direct issuer involvement may be more impactful since lack of issuer requests (3.63) hinder adoption
Voluntary adoption (3.15) is lower compared to the impact of making it compulsory	Mandatory Usage Drives Adoption (Mandated vs. Voluntary - 3.60). If universities or employers mandated DigiLocker, adoption would increase significantly (3.77–3.88). Voluntary adoption (3.15) is lower compared to the impact of making it compulsory
Future Adoption Intent is Weak (2.44)	Lowest-rated category overall. Users do not strongly intend to use DigiLocker more frequently (2.29) or continue using it in the next 6 months (2.47). While users recognize its benefits, they do not feel compelled to continue using it regularly

6 Insights from Issuers and Requesters

The adoption of DigiLocker by institutional stakeholders, particularly universities as issuers and requesters, reveals several systemic challenges and concerns. These perspectives offer a ground-level view of implementation struggles and the operational bottlenecks that can hinder long-term platform integration. Few key insights on challenges they face are discussed below.

Technical and Operational Barriers: Universities highlighted frequent technical errors and API integration failures, resulting in unreliable system performance. The platform is perceived as not readily adaptable to varying workflows and document formats used across different institutions. Institutions reported high error rates (25–50%) during document uploads, leading to inefficiencies and portal downtime, which further disrupts smooth operations.

Lack of Flexibility: Issuers face rigid compliance requirements, especially around document formats and metadata structures. There is limited flexibility in the format of certificates that can be issued, which restricts university autonomy and makes the system feel overly prescriptive. The data upload process is also viewed as lengthy and cumbersome, discouraging proactive use.

Administrative Burdens: Institutions struggle to keep up with frequent format changes, making it difficult to maintain consistency. Moreover, significant internal changes are required at the university level before documents can be issued via DigiLocker, creating a resource-intensive administrative burden that adds to resistance.

Limited Support and Feedback Loops: While the NAD team is considered helpful, issuers reported that hands-on support is lacking during setup and integration. There is no structured feedback mechanism, making it difficult for institutions to get their concerns addressed or improvements implemented in a timely manner.

Low or No Demand from Requesters: One of the most striking concerns is the low demand from recruiters and verifiers to access documents via DigiLocker. Universities noted that employers or scholarship agencies rarely request digital verification through the platform. The fetch rate of documents by external parties is extremely low, indicating poor ecosystem participation and undermining the platform's intended interoperability. As one administrator noted: "We're uploading everything, but no one is fetching it. Unless this changes, we see little value beyond compliance."

Lack of Long-Term Buy-In: Many universities clearly stated that they would not voluntarily continue using DigiLocker for verification unless mandated. Without regular institutional benefits, demand-side usage, or policy-linked incentives, the motivation to remain engaged remains low.

To conclude, universities and institutional issuer's view DigiLocker as a compliance-driven tool. While the system promises digitization and streamlined document issuance, real-world adoption is hindered by technical constraints, rigid workflows, lack of support, and minimal demand from requesters. Institutions experience high administrative burdens and limited flexibility, leading to frustration and disengagement. Without stronger handholding, ecosystem incentives, or user-side demand, issuers are unlikely to voluntarily invest further in DigiLocker beyond what is mandated.

7 DigiLocker Team Perspective: Operational Realities and Focus

To complement user and institutional perspectives, interviews were conducted with members of the DigiLocker implementation team working across MeitY. These discussions offered valuable insights into the platform's development priorities, operational challenges, and ecosystem strategy. Few insights gathered were as follows.

Limited Operational Bandwidth: The DigiLocker team comprises a 47-member in-house unit based in New Delhi, responsible for onboarding, product development, and support. Although expansion to 88 staff is planned, current capacity limits their ability to provide personalized onboarding or real-time technical support to thousands of institutions across India.

Phased Growth and Sectoral Focus: The team emphasized DigiLocker's phased evolution, with initial versions being cost-effective and link based. The current phase, dubbed DigiLocker 2.0, aims for scaling and self-sustainability. Current focus sectors include education, health, and financial services, with expansion into government recruitment and regulatory processes.

Government-Centric Prioritization: Most usage continues to be driven by government departments, particularly during exam results and elections. The system prioritizes high-volume bulk issuance over real-time transaction frequency, making it suitable for administrative tasks but less compelling for everyday user engagement.

Public vs. Private Sector Imbalance: The team acknowledged that while public sector adoption is high, private-sector engagement remains limited as they actively didn't push the DigiLocker adoption to private industry. This creates a dependency on state mandates, and market-driven organic usage is still underdeveloped, which limits broader ecosystem adoption.

Cross-Cutting Systemic Challenges: Beyond these specific perspectives, several systemic challenges persist that affect DigiLocker's scalability and effectiveness: A key concern is the ongoing departmental resistance to data sharing and automation of verification processes, often rooted in legacy practices, security apprehensions, and a preference for manual control.

- Additionally, while the team has made significant strides in expanding API support, many institutions still face difficulties in implementing and integrating these interfaces effectively, pointing to the need for more tailored technical assistance.
- Another major hurdle lies in the dual onboarding process that is distinct for issuers and requesters which, despite its necessity for security and role clarity, is often perceived as complex and insufficiently documented. The DigiLocker team acknowledges these barriers and is actively working toward simplifying onboarding, strengthening support systems, and fostering a culture of data-sharing trust to drive wider adoption.

The DigiLocker team is focused on scaling operations through strategic government partnerships and platform evolution. However, limitations in team capacity, over-reliance on top-down adoption, and low private-sector engagement have constrained the platform's impact. With current priorities centered on bulk issuance and public-sector transactions, the system has yet to fully evolve into a citizen-centric, high-frequency DPI. To ensure broader and sustainable adoption, the team must balance onboarding volume with transaction depth, strengthen API support, and address institutional pain points more proactively.

8 Usage Frequency Patterns and Ecosystem-Driven Adoption Insights

The analysis of DigiLocker's adoption patterns highlights a crucial distinction between the engagement frequency of institutional stakeholders (issuers and requesters) and citizens. Interviews and ecosystem mapping revealed that while issuers and requesters integrate DigiLocker into several of their operational processes with medium to high frequency, citizen interaction with the platform remains largely infrequent and event based.

For issuers, activities such as uploading academic certificates, issuing health records, and providing identity documents are linked to cyclical or periodic activities like admissions, onboarding, examination results, or regulatory compliance submissions. These activities occur systematically, allowing issuers to embed DigiLocker into their workflows. Similarly, requesters such as regulatory bodies, government agencies, and private service providers use DigiLocker for verifying credentials during predictable operational cycles like recruitment drives, financial aid disbursements, and background verifications. In these cases, DigiLocker functions as an efficient enabler, fulfilling medium to high-frequency operational needs with a standardized approach.

However, when observed from the citizen's perspective, the engagement frequency tells a different story. Citizens primarily use DigiLocker at key moments in their lives applying for college admissions, appearing for competitive examinations, seeking government jobs, registering property, or applying for loans or insurance. These interactions are sporadic and tied to major events rather than daily or even monthly needs. Consequently, after their initial registration and use, many citizens either forget about the platform or do not perceive an ongoing need to engage with it. Unlike payment apps, social media, or government service portals that foster daily or weekly interaction, DigiLocker remains passive, only surfacing during specific bureaucratic or legal requirements.

A key reason for this is the limited push from issuers and requesters. Despite institutional adoption, DigiLocker has not been uniformly mandated as the sole or primary mode of verification or document submission. Traditional paper-based processes and alternative digital channels continue to coexist, offering users multiple options. In the absence of strong nudges or mandatory usage requirements, citizens often default to older methods they are familiar with, thereby weakening the platform's relevance in routine digital transactions [13].

While issuers and requesters handle multiple high and medium frequency processes, most citizen-initiated interactions cluster into the low-frequency category. As a result, without proactive external encouragement, citizens have few incentives to develop a habit of using DigiLocker as a regular digital utility.

However, there are notable exceptions where high-frequency citizen engagement has been successfully achieved. The fintech sector, particularly companies offering small-ticket or collateral-free loans, actively integrates DigiLocker into customer onboarding processes. In these cases, citizens are not only encouraged but often incentivized to link their DigiLocker accounts for instant KYC, eligibility verification, and document retrieval. The promise of faster approvals and minimal paperwork creates a win-win situation for both service providers and users. This approach has led to significantly higher daily transaction volumes and increased citizen familiarity with the platform, demonstrating that when the ecosystem actively drives usage and users perceive immediate benefits, adoption rises naturally [14].

This example underscores an important insight: while the DigiLocker platform has the foundational infrastructure, its widespread adoption among citizens is largely dependent on how deeply it is embedded into frequent, user-facing services. Without regular touchpoints, even a robust system risks becoming an occasional-use tool rather than a core part of a citizen's digital ecosystem.

In conclusion, the challenge for DigiLocker is not the lack of issuer or requester participation, but the gap between institutional operations and citizen usage patterns. Moving forward, efforts must focus on creating high-frequency touchpoints for citizens, encouraging mandatory integrations in service delivery, and fostering ecosystem partnerships that make DigiLocker the default method for document exchange and verification across a broad range of daily activities.

9 Conclusion

This study critically examined the adoption of DigiLocker as a foundational element of India's Digital Public Infrastructure, focusing on its usage patterns, institutional integration, and system-level bottlenecks. While the platform offers a robust, secure, and scalable infrastructure for digital document exchange, its real-world adoption remains fragmented and episodic. The research highlighted that much of DigiLocker's usage is driven by top-down mandates and isolated high-demand events, rather than by consistent, voluntary, and habit-forming engagement.

As the visual summary in Fig. 6 illustrates, the core problem lies in limited continuous usage driven primarily by mandates and events, rather than organic demand. From the user side, concerns around data privacy, misunderstandings about utility, and low voluntary engagement persist. Institutions, particularly issuers like universities, report technical barriers, low support, and administrative burdens, while the DigiLocker implementation team grapples with limited capacity and over-dependence on public sector demand.

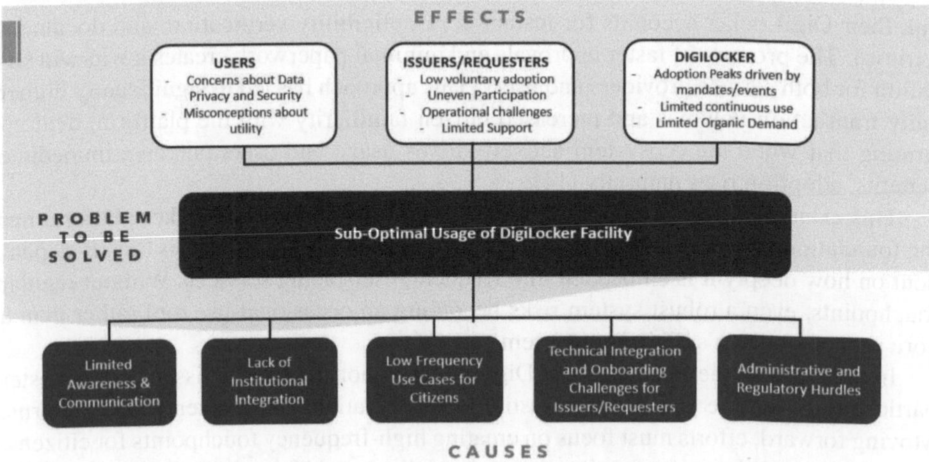

Fig. 6. Causes and effects of sub-optimal use of DigiLocker

From the user side, persistent concerns around data privacy, lack of clarity on utility, and limited awareness have curtailed widespread participation. On the institutional front, particularly among issuers like universities and government departments, adoption is slowed by technical integration hurdles, poor documentation, limited API readiness, and a dual onboarding process that remains cumbersome. The DigiLocker team itself faces capacity constraints, relying heavily on government mandates in the absence of strong private-sector uptake or continuous organic demand.

This weak engagement of the private sector is a factor that sharply contrasts with the core DPI principle of openness to market. For DigiLocker to evolve into a truly inclusive and scalable platform, it must go beyond public-sector compliance and actively foster market participation. The current institutional and technical ecosystem remains inward facing, limiting innovation and the proliferation of diverse, value-added services that could drive everyday relevance and organic user demand.

The findings underscore the need to shift DigiLocker from a compliance-based utility to a citizen- and institution-first service model. This requires addressing both the technical and behavioral dimensions of adoption by simplifying processes, expanding use cases, strengthening support mechanisms, and making the platform more responsive to user and institutional needs. Without this recalibration, DigiLocker risks being confined as a transactional tool rather than evolving into a transformative, embedded layer of India's digital governance landscape. The future of DigiLocker hinges not only on its infrastructure, but on its capacity to deliver relevance, convenience, and agency to all stakeholders in the digital ecosystem.

References

1. TIC Council India: TIC Council Recommendations for a Robust Cybersecurity
2. United Nations Development Programme (UNDP): The DPI Approach- A Playbook (2023)

3. Mazzucato, M., Eaves, D., Vasconcellos, B.: Digital public infrastructure and public value: what is 'public' about DPI? In: Working Paper Series: IIPP WP 2024–05, UCL Institute for Innovation and Public Purpose (2024)
4. Alonso, C., Bhojwani, T., Hanedar, E., Prihardini, D., Uña, G., Zhabska, K.: Stacking up the benefits: lessons from India's digital journey. In: IMF Working Papers 2023 ed., International Monetary Fund (2023)
5. Bandura, R., McLean, M., Sultan, S.: Unpacking the Concept of Digital Public Infrastructure and Its Importance for Global Development (2023)
6. DigiLocker: (2025) (Online). Available: https://www.digilocker.gov.in/web/about/about-digilocker. Accessed Feb. 2025
7. Rajendran, S.: 15 Crore and Counting: DigiLocker Leads the Charge in India's Digital Revolution (2023)
8. Digilocker Authority: Office Order: No. 3(42)/2014-EG-II(Part-II): Meity (2016) (Online). Available: https://www.dla.gov.in/sites/default/files/pdf/aboutUS/preservation-and-retention-of-information-by-intermediaries-providing-digital-locker-facilities-rules-2016.pdf. Accessed Feb. 2025
9. NITI Aayog: Data Empowerment and Protection Architecture—A Secure Consent-Based Data Sharing Framework (2020)
10. Venkatesh, V., Morris, M.G., Davis, G.B., Davis, F.D.: User acceptance of information technology: toward a unified view. MIS Quartely (2003)
11. Eaves, D., Rao, K.: Digital Public Infrastructure: Framework for Conceptualisation and Measurement (2025)
12. Waghmare, A.: ICT skills (2024)
13. Marathe, M., Chandra, P.: Officers never type: examining the persistence of paper in e-governance. In: CHI '20: Proceedings of the 2020 CHI Conference on Human Factors in Computing Systems (2020)
14. Buteau, S., Rao, P., Valenti, F.: Emerging Insights from Digital Solutions in Financial Inclusion. Springer (2021)

Digital Adoption in Public Services: The Case of e-Government in Indonesia

Alvedi Sabani[1(✉)], Mohammad Alamgir Hossain[1], Vinh Thai[1], and Bart J. A. van Bueren[1,2]

[1] RMIT University, Melbourne, VIC 3000, Australia
alvedi.sabani@rmit.edu.au
[2] Monash University, Melbourne, Australia

Abstract. Digital adoption has become a defining challenge and opportunity in public sector reform, particularly as governments integrate emerging technologies such as artificial intelligence, cloud computing, and big data into service delivery. In this context, electronic government (e-Government) has emerged as a central pillar of digital transformation, aiming to improve efficiency, transparency, and citizen engagement. However, the adoption of e-Government services remains inconsistent, especially in developing countries, where infrastructural, institutional, and socio-cultural barriers hinder widespread uptake. This study investigates the determinants of digital adoption in public services by examining e-Government usage in Indonesia, a representative developing country. Extending the Unified Theory of Acceptance and Use of Technology (UTAUT), the study incorporates two endogenous and four exogenous context-specific factors tailored to emerging digital environments. Using survey data from 314 e-Government users and employing structural equation modelling (SEM), the study evaluates the relative influence of these factors on adoption outcomes. The results contribute to a deeper theoretical understanding of digital adoption in the public sector and provide actionable insights for policymakers seeking to advance inclusive and effective e-Government implementation as part of national digital transformation efforts.

Keywords: Digital Transformation · Adoption · e-Government · UTAUT · Developing Countries · SEM

1 Introduction

The ability of society to adopt new technologies determines its capacity for innovation and institutional transformation [1]. In public administration, the success of digital initiatives such as e-Government depends not only on technical infrastructure but on the collective readiness of governments, businesses, and citizens to adopt and use these systems meaningfully [2].

E-Government is broadly defined as the use of ICT for improving the delivery of public services to citizens and businesses [3, 4]. It has numerous benefits for various stakeholders, including public organizations, businesses and citizens. From the public

A. Elbanna et al. (Eds.): TDIT 2025, IFIP AICT 778, pp. 22–38, 2026.
https://doi.org/10.1007/978-3-032-16775-0_2

organization perspective, the development of e-Government enhances information sharing between government institutions [5, 6]. For businesses, e-Government facilitates online public procurement [7] and enables seamless two-way communications between businesses and public organizations [8]. For citizens, e-Government improves the quality of public service delivery [9, 10] and the transparency of public decision-making [11, 12]. It also encourages the involvement of citizens in public administration [13]. Reflecting these benefits, many countries have accelerated the deployment of e-Government platforms to modernize public service delivery and strengthen institutional responsiveness [14].

Despite growing investment in e-Government, adoption outcomes remain inconsistent across contexts particularly in developing countries where infrastructural, institutional, and behavioral challenges persist [10, 15]. While there is consensus on the transformative potential of e-Government, there is less clarity about the determinants that underpin successful adoption in resource-constrained and diverse national settings.

This study seeks to address this gap by evaluating the key determinants of e-Government adoption, using Indonesia as a representative case of the developing country context. As one of the largest and most populous democracies in the world, Indonesia has made substantial efforts to digitize public services. However, its experience also reflects many of the structural and socio-technical challenges typical of emerging economies, making it a relevant and instructive context for broader theory-building and policy learning.

To this end, the study extends the Unified Theory of Acceptance and Use of Technology (UTAUT) [16] by incorporating two endogenous and four exogenous context-specific factors. Drawing on interdisciplinary literature and empirical data from a survey of Indonesian users, it applies structural equation modelling (SEM) to evaluate the significance of these determinants in shaping adoption outcomes. The central research question guiding this investigation is: *What are the determinants that influence the successful adoption of e-Government initiatives in Indonesia?* By addressing this question, the study aims to contribute both to the theoretical advancement of digital government research and to the practical development of more targeted and effective e-Government strategies in developing country contexts.

2 Literature Review

2.1 Adoption of e-Government Services in Developing Countries

The global expansion of e-Government has generated considerable scholarly interest in understanding how such services are adopted across various national and contextual settings. In response, a wide range of models have been proposed to explain the adoption of e-Government from different theoretical and stakeholder perspectives [11, 17, 18]. For instance, Debjani, Umesh [19] proposed a service quality model for assessing e-Government adoption in India. Ahmed and Campbell [20] investigated the perception of citizens on the adoption of e-Government in the Kurdistan Region of Iraq. Alghamdi and Beloff [21] developed a model for evaluating e-Government adoption from the business sector perspective. Alzahrani, Alzahrani, Al-Karaghouli [22] and Sulistyowati, Alrajawy [23] proposed an e-Government adoption model focusing on trust levels. Despite some progress in modelling e-Government adoption, there is a lack of research investigating the citizens' perspective. This is especially evident in developing countries, where e-Government development is commonly stagnant at the transaction stage [24, 25]. At this stage, government services have progressed beyond mere information provision (e.g., static websites) to offer basic digital transactions such as submitting forms, making payments, or requesting services online. However, these services often lack full integration, real-time responsiveness, or personalized interactivity, limiting their effectiveness and perceived value among users. The transaction stage thus represents a critical but transitional phase in e-Government maturity, where adoption challenges are particularly pronounced and user engagement remains fragile.

The aim of this study is to develop an e-Government adoption model for better understanding the adoption of e-Government at the transaction stage from the perspective of citizens in developing countries such as Indonesia. A review of the relevant literature has been conducted to achieve this aim. An extensive literature search was performed across multiple reputational databases, including Emerald, Google Scholar, ScienceDirect, Scopus, Springer and Web of Science, to ensure sufficient review coverage. Search terms were used to ensure that no relevant studies were missed. The terms 'adoption', 'acceptance' and 'implementation' are often used interchangeably in literature. As a result, those terms including 'e-Government adoption', 'e-Government acceptance' and 'e-Government implementation' were used as search terms. The search led to the identification of 4,428 studies related to e-Government adoption published in the last two decades. Figure 1 presents an overview of the e-Government adoption studies and related themes using VOSviewer [26, 27], colors categorize interrelated themes and the size of circles illustrates the number of keywords appearance in publications (larger circles indicates more publications contain such keywords). Three prominent clusters are evident:

- **Cluster 1 (Blue)** focuses on **citizen-centric adoption and behavioral theories**, containing terms such as *e-government adoption, citizen adoption, intention, acceptance, unified theory*, and *design methodology approach.* This cluster reflects the strong influence of models such as UTAUT and Technology Acceptance Model (TAM), which have shaped much of the empirical work in adoption research, especially regarding individual-level determinants like perceived usefulness and behavioral intention.
- **Cluster 2 (Green)** represents themes related to **institutional and project-level implementation**, including keywords such as *e-government project*, *critical success factor*, *initiative*, *barrier*, *stakeholder*, and *ICT*. This cluster highlights organizational and environmental factors, including capacity-building, stakeholder coordination, and infrastructure readiness.
- **Cluster 3 (Red)** centers around **service outcomes and public value**, featuring terms like *effectiveness*, *efficiency*, *innovation*, *satisfaction*, *service quality*, and *platform.* These terms point to performance-oriented evaluations of e-Government and growing interest in the impact of adoption on service delivery and user experience.

These visualizations confirm that e-Government adoption is a multidimensional phenomenon. While behavioral theories dominate individual-level analysis, emerging research increasingly addresses broader implementation challenges and the role of trust, organizational readiness, and contextual fit particularly in developing countries. This reinforces the relevance of the present study, which aims to bridge these perspectives through an extended UTAUT framework tailored to the transactional stage of e-Government services in Indonesia.

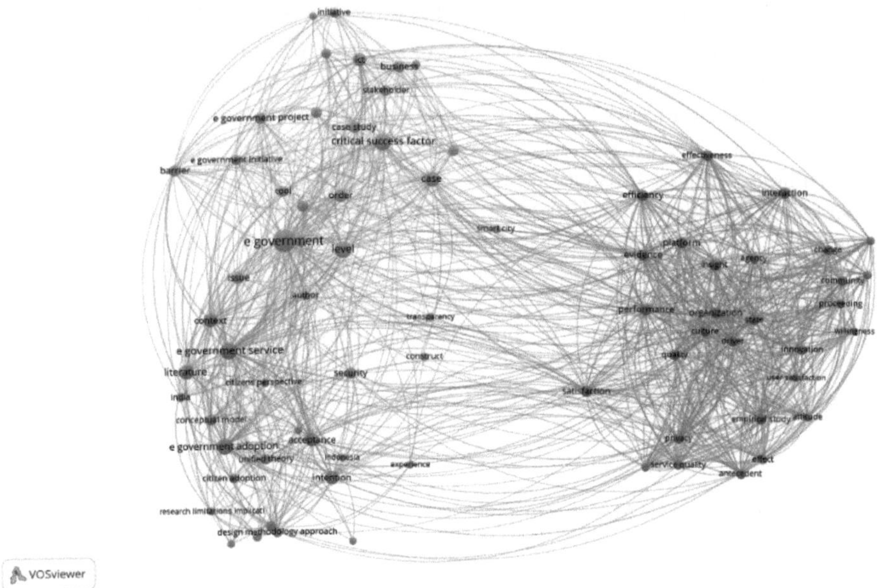

Fig. 1. Network visualization themes on the adoption of E government

2.2 UTAUT Adoption in E-Government Studies

Venkatesh, Morris [16] consolidated the top eight adoption theories to develop the UTAUT model for investigating the adoption of technologies. UTAUT has become one of the most widely used theoretical lenses for investigating the adoption of specific technologies due to its simplicity, consistency and robustness [28, 29]. Four major factors for explaining the adoption of specific technologies using UTAUT are performance expectancy, effort expectancy, social influence and facilitating condition. Performance expectancy is described as the degree to which an individual believes that adopting the technology will result in better performance. Effort expectancy is referred to as the degree of ease in using the technology. Social influence is described as the degree to how an individual feels the importance that others believe they should use the new technology. Facilitating conditions refers to the degree to which an individual believes that a technical infrastructure exists to support the technology. These four factors determine the intention, which is the person's subjective probability of adopting new technologies [16].

The UTAUT has been adopted in e-Government adoption studies worldwide. Gupta, Bhaskar [30], for example, extended UTAUT with trust and citizen satisfaction factors to identify the critical factors influencing e-Government adoption in India. Bhuasiri, Zo [31] integrated UTAUT with self-determination theory (SDT) to examine e-tax-filing acceptance in Thailand. Rodrigues, Sarabdeen [32] applied UTAUT with user satisfaction to examine the adoption of e-Government services from the perspective of citizens in the United Arab Emirates. Lu and Nguyen [33] combined UTAUT and IS Success to investigate the adoption of an online tax-filing service in Vietnam. Further, Rabaa'i [34] adopted UTAUT to identify the cultural factors influencing e-Government adoption in Jordan. Hariguna [35] extended UTAUT with information and service quality factors to study public behavioral intention to use e-Government services in Indonesia. Meanwhile, Kurfalı, Arifoğlu [3] investigated the role of trust in citizens' decisions to adopt e-Government in Turkey. Alharbi, Papadaki [36] extended UTAUT with grounded theory to analyze the effects of security and its antecedents on the intention to use e-Government services in Saudi Arabia. Sabani, Thai [37] applied UTAUT to assess critical factors for adopting e-Government in Indonesia. Garcia-Rio, Palos-Sanchez [38] extend UTAUT with perceived trust, attitude and role of e-Government during COVID-19 to investigate the adoption of e-Government services in Spain during the pandemic. These studies show that the UTAUT model is appropriate for examining the adoption of e-Government in various contexts. Table 1 presents a summary of these studies.

Table 1. A summary of studies using UTAUT for citizen adoption of E government

Reference	Theories	Methods	Factors
Gupta, Bhaskar [30]	UTAUT + Trust and Citizen Satisfaction	Survey	Effort expectancy, performance expectancy, trust in technology, trust in government, citizen satisfaction and facilitating conditions
Bhuasiri, Zo [31]	UTAUT + SDT	Survey	Performance expectancy, facilitating conditions, social influence, perceived credibility, perceived autonomy and perceived competence
Rodrigues, Sarabdeen [32]	Extended UTAUT	Survey	Attitudes, performance expectations, effort expectations, perceived security, facilitating conditions, perceived privacy, perceived uncertainty, trust
Lu and Nguyen [33]	UTAUT + IS Success	Survey	Performance expectancy, social influence, effort expectation, information quality, system quality and service quality

(*continued*)

Table 1. (*continued*)

Reference	Theories	Methods	Factors
Rabaa'i [34]	UTAUT	Survey	Performance expectancy, effort expectancy, social influence and facilitating conditions
Hariguna [35]	UTAUT + Perceived Information Quality	Survey	Performance expectancy, effort expectancy, facilitating conditions and perceived information quality
Kurfalı, Arifoğlu [3]	UTAUT	Survey	Performance expectancy, social influence, facilitating conditions, trust of internet and trust
Alharbi, Papadaki [36]	UTAUT2 + Grounded Theory	Mixed	Performance expectancy, social influence, facilitating conditions, habit, trust, privacy perception, security culture, cybersecurity law, user interface quality, general information security awareness and tangible security features
Garcia-Rio, Palos-Sanchez [38]	UTAUT + Perceived Trust + Attitude	Survey	Performance expectancy, social influence, effort expectancy, facilitating condition, perceived trust, role of e-government during COVID-19, and attitude
Sabani, Thai [37]	UTAUT + IS Success + Contextual Factors	Interview	Performance expectancy, social influence, effort expectancy, information quality, system quality, perceived transparency, and ICT literacy

3 Research Model

In addition to the UTAUT constructs, this research partially adopts the DeLone and McLean model of IS success [39] to better understand citizens' perceptions towards e-Government services at the transaction stage. As a result, two core constructs of the model, information quality and system quality, are adopted in the research model. Further, the proposed model integrates additional factors, including perceived security, ICT literacy and perceived transparency adapted from previous e-Government adoption studies [37, 40, 41]. These additional factors are essential to e-Government adoption research from the perspective of citizens in developing countries. These two factors are deemed to play a vital role in influencing citizens' decision to adopt e-Government. The integration of the UTAUT and these factors would help to achieve more robust explanations of the adoption of e-Government from the perspective of citizens in developing countries. Figure 2 presents the research model for investigating the critical factors for e-Government adoption from the perspective of citizens in developing countries.

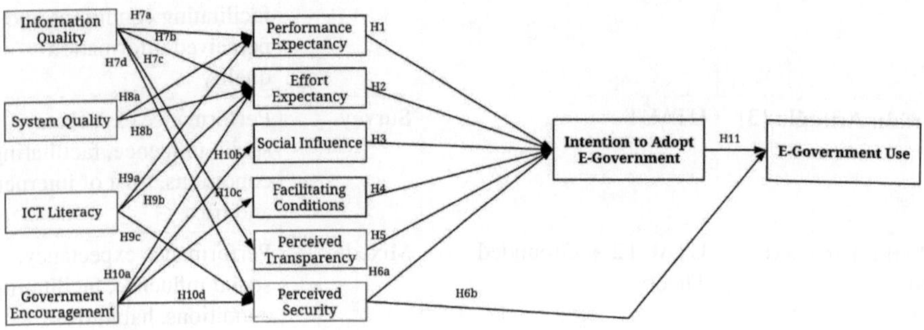

Fig. 2. The research model

Note: Black box indicates core UTAUT constructs, red box indicates endogenous extensions, and blue box indicates exogenous extensions.

The model has eleven major hypotheses, with twenty-one relationships identified. The relationships are derived based on thematic analysis while being grounded in the existing literature. Appendix A provides a summary of the hypotheses developed and the relationship between the constructs.

4 Research Method

4.1 Data Collection

The survey participants were Indonesian citizens. Bahasa Indonesia, the official language of Indonesia, was used for the survey to ensure clarity and facilitate faster response times. The survey was translated using the forward–backward translation method [42] where one translator first translated the instrument from English to Indonesian, and a second translator then independently translated it back into English. This process, conducted by linguistic specialists, ensured semantic equivalence between the English and Indonesian versions of the survey.

The probability sampling technique was used to select the research sampling frame of Indonesian citizens above 18 years old (the minimum age to access e-Government). Determining an adequate sample size is critical to allow findings to be generalized to the entire population with the desired level of precision and confidence [43–45]. The survey was developed using the Qualtrics platform and distributed electronically through social media channels such as Facebook and LinkedIn. A total of 314 valid responses were collected.

4.2 Profile of Respondents

The demographic distribution of respondents was analyzed across age, gender, education, occupation, and frequency of e-Government use. In terms of age, the majority (87%) were young adults aged 21–45 years, with 60% aged 21–30 and 27% aged 31–45. Gender distribution showed 64.2% male, 34.4% female, and 1.4% preferring not to disclose. Most respondents were infrequent e-Government users, accessing services once every six months or less. Specifically, 27.4% used them once in six months, 26.3% once a year, and 8.8% less than once a year. Only 14% used e-Government services monthly, and 20% quarterly. Educationally, nearly three-quarters held a university qualification: 61.4% had a bachelor's degree, 13.33% a master's degree, and 2.46% a doctorate. A further 9.12% held a diploma, 11.93% completed high school, 1.4% junior high school, and 0.35% had no formal education. Occupationally, 46.3% worked in the private sector, 17.2% were self-employed, 12.6% worked in government, 14.4% were students, 4.9% unemployed, and 1.1% retired. Overall, the sample reflects diversity across demographic categories and varying levels of e-Government usage, providing a representative basis for analyzing adoption patterns.

5 Data Analysis

5.1 Preparing for SEM Analysis

To effectively detect outliers, the Mahalanobis distance (D2) for each measurement item is computed [46, 47]. D2 is used to measure the distance between a single observation and the mean of all the observations in a given study [48]. This study assesses D2 of each data case using the chi-square ($\chi 2$) distribution with a P-value (< 0.001) and degrees of freedom equal to the independent constructs number [49, 50]. A particular case is considered an outlier if the D2 of this case is higher than the $\chi 2$ value [50]. As a result, four cases are detected as data outliers in this study, and they are deleted from further analysis. As a result, 48 cases are deleted in the missing data assessment, 4 cases are removed in the assessment of univariate outlier, and 18 cases are deleted in the assessment of multivariate outlier, leading to a total of 244 valid cases to be further analyzed using the SEM technique.

Non-response bias concerns the partiality that exists when a group of respondents differs from another group (Hair et al. 2010). The assessment of non-response bias is important to ensure that the collected data remains representative of the study population [51]. The presence of non-response bias is a concern for researchers when they collect data via a survey instrument. This is because the existence of non-response bias influences the generalisability of the study findings [52]. Non-response-bias tests check whether there is any difference in opinion of the respondents with the non-respondents who could have participated in the survey. Thus, the rationale for this test is that late respondents were likely to have a similar characteristic to non-respondents. Non-response bias is assessed by examining the differences in demographics information between two groups of respondents [52]. A non-response bias is assessed by using the Mann-Whitney U test using SPSS to compare the main demographic information including age, gender, education and occupation of the 200 first responses from the last 44 responses as shown in Table 2.

Table 2. Mann-Whitney U test for early and late samples

	Age	Gender	Education	Occupation
Z	0.187	0.533	0.386	0.318

The results shown in Table 2 indicate that no significant differences can be detected in the main demographic information between the early group of respondents and the latter group of respondents, provided that in each instance, z-values are not significant at 0.05 level. Thus, it would be reasonable to conclude that the nonresponse bias did not arise a problem in this study.

5.2 Assessment of the Measurement Model

Measurement model analysis examines the relationships between an observed variable (measurement item) and a latent variable (construct) in a specific study [52]. An observed variable is usually measured directly through a numerical value obtained from the research participants in response to a certain question in the research survey instrument [52]. A latent variable cannot directly be measured. It is often measured using multiple observed items [52]. In the measurement model, each measurement item should be linked properly to an individual construct for ensuring the validity of the measurement model [53].

The latent variables including performance expectancy, effort expectancy, social influence, facilitating conditions, perceived security, information quality, system quality, perceived transparency, ICT literacy, government encouragement, and the adoption of e-Government, are depicted in the full measurement model with a total of 46 items. The constructs are formative, which were evaluated based on their outer weights, outer loadings and multicollinearity.

In examining the formative indicators, the criteria for measuring the validity and reliability of reflective constructs do not apply [54]. In evaluating formative constructs, the guide given by Hair Jr, Hult [54] was followed. This initiates by measuring the significance of the outer weights of the items of the constructs. If the outer weight is significant, then the item is kept. If the outer weight is not significant, then the outer loading is considered. If the outer loading is greater than 0.5, the item is retained. If the outer loading is less than 0.5 but is significant, the item is kept, otherwise, it is removed [54]. The items on this study have satisfied the criteria.

5.3 Assessment of the Structural Model

To test the research model, the study employed a partial least squares structural equation modeling (PLS-SEM) method, and used SmartPLS 4 software [55]. PLS-SEM was used because of the formative constructs, and complexity of the model (Chin 2010). To assess the measurement and structural model, we followed the guidelines of (Hair et al. 2017) and Petter, Straub, and Rai (2007). First, we checked the formative measurement models for collinearity of items by checking the VIF values. All VIF values were below the threshold of 3.3 (Hair et al. 2017). Harman's single-factor test was performed, and none of the factors exceeded the threshold of more than 50% of the total variance [56]. The use of Harman's single factor and VIF analysis suggests that common method bias is not a concern in this study. These findings show that all the results are satisfactory. Next, using a bootstrapping technique in SmartPLS, we calculated the significance of the outer weights. All indicators were significant at a 5% level. Upon analyzing the result of the hypotheses testing as shown in Fig. 3, 20 out of 21 hypotheses were accepted. The path-coefficient value (β) is shown near to each link among the constructs.

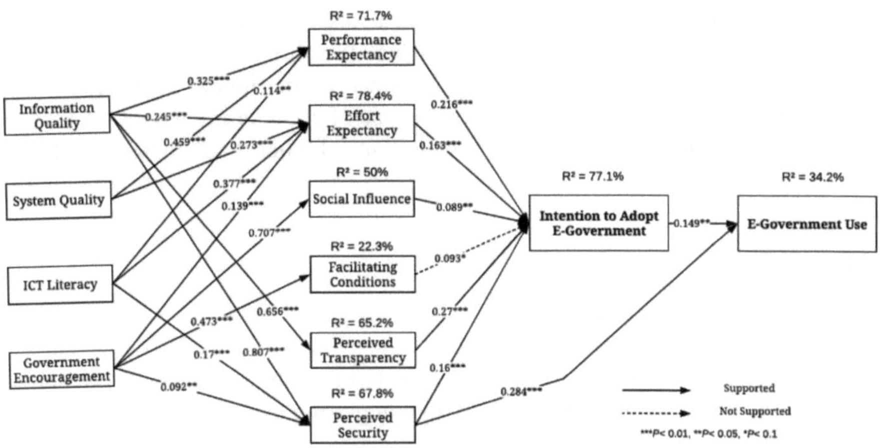

Fig. 3. Structural model

As shown in Fig. 3, only the relationship between *facilitating conditions* and the *intention to adopt* e-government (H4) was not supported. This suggests that *performance expectancy, effort expectancy, social influence, perceived security*, and *perceived transparency* are critical determinants of e-government adoption and use in Indonesia. In addition, *information quality, system quality, ICT literacy* and *government encouragement* emerged as important exogenous factors shaping adoption behavior.

5.4 Coefficient of Determination

The Coefficient of Determination (R^2) explains the combined power of the exogenous variables on the endogenous variable [54]. Using the guidelines written by Chin [57], the values 0.67, 0.33 and 0.19 represent strong, moderate and weak effects respectively. As presented in Table 3, data accounted for 71.7% in variance for the performance expectancy, 78.4% in variance for effort expectancy, 50% in variance for social influence, and 22.3% for facilitating conditions based on their exogenous factors, while explaining 65.2% on perceived transparency and 67.8% on perceived security.

Table 3. R^2 values for the endogenous constructs

	R^2	Effect
Performance Expectancy Factors	0.717	Strong
Effort Expectancy Factors	0.784	Strong
Social Influence Factors	0.500	Moderate
Facilitating Conditions Factors	0.223	Weak
Perceived Transparency Factors	0.652	Moderate
Perceived Security Factors	0.678	Strong

R^2 is also assessed in the structural model analysis. It was conducted to identify the level of strength of the structural model by using R^2 value [52]. R^2 value shows how much variance in endogenous variables is explained by the model [57]. This research model has successfully explained 34.2% on the use of e-Government and 77.1% of the variance in the intention to adopt e-government that is higher than the baseline UTAUT model.

6 Discussion

6.1 Key Findings

This study advances e-Government research from both theoretical and practical perspectives. Theoretically, it extends the UTAUT by integrating exogenous factors including information quality, system quality, and ICT literacy as well as endogenous factors including perceived transparency and perceived security that are particularly relevant in developing country contexts such as Indonesia.

From a practical standpoint, the findings provide actionable insights for government agencies and public organisations seeking to improve e-Government uptake. These insights can inform the development of strategies and policies that enhance the quality, trustworthiness, and accessibility of e-Government services, thereby supporting their sustained use in Indonesia and other developing economies.

The study specifically examined the factors influencing citizens' adoption and use of e-Government services, providing empirical evidence of the relative importance of these determinants in shaping adoption intentions and behaviours.

6.2 Theoretical Contributions

This study extends the UTAUT with the IS Success model to for investigating the citizen adoption and use of e-Government at the transaction stage in developing countries. This research contributes to the theory by confirming the appropriateness of combining theories such as the UTAUT and the IS Success model for investigating the adoption and use of technological innovations in society. This provides a more holistic view of the citizen perspective on e-Government adoption.

Furthermore, this study incorporates additional constructs identified through an earlier literature review and qualitative investigation by Sabani, Thai [37] that have often been overlooked in prior research. These include perceived transparency and perceived security, which were found to directly influence e-Government adoption, and ICT literacy and government encouragement, which exerted indirect effects. The refinement and validation of these constructs represent a meaningful theoretical advancement [58–60], addressing notable gaps in the e-Government literature.

The research model has successfully explained 77.1% of the variance in the intention to adopt e-Government. This result is substantial, compared to the baseline UTAUT that only explains 70% of its intended use [16]. This result is also marginally higher than UTAUT2, which explains 74% of the variance [61], demonstrating the explanatory power of the extended framework in the context of e-Government adoption.

6.3 Practical Implications

The findings have important implications for public organisations, the central government, and technology vendors in promoting e-Government adoption in Indonesia:

- **Public organisations** should adopt a citizen-oriented approach that addresses not only technical readiness but also social and contextual barriers, including limited ICT literacy and resource constraints. Initiatives could include targeted communication campaigns, ICT infrastructure upgrades, and training programs to strengthen citizens' digital competencies.
- **Central government** support is essential for funding, policy alignment, and nationwide awareness campaigns. Providing standardised, secure digital platforms and fostering citizen engagement through education and outreach can significantly enhance trust and adoption.
- **Technology vendors** should focus on developing user-friendly, reliable, and integrated platforms that facilitate seamless access to services. Collaboration with government agencies is critical to ensure scalability, interoperability, and citizen-centred design.

The results reinforce that e-Government adoption is primarily an adaptive challenge requiring coordinated action across policy, infrastructure, and service design domains.

7 Conclusion, Limitations and Future Research

This study develops and tests an extended UTAUT framework for e-Government adoption in a developing country context. By integrating IS Success constructs (information quality, system quality) and context-specific factors (ICT literacy, perceived transparency, perceived security, and government encouragement), the model offers a broader view of citizen adoption behavior.

Survey data from Indonesian citizens, analyzed using PLS-SEM, show that performance expectancy, effort expectancy, social influence, perceived transparency, and perceived security strongly influence adoption intentions, while information quality, system quality, ICT literacy, and government encouragement act as key enablers. The model explains 77.1% of the variance in adoption intention, exceeding the baseline UTAUT and UTAUT2.

While offering important insights, this study has several limitations. First, it is based on cross-sectional data, capturing only a single point in time. In the rapidly evolving digital landscape, shaped by emerging technologies such as generative AI, citizen behaviors and expectations may shift quickly. Future studies should adopt longitudinal designs to track changes in adoption patterns. Second, the research focuses exclusively on citizens' perspectives, omitting other key stakeholders such as businesses and public organizations. Including these groups would provide a more comprehensive view of e-Government implementation. Third, while factors such as ICT literacy, government encouragement, and perceived transparency were examined, future research should explore their interaction and moderating effects, particularly in contexts with uneven digital access. Finally, although the model explains a substantial proportion of variance in adoption intention (77.1%), it accounts for only 34.2% of actual usage. This gap suggests the need to investigate distinct drivers of sustained e-Government use, including the potential role of AI-enabled personalization and adaptive service delivery.

Disclosure of Interests. The authors have no competing interests to declare that are relevant to the content of this article.

Appendix A: Summary of Hypotheses

Construct	Link	H#	Hypothesis statement
Performance Expectancy (PE)	PE → IA	H1	Performance expectancy may have a positive effect on the intention to adopt e-government
Effort Expectancy (EE)	EE → IA	H2	Effort expectancy may have a positive effect on the intention to adopt e-government
Social Influence (SI)	SI → IA	H3	Social influence may have a positive effect on the intention to adopt e-government
Facilitating Conditions (FC)	FC → IA	H4	Facilitating conditions may have a positive effect on the intention to adopt e-government
Perceived Transparency (PT)	PT → IA	H5	Perceived security may have a positive effect on the intention to adopt e-government
Perceived Security (PS)	PS → IA	H6a	Perceived security may have a positive effect on the intention to adopt e-government

(*continued*)

(*continued*)

Construct	Link	H#	Hypothesis statement
	PS → EU	H6b	Perceived security may have a positive effect on e-government use
Information Quality (IQ)	IQ → PE	H7a	Information quality may have a positive effect on performance expectancy
	IQ → EE	H7b	Information quality may have a positive effect on effort expectancy
	IQ → PT	H7c	Information quality may have a positive effect on perceived transparency
	IQ → PS	H7d	Information quality may have a positive effect on perceived security
System Quality (SQ)	SQ → PE	H8a	System quality may have a positive effect on performance expectancy
	SQ → EE	H8b	System quality may have a positive effect on effort expectancy
ICT Literacy (IL)	IL → PE	H9a	ICT literacy may have a positive effect on performance expectancy
	IL → EE	H9b	ICT literacy may have a positive effect on effort expectancy
	IL → PS	H9c	ICT literacy may have a positive effect on perceived security
Government Encouragement (GE)	GE → EE	H10a	Government encouragement may have a positive effect on effort expectancy
	GE → SI	H10b	Government encouragement may have a positive effect on social influence
	GE → FC	H10c	Government encouragement may have a positive effect on facilitating conditions
	GE → PS	H10d	Government encouragement may have a positive effect on perceived security
Intention to Adopt (IA)	IA → EU	H11	Intention to adopt may have a positive effect on e-government use

References

1. Prasad Agrawal, K.: Towards adoption of generative AI in organizational settings. J. Comput. Inf. Syst. **64**(5), 636–651 (2024)
2. Khan, A., Krishnan, S.: Citizen engagement in co-creation of e-government services: a process theory view from a meta-synthesis approach. Internet Res. **31**(4), 1318–1375 (2021)
3. Kurfalı, M., et al.: Adoption of e-government services in Turkey. Comput. Hum. Behav. **66**, 168–178 (2017)
4. Hooda, A., et al.: Clarifying the role of e-government trust in e-government success models: a meta-analytic structural equation modeling approach. Australas. J. Inf. Syst. **27**(0) (2023)
5. Puspitasari, L., Ishii, K.: Digital divides and mobile Internet in Indonesia: impact of smartphones. Telematics Inform. **33**(2), 472–483 (2016)
6. Tran Pham, T.K.: Government administrative capacity, e-government performance and citizen's e-government adoption: evidence from a transition country. Transform. Govt. People Process. Policy **17**(3), 443–458 (2023)
7. Sambasivan, M., Patrick Wemyss, G., Che Rose, R.: User acceptance of a G2B system: a case of electronic procurement system in Malaysia. Internet Res. **20**(2), 169–187 (2010)
8. Susanto, T.D., Goodwin, R.: User acceptance of SMS-based e- government services: differences between adopters and non-adopters. Gov. Inf. Q. **30**(4), 486–497 (2013)
9. Nam, T.: Determining the type of e-government use. Gov. Inf. Q. **31**(2), 211–220 (2014)
10. Al Sayegh, A.J., et al.: Factors affecting e-government adoption in the UAE public sector organisations: the knowledge management perspective. J. Knowl. Manag. **27**(3), 717–737 (2023)
11. Deng, H., Karunasena, K., Xu, W.: Evaluating the performance of e-government in developing countries. Internet Res. **28**(1), 169–190 (2018)
12. Sabani, A.: Investigating the influence of transparency on the adoption of e-Government in Indonesia. J. Sci. Technol. Policy Manag. **12**(2), 236–255 (2021)
13. Heeks, R., Bailur, S.: Analyzing e-government research: perspectives, philosophies, theories, methods, and practice. Gov. Inf. Q. **24**(2), 243–265 (2007)
14. United Nations, *UN E-Government Survey 2024*. 2024, United Nations: New York
15. AbdulKareem, A.K., Oladimeji, K.A.: Cultivating the digital citizen: trust, digital literacy and e-government adoption. Transform. Gov. People Process. Policy **18**(2), 270–286 (2024)
16. Venkatesh, V., et al.: User acceptance of information technology: toward a unified view. MIS Q. **27**(3), 425–478 (2003)
17. AlAwadhi, S., Morris, A.: The use of the UTAUT model in the adoption of E-government services in Kuwait. In: Proceedings of the 41st Annual Hawaii International Conference on System Sciences (HICSS 2008) (2008)
18. Al-Mamari, Q., Corbitt, B., Gekara, V.: E-government adoption in Oman: motivating factors from a government perspective (2013)
19. Debjani, B., Umesh, G., Gupta, M.P.: E-service quality model for Indian government portals: citizens's perspective. J. Enterp. Inf. Manag. **25**(3), 246–271 (2012)
20. Ahmed, K.M., Campbell, J.: Citizen perceptions of E-government in the Kurdistan Region of Iraq. Australas. J. Inf. Syst. **19**(0) (2015)
21. Alghamdi, S., Beloff, N.: Innovative framework for e-government adoption in Saudi Arabia: a study from the business sector perspective. Int. J. Adv. Comput. Sci. Appl. **7**(1), 655–664 (2016)
22. Alzahrani, L., Al-Karaghouli, W., Weerakkody, V.: Analysing the critical factors influencing trust in e-government adoption from citizens' perspective: a systematic review and a conceptual framework. Int. Bus. Rev. **26**(1), 164–175 (2017)

23. Sulistyowati, W.A., et al.: Factors contributing to E-government adoption in Indonesia—an extended of technology acceptance model with trust: a conceptual framework. In: Intelligent Computing and Innovation on Data Science, pp. 651–658. Springer (2020)
24. Obi, T., Naoko, I.: A Decade of World e-Government Rankings. Ringgold Inc, Beaverton (2016)
25. United Nations: United Nations E-Government Survey 2020. In: United Nations E-Government Survey 2020. Department of Economic and Social Affairs, New York
26. Perianes-Rodriguez, A., Waltman, L., van Eck, N.J.: Constructing bibliometric networks: a comparison between full and fractional counting. J. Informet. **10**(4), 1178–1195 (2016)
27. Van Eck, N.J., Waltman, L.: Visualizing bibliometric networks. In: Measuring Scholarly Impact, pp. 285–320. Springer (2014)
28. Williams, M.D., Rana, N.P., Dwivedi, Y.K.: The unified theory of acceptance and use of technology (UTAUT): a literature review. J. Enterp. Inf. Manag. **28**(3), 443–488 (2015)
29. Venkatesh, V.: Adoption and use of AI tools: a research agenda grounded in UTAUT. Ann. Oper. Res. 1–12 (2022)
30. Gupta, K.P., Bhaskar, P., Singh, S.: Critical factors influencing e-government adoption in India: an investigation of the citizens' perspectives. J. Inf. Technol. Res. (JITR) **9**(4), 28–44 (2016)
31. Bhuasiri, W., et al.: User acceptance of e-government services: examining an e-tax filing and payment system in Thailand. Inf. Technol. Dev. **22**(4), 672–695 (2016)
32. Rodrigues, G., Sarabdeen, J., Balasubramanian, S.: Factors that influence consumer adoption of e-government services in the UAE: a UTAUT model perspective. J. Internet Commer. **15**(1), 18–39 (2016)
33. Lu, N.L., Nguyen, V.T.: Online tax filing—E-Government service adoption case of Vietnam. Mod. Econ. **7**(12), 1498 (2016)
34. Rabaa'i, A.A.: The use of UTAUT to investigate the adoption of e-government in Jordan: a cultural perspective. Int. J. Bus. Inf. Syst. **24**(3), 285–315 (2017)
35. Hariguna, T.: Understanding of public behavioral intent to use e-Government service: an extended of unified theory of acceptance use of technology and information system quality. Procedia Comput. Sci. **124**, 585–592 (2017)
36. Alharbi, N., Papadaki, M., Dowland, P.: The impact of security and its antecedents in behaviour intention of using e-government services. Behav. Inf. Technol. **36**(6), 620–636 (2017)
37. Sabani, A., Thai, V., Hossain, M.A.: Factors affecting citizen adoption of E-government in developing countries: an exploratory case study from Indonesia. J. Glob. Inf. Manag. (JGIM) **31**(1), 1–23 (2023)
38. Garcia-Rio, E., et al.: Different approaches to analyzing e-government adoption during the Covid-19 pandemic. Gov. Inf. Q. **40**(4), 101866 (2023)
39. DeLone, W.H., McLean, E.R.: The DeLone and McLean model of information systems success: a ten-year update. J. Manag. Inf. Syst. **19**(4), 9–30 (2003)
40. Shareef, M.A., et al.: E-Government adoption model (GAM): differing service maturity levels. Gov. Inf. Q. **28**(1), 17–35 (2011)
41. Sabani, A., Deng, H., Thai, V.: Evaluating the performance of E-government in Indonesia: a thematic analysis. In: Proceedings of the 12th International Conference on Theory and Practice of Electronic Governance, pp. 435–440. Association for Computing Machinery, Melbourne, VIC, Australia (2019)
42. Bailey, K.: Methods of Social Research. Simon and Schuster (2008)
43. Fowler Jr, F.J.: Survey Research Methods. Sage Publications (2013)
44. Lavrakas, P.J.: Encyclopedia of Survey Research Methods. Sage Publications (2008)
45. Teddlie, C., Yu, F.: Mixed methods sampling: a typology with examples. J. Mixed Methods Res. **1**(1), 77–100 (2007)

46. Hair, J.F., et al.: Multivariate Data Analysis: A Global Perspective, vol. 7. Pearson Education, New Jersey, US (2010)
47. Hadi, A.S.: Identifying multiple outliers in multivariate data. J. Roy. Stat. Soc. **54**(3), 761–771 (1992)
48. Kline, R.B., *Principles and Practice of Structural Equation Modeling.* 2015, New York, US: Guilford Publications
49. Chowdhury, P.: Supply Risk Mitigation and its Impact on Operational Performance of Small- and Medium-sized Enterprises: A Social Capital Approach, in Business IT and Logistics. RMIT University, Australia (2019)
50. Tabachnick, B.G. and L.S. Fidell, *Using Multivariate Statistics.* Inc. 2007, Boston: Pearson Education
51. Okoli, C., Pawlowski, S.D.J.I., and management: The Delphi method as a research tool: an example, design considerations and applications. Inf. Manag. **42**(1), 15–29 (2004)
52. Hair, J.F., et al.: Multivariate Data Analysis. Cengage (2018)
53. Byrne, B.M.: Structural Equation Modeling with AMOS: Basic Concepts, Applications, and Programming, 2 edn. Routledge, New York, US (2013)
54. Hair Jr, J.F., et al.: A Primer on Partial Least Squares Structural Equation Modeling (PLS-SEM). Sage Publications (2016)
55. Ringle, C., S. Wende, and J. Becker. *SmartPLS 4.* 2024; Available from: https://www.smartpls.com
56. Harman, H.H.: Modern Factor Analysis. University of Chicago Press (1976)
57. Chin, W.W.: How to write up and report PLS analyses. In: Esposito Vinzi, V., et al. (Eds.) Handbook of Partial Least Squares: Concepts, Methods and Applications, pp. 655–690 Springer, Berlin, Heidelberg (2010)
58. Reay, T., Whetten, D.A.: What Constitutes a Theoretical Contribution in Family Business? SAGE Publications Sage, Los Angeles, CA (2011)
59. Whetten, D.A.: What constitutes a theoretical contribution? Acad. Manag. Rev. **14**(4), 490–495 (1989)
60. Webster, J., Watson, R.T.: Analyzing the past to prepare for the future: writing a literature review. MIS Quarterly **26**(2), 8–23 (2002)
61. Venkatesh, V., Thong, J.Y., Xu, X.J.M.Q.: Consumer acceptance and use of information technology: extending the unified theory of acceptance and use of technology. MIS Quarterly **36**(1), 157–178 (2012)

Navigating Digital Inequality: A Sequential Mixed-Methods Study of Digital Adoption Antecedents in Marginalized Communities of Jharkhand, India

Munmun Ghosh(✉) and Swetabh Pandey

Symbiosis Institute of Media and Communication, Pune, India
{munmun.ghosh,swetabh.pandey}@simc.edu

Abstract. Marginalized communities often remain excluded from the digital revolution due to socio-economic and structural barriers. This study employs a sequential exploratory mixed-methods design in Jharkhand, India, to investigate antecedents of digital technology adoption in tribal and remote populations. In the qualitative phase, 36 in-depth interviews with government officials, village heads, and community members informed the adaptation of survey instruments to the local context. The quantitative phase analyzed 401 respondents, using exploratory factor analyses, followed by regression modelling and moderation analysis. Results indicate that robust digital infrastructure (e.g., reliable internet and electricity) and supportive government policies significantly enhance digital adoption. In contrast, local socio-cultural factors show a nuanced influence – not directly predicting adoption on average – but become highly significant when moderated by socio-economic background. Higher socio-economic status amplifies the positive effects of infrastructure and culturally relevant content on adoption, while low status can dampen these effects. By integrating the Unified Theory of Acceptance and Use of Technology 2 (UTAUT2) with social exclusion and cultural frameworks, the study reveals a complex interplay between infrastructure, policy, culture, and socio-economic conditions. The findings inform theory by extending UTAUT2 with a socio-economic moderator and guide policymakers toward more inclusive, context-sensitive digital interventions.

Keywords: Digital Adoption · Digital Divide · Marginalized Communities · UTAUT2 · Mixed-Methods · Social Exclusion Theory · Digital Inclusion · Rural India

1 Introduction

Marginalization arises from unequal power dynamics among social groups, and one of the most historically marginalized communities in India is its tribal population (Baah et al. 2018). Tribal societies possess a rich and living cultural heritage; yet, they have long endured poverty, economic isolation, and exclusion from mainstream development

Published by Springer Nature Switzerland AG 2026
A. Elbanna et al. (Eds.): TDIT 2025, IFIP AICT 778, pp. 39–67, 2026.
https://doi.org/10.1007/978-3-032-16775-0_3

processes. Defined by their geographic isolation, socio-economic vulnerabilities, and traditional ways of life, tribal communities have remained on the periphery of regional progress (Sahu 2019). Technology and information are key drivers of societal integration and development in today's globalized world, transforming how individuals communicate and access information (Ghosh 2024). Smartphones, in particular, have made connectivity portable and ubiquitous, allowing most individuals in developed nations to be consistently "online" (Firth 2019). Furthermore, the COVID-19 pandemic accelerated digital transformation, which has been instrumental in popularizing local languages and cultural content (Das 2023), indicating a new cultural dynamic for digital engagement. Concomitant with these global and national innovations, however, marginalized groups face overwhelming obstacles to digital inclusion. Inferior digital infrastructure, combined with socio-economic disadvantages, language exclusion, and deeply entrenched cultural *habitus*, holds these communities back from participating in the digital age. While government policies aim for inclusivity, they often overlook issues such as low literacy rates, infrastructural deficits, and the unique socio-cultural context of tribal societies.

In light of this, the present work is driven by the pressing need to comprehend and resolve digital inequality experienced by marginalized communities in Jharkhand – an eastern Indian state with a significant tribal population. Article 342 of the Indian Constitution recognizes more than 700 Scheduled Tribes (STs) in the country (Ramakrishnappa 2022). Jharkhand alone is home to 32 Scheduled Tribes, including eight classified as Particularly Vulnerable Tribal Groups (Sahu 2019). Long-standing political, educational, and economic marginalization has severely limited the ability of indigenous communities to access digital services and participate in the digital economy (Kulkarni 2019). Economic hardships restrict access to smartphones, computers, and internet services (Ghosh 2024). The COVID-19 pandemic further exacerbated these challenges by disrupting physical infrastructure, social services, and community networks that are critical to marginalized populations (Operario et al. 2020).

Jharkhand is among India's most marginalized states, with tribal peoples comprising over 26% of its population (Census 2011). Despite national progress in expanding digital infrastructure, Jharkhand continues to experience persistent socio-economic inequalities, infrastructural shortcomings, and digital marginalization – especially in its tribal and rural regions. The high concentration of Scheduled Tribes (STs), including Particularly Vulnerable Tribal Groups (PVTGs), makes Jharkhand a crucial location for studying the interaction between digital policy interventions, regional cultural processes, and socio-economic constraints. Research in Jharkhand thus offers valuable insights into the challenges and opportunities of digital inclusion for India's most marginalized areas. Considering the above, this study intends to explore the status of digital technology adoption among marginalized communities (tribal groups and those residing in remote locations) of Jharkhand on the road to digital equality. Through this research, the study intended to investigate two key research questions:

RQ1: How do digital infrastructure, government policies, and local cultural factors influence the digital adoption of marginalized communities?

RQ2: How does socio-economic background shape the relationships between digital infrastructure, government policies, local culture, and the digital adoption process among marginalized communities?

The remainder of this paper is structured as follows: Sect. 2 reviews the relevant literature and theoretical framework. Section 3 outlines the methodology, including the sequential mixed-methods design. Section 4 presents qualitative findings, followed by quantitative analysis in Sect. 5. Section 6 discusses key implications, and Sect. 7 concludes with limitations and future research directions.

2 Literature Review

Building on prior studies, this research employs an integrated theoretical framework to comprehensively examine the digital adoption process from the perspective of marginalized groups. Previous research has utilized models such as Technology–Community–Management (Ale and Chib 2011), the Unified Theory of Acceptance and Use of Technology 2 (UTAUT2) (Ashley Eve Kudiwa 2024), Digital Learning Acceptance Frameworks (Arjumand and Muthulakshmi 2024), and Social Exclusion Theory (Reddick et al. 2020) to explain digital engagement and adoption. Based on these pillars, the current research incorporates fundamental elements of these theories to address the complexities of digital inclusion for marginalized groups. The framework primarily employs UTAUT2 to describe the behavioral intentions and usage patterns of marginalized groups concerning digital technologies. UTAUT2 explains how marginalized people perceive "performance expectancy, effort expectancy, and facilitating conditions" within their socio-economic and cultural contexts. In parallel, the research draws on social exclusion theory to examine how structural barriers, systemic inequalities, and historical marginalization contribute to digital divides, providing a critical lens to evaluate the effects of government policy and digital infrastructure. Additionally, Hofstede's cultural dimensions theory is employed to contextualize digital adoption behaviors further. Specific cultural constructs – such as power distance (hierarchical influences on policy acceptance), uncertainty avoidance (community openness to technological change), individualism vs. collectivism (the role of community-oriented versus individualistic values), and long-term versus short-term orientation (prioritization of immediate versus future benefits) are examined to understand how cultural values shape technology use.

Prior research on marginalized communities has often focused on usage patterns, demographic variables, and access to technology. Recent studies continue to highlight the uneven progress in rural digital adoption across India. For example, Kumar and Sofat (2024) highlight how infrastructural disparities in eastern states hinder meaningful e-inclusion, while Giest (2025) examines how socio-cultural resistance persists even when digital infrastructure is in place. These insights reaffirm the urgency of exploring region-specific antecedents of adoption, particularly in underrepresented tribal areas like Jharkhand. This study thus contributes to this emerging body of work by focusing on both structural and cultural factors in a marginalized state context. According to the study's proposed framework, Digital Infrastructure (DI), Government Policies (GP), and Local Context and Culture (LCC) are primary predictors of Digital Adoption, with Socio-Economic Background (SEB) identified as a crucial moderator. Digital Adoption (DA) (e.g., usage behavior or intention) serves as the outcome variable in the proposed model. This integrated approach offers a comprehensive understanding of how infrastructural, policy-driven, and socio-cultural factors collectively impact digital inclusion among marginalized communities.

2.1 Digital Infrastructure (DI)

Digital infrastructure refers to the technical and organizational resources, such as broadband networks, mobile connectivity, server access, and devices, that are essential for accessing digital services, particularly in regions with infrastructural deficits, which highlight stark urban–rural disparities in infrastructure across states (ICRIER 2023). The digital divide between urban and rural communities remains a persistent global challenge, particularly in developing countries where rural populations often experience lower levels of education and income, exacerbating their digital exclusion (Helsper 2021). Disparities in physical access to the internet and network availability form the initial layer of the digital divide (Ragnedda 2019; Ghosh 2024). In rural India, poor digital infrastructure, characterized by frequent power outages, low bandwidth, and unstable internet connectivity, continues to limit internet penetration and restrict access to the digital economy (Saini and Singh 2021). Recent statistics highlight the severity of this divide: while 64% of urban India has internet access, only 29% of rural India is connected (Patel 2024; Pignot 2024). Globally, India's internet penetration rate stood at 48.7% in early 2023, significantly lower than the United States' rate of 91.8% (Kemp 2023). Recognizing these disparities, the Government of India's *Digital India* initiative aims to achieve citizen empowerment, on-demand governance, and universal access to digital infrastructure (Morte-Nadal and Esteban-Navarro 2022). Notably, between 2015 and 2021, rural internet subscriptions increased by 200%, compared to 158% growth in urban areas, indicating substantial progress (PIB 2023). Still, infrastructure deficiencies remain pronounced in many tribal areas, and considering and based on these insights, the following hypothesis is proposed:

H1: *Digital infrastructure has a significant positive impact on the digital adoption of marginalized communities.*

2.2 Government Policies and Framework (GP)

Government policy includes regulations, subsidies, and public-private partnerships that influence digital service delivery (Bhatia-Kalluri and Caraway 2023). Thus, in the context of digital inclusion, Government policy refers to public initiatives, programs, and frameworks designed to enhance citizens' access to and use of digital technologies. In recent years, the proliferation of digital media has significantly altered the way governments communicate (Flew et al. 2019). Public agencies increasingly leverage digital media's immediate, direct, and interactive capabilities to promote transparency, citizen engagement, and collaborative governance (Bertot et al. 2010). The use of technology to promote good governance and ensure the timely dissemination of information to the public is widely recognized as a critical driver of efficient, goal-oriented development (Soeteman-Hernández et al. 2021).

In India, several national initiatives have played crucial roles in promoting digital adoption. Programs such as the Production-Linked Incentive (PLI) schemes for telecom and networking equipment, as well as projects like *BharatNet*, aim to enhance accessibility, affordability, connectivity, and inclusivity nationwide (KPMG 2023). To further accelerate digital inclusion, the Government of India extended the Digital India initiative for an additional five years (2021–2026) with an outlay of ₹14,903 crore, focusing on expanding public internet access and simplifying digital technologies for citizens (The Hindu Bureau 2023). These top-down efforts have been complemented in some regions by innovative local strategies. For instance, states such as West Bengal created locally relevant applications and decentralized approaches to build trust and encourage rural populations to adopt digital services (Bandyopadhyay et al. 2020). Such localized, culturally adapted frameworks underscore the importance of context-specific implementation in enhancing digital adoption among marginalized groups.

Drawing from current literature and policy analyses, the hypothesis is framed as:

H2: *Government policies and frameworks play a significant role in the digital adoption of marginalized communities.*

2.3 Local Context and Culture (LCC)

Local culture encompasses beliefs, traditions, and communication norms that shape digital behaviors, as framed by Hofstede's dimensions and further explored through regional ethnographic studies (Kalam et al. 2020). Local context and culture encompass the socio-cultural norms, values, traditions, languages, and community dynamics specific to a region, which can influence perceptions and use of technology (Petrova and Pervukhina 2022). A prevalent critique of technology adoption in non-Western contexts is that digital proliferation may erode regional cultural values and norms (Blayone and Olena Mykhailenko 2025). The social constructivist approach challenges technological determinism by emphasizing that technological development is shaped by social, cultural, and economic factors rather than occurring independently of context (Roztocki et al. 2019). As Delanty and Harris (2021) suggest, modern technology – by removing the "aura" historically associated with tradition – can lead to a *"shattering of tradition"* and altered cultural perceptions. Culture indeed plays a crucial role in the adoption of technology. Blut and Wang (2019) discussed how cultural differences significantly affect the perception and utilization of technology. These views suggest that technology both influences cultural practices and is itself shaped by existing cultural frameworks (Ruotsalainen and Heinonen 2015). Empirical evidence over time also supports the culturally contingent nature of technology use (Yang Meier et al. 2020; Jan et al. 2022; Kim et al. 2025).

Furthermore, Social cognitive theory (Bandura 1986) provides a complementary lens, emphasizing the interplay between personal characteristics, behavior, and the social environment. It recognizes the role of social learning and reinforcement in shaping behavioral intentions (Compeau et al. 1999; Chiu et al. 2006). This perspective is valuable for understanding how marginalized populations interact with technology within their unique social contexts (Mehra et al. 2004). In low-income, collective settings, trust in community leaders, preference for local-language content, and peer influence within close-knit groups can all strongly mediate digital uptake (Lyon 2000; Foshay 2016). Thus, digital adoption among marginalized communities is deeply embedded in broader social structures and cultural norms. Based on this understanding, the hypothesis is framed accordingly as:

H3: *Local context and culture have a significant influence on the digital adoption of marginalized communities.*

2.4 Socio-Economic Background (SEB)

Socio-economic background refers to an individual's social and economic circumstances, including factors such as education level, literacy, income, occupation, and social status, which shape access to resources and opportunities (Munir et al. 2023). Socioeconomic factors, such as gender, age, education, occupation, and income, are closely correlated with individuals' access to and use of digital services (Saini and Singh 2021). More affluent or educated groups are typically better positioned to access and benefit from digital technologies. At the same time, marginalized individuals may face barriers such as a lack of awareness, limited accessibility, or lower motivation to adopt such technologies (Paccoud et al. 2021). Gender inequality is yet another important dimension of digital exclusion – historically, women often had lower access and usage rates (Bimber 2000). However, longitudinal analyses have shown that the gender gap in digital adoption is narrowing over time (Ono and Zavodny 2002), and recent evidence even suggests that women can equal or outpace men in specific rural digital adoption metrics (Sindakis and Showkat 2024).

Socioeconomic background (SEB) is increasingly recognized as a critical factor in the adoption of digital technology among marginalized communities. Established models (e.g., UTAUT2) and theories related to social exclusion or digital inequality suggest that SEB influences technology acceptance processes (Mostafa Al-Emran 2023; Ong et al. 2023). For instance, an integration of technology acceptance and diffusion models argues that SEB moderates how perceived usefulness, ease of use, and social influence translate into adoption outcomes (Yusof et al. 2025); similarly, social exclusion theory posits that poverty and low education create a "vicious cycle" in which socioeconomic disadvantage perpetuates digital exclusion (Warren 2007). Empirical evidence supports this view: Kanojia and Lal (2023) found in their study that income and education levels significantly modified the strength of core adoption predictors, with higher-SEB users exhibiting a stronger link between positive attitudes (derived from perceived usefulness) and digital adoption intentions. However, even "easy-to-use" services often see muted uptake in low-SEB communities due to residual barriers (e.g., limited literacy, infrastructure gaps, or cultural reservations) (Yusof et al. 2025). Thus, SEB fundamentally shapes the magnitude and direction of predictor–outcome relationships in technology uptake. Recognizing this moderating influence not only enriches theory but also guides the present methodology, which explicitly tests SEB's conditioning effect on adoption determinants in marginalized settings.

Accordingly, the following hypotheses are proposed:

H4a: *Socio-economic background moderates the influence of digital infrastructure on digital adoption.*

H4b: *Socio-economic background moderates the influence of government policies on digital adoption.*

H4c: *Socio-economic background moderates the influence of local context and culture on digital adoption.*

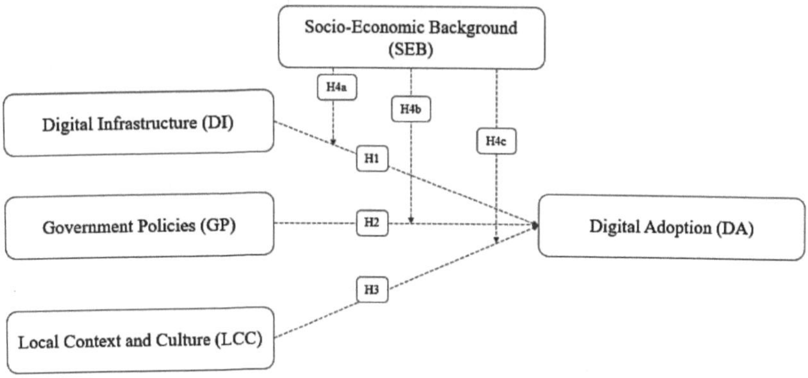

Fig. 1. Proposed framework. Source—Author's Conceptualization

Figure 1 illustrates the initial conceptual framework, depicting H1–H3 as direct effects on Digital Adoption and H4a–H4c as moderating effects of SEB.

3 Methodology

This study employed a sequential exploratory mixed-methods design (Creswell and Creswell 2018) to develop and validate the research instrument systematically. This approach was deemed appropriate because an initial qualitative exploration provides in-depth, culturally nuanced insights that can inform the design of a contextually relevant survey for the subsequent quantitative phase. In other words, starting with qualitative inquiry allowed us to adapt measurement scales to the local cultural setting and ensure that key constructs (such as digital infrastructure, policy, and culture) were operationalized in a way that resonated with participants' lived experiences. The follow-up quantitative phase then tested hypotheses and the measurement model derived from those insights. Such a design is especially justified in marginalized contexts where standardized technology adoption scales (e.g., UTAUT2) might not fully capture local realities without prior exploration.

Phase 1 – Qualitative Exploration

In the initial qualitative phase, we conducted 36 in-depth interviews (continuing until the attainment of saturation) with a purposive sample of stakeholders in Jharkhand.

Participants included government officials involved in digital initiatives, village heads (*Mukhiya*), and general community members across various remote tribal villages. Table 1 provides an overview of the interview sample characteristics. We intentionally sampled a diverse range of informants to gather multiple perspectives on digital adoption barriers and enablers in these communities. Each interview followed a semi-structured protocol that covered topics such as experiences with using (or attempting to use) digital services, perceptions of government digital programs, local attitudes toward technology, infrastructural challenges faced (e.g., connectivity, electricity), and cultural or language factors that affect technology use. Interviews averaged ~ 30 min in length. They were conducted in local languages (primarily Hindi and regional dialects, such as Santhali), with the help of trained translators wherever necessary, to ensure participants could express themselves comfortably. All interviews were audio-recorded with consent, then transcribed and translated into English for analysis.

Table 1. Profile of interview participants (qualitative phase)

Participant category	Description	Count (n = 36)
Government Officials	State and district e-governance officers, ICT program managers	10
Village Heads (*Mukhiya*)	Elected heads of villages/communities	8
Community Members	General residents (mixed ages and genders) from tribal/rural areas	18

The qualitative data are analyzed using interpretative phenomenological analysis (IPA) to derive nuanced insights into participants' experiences with digital media, particularly about the study's key variables (DI, GP, LCC, and SEB). Two researchers independently open-coded the transcripts using NVivo 12 software, identifying recurrent concepts and contextual factors mentioned by participants. Codes were iteratively refined and grouped into emergent themes through discussion and consensus, ensuring reliability of interpretation. This inductive process yielded rich descriptions of each construct in the local setting, informing our operationalization of them in the survey. For example, the interviews highlighted specific facets of *digital infrastructure* (e.g. daily hours of electricity availability, distance travelled to find network signal), *government policy* (awareness of specific schemes, trust in digital services like mobile banking), *local culture* (use of tribal languages online, influence of community leaders), and *socio-economic barriers* (low income, low literacy) that standard questionnaires might not capture. These insights directly shaped the wording and content of our measurement items in the next phase. Below, we summarize key qualitative findings by construct, which also served to refine our hypotheses.

4 Findings

4.1 Qualitative Findings

Digital Infrastructure: Participants reported that despite government efforts to enhance infrastructure, reliable internet access remains a significant barrier. In remote villages, connectivity is so limited that people often have to travel to a community centre or panchayat office to obtain a usable network signal. Electricity supply is also inconsistent – many interior areas receive power for only 5–6 h a day, hindering device charging and stable usage. While smartphone penetration has increased following COVID-19 (mainly due to the push for online education), the combination of limited network coverage and frequent outages significantly impedes regular internet use. Notably, digital adoption appears uneven across generations: younger individuals, driven by the necessity of online classes and opportunities, have become relatively adept at using platforms like Zoom and Google Meet; in contrast, older generations struggle due to limited digital literacy and unfamiliarity. As one middle-aged participant explained, *even after purchasing a smartphone for their children's schooling, poor network coverage and a lack of awareness about available digital services made it difficult for the family to benefit from the device.* Such accounts underscore that structural issues – a weak communication grid and electricity constraints – continue to limit meaningful digital engagement.

Government Policies: Participants acknowledged several government initiatives leveraging digital platforms that have improved service delivery and financial inclusion. Frequently mentioned were e-governance services, mobile banking, and flagship schemes like *Jan Dhan Yojana* (financial accounts for the unbanked) and direct benefit transfers (DBT) of subsidies. Social media, especially X (formerly Twitter), has emerged as a channel for grievance redressal and disseminating information about schemes. However, the impact of these digital government efforts is tempered by low digital literacy and trust issues. Many villagers – especially women and the elderly – are unable or hesitant to fully engage with online services due to fear of scams, lack of cybersecurity awareness, or simple unfamiliarity. For example, one female participant noted that *while UPI mobile payments have made transactions more convenient, she still worries about fraud and thus avoids larger dealings online.* Younger community members increasingly use WhatsApp to receive information and share updates (often related to government programs or job opportunities). In contrast, older generations still rely on traditional face-to-face gatherings at the village *Akhra* (meeting place) for news. Interestingly, an emerging trend noted was that people are joining social media primarily to follow government pages and leaders for relevant updates. In summary, digital platforms are enhancing access to information and services. However, they have not entirely replaced in-person interactions, and in some cases, have additionally introduced new challenges related to trust and digital skills.

Local Context and Culture: Local cultural dynamics shape digital behavior. Participants emphasized the pivotal role of community influencers and trusted leaders in propagating digital literacy. *If a respected village figure advocates a particular app or e-service, others are far more likely to try it.* There is a strong preference for content in regional languages and from familiar sources; engagement spikes when information is presented through culturally proximal channels (*e.g., an audio message in Santhali by a known community worker*). Peer effects are significant: seeing neighbours successfully use a digital tool motivates others. One young participant shared that *observing his friend obtain crop prices via a mobile app convinced him to invest in a smartphone despite his financial constraints*. At the same time, cultural tensions were evident. Several elders voiced concern that the influx of non-native content (mostly Hindi or English) on the internet is eroding indigenous languages and practices. One interviewee expressed concern that local youths, preoccupied with *YouTube and social media, were neglecting the Santhali language and traditional chores, perceiving digital engagement as a threat to cultural preservation*. Overall, the qualitative narratives suggest that digital media open up new opportunities for marginalized groups (including information access, connectivity, and even empowerment), but simultaneously pose challenges to cultural continuity. Interventions that leverage local culture – such as community-led tech workshops or content creation in tribal languages – seem crucial for fostering trust and relevance.

In summary, the qualitative phase revealed that *access barriers, socio-economic factors, local trust structures, and cultural norms* all critically influence digital adoption in Jharkhand's marginalized communities. Digital initiatives tend to succeed when infrastructural improvements are complemented by localized, culturally sensitive efforts that address issues of trust, literacy, and cultural preservation. These findings reinforced our proposed conceptual model and informed the design of the subsequent survey instrument (e.g., including items on electricity reliability, trust in e-services, etc.). Key themes from the interviews were mapped onto our hypotheses: for example, the stories illustrated *why* digital infrastructure (H1) and government support (H2) should matter, *how* local culture might facilitate or hinder adoption (H3), and *in what ways* socio-economic gaps (education, income) could amplify or mute these effects (H4a–H4c).

4.2 Phase 2 – Survey and Quantitative Analysis

Building upon the qualitative insights, we designed a structured survey instrument for the quantitative phase. All survey measures for the primary constructs (DI, GP, LCC, SEB, and DA) were either adapted from established scales in prior literature or newly created based on the interview findings, then refined for cultural relevance and clarity. For example, items measuring *Digital Infrastructure* were tailored to ask about perceptions of network availability and electricity stability in the respondent's locality (rather than generic tech access), and *Local Culture* items probed agreement with statements about preferring local language content or influence of community norms on tech use. The survey was prepared in both English and Hindi; a back-translation method was used to ensure accuracy of the Hindi version. Given the low literacy levels among some target respondents, the survey was administered via face-to-face interviews by trained enumerators (who were from the region and spoke local dialects). The enumerators read questions aloud and recorded responses on tablets. Participants were assured of anonymity and that their responses would be used solely for research purposes.

The target population was marginalized community members in rural Jharkhand who had at least some exposure to digital technology (e.g., owning or having access to a mobile phone). We employed a purposive cluster sampling strategy: several remote villages across different districts (15 districts) were identified in collaboration with local

NGOs, ensuring coverage of areas with high tribal populations and known infrastructural challenges. Within each village cluster, households were approached and one adult respondent (aged 18 or above) was recruited per household (with an effort to balance gender representation). This yielded a sample of 418 respondents for the survey. This sample size exceeds the minimum recommended threshold of ~ 200–300 for analyses involving models of moderate complexity (Hair et al. 2020), providing sufficient statistical power. The demographic attributes of the survey respondents are detailed in Table 2. In brief, the final sample consisted of 58% males and 42% females. Ages ranged from 18 to 67 years (mean ~ 34 years). Approximately two-thirds of respondents had at least a secondary school education, although a significant subset (≈approximately 30%) had not completed high school. The majority were engaged in agriculture or daily wage labor, with low household incomes reflecting subsistence livelihoods. Such diversity in age, gender, and socio-economic status within the marginalized context helps ensure our findings are broadly representative of the target communities. The survey was conducted between September 2024 and February 2025.

Table 2. Demographic profile of survey respondents (quantitative phase)

Characteristic	Category	Percentage of Respondents (N = 418)
Gender	Male / Female	58% / 42%
Age group	18–30 / 31–50 / Above 50	34% / 46% / 20%
Education level	No formal education	12%
	Primary (up to 8th grade)	19%
	Secondary (9th–12th grade)	45%
	Tertiary (college or higher)	24%
Primary occupation	Agriculture (farmer/laborer)	51%
	Non-agricultural labor	22%
	Self-employed/Small business	15%
	Unemployed or homemaker	12%

All survey questions were carefully worded to elicit information pertinent to the research objectives. Given the remote and multilingual setting, the researchers worked closely with local interpreters during data collection to ensure respondents fully understood each item. For instance, technical terms were explained in layperson's terms and analogies (e.g., describing "internet bandwidth" as "speed of phone network" in the local language). This on-ground assistance was essential for reaching marginalized participants who might otherwise be inaccessible due to language or literacy barriers.

Data Analysis Approach – The quantitative data were analyzed using Jamovi (v2.3.28) statistical and analytical software. A preliminary check was conducted, and exploratory factor analysis (EFA) was performed on the multi-item construct measures to validate the factor structure suggested by our theoretical model. Subsequently, a confirmatory factor analysis (CFA) was conducted to verify the measurement model, and then multiple regression analyses (including interaction terms) were run to test the hypotheses. Throughout, recommended procedures for establishing the reliability and validity of the constructs were adhered to as detailed next.

Preliminary Analysis: Of the 418 collected responses, we screened for completeness and quality. Few cases (n≈17) with excessive missing data or straight-line answers were excluded. The distribution of each variable was also examined; a few outliers on continuous measures (e.g., extremely high self-reported usage hours) were identified, but sensitivity tests confirmed they did not substantially distort results, so they were retained. The final dataset (n≈401) was thus deemed suitable for factor analysis and regression.

Exploratory Factor Analysis (EFA) was conducted using principal axis factoring with oblimin rotation to identify the latent structure underlying the survey items. Bartlett's test of sphericity was significant ($\chi^2 = 9882$, df = 190, $p < .001$), and the overall KMO measure of sampling adequacy was 0.772, indicating suitability for factor analysis. Four factors were extracted based on eigenvalues greater than one and supported by the scree plot, cumulatively explaining 75.3% of the total variance. Most items demonstrated strong loadings (> 0.60) on their respective factors, confirming convergent validity. For instance, LCC3 (0.906), SEB1 (0.891), and GP4 (0.822) loaded strongly on Factor 1, while DA1 (0.942), DA2 (0.875), and DA3 (0.707) loaded on Factor 3. Items with high uniqueness or cross-loadings (e.g., DI1 and DI3) were reviewed for potential exclusion in future refinement. These results confirm that the constructs of Digital Infrastructure, Government Policy, Local Context and Culture, Socioeconomic Background, and Digital Adoption exhibit satisfactory construct validity, providing a sound basis for subsequent regression and moderation analyses. (as shown in Table 3 below). All these statistics were considered acceptable (Hair et al. 2020).

Reliability Analysis

Scale reliability was evaluated using Cronbach's α and McDonald's ω, both of which indicated excellent internal consistency. The overall reliability coefficients were $\alpha = 0.877$ and $\omega = 0.894$, exceeding the standard threshold of 0.70 (Hair et al. 2020). These results confirm that the measurement instrument demonstrates strong internal coherence and is suitable for further statistical analysis (Table 4).

Discriminant validity was further assessed using the Fornell–Larcker criterion, which compares the square root of the Average Variance Extracted (AVE) of each construct with its inter-construct correlations. As shown in Table 5, the square roots of AVE values - 0.784 for Local Context and Culture (LCC), 0.806 for Socioeconomic Background (SEB), and 0.847 for Digital Adoption (DA) were all greater than their corresponding inter-construct correlations (ranging from − 0.2215 to 0.128). This confirms that the constructs are empirically distinct from one another, thereby affirming the discriminant validity of the model (Ab Hamid et al. 2017). The AVE for Digital Infrastructure and Government Policy (DI-GP) was not computed due to unstable loading patterns for one or more indicators.

Before regression modelling, multicollinearity among the independent variables (DI, GP, LCC, SEB, plus interaction terms) was checked. All variance inflation factors (VIFs)

Table 3. Factor loadings

	Factor				
	1	2	3	4	Uniqueness
LCC3	0.906				0.1163
SEB1	0.891				0.1507
SEB3	0.878				0.1271
GP4	0.822				0.2060
GP3	0.811				0.2236
LCC2	0.564				0.0526
LCC4	0.507				0.2422
DI3					0.6309
SEB2		0.955			0.0513
LCC1		0.953			0.0500
GP2		0.793			0.3180
DI2		0.768			0.2242
DI4		0.725			0.3225
GP1		0.579			0.3511
DA1			0.942		0.1142
DA2			0.875		0.2531
DA3			0.707		0.0975
SEB4				– 0.815	0.2248
DA4				0.680	0.1891
DI1					0.9960

Note.'Principal axis factoring' extraction method was used in combination with a 'oblimin' rotation

Table 4. Scale reliability statistics

	Cronbach's α	McDonald's ω
Scale	0.877	0.894

were well below 5.0 (maximum ~ 1.8) and tolerances above 0.5, indicating no serious multicollinearity concerns. Thus, the predictors can be included together in the regression models without risk of instability.

Regression Analysis

Hypothesis Testing (Main Effects)

Table 5. Fornell–Larcker criterion for discriminant validity

Construct	√AVE	LCC	SEB	DA	DI-GP
Local Context & Culture (LCC)	0.784	—	0.0915	– 0.175	0.0869
Socioeconomic Background (SEB)	0.806		—	0.128	– 0.1009
Digital Adoption (DA)	0.847			—	– 0.2215
Digital Infrastructure & Government Policy (DI-GP)	—				—

H1–H3 (the direct effects of DI, GP, and LCC on digital adoption) are tested, and the role of SEB as an additional predictor is examined. Given that our dependent variable, Digital Adoption (DA), was measured on a continuous scale (indicating propensity or frequency of using digital services), the study employed a standard multiple regression analysis. Table 6 summarizes the regression results, including standardized coefficients (β) and significance levels for each predictor. The overall model fit was significant: F (4, 413) = 36.6, $p < 0.001$, with an R^2 of 0.512. This indicates that the four predictors together explain about 51.2% of the variance in digital adoption – a substantial effect, suggesting our model has good explanatory power for understanding digital uptake in this context.

Table 6. Regression results – main effects on digital adoption

Model fit measures			
Model	R		R^2
1	0.715		0.512
Predictor	β coefficient	p-value	Hypothesis outcome
Digital Infrastructure (DI)	0.3020	< 0.001**	H1 Supported
Government Policies (GP)	0.3868	< 0.001**	H2 Supported
Local Context & Culture (LCC)	0.0809	0.363	H3 *Not* Supported
Socio-Economic Barriers (SEB)	– 0.2618	< 0.001**	(Direct effect; negative)

Looking at individual hypotheses: Digital Infrastructure (DI) exhibited a positive and highly significant effect on Digital Adoption ($\beta = 0.302, p < 0.001$), supporting H1.

This implies that, holding other factors constant, improvements in local digital infrastructure (better connectivity, electricity, device access) are associated with higher digital adoption among marginalized users. Government Policies (GP) also showed a strong positive effect ($\beta = 0.387$, $p < 0.001$), supporting H2. This suggests that supportive policy frameworks and digital inclusion initiatives (when effectively reaching the community) contribute meaningfully to encouraging technology uptake. In contrast, Local Context & Culture (LCC) had a positive but statistically non-significant relationship with Digital Adoption ($\beta = 0.081$, $p = 0.363$). Thus, H3 was not supported in a direct sense – variations in local cultural or contextual factors did not, on average, predict digital adoption levels in this sample. This is an intriguing result given the theoretical importance of culture; it hints that cultural influences might be more complex (potentially operating through interactions, which we examine shortly). Finally, Socio-Economic Barriers (SEB) had a significant *negative* effect on Digital Adoption ($\beta = -0.262$, $p < 0.001$). In substantive terms, this means individuals with greater socio-economic disadvantages (lower education, income, etc.) tend to have markedly lower digital adoption, all else equal. While we did not hypothesize a direct effect for SEB (since we conceptualized it mainly as a moderator), this finding reinforces the critical role of socio-economic factors as an obstacle to digital inclusion. Overall, the main-effects model confirms that infrastructural and policy factors are key enablers of adoption in marginalized communities, whereas socio-economic deprivation remains a significant impediment. Local cultural context, interestingly, did not show a uniform effect in this linear model, prompting a closer look at the moderation hypotheses.

Moderation Analysis

H4a, H4b, and H4c posited that Socio-Economic Background (SEB) would moderate the effects of DI, GP, and LCC on digital adoption, respectively. Table 7 below shows the testing of these interactions using moderated regression analysis. For each predictor, an interaction term with the SEB variable (after mean-centering the constituent variables to reduce multicollinearity) is created. The regression model was then extended to include these interaction terms. The results for the interaction effects are summarised below (Table 7).

Moderation of DI → DA by SEB (H4a): The interaction term DI ∗ SEB was positive and statistically significant (Estimate = 0.5671, SE = 0.0983, Z = 5.77, $p < 0.001$). This indicates that SEB significantly moderates the relationship between digital infrastructure and adoption. Simple slope analysis further revealed that the effect of DI on DA was stronger at higher levels of SEB (Estimate = 0.732, $p < .001$) and non-significant at lower levels of SEB (Estimate = – 0.269, $p = 0.053$). This suggests that the positive impact of digital infrastructure on adoption becomes more pronounced when social and economic barriers are high. In essence, H4a is supported; the positive influence of infrastructure on adoption becomes *more pronounced* for communities facing greater socio-economic challenges. When people are significantly disadvantaged, having a functional digital infrastructure (even a single village Wi-Fi hotspot or reliable phone network) can make a decisive difference in enabling them to go online. In contrast, people who are socioeconomically better off might find ways to adopt technology even without perfect infrastructure (e.g., by affording alternatives).

Moderation of GP → DA by SEB (H4b): The interaction GP ∗ SEB was *not* statistically significant (Estimate = + 0.035, SE = 0.117, $Z = 0.299$, $p = 0.765$). This means SEB does not significantly moderate the impact of government policies on digital adoption. In other words, H4b is not supported – the effect of supportive digital policies and initiatives appears to be pretty consistent across different socio-economic strata. Indeed, the simple slopes showed that GP had a significant positive effect on adoption at low, medium, and high levels of SEB alike (all $p < 0.001$). This finding suggests that well-designed government interventions (such as free training, subsidized devices, or e-service kiosks) benefit everyone in these communities, regardless of individual background – or put differently, even the poorest can take advantage of good policies if those policies adequately reach them. It underscores the broad importance of inclusive policy implementation.

Moderation of LCC → DA by SEB (H4c): The interaction LCC ∗ SEB was highly significant (Estimate = + 0.749, SE = 0.076, $Z = 9.90$, $p < 0.001$). Thus, SEB strongly moderates the relationship between local cultural context and digital adoption, supporting H4c. The nature of this interaction is particularly interesting: simple slope analysis showed that for individuals with low socio-economic barriers (i.e. relatively better-off), the relationship between LCC and DA was negative and significant (slope $\beta \approx -0.43$, $p < 0.001$); but for those with high socio-economic barriers (very disadvantaged), the relationship turned positive and highly significant ($\beta \approx + 0.89$, $p < 0.001$). In other words, among the poorest segments, a favourable local culture (e.g., strong community support, availability of content in local language, etc.) dramatically boosts digital adoption. However, among the relatively better-off in these communities, local cultural factors – perhaps such as attachment to tradition or skepticism of outside technology – might even slightly hinder adoption (hence a negative association when SEB is low). This flip, in effect, explains why LCC had no net impact in the aggregate: the cultural influence is *contingent on socio-economic status*. Marginal means plots (see Fig. 2) confirmed this crossover interaction: at low SEB, adoption was higher when local culture was less emphasized (possibly indicating these individuals adopt mainstream digital behavior irrespective of local customs), whereas at high SEB (high barriers), adoption was highest when local culture was strongly supportive of digital use. Thus, H4c is supported, highlighting a nuanced interplay between cultural context and socio-economic marginality in shaping digital uptake.

Summarizing the moderation analysis yields the following interpretations:

- **DI ∗ SEB:** Significant moderation – the benefit of digital infrastructure on adoption is *much greater* for individuals facing high socio-economic barriers (who rely heavily on infrastructural improvements to participate digitally).
- **GP ∗ SEB:** No significant moderation – government policy support has a consistently positive effect on adoption across all socio-economic groups, implying such initiatives are broadly effective.
- **LCC ∗ SEB:** Significant moderation – the effect of local culture on adoption flips from slightly negative (for higher-SES individuals) to strongly positive (for lower-SES,

Table 7. Moderation estimates

Study variables	Estimate	SE	Z	p	Remarks
Variable - DI					
DI	**0.2318**	**0.0702**	**3.30**	**< .001**	
SEB	**0.0445**	**0.0377**	**1.18**	**0.238**	
DI * SEB	**0.5671**	**0.0983**	**5.77**	**< 0.001****	**Supported**
Simple slope estimates (DI)					
Average	**0.232**	**0.0744**	**3.12**	**0.002**	
Low (− 1SD)	**− 0.269**	**0.1386**	**− 1.94**	**0.053**	
High (+ 1SD)	**0.732**	**0.0866**	**8.45**	**< 0.0001**	
Variable 2 - GP					
GP	**0.6376**	**0.0761**	**8.378**	**< 0.001**	
SEB	**− 0.1232**	**0.0375**	**− 3.286**	**0.001**	
GP * SEB	**0.0350**	**0.1170**	**0.299**	**0.765**	**Not Supported**
Simple slope estimates (GP)					
Average	**0.638**	**0.0761**	**8.38**	**< 0.001**	
Low (− 1SD)	**0.607**	**0.1559**	**3.89**	**< 0.001**	
High (+ 1SD)	**0.669**	**0.0927**	**7.21**	**< 0.001**	
Variable 3 - LCC					
LCC	**0.228**	**0.0624**	**3.66**	**< 0.001**	
SEB	**0.330**	**0.0966**	**3.42**	**< 0.001**	
LCC * SEB	**0.749**	**0.0757**	**9.90**	**< 0.001****	**Supported**
Simple slope estimates (LCC)					
Average	**0.228**	**0.0702**	**3.26**	**0.001**	
Low (− 1SD)	**− 0.433**	**0.1130**	**− 3.83**	**< 0.001**	
High (+ 1SD)	**0.890**	**0.0754**	**11.80**	**< 0.001**	

Note. Simple Slope Estimates shows the effect of the predictor on the dependent variable at different levels of the moderator (SEB)

high-barrier individuals). In highly marginalized segments, a culturally supportive environment (community encouragement, local language content) is crucial and can substantially elevate adoption. For relatively better-off individuals, local cultural context might matter less or even act as a conservative force relative to external influences.

These nuanced results reinforce that *socio-economic background profoundly shapes how and for whom certain factors matter*. SEB essentially accentuates the importance of infrastructure and cultural relevance for the poorest of the poor, while not altering the universal benefit of sound policy. In practical terms, digital inclusion efforts must pay special attention to those on the lowest rung's socio-economically – in their case, improving infrastructure and providing culturally tailored content can yield disproportionately large gains in adoption. Meanwhile, supportive policies should continue unabated since they help across the board.

5 Discussion

This study examined the factors influencing digital technology adoption among marginalized communities in Jharkhand, India, using an integrated framework of UTAUT2, social exclusion theory, and cultural context. The findings reveal that the considered variables have significant impacts on digital adoption; however, their effects vary across different socio-economic contexts. This section presents the results in light of prior research, discusses theoretical implications, and outlines practical steps forward.

5.1 Digital Infrastructure

The significant role of digital infrastructure aligns with core tenets of UTAUT2, which highlights facilitating conditions as a key determinant of technology use. The quantitative analysis results showed that better infrastructure (stable internet and electricity, device availability) strongly predicts higher adoption ($\beta \approx 0.30$). Qualitative accounts confirmed that basic access remains a gating issue in remote areas – for example, some villagers must travel for network signal, illustrating how infrastructure deficits directly impede usage. This finding resonates with recent studies emphasizing connectivity as critical for rural digital uptake (Sindakis and Showkat 2024). Similarly, Wu and Peng (2024) noted that challenges like poor network coverage continue to hinder meaningful digital engagement in marginalized communities. This research reinforces these observations and extends them to the tribal context of Jharkhand. The takeaway is that *bridging the digital divide begins with bridging the infrastructure divide.* From a theoretical standpoint, this underscores the importance of "facilitating conditions" (in UTAUT2 terms) in extreme contexts. Without a minimum level of connectivity and power, even the most motivated individuals cannot participate online. Practically, the implication is straightforward: continued investment in rural telecom infrastructure, electrification, and maintenance is foundational. The findings suggest that such investments can directly translate into increased digital adoption among the poorest citizens, as they create the enabling environment for any other interventions to take root. So, it means policymakers and development agencies must prioritize closing the rural infrastructure gap as a first step towards digital equity. Innovative solutions like community Wi-Fi centres, solar-powered charging stations, or extending mobile towers to off-grid hamlets are concrete actions that can empower marginalized groups to come online. These improvements are not just technical upgrades; they are social levellers that give marginalized communities the basic opportunity to connect, learn, and engage with the broader world.

5.2 Government Policies

Government initiatives and policy frameworks emerged as another strong driver of adoption ($\beta \approx 0.39$), highlighting the efficacy of inclusive digital programs when implemented well. The data analysis result illustrated how schemes like Jan Dhan Yojana (bank accounts) and various e-governance and digital financial services have started to make inroads, providing tangible incentives for people to embrace digital tools (e.g., to receive benefits or access services). This finding is consistent with the notion in social exclusion theory that structural inclusion efforts (like pro-poor policies) can mitigate digital inequality. It also finds support in recent literature. Sindakis and Showkat (2024) and Ghosh (2024) documented that the Digital India Program (DIP) has played a vital role in empowering rural populations and even helped narrow the gender gap in technology access. In phase one of the research (qualitative phase), many female respondents were using smartphones partly due to government-facilitated programs, echoing that observation. Also, according to Kathuria et al. (2021), they demonstrated how localized digital policy interventions in India (like state-level e-services and training) boosted adoption by building trust and relevance at the grassroots. This is also supported and emerged as one point in the qualitative interviews that policy impact is amplified when coupled with community outreach (e.g., using local influencers to promote schemes). Notably, the moderation results showed policy effects were uniform across socio-economic groups – even the most disadvantaged benefited from well-delivered initiatives. This suggests that government programs, when accessible, can act as a great equalizer in digital inclusion. Thus, it indicates that sustained commitment to inclusive digital policies is justified and necessary. The theoretical implication is that policy support is an exogenous factor that can compensate for specific deficiencies (like low income or education) by lowering barriers (through subsidies, free training, etc.). Practically, governments should expand and refine programs such as digital literacy missions, subsidized smartphones or data plans for low-income households, and community internet centres. Feasible actions include partnering with local NGOs to ensure schemes reach illiterate populations (e.g., via assisted access points at panchayat offices) and tailoring services to local needs (like agricultural market info apps in local languages). Additionally, building robust feedback loops (through village meetings or social media) can improve trust and uptake – as some participants noted, seeing their grievances addressed online increased their faith in digital platforms. The findings of this research thus validate that "digital inclusion policy works", and to maximize impact, such policy must be context-aware and coupled with on-ground facilitation in marginalized regions.

5.3 Local Culture and Context

The influence of local socio-cultural context on digital adoption proved to be complex. In the overall model, LCC did not have a significant direct effect, which initially seems to contradict expectations from cultural theory. However, the moderation analysis revealed that culture matters profoundly, but its effect is conditional on socio-economic status. For the most disadvantaged groups, a supportive local culture (community encouragement, content in one's language, etc.) can significantly boost adoption. It became a strong positive predictor under high barriers. This aligns with the notion that when formal resources are scarce, informal social structures and norms play a crucial role in technology diffusion (Roztocki et al. 2019). Conversely, for relatively better-off individuals in these communities, local cultural factors had a negligible or even slight negative influence, perhaps because these individuals are less constrained by local norms and more influenced by broader (national/global) culture and personal utility considerations. Prior qualitative research emphasizes that technology adoption is culturally contingent, and our findings echo that but add nuance (Blayone and Mykhailenko 2025; Kalam et al. 2020).

Additionally, it was found that trust and social influence in the community – aspects highlighted by social cognitive theory – are key for marginalized users. This resonates with other studies in rural contexts (Nayak and Alam 2022). The study's results provide empirical support for these claims. The "flipped" effect we observed suggests that those with higher education/income might adopt technology regardless of local traditional resistance (or even as a form of differentiation from tradition). In contrast, those with low education/income rely heavily on communal cues and culturally relevant content to adopt. Thus, theoretically, this underscores that digital divide research must account for cultural context *in tandem* with socio-economic status – culture is not a uniform influence but interacts with class and education. From a practical perspective, digital inclusion efforts must be culturally sensitive and community-driven, especially when targeting the poorest segments. Feasible actions include recruiting and training local youth as "digital ambassadors" to teach elders in culturally appropriate ways, developing content (government forms, apps, instructional videos) in local tribal languages and idioms, and leveraging respected community leaders or teachers to endorse new technologies. So, for example, if village chiefs or religious leaders become advocates for certain beneficial digital practices (like telehealth or mobile banking), it can assuage fears and lend legitimacy, catalyzing wider adoption. At the same time, one must be mindful of cultural tensions, as participants during the qualitative interviews raised valid concerns about cultural erosion. Thus, the study's findings highlight that culture can be either a bridge or a barrier in digital adoption, depending on how it is engaged – and for marginalized communities, engaging it the right way (through inclusion of local norms, languages, and social structures) is indispensable for success.

5.4 Socio-Economic Background and Inequality

Perhaps the most salient thread tying the above points together is the role of socio-economic background. This research empirically demonstrated that socio-economic disadvantages (low education, poverty) not only directly reduce digital adoption but also modulate the impact of other factors. This reinforces the idea that the digital divide is fundamentally linked to existing social inequities (Helsper 2021). For marginalized populations, poverty and illiteracy are twin barriers – even if infrastructure is improved and services are offered, those with very low literacy or income may still struggle to adopt without targeted support. The moderation results showed that for people with higher barriers, improving infrastructure or providing culturally relevant content yields disproportionately high returns in terms of adoption. This is an encouraging insight: it suggests that by focusing efforts on the most vulnerable subgroups, one can significantly "move the needle" on inclusion. It also explains why prior research often finds that the digital divide mirrors the socio-economic divide (Reddick et al. 2020). This study extends the literature by quantifying how socio-economic context changes the effects of interventions. Recent evidence from rural technology projects similarly highlights that younger, better-educated individuals tend to be early adopters, while older, less-educated individuals lag without extra help (Sindakis and Showkat 2024).

The implication is that closing the digital divide is not just about technology – it requires tackling underlying social exclusion. Theoretical models of technology acceptance should integrate moderators like education and income (as in this study) to increase their explanatory power in marginalized settings. Practically, digital inclusion initiatives should be tightly coupled with broader development initiatives: improving education and literacy is, in the long run, a digital inclusion strategy. Thus, special measures are needed to include low-SES individuals. For example, this could involve simplifying user interfaces, providing voice-based services for the illiterate, or offering assisted access points where trained personnel can help villagers perform digital tasks (similar to a "digital public library" concept). In addition, economic measures such as microloans, subsidies for device affordability, and free or low-cost internet access can directly alleviate the cost barrier associated with SEB. Ultimately, bridging socio-economic gaps in digital adoption will also yield broader socio-economic benefits – as digital connection becomes increasingly necessary for education, livelihoods, and civic participation, those left offline risk further marginalization. The study's findings thus emphasize that *digital inclusion is both a technical and a social challenge*, one that requires an equity-oriented approach focusing on the poorest and most marginalized.

6 Theoretical Implications

This research offers several contributions to technology adoption theory, especially in the context of underserved communities. First, by integrating UTAUT2 with social exclusion theory and Hofstede's cultural dimensions, we demonstrate that digital adoption in marginalized settings is not merely a function of individual perceptions (as per classical TAM/UTAUT models) but is profoundly shaped by broader socio-cultural and policy environments. The findings extend UTAUT2 by introducing Socio-Economic Background (SEB) as a critical moderating variable. In the original UTAUT2, factors like facilitating conditions and effort expectancy are considered universal predictors; the study's results show that their influence can vary depending on an individual's socio-economic barriers. For example, even if facilitating conditions (infrastructure) improve, a person lacking education or income might still not adopt unless additional support is provided – yet once a threshold of support is met, that same infrastructure improvement has a *greater* impact on someone who was previously excluded. This moderated effect highlights the non-linear, conditional nature of technology acceptance in real-world diverse populations, suggesting that future models should treat socio-economic factors not just as controls but as fundamental context variables.

Second, this research refined social exclusion theory in the digital domain by illustrating how targeted government policies can actively reduce digital exclusion – but importantly, these policies work best when coupled with efforts to build trust and digital capability at the community level. Social exclusion theory posits that structural disadvantages lead to marginalization; this study shows that structural *inclusions* (like pro-poor digital policies) can mitigate those effects, effectively breaking the exclusion cycle if executed well. The consistent positive impact of government support across all groups in the discussion is evidence that *exclusion is not inevitable* – wise policy can empower marginalized citizens to overcome some infrastructural and economic hurdles. This theoretically underscores the role of institutions and governance as mediators in the digital divide, a dimension sometimes underemphasized in purely user-centric adoption models.

Third, the contribution to cross-cultural technology adoption research by shedding light on how *collectivist community values and cultural preservation concerns* mediate technology acceptance in indigenous and rural settings. It is found that cultural context does not uniformly impede or facilitate adoption; rather, its effect is conditioned by other inequalities. This suggests that theories of cultural influence (like Hofstede's dimensions) may need to be applied in a nuanced way within a single cultural region, and subcultural variations (e.g., between more and less educated subsets) can lead to different outcomes. Essentially, culture in this study acted as an amplifier when socio-economic barriers were high, implying a kind of interplay between material and cultural capital. The concept of "technological leapfrogging" often assumes that if infrastructure is given, communities will adopt; this study's findings caution that cultural and socio-economic context will determine if leapfrogging truly occurs. The implication for theory is to encourage more *multi-dimensional models* that include economic, social, and cultural variables concurrently. This study adds empirical backing to this trend and specifically advocates including socio-economic indicators as moderators and cultural factors as either moderators or additional constructs in models aiming to predict technology use in rural or marginalized populations.

Summarizing, the theoretical lenses used in this study converge on a key insight: digital behavior is embedded in a *social system*. For marginalized groups, you cannot separate the user from their environment – adoption (or non-adoption) is the result of an ongoing negotiation between individual agency and structural conditions. The findings of this research will encourage further research to adopt an ecosystem perspective on digital inclusion, examining not just "will someone use a technology," but "under what conditions and for whom" technology delivers its promise of empowerment.

7 Practical Implications

The study's findings yield actionable insights for policymakers, development organizations, and practitioners working to overcome the on-ground digital inequality:

a. Reliable internet connectivity, electricity, and device access are foundational. Government and private sector stakeholders should prioritize extending network coverage to uncovered villages (e.g., through incentive programs for telecom operators or community networks). Off-grid solutions like solar-powered Wi-Fi hotspots and charging stations can address power issues. Even a single mobile tower or public internet kiosk in a cluster of villages can dramatically increase digital participation. Bridging infrastructure gaps will have a direct payoff in adoption rates, as evidenced by the strong effect of DI in our model. Every additional hour of electricity or extra bar of network signal is an hour a marginalized individual can spend online – potentially accessing education, markets, or telehealth.

b. To complement infrastructure, the affordability of digital access must be tackled. Subsidizing smartphones or data plans for low-income households (as some government programs and universal service funds are beginning to do) is crucial. A practical example is setting up *Common Service Centres (CSCs)* in each panchayat, staffed with a trained facilitator who can assist villagers in accessing e-government portals, filling forms, etc. Such centres, aligned with India's Digital India vision, have proven effective in states where they have been deployed, and the study's findings underscore their importance for communities like those in Jharkhand.

c. Building digital skills and trust is as important as building infrastructure. *Community-based workshops* focusing on basic digital literacy, cybersecurity awareness, and the practical benefits of online services should be conducted regularly. A *"train-the-trainer" approach*: identify and train local youth volunteers or teachers who can then teach others in the community in the local language and a culturally appropriate manner. For example, workshops can be held at village gathering spots (like the *Akhra* mentioned by participants) and use analogies or storytelling that resonate culturally. Content should be in tribal languages (e.g., Santhali) where possible. Demonstrating use-cases such as making a mobile payment for market goods or conducting a video call with a doctor – in a hands-on manner will build confidence. These efforts directly address the "digital literacy gap," which often underlies the reluctance we saw among older and female participants.

d. Given the strong interplay between socio-economic factors and digital adoption, interventions should be holistic. For instance, any rural development or poverty-alleviation program (be it in agriculture, health, or education) should have a digital inclusion component. When providing new farming equipment or techniques, also provide training on using mobile apps for weather or price information. When building new schools, ensure they have internet-enabled learning. Conversely, use digital platforms to enhance the delivery of existing schemes (as the government is attempting through direct benefit transfers and digital IDs). In Jharkhand, schemes like Ayushman Bharat (health insurance) and PDS (food distribution) are increasingly linked with digital authentication – ensuring community awareness and the ability to use these digital interfaces will improve service uptake and outcomes. The practical implication here is that *digital inclusion is not a standalone goal* but a means to amplify social inclusion in general. Therefore, stakeholders should mainstream digital capacity-building into all community development projects.

e. While our study found the gender gap narrowing, it still surfaced that women and older adults are more hesitant. Targeted efforts are needed for these groups. For women, creating women-only digital literacy circles or involving female facilitators might foster a more comfortable learning environment. Content highlighting women's success stories through digital tools (for business, education, etc.) can also inspire others. For the elderly, patience and reassurance are key – perhaps school students could be mobilized in an intergenerational learning program, teaching seniors how to use smartphones (this doubles as a youth engagement activity). Additionally, addressing practical constraints like time and mobility (bringing training to someone's doorstep if they cannot easily attend) will help include these often left-behind demographics.

The ultimate practical aim is *inclusive digital empowerment* – everyone, regardless of age or gender, should feel that technology can be for them and can tangibly improve their lives.

f. In implementing these recommendations, it is crucial to work collaboratively with the community. Participatory approaches (e.g., community meetings to identify what digital services are most needed, co-design of interventions) will ensure that actions are culturally appropriate and meet actual needs. When these steps are taken in unison, they create a reinforcing cycle, as more marginalized people come online and see value, demand for digital services grows, which in turn justifies further infrastructure and service improvements. Over time, such efforts can transform digital outsiders into digital citizens, helping to break cycles of marginalization.

8 Conclusion

This research aimed to explore the landscape of digital inequality in marginalized communities, identifying the factors that drive or hinder digital adoption in these areas. Focusing on tribal and rural populations in Jharkhand, India, the study employed a sequential mixed-methods approach to uncover deep insights and robust empirical patterns. The results presented a hopeful yet challenging picture: on one hand, infrastructure and supportive policies are effective; when people have access to a network and relevant services, they tend to go online and benefit. On the other hand, enduring socio-economic and cultural barriers mean that not everyone can seize digital opportunities equally. By exploring those nuances, the study showcased that *digital inclusion is a multi-faceted issue* requiring coordinated solutions. The study contributes to theory by extending mainstream technology adoption models to include the realities of marginalization, and it provides practical guidance for stakeholders aiming to foster an inclusive digital society. Ultimately, bridging the digital divide for marginalized communities is not just about providing technology; it is about *empowerment.* It entails giving people the tools, access, skills, and confidence to make technology work for them. As the findings emphasize, this involves strengthening infrastructure, tailoring interventions to local culture, building human capital, and addressing inequities hand in hand. The case of Jharkhand's communities illustrates both the struggles and the ingenuity of marginalized users: despite weak infrastructure and low income, the stories of villagers finding ways to connect – traveling to a distant hilltop for signal or pooling money to buy a shared smartphone. These stories underline that the appetite for digital participation exists; it is a collective responsibility to lower the barriers and open the digital gates for all. When a tribal farmer can check crop prices on her phone, a young student in a remote hamlet can attend an online class, or an elder can consult a doctor via telemedicine, we move closer to a world where digital justice complements social justice. In sum, the road to digital equality is long and winding, but the study provides map markers showing which paths lead forward.

9 Limitations and Future Research

Despite our best efforts, this study has limitations that must be acknowledged. First, the focus on a single geographic region (Jharkhand) and predominantly tribal communities may limit the generalizability of our findings to other contexts. India is highly diverse;

what holds in Jharkhand's rural areas might differ in other states or countries with different cultural or infrastructural conditions. Future research should extend this work by conducting comparative studies across multiple regions.

Second, the research design was cross-sectional, capturing a snapshot in time. Technology adoption and digital ecosystems are evolving rapidly, especially with post-pandemic shifts. Longitudinal studies would be valuable to observe how digital adoption in marginalized communities changes over time (e.g., does initial adoption lead to sustained usage and skill development, or do some relapse due to barriers?). A longitudinal approach could also better establish causal directions. Tracking communities over time could illuminate these dynamics.

Third, while the mixed-methods design helped contextualize the survey findings, there is always a possibility of measurement bias. Self-reported adoption might not fully capture actual behavior (some respondents may over- or understate their digital engagement due to social desirability or recall issues). Future studies could incorporate objective usage data where feasible (e.g., logging actual usage of a provided app, or community-level internet traffic statistics) to complement self-reports.

Another limitation is that our quantitative model, while reasonably comprehensive, did not include every possible factor. Other constructs might influence digital adoption in marginalized settings – for example, personal innovativeness, trust in technology, or specific skill competencies – which this research did not explicitly model, as the qualitative data hinted at trust and risk concerns. However, the study did not have separate survey scales for "trust in digital services" or "perceived risk", which might be worth including in future research given their importance noted.

In terms of analysis, the study primarily used regression-based moderation to test interactions. Future research could employ more advanced modelling techniques like structural equation modelling (SEM) or multilevel modelling. An SEM approach would allow simultaneous assessment of the measurement and structural models with fit indices and could test mediation pathways. Multilevel models might be relevant if communities or villages can structure data; one could then examine community-level factors alongside individual factors to capture hierarchical effects. Such techniques could provide a more nuanced validation of the relationships we observed. The moderation analysis, while shedding light on interactions, raises new questions: *why* exactly does culture flip its effect based on SEB? Although a plausible interpretation is provided in this study, future qualitative research could delve deeper into that mechanism, perhaps ethnographic studies or focus groups that explore how different socio-economic subgroups within the same culture perceive technology. Similarly, the lack of GP moderation is noteworthy; it suggests that policies are perhaps evenly implemented, but it would be worth investigating whether specific policies unintentionally favor the slightly better-off among the marginalized. A fine-grained study on policy reach and uptake across micro-demographics could inform more equitable policy design.

Another avenue for future research is examining the *outcomes of digital adoption*. This study treated adoption itself as the outcome, but ultimately, it is also important to understand what that adoption leads to (e.g., improved livelihoods, better health information, social empowerment). Does increased digital connectivity strengthen social inclusion or political voice for these groups? Investigating these "downstream" effects will help make the case to governments and other stakeholders that investing in digital inclusion yields tangible benefits for marginalized populations' well-being.

Finally, future researchers can also explore the role of emerging technologies in these settings. For example, with the rise of cheap smartphones, many rural users leapfrog directly to mobile internet (bypassing PCs). How do mobile-specific factors (like interface simplicity, app design) affect marginalized users' adoption compared to traditional factors? Moreover, technologies like vernacular voice assistants or AI chatbots have the potential to bridge literacy gaps – studying their acceptance using our extended framework (with culture and SEB considered) would be timely. As digital ecosystems evolve (e.g., the spread of digital payment systems, telemedicine, online education in rural areas), ongoing research must track how antecedents of adoption might shift or how new antecedents emerge (such as digital trust, data privacy concerns, etc., which may become salient as usage grows).

This study lays the groundwork by identifying and empirically testing key antecedents of digital adoption in a marginalized context. By addressing its limitations and pursuing the outlined research directions, scholars can further unravel the complex phenomenon of digital inclusion and adoption.

Acknowledgements. Disclosure Statements

- The researchers disclose no potential conflicts of interest.
- The author received no funding to research, write, and publish this paper.

References

Ab Hamid, M.R., Sami, W., Mohmad Sidek, M.H.: Discriminant validity assessment: use of Fornell & Larcker criterion versus HTMT criterion. J. Phys: Conf. Ser. **890**(1), 012163 (2017). https://doi.org/10.1088/1742-6596/890/1/012163

Ale, K., Chib, A.: Community factors in technology adoption in primary education: perspectives from rural India. Inf. Technol. Int. Dev. **7**(4), 53–68 (2011)

Arjumand, K., Muthulakshmi, A.P.: Contextual factors shaping digital learning in rural education: government policies, community organizations, and social support. Int. J. Sci. Res. (IJSR) **13**(2), 546–553 (2024). https://doi.org/10.21275/SR24206112111

Ashley Eve Kudiwa.: Technology adoption by rural women: a unified theory of acceptance and use of technology (UTAUT2) analysis. Texila Int. J. Acad. Res. **11**(2) (2024). https://doi.org/10.21522/tijar.2014.11.02.art016

Baah, F.O., Teitelman, A.M., Riegel, B.: Marginalization: conceptualizing patient vulnerabilities in the framework of social determinants of health: an integrative review. Nurs. Inq. **26**(1), e12268 (2018). https://doi.org/10.1111/nin.12268

Bandura, A.: Social foundations of thought and action: a social-cognitive view. Acad. Manag. Rev. **12**(1), 169 (1986). https://doi.org/10.2307/258004

Bandyopadhyay, S., Bhattacharyya, S., Basak, J.: Social knowledge management for rural empowerment. Routledge India (2020). https://doi.org/10.4324/9780429320170

Bhatia-Kalluri, A., Caraway, B.R.: Transformation of the digital payment ecosystem in India: a case study of Paytm. Soc. Incl. **11**(3) (2023). https://doi.org/10.17645/si.v11i3.6687

Bimber, B.: Measuring the gender gap on the internet. Soc. Sci. Q. **81**, 868–876 (2000)

Blayone, T.J.B., Mykhailenko, O.: Using digital technologies for indigenous sociocultural advancement in an era of AI: a systematic critical synthesis. Preserv. Digit. Technol. Cult. (2025). https://doi.org/10.1515/pdtc-2024-0086

Blut, M., Wang, C.: Technology readiness: a meta-analysis of conceptualizations of the construct and its impact on technology usage. J. Acad. Mark. Sci. **48**(4), 649–669 (2019). https://doi.org/10.1007/s11747-019-00680-8

Census: Tribe Specific Data (Jharkhand). Tribal Welfare Research Institute Jharkhand (2024). www.trijharkhand.in/en/tribe-specific-data-jharkhand

Chiu, C.-M., Hsu, M.-H., Wang, E.T.G.: Understanding knowledge sharing in virtual communities: an integration of social capital and social cognitive theories. Decis. Support Syst. **42**(3), 1872–1888 (2006). https://doi.org/10.1016/j.dss.2006.04.001

Compeau, D., Higgins, C.A., Huff, S.: Social cognitive theory and individual reactions to computing technology: a longitudinal study. MIS Q. **23**(2), 145 (1999). https://doi.org/10.2307/249749

Creswell, J.W., Creswell, J.D.: Research Design, 5th edn, pp. 224–225. SAGE Publications (2018)

Das, K.: The Role of Regional OTT Platforms in Promoting Local Languages and Cultures (July 4, 2023)

Delanty, G., Harris, N.: Critical theory and the question of technology: the Frankfurt School revisited. Thesis Eleven **166**(1), 072551362110020 (2021). https://doi.org/10.1177/07255136211002055

Firth, J.: The "online brain": how the internet may be changing our cognition. World Psychiatry **18**(2), 119–129 (2019). https://doi.org/10.1002/wps.20617

Flew, T., Martin, F., Suzor, N.: Internet regulation as media policy: rethinking the question of digital communication platform governance. J. Digit. Media Policy **10**(1), 33–50 (2019). https://doi.org/10.1386/jdmp.10.1.33_1

Foshay, R. (Ed.).: The Digital Nexus: Identity, Agency, and Political Engagement. Athabasca University Press (2016). https://doi.org/10.15215/aupress/9781771991292.01

Ganesan, R.: Digital Inclusion in Rural India: The Key to Unlocking India's Economic Potential. The Times of India (May 23, 2023)

Ghosh, M.: Introduction. In: India's Silver Surfers: Transforming the Digital Inequalities/diversities, pp. 1–17. Springer Nature, Switzerland (2024). https://doi.org/10.1007/978-3-031-71194-7%E2%82%81

Giest, S.: The intersection of digital and social infrastructures in (a)spatial policymaking. Policy Sci. https://doi.org/10.1007/s11077-025-09569-6

Hair, J.F., Black, W.C., Babin, B.J., Anderson, R.E.: Multivariate Data Analysis, 8th edn. Cengage Learning Emea (2020)

Haleem, A., Javaid, M., Qadri, M.A., Suman, R.: Understanding the role of digital technologies in education: a review. Sustain. Oper. Comput. **3**(3), 275–285 (2022). https://doi.org/10.1016/j.susoc.2022.05.004

Helsper, E.: The Digital Disconnect: The Social Causes and Consequences of Digital Inequalities. Sage (2021)

Hyland-Wood, B., Gardner, J., Leask, J., Ecker, U.K.H.: Toward effective government communication strategies in the era of COVID-19. Hum. Soc. Sci. Commun. **8**(1), 1–11 (2021) (Nature). https://doi.org/10.1057/s41599-020-00701-w

ICRIER.: State of India's Digital Economy, pp. 1–144. Indian Council for Research on International Economic Relations - Centre for Internet and Digital Economy (2023)

Jan, J., Alshare, K.A., Lane, P.L.: Hofstede's cultural dimensions in technology acceptance models: a meta-analysis. Univers. Access Inf. Soc. **23**(1), 1–25 (2022). https://doi.org/10.1007/s10209-022-00930-7

Kalam, M.A., Mishra, A., Pal, S., Roy, S.: Culture and demography: a micro-level study between two communities residing in the city of Kolkata, West Bengal. Orient. Anthropol. Bi-Annu. Int. J. Sci. Man **20**(1), 49–59 (2020). https://doi.org/10.1177/0972558x20913701

Kanojia, P., Lal, M.: The moderating effect of demographic factors on the adoption of electronic payments. Int. J. Manag. Pract. **16**(1), 18 (2023). https://doi.org/10.1504/ijmp.2023.127676

Kathuria, R., Kedia, M., Raj, A., Sekhani, R., Sinha, S.: Building an Inclusive Digital Society for Rural India, pp. 41–43. India Council for Research on International Economic Relations (ICRIER) (2021)

Kemp, S.: Digital 2023: The United States of America. DataReportal – Global Digital Insights (February 9, 2023)

Khan, S.A.: Government Initiatives and Affordable Devices are Helping Fuel India's Digital Inclusion (2023, May 20)

Kim, S.J., Lee, Y.E., Chock, T.M.: Cultural differences in the use of augmented reality smart glasses (ARSGs) between the U.S. and South Korea: privacy concerns and the technology acceptance model. Appl. Sci. **15**(13), 7430 (2025). https://doi.org/10.3390/app15137430

KPMG: Expanding Tech Horizons - Unlocking India's Digital Potential, pp. 1–56 (2023). https://assets.kpmg.com/content/dam/kpmgsites/in/pdf/2023/10/expanding-tech-horizons-unlocking-indias-digital-potential.pdf.coredownload.inline.pdf

Kumar, H., Sofat, R.: Analysing consumer behaviour by integrating digital payment awareness into the UTAUT model. Int. J. Electron. Financ. **13**(2), 139–167 (2024). https://doi.org/10.1504/ijef.2024.137633

Krotz, F.: Mediatization: a concept with which to grasp media and societal change. In: K. Lundby (Ed.), Mediatization. Concept, Changes, Consequences. Peter Lang Publishing (2009)

Kulkarni, M.: Digital accessibility: challenges and opportunities. IIMB Manag. Rev. **31**(1), 91–98 (2019). https://doi.org/10.1016/j.iimb.2018.05.009

Lyon, F.: Trust, networks and norms: the creation of social capital in agricultural economies in Ghana. World Dev. **28**(4), 663–681 (2000). https://doi.org/10.1016/s0305-750x(99)00146-1

Al-Emran, M.: Beyond technology acceptance: development and evaluation of technology-environmental, economic, and social sustainability theory. Technol. Soc. **75**, 102383 (2023). https://doi.org/10.1016/j.techsoc.2023.102383

Munir, J., Faiza, M., Jamal, B., Daud, S., Iqbal, K.: The impact of socio-economic status on academic achievement. J. Soc. Sci. Rev. **3**(2), 695–705 (2023). https://doi.org/10.54183/jssr.v3i2.308

Nayak, K.V., Alam, S.: The digital divide, gender, and education: challenges for tribal youth in rural Jharkhand during Covid-19. DECISION, **49**(2) (2022). https://doi.org/10.1007/s40622-022-00315-y

Ono, H., Zavodny, M.: Gender and the internet. Federal Reserve Bank of Atlanta, 1–15 (2002). https://files.eric.ed.gov/fulltext/ED505602.pdf

Ong, M.H.A., Yusri, M.Y., Ibrahim, N.: Use and behavioural intention using digital payment systems among rural residents: extending the UTAUT-2 model. Technol. Soc. **74**, 102305 (2023). https://doi.org/10.1016/j.techsoc.2023.102305

Operario, D., King, E.J., Gamarel, K.E.: Prioritizing community partners and community HIV workers in the COVID-19 pandemic. AIDS Behav. **24**(10), 2748–2750 (2020). https://doi.org/10.1007/s10461-020-02896-0

Patel, S.: Perspective of digital transformation in rural India. Int. J. Sci. Res. **13**(4), 387–390 (2024). https://doi.org/10.21275/sr24402140819

Petrova, Y., Pervukhina, S.: Socio-cultural changes are influenced by information and communication technology. E3S Web Conf. **363**, 04039 (2022). https://doi.org/10.1051/e3sconf/202236304039

PIB Delhi.: Union Cabinet Approves Expansion of the Digital India Programme with an Outlay of ₹ 14,903 Crore. Pib.gov.in (August 16, 2023)

Pignot, E.: Expanding Internet Adoption in Rural India | Action Learning | MIT Sloan. MIT Sloan (2024). https://mitsloan.mit.edu/action-learning/expanding-internet-adoption-rural-india?

Ragnedda, M.: Conceptualising the digital divide. In: Mutsvairo, B., Ragnedda, R. (eds.) Mapping the Digital Divide in Africa: A Mediated Analysis, pp. 27–43. Amsterdam University Press (2019)

Ramakrishnappa, V.: Exclusion of scheduled tribes in access to digital services in India: bottlenecks and the way forward. East Afr. Sch. J. Econ. Bus. Manag. **5**(9), 251–255 (2022). https://doi.org/10.36349/easjebm.2022.v05i09.001

Reddick, C.G., Enriquez, R., Harris, R.J., Sharma, B.: Determinants of broadband access and affordability: an analysis of a community survey on the digital divide. Cities **106**(102904), 102904 (2020). https://doi.org/10.1016/j.cities.2020.102904

Roztocki, N., Soja, P., Weistroffer, H.R.: The role of information and communication technologies in socioeconomic development: towards a multidimensional framework. Inf. Technol. Dev. **25**(2), 171–183 (2019). https://doi.org/10.1080/02681102.2019.1596654

Ruotsalainen, J., Heinonen, S.: Media ecology and the future ecosystemic society. Eur. J. Futur. Res. 3(1) (2015). https://doi.org/10.1007/s40309-015-0068-7

Sahu, S.: Demographic trends and occupational structure of particularly vulnerable tribal groups in Jharkhand. Int. J. Rev. Res. Soc. Sci. **7**(2), 316–322 (2019)

Saini, N., Singh, P.: A study of rural areas towards the growth of digital India in the post-COVID-19 pandemic. PalArch's J. Archaeol. Egypt/Egyptol. **18**(7), 2101–2106 (2021)

Sindakis, S., Showkat, G.: The digital revolution in India: bridging the gap in rural technology adoption. J. Innov. Entrep. **13**(1), 1–28 (2024). https://doi.org/10.1186/s13731-024-00380-w

Soeteman-Hernández, L.G., Sutcliffe, H.R., Sluijters, T., van Geuns, J., Noorlander, C.W., Sips, A.J.A.M.: Modernizing innovation governance to meet policy ambitions through trusted environments. NanoImpact **21**, 100301 (2021). https://doi.org/10.1016/j.impact.2021.100301

The Hindu Bureau. Digital India Expansion Gets ₹14,903 Crore Outlay. The Hindu (August 16, 2023). https://www.thehindu.com/news/national/cabinet-approves-extension-of-digital-india-project-with-outlay-of-14903-crore/article67201285.ece

Warren, M.: The digital vicious cycle: links between social disadvantage and digital exclusion in rural areas. Telecommun. Policy **31**(6–7), 374–388 (2007). https://doi.org/10.1016/j.telpol.2007.04.001

Wu, G., Peng, Q.: Bridging the digital divide: unraveling the determinants of FinTech adoption in rural communities. SAGE Open **14**(1) (2024). https://doi.org/10.1177/21582440241227770

Yang Meier, D., Barthelmess, P., Sun, W., Liberatore, F.: An empirical study on wearable technology acceptance in healthcare: a cross-country analysis between Chinese and Swiss consumers based on differences in national culture(Preprint). J. Med. Internet Res. **22**(10) (2020). https://doi.org/10.2196/18801

Yusof, N.A., Jimainal, M.N.H., Ansar, R., Chekima, B., Phin, N.Y., Shalahuddin, S.: The moderating role of socio-economic status in digital marketing adoption and agribusiness sustainability among rural youth. Int. J. Res. Innov. Soc. Sci. **9**(4), 813–824 (2025). https://doi.org/10.47772/ijriss.2025.90400061

Rethinking Smartness: Towards Inclusive, Affordable, and Human-Centric Smart Societies

Anton Manfreda(✉)

School of Economics and Business, University of Ljubljana, Kardeljeva Ploscad 17, 1000 Ljubljana, Slovenia

anton.manfreda@ef.uni-lj.si

Abstract. Smart city initiatives have often focused on technological complexity and data-driven governance, yet their success in enhancing resident well-being remains limited. This paper argues for a paradigm shift towards inclusive and sustainable smart societies. Focusing on the role of technology and cost-of-living implications, the study critically examines how "smartness" may correlate with affordability and quality of life. Drawing on public perception data and existing literature, the findings highlight that higher smartness rankings are frequently associated with increased living costs, raising equity concerns. A human-centered, affordable approach to smart city development is proposed as essential for resilient inclusive smart places and societies.

Keywords: Smart Cities · Cost of Living · Human-Centered Design · Digital Transformation

1 Introduction

Urbanization has accelerated globally, with projections indicating 68% of the world's population will reside in cities by 2050 [1]. In response, smart cities have emerged as a strategy to address urban challenges through technological innovations. However, the promise of smart cities to enhance residents' quality of life and promote sustainability often falls short when social and environmental dimensions are neglected.

While definitions of smart cities vary, they generally emphasize the use of technology-based solutions to enhance citizens' quality of life, improve interactions with local governments, and promote sustainable development. Smart cities aim to balance social, environmental, and economic factors by integrating processes that efficiently manage key urban assets and resources [2]. This integration relies on various technological solutions, including optic networks, open data analytics, Internet of Things, and other innovative information and communication technologies [3].

Despite the compelling promise of smart cities, many initiatives have fallen short of delivering desired outcomes, often due to an overemphasis on technological solutions at the expense of socio-environmental dimensions critical to sustainable urban

Published by Springer Nature Switzerland AG 2026
A. Elbanna et al. (Eds.): TDIT 2025, IFIP AICT 778, pp. 68–74, 2026.
https://doi.org/10.1007/978-3-032-16775-0_4

living. The transition from smart cities to smart societies represents a necessary evolution, where technology integration is balanced with human-centric principles like social equity, inclusivity, and sustainability.

This paper therefore addresses the following research question: How does smartness align with affordability and quality of life?

This research makes two interrelated contributions. First, it provides an empirical illustration of the trade-off between "smartness" and affordability by integrating global indices on smart city performance, happiness, and cost of living. Second, it advances a conceptual call for reframing smart city development towards an inclusive, affordable, and human-centered "smart society" paradigm. While the empirical part demonstrates the cost-of-living implications of technological advancement, the conceptual framing highlights the broader socio-economic and governance shifts required for equitable smart futures.

By examining technological roles and cost-of-living impacts, it highlights the need for inclusive approaches that balance innovation with affordability and well-being.

2 Literature Review

2.1 The Smart City Concept

The concept of the smart city has emerged as a response to the challenges posed by rapid urbanization and the need for sustainable development. Smart cities are typically defined by their use of technology-based solutions to enhance citizens' quality of life, increase interaction with local governments, and promote sustainability [2]. By leveraging innovative infrastructures like the Internet of Things, optic networks, and advanced information and communication technologies, smart cities manage key assets and resources more efficiently, aiming for a balanced integration of social, environmental, and economic factors [3].

Several authors provide various definitions of smart cities, emphasizing different aspects. Schaffers, Komninos, Pallot, Trousse, Nilsson and Oliveira [4, 5] describe smart cities as innovation-driven ecosystems that enhance community welfare through ICT infrastructure, focusing on sustainable and user-oriented development. On the other hand, some view smart cities as self-monitoring, self-responsive systems integrating critical urban infrastructures to link physical and virtual realms [6].

While definitions vary, common themes among them include sustainability, efficiency, and the importance of citizen collaboration. Smart cities aim to address contemporary urban challenges, fostering environments where residents participate in co-creating solutions to improve the overall quality of urban life.

Yet, challenges persist. Overreliance on technology risks marginalizing social factors like equity and inclusivity. Concerns over data privacy and security further complicate widespread acceptance [7]. Thus, smart cities must evolve beyond technological fixes towards frameworks that integrate societal needs.

2.2 The Role of Technology in Smart Concept Development

Technology has a crucial role in the smart city concept, forming the backbone of the infrastructure and services designed to enhance urban living. Smart cities employ a range of technologies, such as the Internet of Things (IoT), artificial intelligence (AI), big data analytics, and advanced communication networks, all in order to drive efficiency, sustainability, and livability. These tools facilitate real-time data collection and analysis, enabling informed decision-making and more responsive urban management. Technological advancements somehow underpin the smart city concept. IoT facilitates interconnectivity between urban systems, enhancing operational efficiency [8], AI adds predictive capabilities for urban planning and traffic management [9], while big data analytics allows policymakers to derive actionable insights, enabling more responsive governance [10].

However, technological implementation alone does not guarantee sustainable urban environments. For instance, despite advanced traffic systems, many cities still face chronic congestion and pollution [11]. This indicates that technology must be complemented by sustainable urban planning and community engagement.

The COVID-19 pandemic further exposed vulnerabilities in urban systems, highlighting the need for resilience and adaptability in smart city designs [12].

The integration of IoT, AI, and big data analytics is therefore fundamental to the smart city concept, as these technologies collectively enhance urban management and improve the quality of life for residents. The ongoing advancements in these areas promise to further transform urban environments into more efficient, sustainable, and livable spaces.

3 Affordability and Equity: The Cost of Living Factor

3.1 Methodology

While technology-driven urban models aim to improve quality of life, rising costs of living in "smart" cities raise concerns about accessibility and equity.

In this study, the analysis followed a step-by-step approach: (1) data were obtained from the Smart City Index 2023 [13], the Happy City Index 2023 [14] and the Cost of Living 2023 index [15]; (2) for consistency, only cities appearing in all three datasets were retained; (3) rankings and scores were aligned for paired comparison; and (4) correlations between smartness, happiness, and affordability were examined.

3.2 Results

Analysis of global indices show a correlation between higher smartness rankings and increased living costs (Fig. 1). Cities excelling in technological innovation often become less affordable, limiting benefits to wealthier residents. This trend raises critical questions about accessibility and equity in urban environments.

Figure 1 compares "smartness" and the costs of living (ranking). The descending trend (lower numbers represent higher rank) in the scatterplot indicates that cities with better smartness rankings often have higher costs of living, suggesting a trade-off between technological advancement and affordability.

It becomes clear that greater smartness often coincides with higher living costs, suggesting that the quality of life in such cities may be accessible only to those who can afford it. Figure 2 expands on this by presenting scores for smartness and happiness alongside cost-of-living data. This visual representation highlights cases where

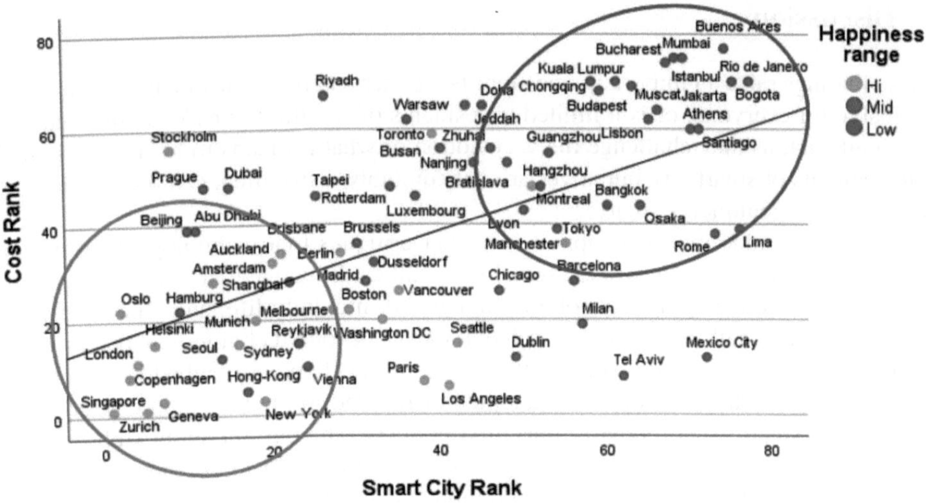

Fig. 1. Comparing "smartness" and the costs of living (ranking).

high smartness scores align with high happiness but also with elevated living expenses, underscoring the complexity of achieving inclusive urban well-being.

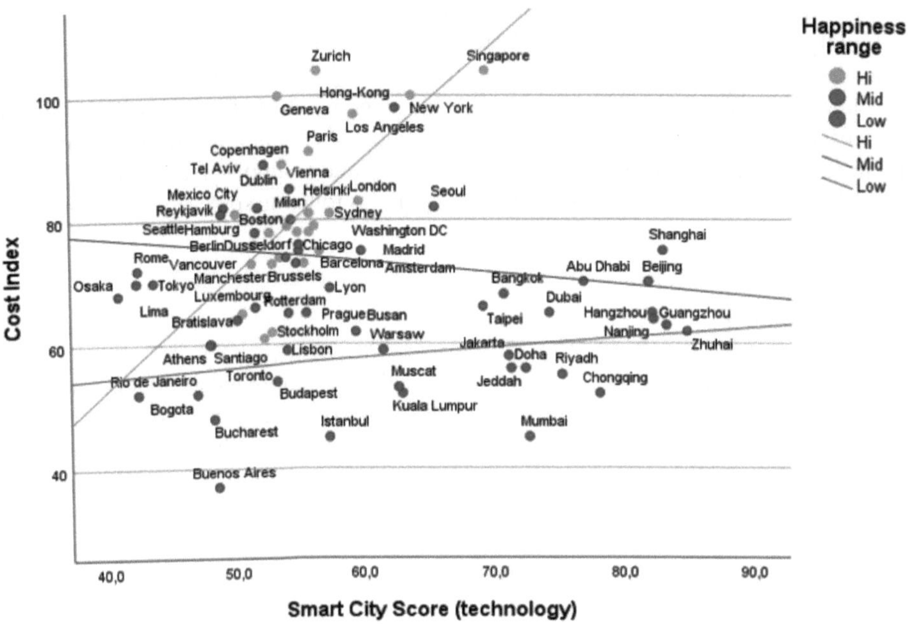

Fig. 2. Comparing "smartness" and the costs of living (scores).

4 Discussion

These findings raise an important question: Is a better and more sustainable future truly attainable for everyone, or is it limited to residents of wealthy cities? The implications are significant, as they challenge the very notion of what it means to be a "smart city." If the benefits of smart city initiatives are not equitably distributed, can these cities still be considered genuinely "smart"?

The results add empirical support to earlier critiques that technology-focused initiatives can unintentionally worsen social inequalities. Elbanna et al. [16] highlight the question how are emerging technologies integrated into daily life, and what effects do they produce and call for future research that moves beyond technological determinism to critically examine whose values, ethics, and perspectives are embedded in emerging technologies, and how these are adopted or resisted in practice, and consequently determining smart users, organizations, and policies. The current study's observation that higher smartness rankings often align with higher costs of living mirrors their call for a sociotechnical perspective, in which human capabilities, institutional design, and equitable access are as central as technical systems.

Similarly, Cranefield and Pries-Heje [17] show that successful digital transformation in urban contexts depends on various dimensions such as leadership strategies that balance innovation with governance, stakeholder engagement and ability to align technical experts and policy makers. The affordability presented in this research can be seen as one such dimension, namely requiring careful policy action to ensure that economic barriers do not weaken the envisioned societal benefits of smart city initiatives.

Finally, Manfreda and Mijač [18] argue that well-being and happiness should be embedded as explicit objectives in smart city planning, rather than assumed outcomes of technological progress. This aligns with the conclusion that a "smart" city that is unaffordable for many fails to fulfill its core mission of enhancing residents' quality of life. Integrating happiness metrics with affordability and technological indicators offers a more holistic measure of smartness, guiding policies towards sincerely inclusive smart societies.

5 Conclusion

The current direction of smart city development calls for a more balanced approach, one that integrates technological advancement with cost considerations and resident well-being. A truly smart city must prioritize inclusivity and accessibility to ensure urban innovations benefit all inhabitants, not just those who can afford them. Without such commitment, the promise of smart cities risks becoming an exclusive ideal.

This evolution should align with the principles of Society 5.0, which envisions a human-centric framework where advanced technologies like AI, IoT, and big data address complex societal challenges. The focus must shift from cities alone to broader societal benefits, fostering well-being, sustainability, and resilience.

The future of urban living depends on creating interconnected systems for efficient resource management and responsive public services, balanced with a strong commitment to social equity. Achieving this vision requires collaboration among governments, private sectors, and communities to co-create environments that are not only technologically advanced but also equitable and livable, harmonizing technology and humanity to build a sustainable and inclusive future for all.

Acknowledgments. The research presented in this paper was financially supported in part by the Slovenian Research Agency under research program No. P2–0037 – Future internet technologies: concepts, architectures, services and socio-economic issues.

Disclosure of Interests. The authors have no competing interests to declare that are relevant to the content of this article.

References

1. United Nations: 68% of the world population projected to live in urban areas by 2050. (2018)
2. Ismagilova, E., Hughes, L., Rana, N.P., Dwivedi, Y.K.: Security, privacy and risks within smart cities: literature review and development of a smart city interaction framework. Inf. Syst. Front. 1–22 (2022)
3. Appio, F.P., Lima, M., Paroutis, S.: Understanding smart cities: innovation ecosystems, technological advancements, and societal challenges. Technol. Forecast. Soc. Chang. **142**, 1–14 (2019)
4. Schaffers, H., Komninos, N., Pallot, M., Trousse, B., Nilsson, M., Oliveira, A.: Smart cities and the future internet: towards cooperation frameworks for open innovation. In: The Future Internet Assembly, pp. 431–446. Springer, Berlin, Heidelberg (Year)
5. Schaffers, H., Komninos, N., Pallot, M., Trousse, B., Nilsson, M., Oliveira, A.: Smart Cities and the Future Internet: Towards Cooperation Frameworks for Open Innovation. Springer, Berlin Heidelberg (2011)
6. Nam, T., Pardo, T.A.: Conceptualizing smart city with dimensions of technology, people, and institutions. In: Proceedings of the 12th Annual International Digital Government Research Conference: Digital Government Innovation in Challenging Times, pp. 282–291 (Year)
7. Neupane, C., Wibowo, S., Grandhi, S., Deng, H.: A trust-based model for the adoption of smart city technologies in Australian regional cities. Sustainability **13**(16), 9316 (2021)
8. Shabrina, W., Andriani, W.: Systematic literature review implementation of the internet of things (IoT) in smart city development. Buana Inf. Technol. Comput. Sci. (BIT and CS) **3**(2), 41–46 (2022)
9. Mashhood, M., Salman, H., Amjad, R., Nisar, H.: The advantages of using artificial intelligence in urban planning–a review of literature. Stat., Comput. Interdiscip. Res. **5**(2), 1–12 (2023)
10. Bibri, S.E.: A novel model for data-driven smart sustainable cities of the future: the institutional transformations required for balancing and advancing the three goals of sustainability. Energy Inform. **4**(1), 4 (2021)
11. Bechle, M.J., Millet, D.B., Marshall, J.D.: Does urban form affect urban NO2? Satellite-based evidence for more than 1200 cities. Environ. Sci. Technol. **51**(21), 12707–12716 (2017)
12. Stan, M.-I., Tasente, T., Rus, M.: Challenges and opportunities regarding the COVID-19 pandemic on urban mobility in Constanta. Romania. Technium Soc. Sci. J. **42**, 1 (2023)
13. IMD World Competitiveness Center: IMD Smart City Index 2023 (2023)
14. Institute for Quality of Life: Happy City Index. Institute for Quality of Life (2023)
15. Economist Intelligence Unit: Worldwide Cost of Living 2023 (2023)
16. Elbanna, A., Dwivedi, Y., Bunker, D., Wastell, D.: The search for smartness in working, living and organising: beyond the 'Technomagic' editorial for special issue of information systems frontiers. Inf. Syst. Front. **22**(2), 275–280 (2020)

17. Cranefield, J., Pries-Heje, J.: Boundary management strategies for leading digital transformation in smart cities. MIS Q. Exec. **22**(2), 129–146 (2023)
18. Manfreda, A., Mijač, T.: Highlighting gaps in technology acceptance research: a call for integrating happiness and well-being into smart city development. J. Innov. Knowl. **9**(4), 100585 (2024)

The Interplay Between Job Applicants and Hiring Algorithm: A Perspective from Structuration Theory

Trinh Nguyen[1(✉)] and Amany Elbanna[2]

[1] Royal Holloway University of London, Egham TW20 0EX, UK
trinh.nguyen.2021@live.rhul.ac.uk
[2] University of Sussex, Brighton BN1 9SL, UK
a.elbanna@Sussex.ac.uk

Abstract. The integration of Artificial Intelligence (AI) into job hiring and selection is growing exponentially. While it sparked heated debates on its impact, little is known on job applicants' experience. This study investigates job applicants' experience of using a particular AI system typically used by large companies in the process of selecting job applicants. The research findings reveal that the use of AI system shapes applicants' behaviors. However, however job applicants actively responds to re-shape their own experience. The study contributes to extant literature on the use of AI and provide guidance for practitioners to enhance job applicants' experience and the effectiveness of AI system in their selection process.

Keywords: Hiring Algorithm · Human AI Interaction · AI Game-based Assessment

1 Introduction

There is a growing interest in the adoption of AI in job hiring and selection [1–3], particularly in its use to assess job applicants' behavior, personality and skills to predict their suitability for a given position [4, 5]. Several AI-based applications are utilized in the selection process including asynchronous video interview, resume screening, chatbots, social media screening, and game-based assessment [6, 7]. They have been adopted in the job hiring of various countries, including those in North America, Europe, and Asia [8], and has become a prominent trend within the recruitment industry [9]. AI Game-based Assessment (AI-GBA) is one of the AI systems commonly in use in the hiring process. It refers to AI system that is integrated into game-based assessments, employing machine learning scoring systems to evaluate applicants' behaviors and personal traits, rather than simply tallying correct and incorrect answers as in traditional GBA processes [6, 10, 11]. Despite the wide spread adoption of AI-GBA in practice, its impact on job applicants' has received little academic attention and understanding of job applicants' experience [12, 13]. Previous research has conceptually examined GBA alone to suggest

Published by Springer Nature Switzerland AG 2026
A. Elbanna et al. (Eds.): TDIT 2025, IFIP AICT 778, pp. 75–87, 2026.
https://doi.org/10.1007/978-3-032-16775-0_5

a range of potential benefits and drawbacks [6, 14, 15]. However, the intersection of AI and GBA introduces a new layer of complexity, particularly regarding the opaqueness and lack of transparency [3, 16, 17]. AI-GBA is not only opaque to applicants but also disguised within a format of series of computer games. Despite its critical role in securing employment, recent research highlights the lack of empirical understanding of how applicants engage with AI-GBA in practice [18]. This misses opportunities to inform and improve its use in practice and to contribute evidence to the broader societal debate. Therefore, this study explores job applicants' lived experience of using AI-GBA during their application process and aims to answer the research question: *How do job applicants interact with AI-GBA system during their job application?*

Following the introduction, section two reviews relevant literature on AI-GBA and users' reaction towards algorithmic hiring. Section three briefly discusses the adopted theoretical lens—Structuration Theory. Section four describes the research methodology. Section five presents the research findings, while section six provides discussions and implications. The final section outlines research limitations and proposes avenues for future research.

2 Literature Review

AI-GBA has become a leading trend in recruitment in recent years [19]. It uses machine learning algorithms to evaluate candidates' behaviors and abilities based on their game-play interactions [6, 11]. In this process, digital trace data from job applicants such as their movements, mouse-clicking speed, and interactions with in-game objects are collected, analyzed and interpreted to assess their personal traits and capabilities [20, 21]. The official website of an AI-GBA platform named Pymetrics, notes that "each game captures thousands of behavioral data points, then builds a profile of what makes a person and job unique" [22].

Empirical research on AI-GBA is currently limited, with existing studies primarily quantitative. Despite being a crucial stakeholder in the hiring process, research has largely overlooked the perspectives of job applicants towards this new assessment approach [11]. Scholars mostly discuss conceptual issues related to fairness and lack of transparency [8, 12, 21, 23, 24], as well as the advantages and disadvantages of the system in use [11, 24, 25]. Among the advantages, AI-GBA can analyze large volumes of applicants' data to assess suitability for specific roles [24, 26], assist hiring managers in decision-making [27], improve applicants' experience and free the hiring process from human-bias [11]. However, there are notable disadvantages. While AI-GBA can reduce human biases, it may introduce other type of algorithmic bias and discrimination in addition to digital faults [24]. In addition, data privacy concern related to AI-GBA could deter suitable job applicants from applying [26, 28, 29].

It is important to empirically explore how job applicants experience the use of AI-GBA during their job application process to inform its adoption and promote fair use. Understanding such experience can provides insight on job applicants perceptions of transparency, fairness, trust, and opportunities in the job market.

3 Theoretical Grounding

Structuration theory, developed by sociologist Anthony Giddens, examines the dynamic relationship between individual actions and social structures [30]. It rejects the traditional dualist perspective that views social practices is determined by either social structure or human agency, instead argues that and social practices are the product of the interplay between social structure and agency through social practices took place over time and space [31]. In this regard, social structures are both the medium through which practices are produced and also the outcome of the practices; a concept known as the "duality" of structure (Fig. 1). While social structures shape individual actions, these actions simultaneously reproduce or transform the structures. Scholars highlighted that the modification and reshaping of social practices might occur in two modes: conscious and/or unconscious collaboration by the agentthat leads to intended and/or unintended consequences, respectively [30].

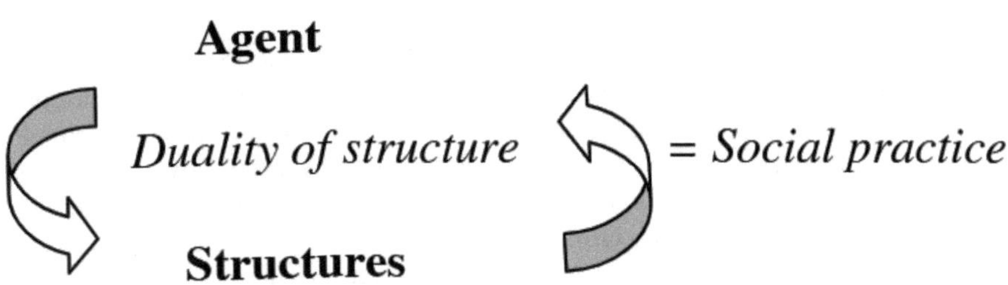

Fig. 1. Theory of structuration: agency-structure duality. *Source* Orlikowski [32]

While the term "structure" suggests something stable and fixed, "structuration" refers to a dynamic and ongoing process [33]. Social structures are initially shaped by two main factors: the structured habitus; meaning the ingrained mindsets and dispositions that guide human agency and the forms of capital (such as social or material resources) that individuals possess. Although these factors influence people's understanding and range of actions, the outcomes ultimately depend on how human agency mobilizes and allocates these resources [34]. Structuration theory therefore reveals the underlying structure from three interrelated dimensions: meaning, power, and legitimation [33].

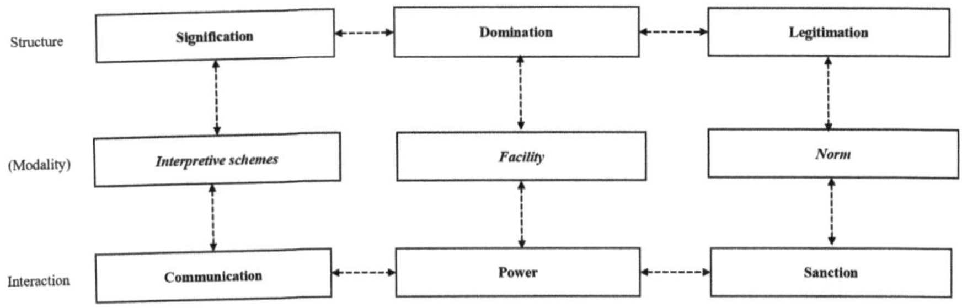

Fig. 2. The dimension of the duality of structure. *Source* Giddens [30]

According to Structuration Theory, the process of social structuring involves three interrelated dimensions: Signification, Domination, and Legitimation [30]. These dimensions correspond respectively to the individual actions of Communication, Power, and Sanction, and are mediated through specific modalities known as Interpretive Schemes, Facilities, and Norms (Fig. 2) [30, 35]. Social structures are not static; they continuously evolve and transform, depending largely on how agents interact with them and pursue their goals [36, 37]. Signification concerns the production of meaning. While social structures shape meaning through shared interpretive schemes, individuals actively interpret and reproduce these meanings in their interactions, which can in turn reshape collective understanding. Domination relates to the distribution and exercise of power through control over resources, whether material or authoritative. Individual actions can reallocate or mobilize these resources to influence social relations and challenge existing power configurations. Legitimation involves the establishment and reinforcement of social norms and rules that sustain the structure. However, through critical engagement and resistance, individuals can contest these norms, leading to their redefinition and the development of new normative frameworks.

The theory has been widely adopted in information systems (IS) and organizational studies to explain how technology and social practices influence each other in the context of IS development, implementation and use [31, 33, 38]. In this regard, technology is treated as a structure that influence and is influenced by users. Two main streams of research build upon this theoretical foundation: one is based directly on Giddens's original work or its adaptation by Orlikowski and Robey [39], and the other is based on DeSanctis and Poole [40] concept of Adaptive Structuration Theory. This study follows the first stream, emphasizing the concept of the duality of structure, wherein the AI-GBA system functions as a social structure in its own right. Unlike the second stream, which addresses internal organizational issues, our approach is more attuned to understanding the social consequences of interacting with this new technology from the perspective of job applicants.

4 Research Methodology

This study adopts an interpretive approach to explore the lived experiences of job applicants as they interact with AI-GBA systems during the application process [41]. This approach allowed us to deeply explore the subjective meanings people assign towards phenomenon as well as their personal experience and viewpoints, which aligns with the study's objectives [41].

To minimize variations associated with different technologies that can impact the results, the research focuses on a single AI-GBA system; namely Pymetrics. Pymetrics is an AI Game-based Assessment platform that widely used by multinational corporations such as British American Tobacco (BAT), Heineken, AB InBev, Jardines, and Unilever for selecting job applicants. This study investigates applicants' interactions with Pymetrics during the internship application process, namely for the Management Trainee Program (MTP) in Vietnam. Pymetrics comprises of a series of 12 individual games embedded with AI algorithms that evaluate nine intrinsic qualities of job applicants [42, 43]. During the gameplay, applicants receive immediate feedback after each game, which reflects their characteristics based on their performance. Upon completing all 12 games, applicants receive a report highlighting their three main traits, along with explanations for each trait [42]. The system identifies applicant traits, assesses their suitability for specific job roles and offers decisions to recruiters. This study focuses on Vietnamese context, as there are several multinational companies operating in Vietnam use Pymetrics to support their mass recruitment activities, and the legal framework related to AI use remains relatively open in this area [44] (Table 1).

Table 1 Summary of data collection phases

Phase	Period	Interviews	Documents and observations
1	May 2023 to June 2023	8	Corporate news, social media observations, system reviews, and document reviews
2	January 2024 to February 2024	18	Corporate news, social media observations, system reviews, and document reviews
3	June 2024 to July 2024	19	Corporate news, social media observations, system reviews, and document reviews
Total		45	

Data were collected from multiple sources, including interviews, social media observations, as well as reviews of documents, news items, and vendor resources [45, 46]. This multi-source approach was employed to triangulate evidence [41, 47] and enhance the validity and credibility of the study [48]. Semi-structured interviews were conducted with 45 participants, allowing for open and conversational discussions that enabled respondents to freely express their views and highlight what they considered important or concerning [49]. This in-depth approach is recommended for exploring new phenomena [50]. Participants were selected based on two criteria: (1) aged between 22 and 25 years who applied for the MTP in Vietnam; and (2) both successful and unsuccessful applicants of Pymetrics. The initial eight participants were recruited using snowball sampling, where existing participants nominated others who might be suitable [51]. Recognizing that snowball sampling can introduce bias—since respondents may refer individuals with similar characteristics or viewpoints [52, 53]—we diversified our recruitment methods by engaging different social media platforms, including Facebook groups and LinkedIn. This helped broaden the participant pool and mitigate sampling bias. All participants belong to the young Generation (Gen Z) and share common characteristics regarding technology. They are considered as "digital native", demonstrating high familiarity with technology in both work and daily live, as well as a strong attachment towards digital environments [54, 55].

Additionally, observation data were gathered from online discussions on Facebook groups, comments on YouTube videos, and LinkedIn posts. Scholars consider social media as an effective source for qualitative data, as it facilitates access to varied perspectives and insights about events and systems [56]. To deepen understanding, we also participated in playing the Pymetrics games gaining firsthand experience of the applicant's perspective and the system's vagueness. Lastly, reports sent to applicants by Pymetrics, recruiters and partner organizations were reviewed to further insight into the evaluation process and feedback format.

All interviews were recorded, transcribed verbatim, and stored anonymously to protect participants' privacy. Data collected from interviews were analyzed and managed using NViVo software. This study follows abductive method which is known as an iterative process between empirical observations and a set of theoretical propositions aiming to generate new theoretical insights [57, 58]. The data analysis followed Gioia Methodology to develop data structure in three rigor steps providing a clear guideline on how data is analyzed [59].

5 Research Findings

This section employs Structuration Theory to reveal the way through which the applicants' experience of AI-GBA is shaped. Although the analysis is structured around specific conceptual categories, these concepts are interconnected and integrated and are delineated separately here to enhance analytical clarity.

5.1 Signification and Production of Meaning

Signification concerns how applicants interpret and assign meaning to the AI-GBA system, shaping their actions in the process. Although all applicants engaged with the same AI-GBA system (Pymetrics), their interpretations evolved and varied over time.

Upon progressing past the first stage of recruitment, applicants were told that subsequent assessments would involve Pymetrics. Most were already familiar with gamified assessments and initially viewed Pymetrics as comparable to previous systems, often describing it as entertaining and "game-like." However, once they began interacting with the system and encountered its ambiguity, their perceptions shifted. As one participant described: "First, I thought this test was similar to other normal tests I have done before. However, after participating in game, I found it completely different" (Participant 15).

Participants noted that the instructions provided were overly simplistic and lacked sufficient context. For example, some were simply told to "click the spacebar continuously for one minute" with no further explanation. This vagueness led to confusion about the game's meaning and purpose. Applicants struggled to prepare in advance, in contrast to traditional or other gamified assessments that feature clear instructions and expectations. This difficulty is illustrated by another participant: "I was able to understand certain parts of some Pymetrics games, but for others, I could not interpret what the recruiters were expecting from me" (Participant 27).

After each game, applicants received immediate brief feedback on their characteristics, raising questions about how the system derived such detailed personal information from their gameplay. As one remarked: "I found that the system generated outcome indicating my personality immediately after each game I played; this was surprising, what did

I do in the game to get this!" (Participant 1). This heightened awareness prompted applicants to approach subsequent games with greater caution as they attempted to interpret the system's scoring methods. These perceptions underscore how the meanings assigned to the system actively shape applicants' understanding and responses throughout their interactions.

5.2 AI-GBA Domination and Job Applicants' Power

This dimension illustrates how applicants negotiate with the AI-GBA system, believing they can influence its outcomes even as its capabilities tend to dominate the process. Unlike traditional tests with fixed answers, Pymetrics assesses how scores are achieved, not just the final results, making identical scores open to different evaluations. Applicants sensed that every action was scrutinized, creating discomfort and uncertainty. "I felt quite worried because the machine can evaluate every gesture" (Participant 15). "This game is more difficult…because it interacts with you more and assesses every move you make" (Participant 4). As one participant explained, "I felt that all of my actions were being recorded and assessed…leading me to believe that the game could analyze every aspect of a job applicant's behavior. However, I was unsure how to respond to this properly, so I simply attempted to maximize my score" (Participant 34).

To navigate the system, applicants tried to uncover hidden rules, sometimes succeeding—"In the Balloon Game, I was able to recognize patterns based on the balloon colors…I simply just followed that pattern" (Participant 26)—and sometimes adjusting through experimentation. "I tried flipping each card five times because…when I flipped it six times, I lost money, but when I flipped it four times, the result was still positive. So I thought five was a good number…" (Participant 36).

Strategies ranged from probing the algorithm's logic to simply following instructions. "I just read the instruction to know how to do it" (Participant 6). Some adopted a passive approach: "I did not think too much and had no understanding of what AI is" (Participant 4), seeing results as mere reflections of company needs: "If I pass, it means I am suitable for the company. If I don't pass, then I am not suitable…" (Participant 2). Many regarded their personality feedback as tied to organizational requirements: "I think I failed this test because my personality didn't align with their company culture" (Participant 26).

Applicants often tailored their responses to align with the recruiter's desired profile: "If I liked that company…I would express myself in the direction that company wants" (Participant 7). Some strategically planned moves to display certain qualities: "Because I want to prove the system that I am a fair person and consistent…" (Participant 36). Many believed they could decipher and steer the system: "I know what the purpose of these games is, so I can navigate the results to the way I want it to be" (Participant 18).

Self-assessment was a key strategy, as applicants reflected on traits like risk aversion to match expected profiles: "I first asked myself how risk-averse I am and compared with what the company might expect…so I decided…medium level of risk aversion" (Participant 35). Pymetrics' opaque algorithms made its evaluations unpredictable, prompting varied interpretations and attempts to present themselves favourably through inferred logic and trial.

5.3 Job Applicants' Resistance

Applicants resisted the uncertainties and opacity of the AI-GBA games through various strategies aimed at improving their performance and understanding the system's evaluation process. Many created multiple profiles using different email addresses and resumes to retake the tests and compare results. As Participant 3 explained, "We will usually have a way to circumvent the rules by creating other emails and submitting a resume together. I also borrowed a friend's account." This approach allowed for repeated attempts and deeper insights: "In general, I did this test many times. You know, when doing the Pymetrics game, you can change your email so you can do it over and over again. I often change my email address and then I can replay. From there, I learn how to change my profile" (Participant 5). Similarly, Participant 39 shared, "After initial rounds, I know the patterns of the balloon game and try to apply it to the following rounds."

Other strategies included distorting play behaviors to fit role profiles, imitating recommended behaviours from online discussions, and maneuvering around game rules. For instance, Participant 4 said, "In the Money Exchange game, I wanted to demonstrate that I am a generous person. I chose to give more to the virtual player than to keep the money for myself…giving it to others could signal generosity." Some deliberately disregarded instructions, such as not writing down answers: "I intentionally wrote the numbers wrong so that the system wouldn't know that I cheated in this game" (Participant 19).

Applicants also collaborated by playing in groups with family or friends and shared feedback to help others adapt their behaviours. Experiences and strategies were frequently exchanged on social media and in online communities: "I joined in a Facebook group to explore what other applicants share and learned from their experience with the Pymetrics games" (Participant 33). These collective practices of resistance including bypassing rules, creating new accounts, sharing resumes and tips became normalized, shaping perceptions and future strategies not only for Pymetrics but also for other algorithmic hiring systems.

6 Discussions

The findings reveal that interactions between job applicants and the AI-GBA system unfold across three interlinked dimensions: meaning-making, struggles over power, and the legitimation of resistance. Although AI-GBA acts as a latent assessment system concealing its decision criteria, applicants actively seek to resist and influence its dominance in the hiring process. Their actions, both shaped by and responding to the system, often legitimize resistance and reshape the dynamics of application. This evolving relationship offers insights into how applicants adapt their strategies when engaging with AI-driven selection tools. Regarding meaning-making, applicants' interpretations of Pymetrics varied and evolved across different phases of use. Their understanding emerged from information provided by the system such as design, feedback, and vagueness and their own actions like seeking knowledge, recalling past experiences, and reflecting with others. Individual interpretive schemes continuously shape how meaning is produced and reproduced over time. With respect to domination, while Pymetrics exerts control through behavioural tracking, profiling, and job-fit analysis, applicants push back by exploring game rules, ignoring uncertainties, testing algorithmic patterns, self-assessing, and engaging in resistance strategies. In terms of legitimation, applicants frame their resistance, such as sharing feedback, creating multiple accounts, or collaborating on gameplay, as valid responses to the system. These practices contribute to new norms around engaging with AI-GBA systems and foster a sense of agency among applicants. As depicted in Fig. 3, these interactive dimensions show how the applicant-system relationship can evolve, originating from personal interpretations and spreading through collective practices, ultimately influencing established norms for using AI-driven hiring tools.

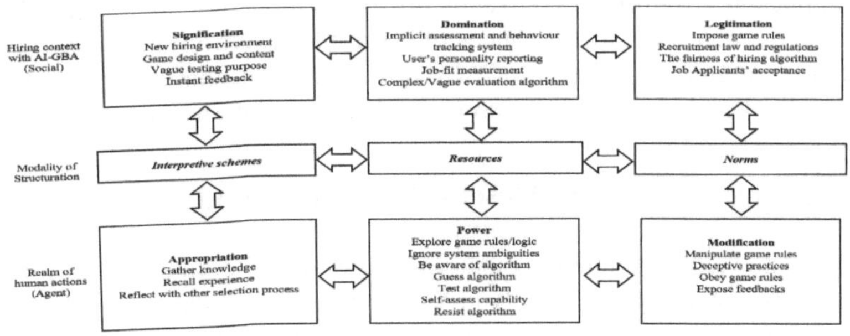

Fig. 3. Framework of the interaction between job applicants and AI-GBA

This research expands current understanding by highlighting the dynamic and reciprocal relationship between applicants and AI-GBA systems. Unlike prior studies focused mainly on user reactions, this work shows that in compulsory application contexts, applicants' relationship with the system continually adapts even in the absence of direct changes to the AI itself. For example, during preparation, many seek advice from friends or social media, shaping their initial perceptions and relationship with the tool. This dynamic interplay is moderated by individual interpretive schemes, resource access, and prevailing social norms (Fig. 3). These factors interact, shifting influence between the applicant and the system based on how applicants utilize available resources.

This research presents significant theoretical and practical contributions. From a theoretical perspective, it extends knowledge on how users respond to algorithmic black boxes during job applications, building on prior research focused on algorithm opacity [60, 61], [62], AI-driven health diagnostics [17], and AI resume screening in recruitment [60]. The study identifies three distinct stages of applicant response to the opacity of AI-GBA systems: Appropriation, where applicants interpret the system's meaning; Power, where they assert agency to manage its influence; and Modification, where they engage in practices that reshape legitimation and institutional norms around AI-GBA. Importantly, the relationship between applicants and AI-GBA is shown to be dynamic, evolving continuously across pre-engagement, engagement, and post-engagement stages, even without modifications to the underlying AI technology itself. This highlights the fluid, reciprocal nature of human-algorithm interaction. Further, the study theorizes this relationship through the lens of structuration theory, emphasizing the co-evolution of system capabilities and user agency and contributing to IS literature by applying this theory in contemporary digital recruitment contexts.

Practically, these findings provide valuable insights for employers, regulators, and policymakers regarding the lived experience of applicants navigating ambiguous, gamified AI-GBA systems. While applicants show resistance and employ strategies to counterbalance algorithmic control, the research underscores a critical need for clearer instructions and guidance. Enhanced transparency would support applicants in developing relevant skills and preparing more effectively for AI-driven assessments. This, in turn, can improve the fairness and user-friendliness of AI-GBA systems, promoting more equitable hiring processes. By fostering better understanding of how the system operates, applicants are empowered to authentically demonstrate their skills and characteristics, thereby increasing their chances of favorable selection outcomes. Ultimately, these insights can guide the design of AI recruitment tools that are more transparent, supportive, and aligned with ethical standards of fairness and inclusivity.

7 Limitations and Future Research Recommendations

This study acknowledges limitations that open avenues for future research. First, as a qualitative study conducted exclusively in Vietnam, its findings are context-specific and aimed at developing theoretical insights rather than producing broadly generalizable conclusions [61]. Future research could adopt quantitative methods to validate and expand these findings across larger and more diverse populations. Second, focusing solely on Vietnam leaves unexplored how applicants from different countries may perceive and experience AI-GBA systems differently, given variations in cultural, economic, and technological contexts. Third, this study concentrated on Generation Z applicants, who are "digital natives" with high digital literacy. Future research should consider other generations with varying technological skills to understand how demographic differences affect perceptions and strategies. Additionally, while this study examined applicants' experiences, investigating the perspectives of recruiters and hiring managers who engage with AI-GBA systems could provide a more comprehensive understanding of how these technologies impact organizational decision-making and practices. Overall, it is hoped that this study will stimulate further discussion on the use, legitimacy, and social implications of AI-GBA in employment processes.

References

1. Pan, Y., Froese, F.J.: An interdisciplinary review of AI and HRM: challenges and future directions. Hum. Resour. Manag. Rev. **33**(1), 100924 (2023)
2. Hemalatha, A., et al.: Impact of artificial intelligence on recruitment and selection of information technology companies. In: 2021 International Conference on Artificial Intelligence and Smart Systems (ICAIS). IEEE (2021)
3. Lacroux, A., Martin-Lacroux, C.: Should I trust the artificial intelligence to recruit? Recruiters' perceptions and behavior when faced with algorithm-based recommendation systems during resume screening. Front. Psychol. **13**, 895997 (2022)
4. Rasipuram, S., Jayagopi, D.B.: Automatic assessment of communication skill in interview-based interactions. Multimed. Tools Appl. **77**, 18709–18739 (2018)

5. Zhang, L., Yencha, C.: Examining perceptions towards hiring algorithms. Technol. Soc. **68**, 101848 (2022)
6. Albassam, W.A.: The power of artificial intelligence in recruitment: an analytical review of current AI-based recruitment strategies. Int. J. Prof. Bus. Rev. **8**(6), e02089–e02089 (2023)
7. Daryani, C., et al.: An automated resume screening system using natural language processing and similarity. In: Ethic and Information Technology [Internet]. Volkson Press, p. 99–103 (2020)
8. Sánchez-Monedero, J., Dencik, L., Edwards, L.: What does it mean to 'solve' the problem of discrimination in hiring? Social, technical and legal perspectives from the UK on automated hiring systems. In: Proceedings of the 2020 Conference on Fairness, Accountability, and Transparency (2020)
9. Nugent, S.E., Scott-Parker, S.: Recruitment AI has a disability problem: anticipating and mitigating unfair automated hiring decisions. In: Towards Trustworthy Artificial Intelligent Systems, pp. 85–96. Springer (2022)
10. Landers, R.N., et al.: Theory-driven game-based assessment of general cognitive ability: design theory, measurement, prediction of performance, and test fairness. J. Appl. Psychol. **107**(10), 1655 (2022)
11. Leutner, F., et al.: Game based assessments of cognitive ability in recruitment: validity, fairness and test-taking experience. Front. Psychol. **13**, 942662 (2023)
12. Raghavan, M., et al.: Mitigating bias in algorithmic hiring: evaluating claims and practices. In: Proceedings of the 2020 Conference on Fairness, Accountability, and Transparency (2020)
13. Kim, F.: The Impact of AI on Modern Recruitment Practices: A Comprehensive Overview (2024). Available from: https://www.expresscomputer.in/guest-blogs/the-impact-of-ai-on-modern-recruitment-practices-a-comprehensive-overview/107961/
14. Chow, S., Chapman, D.: Gamifying the employee recruitment process. In: Proceedings of the First International Conference on Gameful Design, Research, and Applications (2013)
15. Klein, R.M., et al.: The AttentionTrip: a game-like tool for measuring the networks of attention. J. Neurosci. Methods **289**, 99–109 (2017)
16. Möhlmann, M., et al.: Algorithmic Management of Work on online labor platforms: when matching meets control. MIS Q. **45**(4) (2021)
17. Lebovitz, S., Lifshitz-Assaf, H., Levina, N.: To engage or not to engage with AI for critical judgments: how professionals deal with opacity when using AI for medical diagnosis. Organ. Sci. **33**(1), 126–148 (2022)
18. Ohlms, M.L., Melchers, K.G., Kanning, U.P.: Can we playfully measure cognitive ability? Construct-related validity and applicant reactions. Int. J. Sel. Assess. (2023)
19. Armstrong, M.B., Landers, R.N. Collmus, A.B.: Gamifying recruitment, selection, training, and performance management: Game-thinking in human resource management. In: Emerging Research and Trends in Gamification. IGI Global Scientific Publishing, pp. 140–165 (2016)
20. Predicts, A.F.-D.S.G.: Measuring working memory is all fun and games. Exp. Psychol. **61**(6), 417–438 (2014)
21. Auer, E.M., et al.: Using machine learning to model trace behavioral data from a game-based assessment. Int. J. Sel. Assess. **30**(1), 82–102 (2022)
22. Pymetrics (2023). Available from: https://www.pymetrics.ai/assessments
23. Trindel, K., Polli, F., Glazebrook, K.: Using Technology to Increase Fairness in Hiring. What Works, p. 30 (2019)
24. Wilson, C., et al.: Building and auditing fair algorithms: a case study in candidate screening. In: Proceedings of the 2021 ACM Conference on Fairness, Accountability, and Transparency (2021)
25. Yam, J., Skorburg, J.A.: From human resources to human rights: impact assessments for hiring algorithms. Ethics Inf. Technol. **23**(4), 611–623 (2021)

26. Hu, Q.: Unilever's practice on AI-based recruitment. Highlights Bus., Econ. Manag. **16**, 256–263 (2023)
27. Mainka, S.M.: Algorithm-based recruiting technology in the workplace. Tex. A&M J. Prop. L. **5**, 801 (2019)
28. Harris, M.M., Hoye, G.V., Lievens, F.: Privacy and attitudes towards internet-based selection systems: a cross-cultural comparison. Int. J. Sel. Assess. **11**(2–3), 230–236 (2003)
29. Stone, D.L., Lukaszewski, K.M., Isenhour, L.C.: e-Recruiting. The Professional Practice Series, p. 22 (2005)
30. Giddens, A.: The Constitution of Society: Outline of the Theory of Structuration. Polity, 1984
31. Jones, M.R., Karsten, H.: Giddens's structuration theory and information systems research. MIS Q. 127–157 (2008)
32. Orlikowski, W.J.: The duality of technology: rethinking the concept of technology in organizations. Organ. Sci. **3**(3), 398–427 (1992)
33. Whittington, R.: Giddens, Structuration Theory and Strategy as Practice. Cambridge handbook of strategy as practice, pp. 109–126 (2010)
34. Bourdieu, P.: Homo Academicus. Stanford University Press (1988)
35. Jones, M.: Structuration Theory. The Oxford handbook of management information systems, pp. 113–137 (2011)
36. Battilana, J.: Agency and institutions: the enabling role of individuals' social position. Organization **13**(5), 653–676 (2006)
37. DiMaggio, P.J.: Interest and Agency in Institutional Theory. Institutional patterns and Organizations, pp. 3–21 (1988)
38. Champion, D.: Structuration Theory and Conversation Modelling: A Possible Interpretivist Approach to Bridging the Gap in Information System Design. Information Systems The Next Generation, University of York (1999)
39. Orlikowski, W.J., Robey, D.: Information technology and the structuring of organizations. Inf. Syst. Res. **2**(2), 143–169 (1991)
40. DeSanctis, G., Poole, M.S.: Capturing the complexity in advanced technology use: adaptive structuration theory. Organ. Sci. **5**(2), 121–147 (1994)
41. Myers, M.D., Avison, D.: Qualitative Research in Information Systems: A Reader. Sage (2002)
42. iPREP: Free Pymetrics Games Test Practice: 2023 Prep Guide (2023). Available from: https://www.iprep.online/courses/pymetrics-games-test-assessment/?gad_source=1&gclid=EAIaIQobChMIq6yS_ezVggMV2_d3Ch1-2gh5EAAYASAAEgKuqfD_BwE
43. Ghosh, C.W.A.M.A., Jiang, S.: Auditing the Pymetrics Model Generation Process (2020)
44. Dang, H.B., Pham, T.T.Q., Nguyen, V.P., Nguyen, V.H.: Regulatory impact of a governmental approach for artificial intelligence technology implementation in Vietnam. J. Infrastruct., Policy Dev. (2024)
45. Denzin, N.K.: The Research Act: A Theoretical Introduction to Sociological Methods. Routledge (2017)
46. Yin, R.K.: Case Study Research: Design and Methods vol. 5. Sage (2009)
47. Polit, D.F., Beck, C.T.: Nursing Research: Generating and Assessing Evidence for Nursing Practice. Lippincott Williams & Wilkins (2008)
48. Noble, H., Heale, R.: Triangulation in Research, with Examples. Royal College of Nursing, pp. 67–68 (2019)
49. Myers, M.D., Newman, M.: The qualitative interview in IS research: examining the craft. Inf. Organ. **17**(1), 2–26 (2007)
50. Newcomer, K.E., Hatry, H.P., Wholey, J.S.: Handbook of Practical Program Evaluation. Wiley Online Library (2015)
51. Noy, C.: Sampling knowledge: the hermeneutics of snowball sampling in qualitative research. Int. J. Soc. Res. Methodol. **11**(4), 327–344 (2008)

52. Etikan, I., Alkassim, R., Abubakar, S.: Comparision of snowball sampling and sequential sampling technique. Biom. Biostat. Int. J. **3**(1), 55 (2016)
53. Voicu, M.-C., Babonea, A.-M.: Using the snowball method in marketing research on hidden populations. Soc. Probl. **44**(2), 1341–1351 (1997)
54. Lazar, M.-A., Zbuchea, A., Pînzaru, F.: The emerging generation Z workforce in the digital world: a literature review on cooperation and transformation. In: Proceedings of the International Conference on Business Excellence. Sciendo (2023)
55. Turner, A.: Generation Z: technology and social interest. J. Individ. Psychol. **71**(2), 103–113 (2015)
56. Goncalves, M., Cornelius Smith, E.: Social media as a data gathering tool for international business qualitative research: opportunities and challenges. J. Transnatl. Manag. **23**(2–3) (2018)
57. Earl Rinehart, K.: Abductive analysis in qualitative inquiry. Qual. Inq. **27**(2), 303–311 (2021)
58. Tavory, I., Timmermans, S.: Abductive Analysis: Theorizing Qualitative Research. University of Chicago Press (2014)
59. Gioia, D.A., Corley, K.G., Hamilton, A.L.: Seeking qualitative rigor in inductive research: notes on the Gioia methodology. Organ. Res. Methods **16**(1), 15–31 (2013)
60. Armstrong, L., Everson, J. Ko, A.J.: Navigating a Black Box: Students' Experiences and Perceptions of Automated Hiring (2023)
61. Mwita, K.: Strengths and weaknesses of qualitative research in social science studies. Int. J. Res. Bus. Soc. Sci. (2147–4478) **11**(6), 618–625 (2022)

Open Data Platforms Engagement: An Integrative Review of Citizens' Motivations Inhibiting and Accelerating Adoption

Budi Satrio(✉), Fernando Kleiman, and Marijn Janssen

Faculty of Technology Policy and Management, Delft University of Technology, Delft, the Netherlands
{b.satrio,f.kleiman,m.f.w.h.a.janssen}@tudelft.nl

Abstract. Governments are increasingly deploying open data portals and platforms as a technological innovation to empower citizens by providing access to data. Yet, engagement with these portals remains low, suggesting that current approaches may not adequately map the issues surrounding the adoption of these tools. Research on open data has been conducted to overcome the technical and institutional barriers to adopting open data portals and platforms. However, there is a void in the literature about research on the citizens' motivations that support or inhibit their adoption. This study addresses this gap by drawing on the Self-Concordance Model, a motivational theory that explores the alignment of an individual's goals and values, to explain citizens' motivations better. Through an integrative literature review, we conceptualized citizens' motivational factors, linked them with corresponding barriers, and organized them into a taxonomy that reflects their role across different stages of the adoption process. Our analysis reveals that identified and intrinsic motivations play distinct roles in both pre-adoption and post-adoption phases, suggesting that tailored design strategies targeting these motivations could effectively initiate and sustain citizen engagement. This study advances open data research by connecting motivation and use of motivation theory to map the citizens' behavioral dynamics underlying their adoption. Our proposed taxonomy provides a foundation for future research into motivation-driven strategies in designing open data portals and platforms' interventions to increase citizens' engagement.

Keywords: Citizens Engagement · Open Data Portals · Platforms · Motivations · Barriers · Self-Concordance Model · Adoption Process Stages

1 Introduction

Governments can engage citizens by opening their data through portals and stimulating engagement on open data platforms [1]. Open data is broadly understood as data that is freely available for anyone to use, reuse, and redistribute without significant restrictions [2] commonly provided by government organizations [3]. Open data portals and

Published by Springer Nature Switzerland AG 2026
A. Elbanna et al. (Eds.): TDIT 2025, IFIP AICT 778, pp. 88–102, 2026.
https://doi.org/10.1007/978-3-032-16775-0_6

platforms are systems that provide the public with free access to data produced or commissioned by government entities [4]. Once an emerging innovation over a decade ago [5], open data portals and platforms have now become globally available. The Open Data Barometer [6] found that out of 115 countries surveyed, 79 countries had an open data portal, demonstrating a collective effort to make governmental data accessible to citizens worldwide. However, often these portals have not achieved the desired level of citizen interaction [7].

Much research has focused on open data barriers and overcoming them, including data quality. [8, 9], portal usability [10, 11], and data literacy [12, 13]. Yet, the motivation of users has been given scant attention. Although the infrastructure can be available, there is a need for users to be motivated to use open data. To the best of our knowledge, research on the motivations to engage with open data focuses on the technical users, such as developers [14] or government institutions [15]. No research has focused explicitly on citizens' motivation-centered adoption of open data portals and platforms. The motivation for using open data is particularly important since it accounts for personal interests and values [16], which influence how citizens adopt open data portals and platforms.

This paper aims to understand the dynamics that influence citizens' engagement with open data portals and platforms. Specifically, how do motivations shape citizens' participation throughout the adoption process? To answer this, we conduct an integrative literature review to identify motivational and inhibiting factors reported in prior research. Rather than simply listing these factors, we conceptualize them into a taxonomy that reflects their role at each stage of the adoption process. This approach brings structure to complex findings that inform both theory and practice.

To guide this conceptualization, we draw on the Self-Concordance Model (SCM), which explains how individuals are more motivated when their goals are aligned with personal values, pursuing enjoyment, or driven by external rewards or ego [16]. SCM classifies internal motivational processes that precede citizens' evaluation of open data portals. In this sense, SCM provides a motivational lens for understanding why individuals are inclined to engage in the first place. While SCM provides the foundational insight into motivation, it has also demonstrated relevance across various digital contexts. For instance, as a strong moderating factor in the acceptance of generative AI [17], where its parent theory, Self-Determination Theory (SDT) [18], has shown significant effects; as a strong predictor of continuance intention to use smart learning platforms [19]; and as a valuable framework for mapping motivations in gamified citizens' engagement [20]. In our framework, SCM complements other theories such as the Technology Acceptance Model (TAM) and Task-Technology Fit (TTF) as moderating effects [17] of citizens' perceptions on the usefulness and ease of use of open data portals and platforms [21, 22] or as supporting variables for citizens' task performance [23].

Building on this theoretical framework, the remainder of the paper unfolds as follows: the next section presents the research approach, highlighting the use of the PRISMA method. Then, we outline the findings before discussing them. The last section is the conclusion of the review.

2 Research Approach

To answer the main question introduced in the previous section, we systematically integrate and review the literature to conceptualize the motivations and their corresponding barriers influencing citizens' adoption. We employed the PRISMA framework, which enhances the reproducibility of the review process [24]. This framework aligns with our objective to comprehensively address our sub-questions guiding this study:

1. SQ1: What are the citizens' motivations for engaging with open data portals and platforms?
2. SQ2: What barriers hinder citizens' motivation with open data portals and platforms?
3. SQ3: How do motivations and barriers shape the open data portals and platforms' adoption process?

By utilizing the PRISMA framework, we structured our review process across four phases: identification, screening, eligibility, and inclusion [24]. In the first phase, identification, we identify potential studies by searching using the broadly recognized databases for academic literature: Scopus and Web of Science (WoS) [25]. We then defined key terms to be used in the search, focusing on citizens' interaction with open data portals, including motivations and barriers. Therefore, our search strings involved six sets of key terms: 'open data', 'portals/platforms', 'interaction', 'citizen', and 'engagement', as detailed in Table 1. 'Open data' and 'portals/platforms' directly correspond to the technological innovation in this study [26, 27], capturing the context in which citizen engagement occurs. 'Citizen' anchors the search in the target user group, while 'engagement' reflects the behavioral interaction with the open data portals and platforms. 'Motivations' and 'barriers' were included to understand factors influencing citizens' decisions to interact with open data portals [28]. In both databases, we restricted the language to English because studies indicate there is no evidence of systematic bias from using only English [29, 30]. We excluded conference reviews in Scopus and review articles in WoS, as our focus was on empirical and case studies. We also limited searches from the past 15 years to ensure they are relevant to the latest knowledge.

Table 1. Key terms used in the search string.

Key terms	Keywords in the search string
Open data	open data OR open government data
Portals/platforms	portal* (portal OR portals) OR platform* (platform OR platforms)
Interaction	incentive* (incentive OR incentives) OR driver* (driver OR drivers) OR reason* (reason OR reasons) OR barrier* (barrier OR barriers) OR inhibit* (inhibit OR inhibits OR inhibitor OR inhibitors)
Citizen	citizen*(citizen OR citizens)
Engagement	engag*(engage OR engages OR engagement OR engaging) OR participat* (participate OR participates OR participation OR participating) OR interact* (interact OR interaction OR interacting)

For each key term in the table, we provided multiple related keywords. For example, in the 'interaction' term, we listed 'incentive', 'driver', 'reason', 'barrier', and 'inhibitor' with each variation. Our goal is to capture relevant literature based on the key terms about citizens' engagement with open data portals and platforms.

In the second phase, screening, we excluded studies that did not meet the relevance to the research question. In the third phase, eligibility, we further assessed the remaining studies for their relevance and quality. Studies that did not align with the research objectives were excluded. The reasons for exclusion were documented to ensure transparency. Finally, in the fourth phase, inclusion, studies that met all the inclusion criteria were included in the review. This phase involved a detailed examination of the selected studies to extract relevant data on the benefits and barriers to citizen engagement with open data portals.

3 Findings

By using the established search strings defined previously in the research approach, we outlined our PRISMA flow screening process as depicted in Fig. 1.

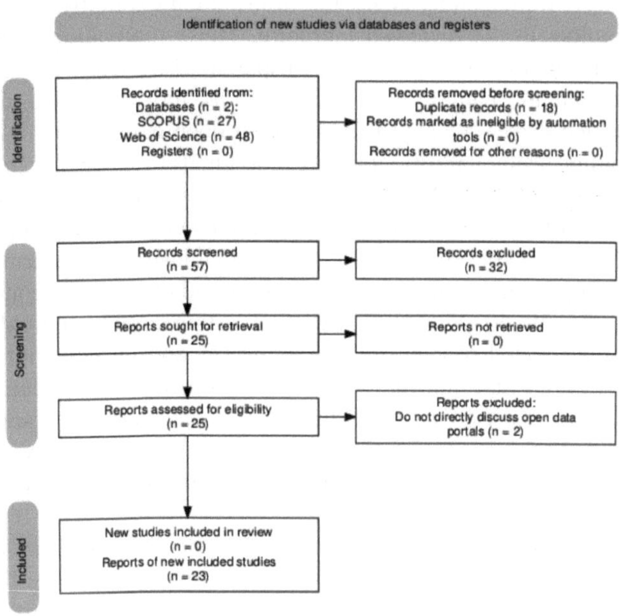

Fig. 1. PRISMA Flow Diagram of motivations influencing citizens' engagement with open data portals. This diagram was created using an online PRISMA flow diagram [31].

Using the PRISMA framework, we identified 75 new records from SCOPUS and Web of Science databases. We excluded 18 reports due to duplicates and 32 since their abstracts do not relate to open data portals and platforms. After reading the content, we excluded two reports because they do not directly discuss engagement with open data portals and platforms. The final number of literature to be reviewed is 23.

3.1 Bibliometric Analysis

Of the 23 reports reviewed, 18 were case studies, 12 employed empirical methods, and the rest were literature reviews, with 12 integrated multiple approaches. Besides the peak in 2018 and the decline in 2020, possibly due to the COVID-19 situation, the frequency of publication remained relatively consistent in the other years. This suggests that researchers have maintained a continuous interest in open data portals' and platforms' engagement. The search results also show a higher number of journal articles (18) than conference papers (6), with one book chapter, suggesting that both journals and conferences play important roles in disseminating research. We also noticed that more datasets used in the studies are from the global north: eleven, compared to seven from the global south countries. One paper analyzed data from both the global north and south. This finding suggests that open data portals in the global north generate more data to be researched.

3.2 Citizens' Motivations to Engage with Open Data Portals and Platforms

To identify citizens' motivations for engaging with open data portals and platforms as guided by our SQ1, we began by analyzing information explicitly stated or implicitly suggested by authors in the reviewed literature. These motivations range from civic curiosity [32] and recognition [33] to better transparency [4, 34, 35]. From these findings, we synthesized thematic patterns and developed six motivational dimensions. First, Civic Values, which drive citizens to engage with open data portals for transparency, oversight, and public accountability, enabling individuals to scrutinize and participate in institutional processes [2, 34–42]. Second, Co-creation, which captures citizens' desire to collaborate and offer feedback that addresses civic challenges through open data portals [2–4, 32, 34, 35, 37, 42–49]. Third, at a more personal level, Empowerment, represents citizens' pursuit of personal growth or feeling pressured by others to contribute or to be informed [4, 32, 36, 38–40, 42, 43]. Fourth, Social Impact, which highlights citizens' intentions to solve societal problems, drive inclusion, and improve public welfare [3, 33, 34, 37, 40, 41, 48]. Fifth, Innovation, which stems from entrepreneurial and creative impulses, where citizens use open data API or tools to create services or apps that advance public benefit [2, 3, 33, 34, 36, 38, 39, 42, 44–47, 49]. Lastly, Community revolves around relationship building with other citizens and feeling connected in broader civic networks [2, 4, 32, 38, 39, 43–49].

To conceptualize these dimensions, we applied the Self-Concordance Model (SCM), which focuses on the alignment of personal values and goals [16]. This theoretical stance is particularly relevant given that engagement with open data is often self-initiated and driven by personal or societal ideals [14, 50]. In other contexts, SCM has been used to map individuals' motivations, such as in language learning [51] or in gamified citizens' engagement [20]. In this sense, SCM offers a psychologically grounded model for understanding the motivational drivers behind citizens' engagement with open data portals and platforms.

Using SCM, we conceptualized the six dimensions of citizens' motivations into external, introjected, identified, and intrinsic [16]. External motivation refers to engagement with open data portals driven by external rewards, such as recognition from others. For example, a citizen may engage with an open data portal to develop apps or to fulfill work-related requirements [33]. Introjected motivation arises from internalized pressure, such as feelings of obligation. For instance, individuals might use open data portals because others are doing so [32]. Intrinsic motivation, conversely, refers to the enjoyment in the activity, such as exploring data for personal curiosity [32]. Lastly, identified motivation occurs when individuals recognize the personal value of an activity, such as using open data to address local issues they deeply care about [41]. We mapped the dimensions and each SCM classification as outlined in Table 2.

Table 2. The dimensions of citizens' motivations conceptualized using SCM.

Dimensions	SCM classification	Information and source
Civic Values	Identified	Citizens engage with open data portals because they value transparency and accountability, which are personally endorsed goals [36]
Co-creation	Intrinsic/Identified	Citizens collaborate and give feedback [45], highly motivated for enjoyment (intrinsic), but they can also believe in civic collaboration (identified) [47]
Empowerment	Identified/Introjected	Citizens using open data portals are driven by personal growth (identified) [32], but sometimes by social pressure to contribute or be informed (introjected) [38]
Social Impact	Identified	Citizens are motivated by alignment with values such as inclusion and community well-being [41]
Innovation	External/Identified	Some citizens pursue innovation for prizes or recognition (external) [33], while others do so because they believe in improving services (identified) [48]
Community	Intrinsic/Identified	Citizens may enjoy dialogue and connection (intrinsic) [32] or value shared purpose (identified) [47]

Our findings revealed that the Civic Values and Social Impact dimensions were closely related to the identified motivation, which stemmed from the personal value of citizens. The external motivation, resulting from the external rewards of using open data portals and platforms, was related to the Innovation dimension. While intrinsic motivation, which focuses on enjoyment, could arise in the Co-creation and Community dimensions. By framing using SCM, we provided a deeper understanding of citizens' motivations in each of the dimensions.

3.3 Barriers that Hinder Citizens' Motivations to Engage with Open Data Portals and Platforms

Although we have outlined citizens' motivations from the literature, a holistic understanding of engagement requires identifying the factors that inhibit it. Therefore, we examined the barriers to citizens' motivations as guided by our SQ2. We analyzed the literature, aiming at both explicit statements and implicit suggestions made by authors across the reviewed studies to uncover inhibitors that hinder motivations. These barriers include issues such as a lack of skills to use open data portals [42], poor digital infrastructure [40], or legal concerns [52]. From these findings, we analyzed similar themes and developed more generic dimensions of barriers. First, Institutional Barriers, which stem from the reluctance of governments to open their data and political resistance, often result in mismatches between data offerings and citizen needs. Second, Technical Limitations, which refer to flaws in the technical layer, such as poor portal design, lack of visualization tools, and non-machine-readable formats that undermine accessibility. Third, Data and Skill Gaps highlight the lack of citizens' technical expertise and the inaccurate, incomplete, or low data quality. Fourth, Legal Concerns involve unresolved security risks, privacy, legal ambiguities, and the lack of feedback mechanisms. Fifth, Communication Challenges arise when outreach efforts fall short, engagement is low, collaboration is limited, and the value of open data remains poorly understood. Lastly, Resource Constraints, which point to the burden of time-consuming data cleaning, poor administrative support, and costly data transformation. We mapped the dimensions as outlined in Table 3.

Table 3. The dimensions of barriers to citizens' motivations.

Dimensions	Information and source
Institutional barriers	Bureaucratic issues, centralized systems, and political resistance reflect norms and reluctance to change [2, 3, 33–36, 40, 42–47, 49, 52]
Technical limitations	Poor design, low interoperability, and infrastructure gaps make open data portals hard to use [2, 3, 32, 38–43, 47–49, 52, 53]
Data and skill gaps	High skill requirements and poor data quality create usability challenges [2–4, 33, 35, 39, 40, 42, 44, 45, 47–49, 53]
Legal concerns	Legal issues and security fears increase perceived risk and reduce adoption [3, 4, 33, 34, 36, 38–41, 47–49, 52, 53]
Communication challenges	Weak outreach and low perceived relevance diminish the value of open data portals [4, 32, 34–36, 38–40, 43–46, 52, 53]
Resource constraints	Time-consuming processes and a lack of support make adoption difficult [36, 52]

Our finding shows a strong research emphasis on institutional barriers, technical limitations, legal concerns, data and skill gaps, and communication challenges related to open data adoption. However, there is limited attention to resource constraints, such as time and support, as barriers to citizen motivation. This gap suggests further research is needed on individuals' experience, specifically on the time-consuming process and the usefulness of open data portals and platforms' support.

3.4 Adoption Process of Open Data Portals and Platforms

After conceptualizing the drivers and barriers of citizens' motivations to engage with open data portals and platforms, our next approach is to answer our SQ3 by connecting them into a structured taxonomy. We applied Rogers' five stages of the technology adoption process: knowledge, persuasion, decision, implementation, and confirmation [54]. Rogers' model is particularly relevant in open data studies since it captures the evolving nature of open data portals and platforms' adoption [11, 55].

By using Rogers' model, our analysis is framed as follows: 1) In the knowledge stage, we explore factors related to awareness and initial interest in engaging with open data portals. 2) In the persuasion stage, we identify elements that shape opinions and attitudes toward using the portals. 3) In the decision stage, we examine the factors that influence citizens' choices to engage or not. 4) In the implementation stage, we investigate aspects affecting the active use of the portals by citizens. 5) Finally, in the confirmation stage, we focus on reflections and factors that reinforce citizens' decisions to continue engaging with open data portals. Drawing from our findings, we connect the adoption process stage with the motivations and barriers as a taxonomy detailed in Table 4.

Table 4. Proposed taxonomy of open data platforms engagement for each adoption process stage.

Adoption stage [54]	Conceptualized motivations [16]	Dimensions of motivations	Dimensions of barriers
Knowledge	• Identified • Intrinsic	• Civic values • Co-creation	• Institutional barriers • Communication challenges
Persuasion	• Identified • Intrinsic • Introjected	• Co-creation • Empowerment • Community	• Data and skill gaps • Legal Concerns
Decision	• Identified • External	• Civic Values • Community • Innovation	• Institutional barriers • Legal concerns
Implementation	• Identified • External • Introjected	• Empowerment • Social impact • Innovation	• Technical limitations • Data and skill gaps • Resource constraints
Confirmation	• Identified • Intrinsic	• Social impact • Community	Resource constraints

The finding shows that each stage of the adoption process has its specific motivations and barriers. In the Knowledge stage, citizens first encounter open data portals and platforms as a concept. If they value transparency (identified) [3, 4, 34–38, 40] or are curious (intrinsic) [32], they will explore. However, bureaucratic issues [52] and poor communication [32] can block awareness. In the Persuasion stage, citizens begin evaluating open data portals' usefulness. If they feel empowered (identified) [38, 40, 42], pressured to be informed (introjected) [40], or enjoy civic dialogue (intrinsic) [4, 44], they use the portals. However, skill gaps [3, 33, 35, 36, 42, 44, 48, 53] and legal concerns [33, 34, 43, 52] can erode confidence. During the Decision stage, citizens decide whether to engage. If they believe in civic duty (identified) [48] or seek recognition (external) [33], they are more likely to commit. However, institutional resistance [40] and legal concerns [34, 52] can stall adoption. In the Implementation stage, citizens begin using data to build apps, solve problems, or learn. Motivation may stem from values (identified) [46], rewards (external) [33], or social obligation (introjected) [33]. However, poor infrastructure [40], time constraints [41], and low skills [3, 35] can hinder engagement. Finally, in the Confirmation stage, citizens reflect on outcomes. If they enjoy the communication (intrinsic) [32] or see alignment with values (identified) [37, 47], they will continue to use the portals. However, resource constraints [32, 52, 53] can lead to disengagement. We observed that the combination of citizens' identified and intrinsic motivations plays a role in starting and sustaining their engagement with open data portals and platforms, which highlights the importance of leveraging these motivations in designing open data portals and platforms.

4 Discussion

Our findings suggest variations in motivations and barriers across each stage of the open data portals and platforms' adoption. In the early stages, Knowledge and Persuasion, citizens are becoming aware of the innovation, and their motivation starts from internal relevance (identified and intrinsic) and slowly shifts toward external pressure (introjected). However, their resistance often stems from limited awareness, institutional and legal barriers, and a lack of skills in using open data portals and platforms. This means that campaigns about open data portals should not only provide information, but also make it personally meaningful for citizens with a clear legal support and training to use them. This proposition is supported by research on the open data portal in Bahrain, which highlights the need to raise citizen awareness and address their personal values for balanced information related to the data provision aspect of the portal [56].

In the Decision stage, their motivation varies from rewards (external), personal values (identified), to genuine enjoyment (intrinsic), underscoring the importance of legal concerns and minimizing institutional barriers. This aligns with the argument that enjoyment, social altruism, and social influence are crucial factors in engagement [57]. Simonofski et al. [58] even show preliminary results that gamification, a motivation-driven design strategy, has a high potential to make open data more enjoyable and enhance user experience, thereby making lay citizens decide to engage with open data portals and platforms.

During the Implementation stage, resistance tends to be technical and linked to the citizens' skills and resources, while motivation ranges from obligation to external rewards. Finally, in the Confirmation stage, citizens may reassess their experience. Motivation depends on the user satisfaction (intrinsic) and perceived value (identified), and resource constraints inhibit them from continuing to engage with open data portals. This insight is similar to Liang et al. [2] findings that in the open data post-adoption, the benefit of saving time and a high user satisfaction and perceived value drive citizens to sustain engagement.

The findings from this integrative literature review indicate that increasing citizen engagement with open data portals requires addressing the specific motivations and barriers at each stage of the adoption process. Specifically, the role of intrinsic and identified motivations, along with their institutional, legal, and resource barriers, which affect the pre- (knowledge stage) and post-adoption (confirmation stage) of open data portals. This approach diverges from existing research, which often centers on data-centric perspectives [8], technical users [14], or institutional barriers [15], and assumes uniform conditions across portals, overlooking the variations in motivations and barriers associated with different stages. Recognizing these differences is essential for designing tailored strategies that increase citizen engagement. Therefore, we recommend that future studies explore motivation-driven approaches to design a more effective engagement solutions for open data portals.

5 Conclusions

Open data research gives scant attention to personal motivations. This integrative literature review highlights the dynamics associated with citizens' motivations across each stage of the open data portals and platforms' adoption process. To address our central question, how do citizens' motivations shape the engagement throughout the adoption process, we propose a taxonomy of open data platforms engagement that maps motivations and barriers at each stage. We begin by examining citizens' motivations, conceptualizing them using the Self-Concordance Model, and exploring their corresponding barriers. Finally, we exhibit their relationship in a taxonomy of citizens' motivations and barriers for each stage of the open data portals and platforms' adoption process.

A key contribution of our study lies in the domain-specific understanding of self-motivations in open data portals and platforms' engagement. We highlight the combination of intrinsic and identified motivations to jumpstart and sustain engagement, but institutional, legal, and resource barriers often constrain these motivations. This motivational dynamics slightly differs from other domains, such as in language learning, where identified motivation (personally meaningful) is more likely to maintain user engagement [51], or in smart learning platforms, where intrinsic motivation (enjoyment) plays a more dominant role [19]. Given our findings, we suggest further research into motivation-driven strategies for designing open data portals and platforms' interventions, as they resonate deeper with individuals' motivations. For example, gamification has shown promise in increasing engagement by tapping into the motivation of lay citizens [58].

Despite these findings, we acknowledge our limitations in this study, including selection bias from our search, inclusion, and exclusion process, which may not represent all available studies, and reporting bias from our assessment of each study, which may select studies that only show significant output with positive outcomes. However, we mitigate this by showing the rigour of our study selection process and outlining the findings as transparently as possible. Moreover, our study highlights that existing research predominantly focuses on countries in the global north with mature open data infrastructures, revealing a gap in understanding how these portals function in diverse socio-economic and cultural settings of the global south.

Future research should focus on collecting empirical data, especially from the global south, to enrich the current knowledge base and provide comprehensive strategies for

engaging citizens. Ultimately, our taxonomy should be tested, leading to more effective engagement of citizens with open data portals.

Acknowledgments. We thank the reviewers for their valuable guidance during the revision process and our colleagues for their valuable suggestions during the conduct of this study.

Contributor Statement First Author: Writing – original draft, Formal analysis. Second Author: Writing – review & editing, Supervision, Conceptualization. Third Author: Writing – review & editing, Supervision

Funding or Grant This work presented herein was funded by the Indonesia Endowment Fund for Education (LPDP) grant number: 202308221741246.

Disclosure of Interests. Author 1 reports financial support was provided by the Indonesia Endowment Fund for Education (LPDP) grant number: 202308221741246. If there are other authors, they declare that they have no known competing financial interests or personal relationships that could have appeared to influence the work reported in this paper.

Supplementary Material. Supplemental materials of the selected studies are available through https://doi.org/10.4121/1a79b442-a00e-40a8-99d9-bb6da161a62c

Use of AI. During the preparation of this work, the author(s) used Rewrite/Copilot in order to improve readability. After using this tool/service, the author(s) reviewed, edited, made the content their own and validated the outcome as needed, and take(s) full responsibility for the content of the publication.

References

1. Janssen, M., Charalabidis, Y., Zuiderwijk, A.: Benefits, adoption barriers and myths of open data and open government. Inf. Syst. Manag. **29**, 258–268 (2012)
2. Liang, Y., Cao, Y., Chen, M., Dong, H., Wang, H.: Determinants of open government data continuance usage and value creation: a self-regulation framework analysis. Gov. Inf. Q. **42**, 102022 (2025). https://doi.org/10.1016/j.giq.2025.102022
3. Rudmark, D., Lindgren, R., Schultze, U.: Open data platforms: design principles for embracing outlaw innovators. J. Strateg. Inf. Syst. **33**, 101850 (2024). https://doi.org/10.1016/j.jsis.2024.101850
4. Cordasco, G., Malandrino, D., Pirozzi, D., Scarano, V., Spagnuolo, C.: A Layered architecture for open data: design, implementation and experiences. In: Proceedings of the 11th International Conference on Theory and Practice of Electronic Governance. pp. 371–381. ACM, Galway Ireland (2018). https://doi.org/10.1145/3209415.3209466
5. Krishnamurthy, R., Awazu, Y.: Liberating data for public value: The case of Data.gov. Int. J. Inf. Manage. **36**, 668–672 (2016). https://doi.org/10.1016/j.ijinfomgt.2016.03.002
6. Open Data Barometer: Global Report—Open Data Barometer. Open Data Barometer (2018)
7. Schwoerer, K.: Whose open data is it anyway? An exploratory study of open government data relevance and implications for democratic inclusion. Inf. Polity. **27**, 491–515 (2022). https://doi.org/10.3233/IP-220008

8. Máchová, R., Lnenicka, M.: Evaluating the quality of open data portals on the national level. J. Theor. Appl. Electron. Commer. Res. **12**, 21–41 (2017). https://doi.org/10.4067/S0718-18762017000100003
9. Raca, V., Velinov, G., Dzalev, S., Kon-Popovska, M.: A framework for evaluation and improvement of open government data quality: application to the Western Balkans national open data portals. SAGE Open **12**, 21582440221104812 (2022). https://doi.org/10.1177/21582440221104813
10. Nikiforova, A., McBride, K.: Open government data portal usability: a user-centred usability analysis of 41 open government data portals. Telematics Inform. **58**, 101539 (2021). https://doi.org/10.1016/j.tele.2020.101539
11. Weerakkody, V., Irani, Z., Kapoor, K., Sivarajah, U., Dwivedi, Y.K.: Open data and its usability: an empirical view from the Citizen's perspective. Inf. Syst. Front. **19**, 285–300 (2017). https://doi.org/10.1007/s10796-016-9679-1
12. Santos-Hermosa, G., Quarati, A., Loría-Soriano, E., Raffaghelli, J.E.: Why does open data get underused? A focus on the role of (open) data literacy. In: Raffaghelli, J.E., Sangrà, A. (eds.) Data cultures in higher education. pp. 145–177. Springer, Cham (2023). https://doi.org/10.1007/978-3-031-24193-2_6
13. Wylie, C., Neeley, K., Ferguson, S.: Beyond technological literacy: open data as active democratic engagement? Digit. Culture Soc. **4**, 157–182 (2018). https://doi.org/10.14361/dcs-2018-0209
14. Kassen, M.: Understanding motivations of citizens to reuse open data: open government data as a philanthropic movement. Innovation **23**, 44–70 (2021). https://doi.org/10.1080/14479338.2020.1738940
15. Altayar, M.S.: Motivations for open data adoption: an institutional theory perspective. Gov. Inf. Q. **35**, 633–643 (2018). https://doi.org/10.1016/j.giq.2018.09.006
16. Sheldon, K.M., Elliot, A.J.: Goal striving, need satisfaction, and longitudinal well-being: the self-concordance model. J. Pers. Soc. Psychol. **76**, 482 (1999)
17. Zheng, Y., Wang, Y., Liu, K.S.-X., Jiang, M.Y.-C.: Examining the moderating effect of motivation on technology acceptance of generative AI for English as a foreign language learning. Educ. Inf. Technol. **29**, 23547–23575 (2024). https://doi.org/10.1007/s10639-024-12763-3
18. Wan, P., Wen, T., Zhang, Y., Gao, H., Wang, J.: Goal self-concordance model: what have we learned and where are we going. Int. J. Mental Health Promotion **23**, 201–219 (2021). https://doi.org/10.32604/IJMHP.2021.015759
19. Li, J., Jin, M., Chen, X.: Understanding continued use of smart learning platforms: psychological wellbeing in an extended TAM-ISCM model. Front. Psychol. **16**, 1521174 (2025). https://doi.org/10.3389/fpsyg.2025.1521174
20. Satrio, B., Kleiman, F., Janssen, M.: Game elements enabling citizens' engagement: an integrative literature review into elements, motivations, drivers and barriers. DGO 1 (2025). https://doi.org/10.59490/dgo.2025.974
21. Zuiderwijk, A., Janssen, M., Dwivedi, Y.K.: Acceptance and use predictors of open data technologies: drawing upon the unified theory of acceptance and use of technology. Gov. Inf. Q. **32**, 429–440 (2015). https://doi.org/10.1016/j.giq.2015.09.005
22. Weerakkody, V., Kapoor, K., Balta, M.E., Irani, Z., Dwivedi, Y.K.: Factors influencing user acceptance of public sector big open data. Prod. Plan. Control **28**, 891–905 (2017). https://doi.org/10.1080/09537287.2017.1336802
23. Bankuoru Egala, S., Afful-Dadzie, E.: Performance of open government data in a developing economy: a multi-stakeholder case analysis of Ghana. TG. **16**, 318–333 (2022). https://doi.org/10.1108/TG-10-2021-0158
24. Moher, D., Liberati, A., Tetzlaff, J., Altman, D.G.: PRISMA Group*, t: preferred reporting items for systematic reviews and meta-analyses: the PRISMA statement. Ann. Int. Med. **151**, 264–269 (2009)

25. Martín-Martín, A., Orduna-Malea, E., Thelwall, M., López-Cózar, E.D.: Google Scholar, Web of Science, and Scopus: a systematic comparison of citations in 252 subject categories. J. Inf. **12**, 1160–1177 (2018)
26. Chan, C.M.L.: From open data to open innovation strategies: creating E-services using open government data. In: 2013 46th Hawaii International Conference on System Sciences. pp. 1890–1899. IEEE, Wailea, HI, USA (2013). https://doi.org/10.1109/HICSS.2013.236
27. Amugongo, L.M., Nggada, S.H., Sieck, J.: Open data portal—A technical enabler to drive innovation in Namibia. In: 2016 2nd International Conference on Open and Big Data (OBD). pp. 80–86. IEEE, Vienna (2016). https://doi.org/10.1109/OBD.2016.19
28. Dove, G., Shanley, J., Matuk, C., Nov, O.: Open data intermediaries: motivations, barriers and facilitators to engagement. Proc. ACM Hum.-Comput. Interact. **7**, 1–22 (2023). https://doi.org/10.1145/3579511
29. Morrison, A., et al.: The effect of English-language restriction on systematic review-based meta-analyses: a systematic review of empirical studies. Int. J. Technol. Assess. Health Care **28**, 138–144 (2012)
30. Jüni, P., Holenstein, F., Sterne, J., Bartlett, C., Egger, M.: Direction and impact of language bias in meta-analyses of controlled trials: empirical study. Int. J. Epidemiol. **31**, 115–123 (2002)
31. Haddaway, N.R., Page, M.J., Pritchard, C.C., McGuinness, L.A.: PRISMA2020: an R package and Shiny app for producing PRISMA 2020-compliant flow diagrams, with interactivity for optimised digital transparency and open synthesis. Campbell Syst. Rev. **18**, e1230 (2022). https://doi.org/10.1002/cl2.1230
32. Birghan, F., Hettenhausen, R., Meschede, C.: Challenges, barriers, and approaches for providing digital citizen information. a case-study in North Rhine-Westphalia, Germany. In: Bui T.X. (ed.) Proceedings of Annual Hawaii International Conference on System Sciences, pp. 2143–2152. IEEE Computer Society (2021)
33. Mergel, I.: The long way from government open data to mobile health apps: overcoming institutional barriers in the US Federal Government. JMIR mHealth uHealth. **2**, e58 (2014). https://doi.org/10.2196/mhealth.3694
34. Saxena, S.: Proposing a total quality management (TQM) model for open government data (OGD) initiatives: implications for India. Foresight **21**, 321–331 (2019). https://doi.org/10.1108/FS-07-2018-0073
35. Hogan, M., Ojo, A., Harney, O., Ruijer, E., Meijer, A., Andriessen, J., Pardijs, M., Boscolo, P., Palmisano, E., Satta, M., Groff, J., Baker, M., Détienne, F., Porwol, L., Scarano, V., Malandrino, D.: Governance, transparency and the collaborative design of open data collaboration platforms: understanding barriers, options, and needs. In: Ojo, A., Millard, J. (eds.) Government 3.0—Next Generation Government Technology Infrastructure and Services. pp. 299–332. Springer, Cham (2017). https://doi.org/10.1007/978-3-319-63743-3_12
36. De Donato, R., Ferretti, G., Marciano, A., Palmieri, G., Pirozzi, D., Scarano, V., Vicidomini, L.: Agile production of high quality open data. In: Proceedings of the 19th Annual International Conference on Digital Government Research: Governance in the Data Age. pp. 1–10. ACM, Delft The Netherlands (2018). https://doi.org/10.1145/3209281.3209352
37. Schmidthuber, L., Stütz, S., Hilgers, D.: Outcomes of open government: does an online platform improve citizens' perception of local government? IJPSM. **32**, 489–507 (2019). https://doi.org/10.1108/IJPSM-02-2018-0056
38. Herrera-Melo, C., González-Sanabria, J.: Proposal for the evaluation of open data portals. In: Revista Facultad de Ingenieria, vol. 29. Universidad Pedagogica y Tecnologica de Colombia (2019) https://doi.org/10.19053/01211129.v29.n0.2020.10194
39. Sangiambut, S., Sieber, R.: The civic open data and crowdsourcing app ecosystem: actors, materials, and interventions. J. Urban Regional Inf. Syst. Assoc. 28 (2017)

40. Temba, R.S., Di, L.: The role of open government data in advancing public sector transparency and accountability: evidence from Tanzania Agricultural Hub. Information Development. 02666669251350664 (2025). https://doi.org/10.1177/02666669251350664
41. Saxena, S.: Drivers and barriers towards re-using open government data (OGD): a case study of open data initiative in Oman. FS **20**, 206–218 (2018). https://doi.org/10.1108/FS-10-2017-0060
42. Craveiro, G.S., Martano, A.M.R.: Caring for my neighborhood: a platform for public oversight. In: Koch, F., Meneguzzi, F., Lakkaraju, K. (eds.) Agent Technology for Intelligent Mobile Services and Smart Societies. pp. 117–126. Springer, Berlin, Heidelberg (2015). https://doi.org/10.1007/978-3-662-46241-6_10
43. Ali, M., et al.: A framework for the multi-dimensional assessment of interoperability for open data ecosystems development. Inf. Polity **29**, 439–466 (2024). https://doi.org/10.1177/15701255241297172
44. Kassen, M.: Adopting and managing open data: Stakeholder perspectives, challenges and policy recommendations. AJIM **70**, 518–537 (2018). https://doi.org/10.1108/AJIM-11-2017-0250
45. Jussila, J., Kukkamäki, J., Mäntyneva, M., Heinisuo, J.: Open data and open source enabling smart city development: a case study in Häme Region. TIM Review **9**, 25–34 (2019). https://doi.org/10.22215/timreview/1266
46. Kassen, M.: Open data in Kazakhstan: incentives, implementation and challenges. ITP **30**, 301–323 (2017). https://doi.org/10.1108/ITP-10-2015-0243
47. Ruijer, E., Grimmelikhuijsen, S., Van Den Berg, J., Meijer, A.: Open data work: understanding open data usage from a practice lens. Int. Rev. Adm. Sci. **86**, 3–19 (2020). https://doi.org/10.1177/0020852317753068
48. Saxena, S.: Open government data (OGD) in six Middle East countries: an evaluation of the national open data portals. Digit. Poli. Regul. Govern. **20**, 310–322 (2018). https://doi.org/10.1108/DPRG-10-2017-0055
49. Saxena, S.: “Usage by stakeholders” as the objective of “transparency-by-design” in open government data: case study of Sri Lanka’s open data initiative. ILS **118**, 420–432 (2017). https://doi.org/10.1108/ILS-05-2017-0034
50. Cabitza, F., Locoro, A., Batini, C.: Making open data more personal through a social value perspective: a methodological approach. Inf. Syst. Front. **22**, 131–148 (2020). https://doi.org/10.1007/s10796-018-9854-7
51. Henry, A., Thorsen, C., Uztosun, M.S.: Exploring language learners’ self-generated goals: Does self-concordance affect engagement and resilience? System **112**, 102971 (2023). https://doi.org/10.1016/j.system.2022.102971
52. Parung, G.A., Hidayanto, A.N., Sandhyaduhita, P.I., Ulo, K.L.M., Phusavat, K.: Barriers and strategies of open government data adoption using fuzzy AHP-TOPSIS: a case of Indonesia. Trans. Gov. People Process Policy. **12**, 210–243 (2018). https://doi.org/10.1108/TG-09-2017-0055
53. Sugg, Z.: Social barriers to open (water) data. WIREs Water **9**, e1564 (2022). https://doi.org/10.1002/wat2.1564
54. Rogers, E.M., Singhal, A., Quinlan, M.M.: Diffusion of innovations. In: An integrated approach to communication theory and research. pp. 432–448. Routledge (2014)
55. Anttila, E.: Perceptions of open data in the tourism industry in Finland: implementation, use, and links with sustainable tourism development (2020)
56. Katbi, A.-K., Al-Ammary, J.: Open government data in kingdom of Bahrain: Towards an effective implementation framework. In: Reis L.P., Costanzo S., Adeli H., and Rocha A. (eds.) Advances in Intelligent Systems and Computing. pp. 699–715. Springer (2019). https://doi.org/10.1007/978-3-030-16181-1_66

57. Rasool, T., Sajid, M., War-Raich, N.F.: Factors influencing the citizens' satisfaction towards the use of open government data: a systematic literature review. eJ. eDemocracy Open Gov. **14**, 167–196 (2022). https://doi.org/10.29379/jedem.v14i2.705
58. Simonofski, A., Zuiderwijk, A., Clarinval, A., Hammedi, W.: Tailoring open government data portals for lay citizens: a gamification theory approach. Int. J. Inf. Manage. **65**, 102511 (2022). https://doi.org/10.1016/j.ijinfomgt.2022.102511

Artificial Intelligence in Crisis Communication: Through the Dual Lens of Journalism and Public Relations

Geetanjali Panda[✉] and Ashwani K. Upadhyay

Symbiosis International University, Pune 412115, India
geetanjali.panda2595@gmail.com

Abstract. We live in times characterised by volatile global crises and accelerating digital disruptions, where amalgamation of Artificial Intelligence (AI) into the dynamics of crisis communication and strategizing poses with possible transformative opportunities while pressing on ethical deterrents. Despite the proliferation of AI tools for sentiment analysis, real-time monitoring and content generation, no existing studies have thoroughly explored their dual impact on empathetic narrative framing and institutional trust-building during crisis management; especially in the Indian market. Addressing this gap, the study explores on how automation is reshaping the practices of Public Relations (PR) industry and Journalism during public crisis. This study advances the theoretical discourse by introducing a hybris human-AI crisis communication framework which is grounded in situational crisis communication theory (SCCT). Drawing on in-depth qualitative interviews with 30 journalists across entry, mid and senior levels, the research aims at investigating the potential of AI disrupting the navigation process of a public crisis while adhering to the challenges it proposes. The findings reveal a growing dependence on automation for efficiency and scale yet contesting the lack of empathy, cultural insensitivity, misinformation, and erosion of trust that automation brings into the picture. As crisis communication is evolving in this age of digitized communication, the future demands adaptive and critically aware professionals who can balance integrity with an AI enhanced media ecosystem.

Keywords: Artificial Intelligence · Public Relations · Journalism · Crisis Management

1 Introduction

An age marked by unprecedented global disruptions across industries, ranging from global pandemics to climate change disasters to unpredictable political unrest and armed conflicts, the need for effective crisis communication is more dire than ever. As companies and various cultural societies wrestle with increasingly complex tragedies, the role of Artificial Intelligence (AI) in crisis management is gaining momentum. With its multiple branches in predictive modelling, real-time reporting, and automated mass communication, AI is being integrated into all possible strategies across industries. From being able

A. Elbanna et al. (Eds.): TDIT 2025, IFIP AICT 778, pp. 103–121, 2026.
https://doi.org/10.1007/978-3-032-16775-0_7

to scan social media for early signs of a PR disaster to automated press releases addressing the ongoing advancements in the world, AI tools hold immense potential to disrupt and revolutionize how crises in any form can be managed, anticipated, and dealt with. This ground-breaking power still has not yet found a stable acceptance among the peers of PR professionals and journalists, the two frontliners in crisis communications. Previously, Management Information system (MIS) research has emphasized AI and machine learning aids with real-time monitoring and responding to critical outbreaks but notes that ethical implementation challenges remain unresolved (Hossain et al. 2025). Similarly, studies from public relations highlights the organizational vulnerabilities when AI misfires, demanding a strategic crisis responses altered by human interventions to mitigate AI accountability (Prahl et al. 2021). Crisis management is based exclusively on accuracy, trust, speed, and emotional intelligence. These qualities traditionally supported the PR and journalism industry and are responsible for navigating through complex social undercurrents, contextual cues, and emotional duress. Automation in crisis management has added a new dimension to this process. When used correctly, algorithms can process massive volumes of information, identify anomalies, and offer strategic insights when demanded. AI offers PR professionals significant leverage in crisis management with its mood-measuring analytics that guide them through stakeholder and public management for better perception. Similarly, with journalists, AI offers various tools that help track developments on a story in real-time while helping generate data-driven stories with accurate data points. However emerging scholarly research in journalism underscores the promise of culturally tailored, multilingual AI tools for public crisis communication—especially is disaster scenarios, but indicates limited insight on their adoption across the sector, lacking critical AI literacy (Hollanek et al. 2025). One of the primary concerns of automation without human intervention is the reliability of the result presented. The information that circulates during a crisis is generally fluid and emotionally charged. AI tools trained before their launch are often biased while crunching data, as not every tool is generative and can factually analyse the current data. Crucially, there's a lack of comparative research differentiating between public crisis communication (natural disasters, health emergencies) and organisational crisis communication (reputational scandals, operational failures, and how AI intervened crisis management in these scenarios varies across context. In the context of a PR professional, it might mean either simmering down the crisis or exacerbating the situation. Journalists unthinkingly relying on imperfect AI-generated content could compromise journalistic integrity in reporting and hamper the public trust. Additionally, AI lacks a cultural, emotional, and ethical stance in a either of the crisis. While it can recognize patterns and trends through data feeds, it still has not developed enough to comprehend the complex human emotions in a high-stakes situation. The evolving role of AI is also redesigning the professional characteristics of PR professionals and journalists. The PR industry is gradually expected to possess strong communication skills and hands-on skills in data analytics, machine learning, and digital ethics (Panda et al. 2019). On the other hand, journalists face the dual challenge of using AI as a tool for research and reporting while also being able to scrutinize AI-related expansions as part of their responsible and ethical reporting of news pieces. Addressing this gap, the study explores the multi-layered implications of automation in various sectors of crisis management with the changing dynamics of the PR industry and Journalism. It throws light on the technological opportunities and examines the trade-offs between AI's efficiency in identifying the category of issue and its potential for empathetic or culturally sensitive communication.

2 Literature Review

2.1 AI in PR (Monitoring, Automation and Predictive Tools)

With technology evolving at a rapid pace, much recent study shows a growing trend analysis in which it showcases the adoption of AI tools in the industry of PR for many mundane activities like real-time monitoring, stake holder analysis, chatbot deployment, message customization during events of crisis for better trackability (Marques and Batista 2022; Swiatek et al. 2014). Marques and Batista (2022) also detailed various uses of applications such as analysis of sentiment and automated content creation, while mentioning significant ethical implications involving transparency and bias. They also talk about AI-driven media monitoring platforms like Meltware and Cision that enable PR teams to detect misinformation online and start shaping communication strategies during emergencies like the colonial pipeline ransomware attack; where they filtered noise, ranked proper sources and tracked narrative trajectories (IABC 2025). Loof et al. (2023) examined the effects of crisis responses formulated through AI vis-à-vis those created by humans. Their study evaluated that while factual clarity in AI-generated responses created a sense of clarity, empathy, a key feature of effective crisis management, was significantly lacking. Similarly, Swiatek et al. (2023) also analysed the disruption caused by the humanoid robots trying to replace traditional PR practitioners in important events of press briefings, raising questions about ethical authenticity, professionalism, and media reception of the measure they suggested. Xiao and Yu (2025) further confirmed this relational gap by emphasizing that the involved stakeholders' fulfilment hinges on apparent and perceived accountability with emotional cognisance. In this area, automated responses struggle the most. Additional contributions included by Nurjanah et al. (2021), who discussed in a case study that the practice of AI during COVID-19 by the Indonesian public health sector strongly addressed the issues of localization, cultural sensitivity, and language alignment, which are critical requirements for the message to be accepted among the targeted audience. Lee et al. (2022) also proposed an ethical AI communication framework where inclusiveness and transparency are essential for risk management during PR disasters. From a broader academic perspective, all of the growth in the digital space leading up to the intervention of AI, falls under the umbrella of Information System (IS), which further in literature offers a responsible AI roadmap that emphasizes on fairness, explainability, privacy, equity and cross agency coordination for crisis resilience management (Lee et al. 2022).

2.2 AI in Journalism (Authorship, Bias, Ethical Oversight)

The second most crucial step for accepting information disseminated during a crisis is the journalistic assessment of PR content. Recently, journalists have constantly faced the pressure to verify and authenticate the data floating around digitally. Journalistic research emphasizes both opportunities and threats in AI-assisted reporting. Waddell (2018) studied the fact that AI-generated news content is usually considered technically sound, but it is still perceived as less credible than human-authored news. This finding is also credited by Huschens et al. (2023), where it is agreed upon that although the transcripts generated by ChatGPT are often considered clean and competent for use, they often fall short in the areas of reliability and emotional nuances expected in journalistic discourse. Automated news generation and fact-checking tools can augment new room efficiencies, but it also raises concerns around ethics, transparency and deskilling. Graefe et al. (2016) talk about the public acceptability of news that is generated algorithmically, determining that although automated factual reporting may be operative and time-saving, storytelling and crisis interpretation still require human intervention to be conceived effectively. Giraldi et al. (2025) also highlight the issue of trustworthiness in AI transparency, signifying that the target audience engagement constantly improves when AI authorship is disclosed. Goyanes et al. (2025) conducted a detailed systematic review of the literature to identify the credibility of automated detection tools and how AI helps combat and contribute to online misinformation, ultimately making the journalistic verification process overtly complicated. A growing discourse highlights the necessity for human-in the loop models, underscoring the importance of human oversight in AI outputs, especially for nuanced and emotionally stimulating content. Efforts to foster critical AI literacy among the industry of journalism will further help in integration of AI as part of creating socio-technical synergy among humans and automation; while easing out on the resistance on Techo-Solutionism and reinforce democratic accountability (Hollanek et al. 2025). Hua (2025) further expanded on the perception of human and AI-generated news content by theoretically comparing news authored by both sides by side, finding that algorithmic efficacy often leads to oversight in ethical distinction, specifically under the pressure of crisis. Carlson (2017) further provides a deep perspective into the qualitative aspect, probing how journalists perceive the ethical boundaries of AI integration in their workspace. His interviews highlight the looming unease amongst the journalists about the erosion of the core journalistic values that revolve around contextual understanding and source accountability.

2.3 Concerns Regarding Ethical and Social Biases

Across journalism and PR, ethical dilemmas have always dominated the scholarly debate. In PR, scholars have documented challenges like ethical authenticity, inclusion and transparency in AI-generated messaging during crisis. In crisis resilience management, stakeholders trust hinges on algorithmic fairness and transparency which is vital for efficiency in urgent emergency scenarios (Srinivasan 2023). Dwivedi et al. (2021) proposed a multidisciplinary analysis, arguing that the current AI tools, while offering sufficient effectiveness, are still prone to socio-economic disruptions, biases, and sensory denseness, such as the de-skilling of communication practitioners. Huang and Rust (2021) argue that the limitations of AI with context to emotional understanding of a situation in the service and communication sectors remain a hurdle that has not been crossed. The Columbian Journal Review (2024) and the Associated Press (2023) have proposed new room guidelines, publicly outlining the responsible use of AI and automation in content creation for gaining public trust through transparency. These guidelines include fully automated reporting on news related to a crisis while maintaining a dedicated team of human editorial oversight to preserve integrity and sensitivity in these delicate situations. In the public relations industry, Arendt et al. (2021) elucidate that many companies/agencies use their own AI systems while responding to the crisis. The study revealed a constant stiffness between deflecting blame and recognizing the errors by AI, with implications for public trust and corporate responsibility. Chesney and Citron (2019) explored the murkier side of automation by analysing deepfakes in crisis management, cautioning about their manipulative potential for controlling the public narrative, and urging proactive regulation. Lee et al. (2022) recommended various principles that revolve around auditability, inclusivity, and cultural contextualization to minimize AI damages during the delicate public crisis.

The literature review revealed a pattern of promises and perils that AI integrations offer during crisis communication. PR professionals generally leverage automation for real-time narrative control and promptly drive the crisis, but the apprehensions about empathy, credibility, and trust remain unanswered. Meanwhile, journalists are constantly challenged to verify and accredit the regular inflow of data and information, while reporting with sturdy editorial standards and reliability. Across both domains, transparency protocols and an ethical framework are deemed essential for preserving integrity. Therefore, the current study explores AI adoption's benefits, limitations, challenges, and applications in crisis management through journalism and PR.

The study aims to address the following research questions:

1. How are PR professionals integrating AI tools into crisis communication strategies?
2. How do journalists assess the authenticity and credibility of AI-generated or assisted PR content during a crisis?
3. What ethical or practical concerns do both groups raise regarding AI's role in shaping crisis narrative?

3 Materials and Methods

This exploratory study uses a qualitative research strategy. Qualitative interviews can be categorized into unstructured, semi-structured, and structured. This study uses semi-structured interviews to collect qualitative insights from experts and professionals working in the journalism industry, as it enables in-depth exploration of professional's nuanced perceptions of a digital disruption in the form of AI in crisis communication. This is method is valuable when aiming to explore and generate and understand the psychologically and sociologically rich, context-driven insights rather than test pre-determined hypothesis. The interviewer has asked several pre-set but open-ended questions (Given 2008). It also aligns with guidance from Creswell (1998), who recommends semi-structured designs for studies that balance structure with flexibility and potential. More so, this approach falls in line with the principles of grounded theory, as it allows themes to emerge inductively from interviews. In the interviewing method, predetermined questions were systematically asked to extract valuable insights about the pertinent issues that the interviewer is studying and exploring. A pilot study was conducted with 10 respondents to ensure the validity and propriety of questions. A discussion guide (Annexure I) with open-ended questions was framed and finalised based on the responses of the pilot study. The duration of the interview was about 25 min. The recording device captured the interviews with prior permission and proper annotations.

3.1 Participants

Journalists working in various media houses were recruited for the study using goa-directed and snowball sampling. Marshall et al. (2013) recommended that for in-depth qualitative research based on grounded theory, an average sample of 30 is sufficient. This suggestion was further recommended by Goulielmos (2004). The assumption of 30 samples is based on the theory of circularity. This theory suggests that while conducting in-depth interviews, after a specific count, repetition of responses starts to hinder the process, with no new insights being generated (Table 1).

Table 1. Participant characteristics

Level	Count	Education	Avg. experience
Entry-level	10	Primarily graduates	2.5 years
Mid-level	16	Mix of diploma certification & PG	5 years
Senior-level	4	Post graduates	10 years

In total, 30 journalists from entry level (10), mid-level (16), and senior level (4) were interviewed for this study based on purposive and snowball sampling. This group size was selected as these professionals are doing the ground-level work in journalism and are aware of the ongoing technological changes in their day-to-day work environment. Entry-level journalists were interviewed as young practitioners who often deal with menial tasks; hence, the young blood in journalism with well-adjusted technological skills will be able to offer more insights on adopting new changes. The education and experience profiling of the interviewees is further segregated based on the level of their acquired educational qualifications and years of experience. At the senior level, out of four participants, all have a postgraduate degree. The average experience of senior-level employees who were interviewed is 10 years. At mid-level, out of 16 participants, 8 are graduates, 5 have postgraduate diplomas, and 3 have postgraduate degrees. The average experience at mid-level is 5 years. The average experience is 2.5 years at the entry level, with mainly fresh graduates. This sample size further aligns with the qualitative benchmarks- as samples beyond 30 typically reach both data and theoretical saturation, especially when data quality is high and participants are relatively homogeneous (Wutich et al. 2024). For this study, we have defined the entry level as having less than three years of experience, the mid-levels having between three and six years, and the senior level having more than eight years of on-ground journalistic experience. The classification was done based on data collected during the pilot study. The study monitored theoretical saturation through analysis, the point where no new themes emerged – even though it is inherently context driven and contingent on researcher judgement (Bouncken et al. 2025).

3.2 Interview Questions

A questionnaire was used during the pilot study to analyse the suitability of participants required for the study. A total of 12 questions were used to secure and collate the responses, ranging from their understanding of technological shifts in terms of automation to the implications of technological shifts with AI impacting their jobs and peripheral work relations.

3.3 Procedure

The interviews were recorded with prior permission, transcribed verbatim, and then analysed. Based on Creswell's (1998) guidelines for coding of data, the collected answers were analysed into subsections and further coded to understand the identified patterns. The emerging categories and patterns were grouped to identify the co-existing themes using the inductive approach. Two coders were used to check the reliability of the created codes, categories, and themes. The study employed elements of thematic analysis, iteratively refining themes and using notes and peer debriefing to support reliability. To ensure transparency, both coders compared themes and resolved discrepancies collaboratively. The study's approach reflects best practice in quality rigor as programs like NVivo was used to provide more structure to coding and streamlining the transcripts (Table 2).

Table 2. Coding Framework and Identified Themes

Theme	Sub-theme	Code from quotes
Empathy versus automation	Tone and emotion	'tone-deaf', 'Insensitive messaging', 'blame shifting', 'inauthentic apology', 'lack of remorse', 'no empathy', 'mass ambiguity', 'overtly diplomatic'
Speed versus accuracy	Verification	'Automated but unchecked', 'repeating whatever is circulating online', 'no fact-checking', 'zero understanding of ground reality', 'unvetted statements'
Trust versus accountability	Disclosure and transparency	'Lack of acknowledgment', 'no prior disclosure of AI generated content', 'blatant addressing of events', 'not understanding the emotional damage', 'false narrative spread', 'linguistic bias

4 Analysis and Results

The following summary and analysis have been derived and presented from the coded, underlining the themes as follows:

RQ1: How are PR professionals integrating AI tools into crisis communication strategies?

4.1 Integration of AI Tools into Crisis Communication by PR Professionals

Theme: Routine Automation for Monitoring and Sentiment Analysis of Raw Data and Interpretation

Most journalists felt that while they deal with PR professionals almost daily, they understand the need and utility that AI offers for the PR industry. PR professionals are well acquainted with and exposed to the new digital shifts with AI happening across industries. From the data collected via interviews, PR professionals are slowly taking steps towards adopting automation in handling various sectors of the industry's reputation management functionality.

One senior-level journalist said, "Technology has inadvertently taken over almost every sector of our day-to-day life, and it is impossible not to take it into consideration when it comes to our work and how it may affect the people we are working with".

Another senior-level executive added, "Many media houses in the West have seamlessly adapted to automation. The Indian media houses must also understand and replicate the need for quick responsiveness and adapt to the offered solutions".

In totality, the interviewees agreed that the intervention of automation while dealing with a crisis scene has proven helpful. Automation positioned as an essential aid, especially for managing large scale data flows, suggesting a shift in PR strategy towards anticipatory and data informed practices more importantly during crisis.

One of the mid-level journalists agreed that, "the younger generation of journalists do understand that a full-blown automation in content creation won't be as effective and the ones that are human produced, but there are tasks and activities that AI can do and make the work less tiresome".

Another entry-level professional suggested that, "both the PR industry and the journalism industry are at the brink of another technological shift. Denying it will not do either party any good. However, what we can do, as two industries whose jobs are intertwined, is to understand and utilize it to our benefit and help make the transaction easier".

A senior-level journalist added, "Many of my friends are in the PR industry. The kind of influx of data that they have to deal with daily with multiple clients is insane. They have to have some level of automation integrated into their profiling because there is no way they can know what is happening where and with which client, especially on social media; and because of that by transitivity, we as journalists who are expected to report with honesty, also need some level of automation to help us give leverage in maintaining credibility of what we put out there. Multiple tools like Brandwatch and Talkwalker, I know of currently, can help further build this symbiotic work culture".

These insights are mediated through journalist's observations and experience from interacting with PR practitioners from various agencies and corporate communication sectors. Therefore, this study's interpretations of PR use remain indirect.

Monitoring, Early Detection, and Sentiment Analysis

Automation in the PR industry has a vast scope, making the mundane activities of PR professionals faster and quicker. AI tools can help PR teams proactively detect quick warning signs in scenes of reputational crisis. Many present tools like Meltwater, Talkwalker, and Brandwatch use natural language processing (NLP) and machine learning algorithms to track brand mentions, identify specific keywords, and report on public sentiment (with current upgrades) across social media, news articles, and mention in real time (Nkembuh 2024). These tools allow the teams to communicate and identify a possible crisis and avert it before it spirals into a full-blown crisis.

For instance, amidst the 2018 Facebook-Cambridge Analytica data breach, their PR teams heavily depended on various sentiment analysis tools, which helped them track constant narratives and the public's perceptions about the data breach. They witnessed significant spikes in keywords such as "privacy violation", "data misuse", and "Zuckerberg testimonials", which helped the communications team shape the narrative and helped Facebook respond proactively (Isaak and Hanna 2018).

Real-time tracking of data on social media platforms has helped PR professionals visualize how the conversations are shaping. This allows the teams to create and adapt to various communication strategies proactively.

AI-Powered Content Generation

Theme: AI in Content Crafting and Crisis Messaging

Today, we have multiple generative AI tools such as ChatGPT, Jasper, and Copy.ai, which constantly prompt emails, press releases, talking points, social media posts, etc. These tools help quickly create different kinds of messages, tailored for different audiences, improving response time by a significant margin (Marques and Batista 2022).

As we saw during the onset and peak of the COVID-19 pandemic, many brands that were essential and required to function, like the industry of aviation and healthcare, were using AI to automatically generate customer support messages regarding flight scheduling, cancellations, refunds, and multiple safety protocols. These messages were also constantly being updated with the changing government guidelines. Even though AI generated the messages, the final approval remained with human teams. (Dwivedi et al. 2021).

An entry-level journalist adds, "The main medium of communication changed. Everything happens on social media, and everyone is consuming everything on these platforms. It is physically impossible for a human to sit behind a screen and filter and respond to everything being put out every second. We need AI here. We need tools to help us navigate the mundane so humans can work on creative and important messaging".

A lot of tedious message circulation and creation is repetitively required to be put out on various platforms for mass consumption and prompt replies. While speed is a benefit, AI-generated content still requires human intervention to avoid tone deaf messaging.

Interpretation

From journalistic POV, PR professionals have started to indulge in use generative AI tools for crafting communications with the public yet human understanding especially in tone and sensitivity is deemed indispensable.

Predictive Modelling and Crisis Simulation

Many journalists working in media houses under the entertainment division suggested that PR teams also use AI for predictive modelling, i.e., anticipating the possible scenarios of various crisis strategies. AI systems like IBM Watson or Salesforce Einstein can simulate how the target audience might respond to the desired messaging or campaigns by exploring the large volumes of historical and current data on digital platforms.

A senior journalist added, "Recently, I travelled abroad and met a PR guy from an agency in the US. He told me how they dealt with a contamination issue with one of their clients in the food and beverage industry. They used the Salesforce prompt to simulate how stakeholders might respond to a public recall notice versus a low-profile fix. This is the kind of automation we are using right now. Moreover, how well it can help the agencies and the company is brilliant. While it eases the road for the PR people, we as journalists must also comprehend and use such tools to report the truth with integrity".

Interpretation

Predictive simulation tools are enhancing PR's strategic agility, further enabling proactive rather than reactive crisis response. While it adds on the dexterity in responsiveness during crisis; helping a better narrative setting but at the same time it also raises concerns of accountability and actually understanding the emotional tonality of the responses.

RQ2: How do journalists assess the authenticity and credibility of AI-generated or assisted PR content during a crisis?

4.2 Journalist's Assessment of AI-Generated/Assisted PR Content

Authenticity and Credibility Concerns

Theme: Authenticity and Emotional Profiling

From the data collected, it was evident that the new age journalists are increasingly aware that the press releases, quotes, comments, data points, and corporate statements they receive from various agencies and reputable brands may be generated or created with the help of AI. This raises important questions on the tonality, authenticity, and credibility of the news they will create and put out for consumption. Journalists assess these aspects using a combination of cross-referencing, professional intuitions, and in some cases, AI detection software tools.

A mid-level journalist commented, "I am mostly sure that almost 90% of the things I receive from brands and other sources have something to do with AI, until I have received the information from my reliable source. There was this one crisis that I had helped report on, a big pharmaceutical company had received a huge public backlash for increasing the price of the drug they were selling. The statement they put out that was sent to various media houses for circulation was heavily criticised by the journalists for being overtly diplomatic and lacking emotional sentiment. Upon further follow-ups, it was revealed that it was a draft not proofed by their team and was circulated as it was generated by whatever tool they were using for immediate relief. Human intervention means this, and emotional sincerity is important amid a public crisis. There is only so much machines can do."

Such events lead journalists to be more vigilant about detecting patterns of language, lack of emotional nuance, or generic paraphrasing by the AI-generated content and call out such actions to maintain a sense of sincerity and authenticity during a public backlash.

Source Attributions and Transparency

The sudden use of automated messaging, especially during a crisis, has shaken the foundation of journalistic sourcing. Journalists rely heavily on clear provenance and accountability in the field of reporting. However, with the constant deployment of AI-generated content, the lines between the author, accreditor, and automated device get blurred (Carlson 2020).

As the senior-level journalists addressed this issue, they asked some valid concerns, "If a statement or a press release contains automated messaging that sounds misleading or inaccurate, who is to be held accountable? The organizations? Their PR team? The tool that they used? The journalists who could not detect and trace back to the author? This is where ethical use of AI needs to intervene in our journalistic work. This is where we, as news reporters, can use automation to track back on the lies that sometimes industries spread during a crisis to avoid backlash. To maintain trust and avoid mass ambiguity, crisis reporting must be accurate and transparent."

To navigate this issue, some journalists slowly understand the need to integrate AI in their reporting and advocate for clearer disclosure practices where they want the organizations and the PR teams to disclose any use of AI in narrative control.

Framing and Bias Detection

Many existing AI tools have some embedded biases in their training dataset. This bias then affects the user's output, which means even the 'diplomatic' or 'neutral' analysis generated by the tool will have implicit and institutional biases (Marques and Batista 2022).

Journalists also threw light on these identified biases in their interviews. An entry-level journalist said, "Much generated content has a certain linguistic bias. Certain words like 'operational dispute' or 'temporary dissatisfaction in employees', etc., are some examples that immediately come to my mind. Using such diplomatic terms during a public meltdown ups the issue's magnitude, which tends to escalate the response from the messaging further. During a crisis, it is essential not to undermine the issue, be complacent about the faults, and understand where the issue stems from".

Interpretations

This unfolds a new layer of requirement for a detailed editorial scrutiny from the house of media before reporting. They must not only fact-check but also understand the rudimentary basis that may lead to escalation in a crisis. As AI generated content remains to be on a steady growth curve, it is very important to understand that transparency is something that is vital while dealing with a public crisis. Strictly fact checking and addressing the raised concerns may lead to a tone-deaf response leading to a louder outcry. Hence the requirement of putting out statements and narratives with empathy and a social understanding of the audience is vital.

RQ3: What ethical or practical concerns do both groups raise regarding AI's role in shaping crisis narrative?

4.3 Ethical Concerns for PR Professionals

Presence of Empathy and Contextual Awareness

Theme: Transparency, Trust and Accountability

Most journalists unanimously agreed that it is vital for PR professionals not to lose sight of empathy while handling a crisis. In today's time, when they are constantly under scrutiny of every user on social media platforms, journalists feel that PR teams forget they are dealing with real-life problems that involve real people's livelihoods at stake. They tend to focus on calming the chaos, forgetting that their statements and reasoning can make or distort the day-to-day lives of people involved in the crisis.

A mid-level journalist adds on," I remember a case which involved a fatal accident in the workplace. The company ended up putting out an auto generated message offering condolence. It was very heavily criticized for its tone-deafness in a harrowing situation like this. Although the entire message wad grammatically sound and passed all the hygienic requirements for a public statement, it somehow failed to express genuine regret and lacked authentic empathy which led to an intensified public outrage. They eventually had to ask the CEO to do a press conference and address the issue with more sincerity."

Even though AI helps with its promptness and clarity in various situations, PR professionals still need to intervene and comprehend a situation before putting out an AI-generated message without authentic checks.

Dilemma of Transparency and Situational Discourse

While journalists understand the need for AI usage in PR, they also want the teams to understand the need for journalists to disclose the extent of the usage of automation. Journalists talked about how some PR professionals they deal with regularly advocate for transparency around AI usage. However, some agencies are reluctant to disclose this information for fear of credibility loss and the replacement of jobs by AI.

The Public Relations Society of America (PRSA) found out in a survey that only 38% of PR practitioners were on board with disclosing AI contribution in press releases, citing a significant threat to their job and the authenticity of their work (PRSA 2022).

Adopting automation across various sectors has raised fears of job displacement, especially among entry-level PR professionals. Most junior-level PR professionals deal with content creation at a base level, dossier creation and analysis, tracking of clients and their branding online, and more menial job profiling, which the tools offered by AI are slowly taking over. While AI cannot replace strategic thinking roles, involving a creative spread of campaign planning, human interaction, communication building, reputation management, crisis building etc., it may replace routine content creation and menial tasks; reducing opportunities for new entrants to learn the field and create a foundation (Huang and Rust 2021).

An entry-level journalist said, “Regarding job anxiety around AI, it is a legit fear that PR professionals have and people across industries have. AI is slowly developing into powerful tools that can do most entry-level jobs in various job profiles, eradicating the need for freshers and helping the companies save on recruiting and training costs”.

Ethical Concerns from Journalists

Journalists are constantly fighting the war of fact-checking. If a journalist mistakenly reports on AI-generated PR information that has circulated online without knowing or disclosing it, they risk the entire media house’s reporting credibility. No matter how small the piece of information might be, if a media house reports it, it needs to be fact-checked and its source must be identified before publishing it. Transparency is a core principle of journalism that must be strictly followed in this age of automated content creation. Failing to do so can undermine the authenticity of reporting and media. (Diakopoulos 2019).

A senior-level journalist agreed on this and added, “I have noticed recently that this has become a trend in PR handling, especially during a crisis, that they mindlessly float anything on social media to attain the goal of popularity and keeping their client talked about. They make and float ridiculous reels and random information, which is pure speculation 90% of the time, to keep their client relevant in pop culture. As journalists who do serious reporting, it becomes imperative that we do not believe everything we read and see and immediately report it. We need to backtrack the source, confirm, cross-check it with various other resources and then report. Mindlessly jumping on the ‘speculation bandwagon’ will make us look silly and unserious”.

However, as AI content filters every platform, keeping track of everything being uploaded becomes increasingly tedious. Journalists must spend more time verifying and contextualising the material before reporting on it. This is also adding to their extensive workload, creating a practical impasse: the need for faster crisis coverage while maintaining the accuracy and integrity of the new piece that is being reported.

Speed Versus Accuracy

As AI has made it easier to create and circulate content effortlessly, the data overload in the form of disinformation and misinformation has also increased. Generative tools like ChatGPT can produce confidant yet incorrect accounts, a phenomenon known as “digital hallucinations” (OpenAI 2023). A delicate crisis can lead to significant public meltdowns and may induce an entirely different sentiment among the audience in their pursuit of information.

A mid-level journalist said, “I’ll take the example of case that happened before tools like ChatGPT existed. The Jhonny Depp vs Amber Heard case. It was such a sensitive issue involving two people caught in a toxic marriage of domestic violence, and did you follow what happened? Instead of understanding what happens behind the close doors with a DV victim, it was made into a spectacle. The only reason Depp won was because he won the public court of opinion through his extensive PR campaigns on social media. Even media houses failed to report authentically on facts and evidence presented, instead they also gave into the social media meme fest against Heard and completely downplayed something as serious as DV. These are the kinds of times we live in. We as journalists have to be very mindful of what we put out because we have the power to shift narratives".

Shedding light further on how legal systems lag in technological advancements, AI-generated spamming on the internet still goes uncontested.

An entry-level journalist asked, "If a defamatory statement is published and attributed to AI, who will take the accountability? The PR firm? The AI vendor or the company? These uncertainties play a very vital role in crisis management in today's times."

Interpretation

Journalists have often questioned who is responsible when AI generated statements misfire—PR firms, corporations, AI companies or the lack of governance around AI. This emphasizes a growing demand for transparency and trust markers such as AI disclosures on contents during crisis communication. Credibility hinges not just on message accuracy but also on clearly identifiable authorship and intent, demanding new norms around AI and automation.

5 Discussion

In conclusion, incorporating AI into crisis management offers a transformative shift that offers considerable leverage wrapped up in multifaceted challenges. Both journalists and PR professionals face multiple questions, such as whether the tool can report and interact with the target audiences better than humans during a crisis. Can a fully automated PR agency handle a full-blown crisis in today's market? How fast can a crisis be predicted and avoided? How accurate will the reporting of AI-assisted crises be? How can journalists maintain constant authenticity while reporting in an AI-assisted crisis without the help of AI?

From the exploratory research, it was evident that the journalists and the PR professionals are aware of and accepting of the powerful capabilities of AI. From real-time data processing for quicker response to predictive analytics for better handling of the crisis, these technologies can enhance decision-making by predicting an early onset of a crisis, monitoring the public narrative, and streamlining the communication strategies in the industry. For PR professionals, this means that they will gain an unprecedented momentum in detecting reputational risks and craft better campaigns with deployed targeted messaging. Journalists also benefit from the intervention. They use AI tools while navigating the overflow of data sets on social media platforms, which will help them draft better and more informed reports after considering everything available.

The slow integration of automation into crisis management in today's time fundamentally changes the PR landscape in dealing with its target audience. While AI has the potential tools to deal with and assist with real-time monitoring and sentiment analysis for better damage control, it also comes with a different set of challenges. It is difficult to find PR professionals with accurate programming and analytical skills to deal with the tools while navigating through a crisis in the public forum. However, the pressure to respond instantly while maintaining authenticity amongst the public requires a hybrid skillset of technological proficiency and human empathy. Another hindrance is the lack of accountability of the current AI systems and the inability to maintain synergy with automation usage and human compassion during a crisis. PR professionals are also struggling to advocate for AI's ethical use to maintain transparency in their campaigns. At the same time, some are more interested in using AI to their benefit without acknowledging the more substantial leverage in delicate situations.

For journalists, AI offers bright opportunities but with some underlying threats. While AI can help in mass data crunching on social media platforms for better and faster reporting, it also risks the authenticity of the news piece. Risk of misinformation, AI-based biases, and deepfakes complicates the verification process of the information. Journalists are standing at the brink of AI intervention in their industry, where they need to find a balance between using AI for quicker response time while not breaching the public's trust through their reporting. AI has the potential to revolutionize crisis management. However, it also hosts many challenges that require ethical manoeuvring from both the PR and journalism industries to handle the crisis accurately.

5.1 Ethical AI and Trust Framework

However, these advancements are accompanied by unavoidable hindrances. AI is still very dependent on what is being fed to the tool. The higher the quality, the more accurate the analysis will be. However, at the same time, social media constantly has an influx of data, which can be misinformation and false speculation, affecting the final crunching. The tool's lack of emotional and contextual understanding has often made the crisis worse in the public's eye. The algorithms' density raises concerns about spreading misinformation without proper verification. PR professionals have struggled with automated help and maintaining their sincerity. They are constantly under pressure to ensure timely action on a crisis while upholding the campaign's cultural sensitivity. Similarly, journalists are confronted with the burden of verifying the information they are being fed, like high-quality AI-generated material, while combating misinformation. The ethical consequences of surveillance, privacy breaches, and potential loss of trust in the public forum further complicate the use of AI in public crisis management. Moreover, both industries face a steep learning curve in acquiring the required skillset to deal with AI-powered job profiling and navigate the technological shifts that might affect jobs. Another challenge a mid-level journalist discusses is the over-reliance of humans on automation. There needs to be a symbiosis of human-created and AI-generated content in crisis to maintain the accuracy and hygiene check required for reporting and press releases, while still holding a sense of human judgment and empathy. This study confirms findings from AI ethics literature emphasizing the importance of trust, transparency and accountability in digital communication systems (Comes 2024).

5.2 Findings and Existing Theory

The results align with Situational Criss Communication Theory (SCCT), which advises tailoring responses based on reputational threat and crisis type. Yet, AI's automation could misalign credibility and empathy, especially when crisis attribution requires nuanced messaging (Coombs 2022). Similarly, the study also extends further on responsible AI roadmap for crisis resilience, highlighting key values like explainability and fairness; but the study underscores that in crisis additional principles such as solidarity and humanity must also be embedded in AI protocols (Comes 2024).

Thus, the future of crisis communication lies in a hybrid tactic that leverages AI's efficacy and data analysis and humans' matchless qualities of intuition, empathy, compassion, and narrative craft. Integrating AI into crisis management is not about replacing humans but supplementing them. Requiring professionals at all levels to adapt, upskill, and remain critical of the technology that they use. AI and automation serve as tools that improve, not compromise, the integrity and efficiency of crisis management in a progressively digital world.

5.3 Implications for Policy, Education and Practice

The findings also throw light on policy makers and how there is a dire need for an explicit set of AI guidelines emphasizing the ethical and emotional dimensions of automation. This approach will help in streamlining the constant and overuse of automation digitally and will help in setting a more standardised understanding of the use of AI. Journalistic and PR training programs must have advanced AI literacy skill enhancing rigour equipping professionals to critically assess AI tools much like recent educational frameworks proposed for some higher education degrees (Chan 2023). Upskilling initiatives like those by Indeed and Google, offer models for fostering broader AI fluency in the workforce (Reuters 2025).

6 Future Directions

As this study primarily focuses on journalist's understanding of AI while dealing with crisis communication and their relation with PR professionals, the needs remains a gap of PR professionals and their dependence on AI during crisis. There can also be a more detailed analyses on quantitative or experimental research could compare AI assisted versus human-driven crisis messaging to assess audience trust and emotional resonance. Additional qualitative work can be incorporated for better understanding of PR professionals' perspective to triangulate with this study's journalistic point of view. Future researchers might test frameworks like Universal Adaptive Crisis Communication (UACC), assessing how emotional intelligence and cultural sensitivity can be systematically embedded in AI tools.

Crisis demand not just speed, but authentically empathetic and value driven communication. The future rests on a hybrid model that harnesses AI's efficacy while honouring human judgement and sentiments. This balance ensures that any technological disruptions, irrespective of its scale, enhances and not erodes the integrity of crisis communication in our increasingly digital world.

Funding and Acknowledgements. The authors received no financial support for the research, authorship, and/or publication of this article.

Declaration of Interests The authors declared no potential conflicts of interest with respect to the research, authorship, and/or publication of this article.

References

Akeel, M.: Championing Responsible AI: A Global Commitment for the Communication Profession. https://www.iabc.com/catalyst/article/championing-responsible-ai-a-global-commitment-for-the-communication-profession. Last accessed 08 Aug 2025

Associated Press Newsroom: AP's Guidelines on AI in Journalism: Balancing Innovation with Integrity. https://apnews.com (2023)

Bouncken, R.B., et al.: Purposeful sampling and saturation in qualitative research methodologies: recommendations and review. Rev. Manag. Sci. 1–37 (2025). https://doi.org/10.1007/s11846-025-00881-2

Cai, K.: Google Pushes Global Agenda to Educate Workers, Lawmakers on AI. https://www.reuters.com/technology/artificial-intelligence/google-pushes-global-agenda-educate-workers-lawmakers-ai-2025-01-25/ (2025)

Carlson, M.: Automating judgment? Algorithmic judgment, news knowledge, and journalistic professionalism. New Media Soc. **20**(5), 1755–1772 (2017). https://doi.org/10.1177/1461444817706684

Cecilia, C.: A Comprehensive AI Policy Education Framework for University Teaching and Learning. https://arxiv.org/abs/2305.00280?utm_source

Chesney, R., Citron, D.K.: Deep fakes: a looming challenge for privacy, democracy, and national security. SSRN Electron. J. **107**, 1753 (2019). https://doi.org/10.2139/ssrn.3213954

Comes, T.: AI for crisis decisions. Ethics Inf. Technol. **26**, 1 (2024). https://doi.org/10.1007/s10676-024-09750-0

Coombs, W.T.: Situational crisis communication theory (SCCT). In: The Handbook of Crisis Communication, pp. 193–204 (2022). https://doi.org/10.1002/9781119678953.ch14

Creswell, J.W., Poth, C.N.: Qualitative Inquiry and Research Design: Choosing Among Five Approaches. Sage Publications, Los Angeles (2018)

Diakopoulos, N.: Automating the News: How Algorithms Are Rewriting the Media. Harvard University Press, Cambridge, Massachusetts (2019)

Dwivedi, Y.K., et al.: Artificial intelligence (AI): multidisciplinary perspectives on emerging challenges, opportunities, and agenda for research, practice and policy. Int. J. Inf. Manag. **57**, 101994 (2021). https://doi.org/10.1016/j.ijinfomgt.2019.08.002

Gilardi, F., et al.: Willingness to Read AI-Generated News Is Not Driven by Their Perceived Quality. https://arxiv.org/abs/2409.03500. Last accessed 05 May 2025

Given, L.: The SAGE Encyclopedia of Qualitative Research Methods, vol. 2, p. 1 (2008). https://doi.org/10.4135/9781412963909

Goulielmos, M.: Systems development approach: transcending methodology. Inf. Syst. J. **14**(4), 363–386 (2004). https://doi.org/10.1111/j.1365-2575.2004.00175.x

Goyanes, M., et al.: Artificial intelligence in journalism: a systematic literature review of global trends, regulatory challenges, and ethical concerns. Societo Commun. J. (2025). https://doi.org/10.31235/osf.io/6sa9e

Graefe, A., et al.: Readers' perception of computer-generated news: credibility, expertise, and readability. Journalism **19**(5), 595–610 (2016). https://doi.org/10.1177/1464884916641269

Hollanek, T., et al.: AI, journalism, and critical AI literacy: exploring journalists' perspectives on AI and responsible reporting. AI Soc. (2025). https://doi.org/10.1007/s00146-025-02407-6

Hossain, M.Z., et al.: Artificial intelligence and machine learning in crisis communication: a management information system perspective. Eur. J. Innov. Stud. Sustain. **1**(3), 149–163 (2025). https://doi.org/10.59324/ejiss.2025.1(3).12

Huang, M.-H., Rust, R.T.: A strategic framework for artificial intelligence in marketing. J. Acad. Mark. Sci. **49**(1), 30–50 (2021). https://doi.org/10.1007/s11747-020-00749-9

Huang, M.-H., Rust, R.T.: Engaged to a robot? The role of AI in service. J. Serv. Res. **24**(1), 109467052090226 (2021). https://doi.org/10.1177/1094670520902266

Huschens, M., et al.: Do You Trust ChatGPT?—Perceived Credibility of Human and AI-Generated Content. arXiv (Cornell University). https://doi.org/10.48550/arxiv.2309.02524 (2023)

Isaak, J., Hanna, M.J.: User data privacy: Facebook, Cambridge Analytica, and privacy protection. Computer **51**(8), 56–59 (2018)

Lee, C.-C., et al.: Roadmap Towards Responsible AI in Crisis Resilience Management. https://arxiv.org/abs/2207.09648?utm_source. Last accessed 08 Aug 2025

Lee, J., et al.: Building ethical AI communication frameworks for public risk management. Public Relat. Rev. **48**(3) (2021). https://doi.org/10.1016/j.pubrev.2022.102114

Li, S., et al.: Addressing consumer needs: effects of firms remediation strategies on satisfaction and brand usage intent in AI-powered voice assistant service failures. Int. J. Inf. Manage. **85**, 102951 (2025). https://doi.org/10.1016/j.ijinfomgt.2025.102951

Loof, T., et al.: The Use of Artificial Intelligence in Crisis Communication: A Study of Public Perceptions and Trust of AI. https://scholarworks.uni.edu/ijc/vol55/iss2/4. Last accessed 10 Jul 2025

Marques, R., Batista, F.: Artificial intelligence and public relations: a systematic review of tools, ethics, and applications. Public Relat. Inq. **12**(1), 56–78 (2022). https://doi.org/10.1177/2046147X23114941

Marshall, B., et al.: Does sample size matter in qualitative research? A review of qualitative interviews in is research. J. Comput. Inf. Syst. **54**(1), 11–22 (2013). https://doi.org/10.1080/08874417.2013.11645667

Nkembuh, N.: Leveraging predictive analytics for strategic corporate communications: enhancing stakeholder engagement and crisis management. J. Comput. Commun. **12**(10), 51–61 (2024). https://doi.org/10.4236/jcc.2024.1210005

Nurjanah, N.: Leveraging predictive analytics for strategic corporate communications: enhancing stakeholder engagement and crisis management. J. Asian Public Policy 51–61 (2024). https://doi.org/10.4236/jcc.2024.12100054

OpenAI: GPT-4 Technical Report. OpenAI (2023)

Panda, G., et al.: Artificial intelligence: a strategic disruption in public relations. J. Creat. Commun. **14**(3), 196–213 (2019). https://doi.org/10.1177/0973258619866585

Prahl, A., Goh, W.W.P.: "Rogue machines" and crisis communication: When AI fails, how do companies publicly respond? Public Relat. Rev. **47**(4), 102077 (2021). https://doi.org/10.1016/j.pubrev.2021.102077

PRSA: AI and PR: Survey on Disclosure and Ethical Concerns in Public Relations. Last accessed 2022

Scott, L.: How Local Reporters Manage the Dangers of Covering Extremism. https://www.cjr.org/analysis/local-reporters-dangers-covering-extremism.php. Last accessed 09 Jul 2025

Srinivasan, S.: View of Crisis Communication in the Age of Artificial Intelligence: Exploring the Ethical Implications of AI-driven Risk Management. https://jicrcr.com/index.php/jicrcr/article/view/3025/2609. Last accessed 08 Aug 2025

Swiatek, L., et al.: Robot press briefings and the future of media relations. Public Relat. Rev. **50**(1) (2023). https://doi.org/10.1016/j.pubrev.2023.1019608

Waddell, T.F.: A robot wrote this? Digit. Journal. **6**(2), 236–255 (2018). https://doi.org/10.1080/21670811.2017.1384319

Wutich, A., et al.: Sample sizes for 10 types of qualitative data analysis: an integrative review, empirical guidance, and next steps. Int J Qual Methods **23**, 1–14 (2024). https://doi.org/10.1177/16094069241296206

Xiao, Y., Yu, S.: Can ChatGPT replace humans in crisis communication? The effects of AI-mediated crisis communication on stakeholder satisfaction and responsibility attribution. Int. J. Inf. Manage. **80**, 102835 (2025). https://doi.org/10.1016/j.ijinfomgt.2024.102835

Digital Entrepreneurship and Innovation

Distorted Diffusion: Revisiting Rogers's Diffusion of Innovation Theory in the Age of Mis/Disinformation and AI-Amplified Media

Lucy Griffiths(✉) and Elvira Ismagilova

School of Management, Swansea University, Bay Campus, Swansea, UK
{2275533,elvira.ismagilova}@swansea.ac.uk

Abstract. Grounded in Diffusion of Innovation (DOI) theory, this paper critically reassesses its assumptions within contemporary environments characterised by mis/disinformation and AI-amplified media. Using a conceptual synthesis supported by illustrative case studies on generative AI and 5G technologies, we demonstrate how misleading narratives distort perceptions of innovations, leading to delayed, distorted, or derailed adoption. The paper concludes with theoretical implications highlighting specific DOI assumptions challenged by misinformation and practical recommendations for managing digital technology diffusion in an era of pervasive 'post-truth' information disorder.

Keywords: Diffusion of innovation · Misinformation · Disinformation · Artificial intelligence · Social media · Networked publics · Digital adoption · Epistemic trust · Generative AI · Recommender systems

1 Introduction

Innovations in digital technology promise substantial economic and societal benefits (Atkinson and Castro 2008), but their successful diffusion may be impacted by changes in the information environment (McHale 2019). In recent years, misinformation and disinformation have proliferated on social media (Aimeur et al. 2023; Lim et al. 2024), often accelerated by AI-driven platforms (Bontridder and Poullet 2021; Jaidka et al. 2024; Monteith et al. 2023), contributing to confusion about new technologies. The World Economic Forum warned in early 2024 that "misinformation and disinformation is the most severe short-term risk the world faces" and that "AI is amplifying manipulated and distorted information that could destabilize societies" (Torkington 2024). Platform-based algorithmic curation of information, optimized for engagement rather than accuracy, has introduced new distortions in how innovations are communicated. Traditional diffusion models did not account for these dynamics. Recent studies show that algorithm-driven social media can amplify sensational false content over factual updates (Corsi 2024), underscoring the need to update diffusion theory for the platform economy era. This combination of potentially false information and AI amplification creates a new set

Published by Springer Nature Switzerland AG 2026
A. Elbanna et al. (Eds.): TDIT 2025, IFIP AICT 778, pp. 125–143, 2026.
https://doi.org/10.1007/978-3-032-16775-0_8

of challenges for innovations as they enter the public sphere. In response this paper asks: How might we need to adapt classical innovation diffusion theories in response to 'post-truth' information disorder (Foroughi et al. 2019; Monsees 2021)? In what ways do AI technologies amplify the spread of misleading information about innovative technologies (including AI itself), and with what impact on public understanding and adoption of them?

As a conceptual essay, we address these questions by integrating classical DOI theory with insights on misinformation, social networks, and algorithmic media. This paper offers several contributions:

- Extending Diffusion Theory: We augment Rogers's DOI framework by identifying how mis/disinformation and AI-driven curation distort each stage of the innovation adoption process, anchoring our work in recent theoretical extensions that consider platform-mediated diffusion.
- Illustrative Cases: We present two contrasting case studies—generative AI (deepfakes) and 5G wireless—selected for their salience and contrast.
- Practical Strategies: We provide actionable recommendations for stakeholders.
- Research Agenda: We outline a future research agenda with testable propositions derived from our framework.

2 Theoretical Foundations

2.1 Diffusion of Innovation Theory Overview

Diffusion of Innovation (DOI) theory explains how new ideas and technologies spread through social systems over time. Diffusion refers to "the process by which an innovation is communicated through certain channels over time among members of a social system" (Rogers 2003, p. 5). An innovation's adoption typically follows an S-curve: a small group of early adopters is followed by wider uptake as the innovation gains visibility and credibility, eventually reaching saturation. Rogers identified five adopter categories: innovators, early adopters, early majority, late majority, and laggards, each with characteristic attitudes and risk tolerances (Kaminski 2011). Diffusion involves five stages in the individual adoption decision process (García-Avilés 2020):

- Knowledge—the individual is exposed to the innovation and gains some understanding of "what it is" and "how it works."
- Persuasion—the individual forms an attitude (positive or negative) toward the innovation, weighing information and opinions.
- Decision—the individual decides whether to adopt or reject the innovation (this may include trying it on a limited basis).
- Implementation—the innovation is actually used. The individual (or organization) puts the innovation into practice.
- Confirmation—the individual seeks reinforcement for the adoption decision and continues (or discontinues) use of the innovation

Underpinning successful diffusion are several assumptions about a healthy information environment. Rogers highlighted that potential adopters evaluate innovations based on perceived attributes such as relative advantage, compatibility, complexity, trialability, and observability (Kaminski 2011). If an innovation is perceived as having high relative advantage (better than what came before), compatible with users' values/needs, not overly complex, trialable, and with observable benefits, it is more likely to be adopted. Importantly, these are perceptions—subjective judgments formed by individuals based on the information available to them. DOI theory assumes that through communication channels (mass media and interpersonal networks), accurate knowledge about the innovation's benefits and risks will spread to the social system, allowing individuals to form reasonably correct perceptions and make rational adoption decisions. Furthermore, opinion leaders and change agents play a role in influencing others; in classical diffusion, these tend to be respected figures who advocate the innovation based on credible information and their own positive experiences (Kaminski 2011).

2.2 Evolution of Diffusion Theory: From Mass Media to Algorithmic Media

Rogers's original DOI framework was rooted in a mass-media-dominated era of communication. Early diffusion studies assumed a top-down flow of information (e.g. via print, radio, television) and the presence of human gatekeepers or change agents ensuring message quality. Over time, diffusion theory expanded to incorporate interpersonal networks and two-step flows, acknowledging that peers and social contacts play crucial roles alongside mass media (Valente 1996). The advent of the Internet and Web 2.0 marked a dramatic shift: information dissemination became many-to-many, user-generated content and online social networks enabled innovations (and rumors about them) to spread virally with less oversight. Researchers began to observe diffusion dynamics such as viral growth, network cascades, and echo chambers that were not accounted for in Rogers's initial framing. Next concepts like the "infodemic" (an epidemic of information, often false) emerged, especially during events like the COVID-19 crisis (Cinelli et al. 2020), highlighting how information overload and misinformation can accompany the rapid diffusion of ideas online.

In the current AI-driven, algorithmic media context, diffusion processes are further altered. Digital platforms act as curators of information: their recommendation algorithms (e.g. social media news feeds, search rankings) selectively amplify certain messages and innovations. These algorithms often prioritize engagement, which can inadvertently favor controversial or misleading content (Corsi 2024). The diffusion of innovations today occurs in an environment of platform gatekeeping and algorithmic biases unlike the relatively linear, broadcast environment of Rogers's time. Figure 1 provides a summary of this evolution, contrasting the classical diffusion context with the Web 2.0 social media era and the current AI-algorithmic era.

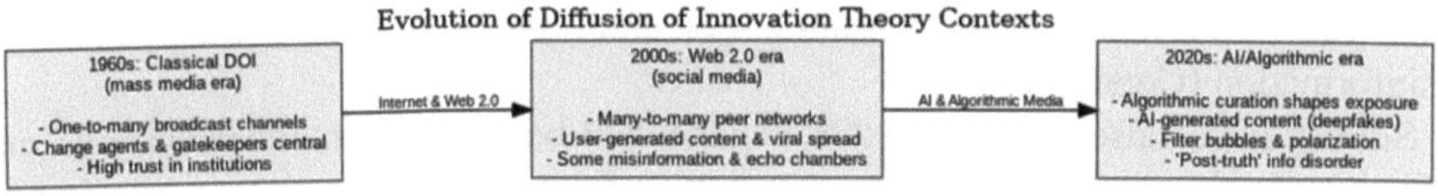

Fig. 1. Evolution of diffusion of innovation theory contexts.

2.3 Misinformation and Disinformation in the Information Ecosystem

The contemporary reality of "post-truth" information disorder challenges Rogers's assumptions of a well-functioning communication environment. It is crucial to distinguish misinformation from disinformation (Wardle and Derakhshan 2017). Misinformation refers to false or misleading information shared unintentionally (Ebrahimi 2022). For instance, an ordinary user unknowingly sharing a false rumour. In contrast, disinformation is false information intentionally created or spread to mislead people (Ebrahimi 2022; Karlova and Fisher 2013). Misinformation and disinformation contribute to an overall environment of information disorder (Wardle and Derakhshan 2017).

In the context of innovation diffusion, the primary concerns are mis- and disinformation that distort public understanding of new technologies. These can take many forms—rumours, conspiracy theories, fabricated content, doctored images or deepfake videos to name a few. Notably, much "fake news" is not entirely fabricated; a kernel of truth may be warped into misleading content, making it more believable. This complicates the task of individuals at the knowledge and persuasion stages of adoption: separating fact from fiction becomes difficult when some falsehoods are packaged as news or expert opinion (Wardle and Derakhshan 2017).

Research shows that misinformation spreads easily through social media and can have significant real-world consequences (Firdaus et al. 2024; Johnson et al. 2022; Muhammed and Mathew 2022). During the COVID-19 pandemic, for instance, health misinformation led people to decline vaccines, reject public health measures, and even embrace unproven treatments, worsening the crisis (Office of the Surgeon General 2025; Skafle et al. 2022). In the context of technological innovations, this means a novel technology might be accompanied by a flood of user-generated content, some of it false or misleading, which shapes public perceptions from the outset. Rogers' model did emphasize communication channels and peer networks, but it assumed that factual information would be transmitted (via mass media or change agents) to raise awareness. Today, however, those channels can just as readily transmit false or fear-based narratives, which may impact diffusion.

2.4 AI's Role: Recommender Systems and Generative AI

Compounding the misinformation challenge is the mediating role of artificial intelligence in today's information ecosystem. AI technologies influence both what information people see and what information exists about innovations. Modern social media platforms rely heavily on AI-driven recommender systems, algorithms that curate news feeds, search results, and content recommendations based on engagement metrics and user profiles. These algorithms are optimized for engagement (capturing user attention), which can inadvertently favor sensational or emotionally charged content, including misinformation (Corsi 2024).

Studies have raised concerns that engagement-based recommender systems may create filter bubbles or echo chambers that amplify false or extreme content while limiting exposure to corrective information (Anandhan et al. 2018; Corsi 2024; Islam et al. 2019; Chen et al. 2023). A study conducted by Corsi (2024) observed that on Twitter (now X), tweets linking to low-credibility domains tended to receive higher algorithmic amplification (impressions) than those linking to high-credibility sources, especially when promoted by influential accounts. In other words, the platform's AI-driven ranking system "facilitated the diffusion of false content by amplifying the visibility of low-credibility content" (Corsi 2024, p. 1). The very architecture of social media can thus bias the diffusion process in favour of misinformation, unless countermeasures are in place.

AI is now also a producer of information (and disinformation) via generative AI. Powerful generative models can create realistic text, images, audio, and video—from chatbots that generate authoritative-sounding answers (which may include falsehoods) to "deepfake" video tools that swap faces or clone voices (Farid 2022; Jadhav et al. 2024). This raises concerns that misinformation could be "supercharged" by AI due to increases in the quantity, quality, and personalization of false content (Simon et al. 2023). While some scholars argue that fears of an AI-driven misinformation apocalypse are overblown (pointing out that distribution of content remains a bottleneck, and that human factors like confirmation bias are still pivotal) (Kapoor and Narayanan 2024), the potential for AI to erode trust is undeniable. A particularly pernicious outcome is the "liar's dividend," whereby the mere knowledge that convincing deepfakes exist allows bad actors to dismiss authentic evidence as fake (Williamson 2022). In summary, AI is a double-edged sword: recommender algorithms can preferentially spread misinformation, and generative models can create ever-more-plausible falsehoods, undermining the information quality that diffusion theory takes for granted.

2.5 Networked Publics and Epistemic Trust

In a networked public sphere, individuals are not passive recipients of information but active participants in creating and sharing it. This networked dynamic means that misinformation can spread virally through peer-to-peer exchanges, often within homophilous communities. Homophily in social networks, a tendency to connect with similar others, can lead to echo chambers where people primarily receive information that reinforces their existing beliefs (Cinelli et al. 2021; Cota et al. 2019). Echo chambers have been shown to facilitate the spread of misinformation and contribute to polarization (Cota et al. 2019). In tightly knit online communities (for example, a forum of anti-vaccine activists or a partisan Facebook group), false claims may circulate widely and face little internal challenge, while corrective information from outside sources is dismissed or not encountered at all (Ecker et al. 2022; Pennycook and Rand 2021). Such closed information loops make certain subgroups impermeable to corrections, a reality that complicates the diffusion of innovations that require broad societal uptake. If a critical mass within a community rejects an innovation due to misinformation, network effects can prevent even willing individuals from benefitting (e.g., a digital payment system is less useful if many in your network refuse to adopt it due to conspiratorial fears) (Steinmetz et al. 2021).

Closely tied to this is the issue of epistemic trust—the trust that people have in sources of information and in institutions of knowledge (science, journalism, government). The epistemic fragility of networked publics refers to how easily trust can be undermined in a fragmented media landscape (Scheufele and Krause 2019). Repeated scandals of data misuse, partisan propaganda, and algorithmic echo chambers have eroded trust in traditional authorities and expertise (Tambini 2021; Allington et al. 2021). In the context of diffusion, this means the source of communications about the innovation matters greatly. If official sources (scientists, government agencies, companies) are not trusted, and if informal sources (friends, influencers) are propagating misinformation, then potential adopters face an epistemic dilemma. Whom do they believe? Trust becomes a deciding factor in whether accurate information or misleading claims will guide one's attitude (van Prooijen et al. 2022; Eysenbach 2020). Misinformation often exploits emotional appeals and confirmation bias—people tend to accept information that aligns with their prior beliefs, further entrenching false narratives (Carrasco-Farré 2022; Zhou and Shen 2022). The result can be polarized interpretations of the innovation's value across different segments of the public (e.g., one subpopulation believes a new technology is a dangerous hoax, while another hails it as game-changing, and each dismisses the other's evidence). This polarization undermines the inclusive, collective advancement that diffusion of beneficial innovations is supposed to achieve.

In sum, the diffusion of innovations today occurs in an information environment fundamentally more chaotic and adversarial than in Rogers's time. False information can outpace truth, AI-driven systems can amplify noise over signal, and social networks can divide audiences into information silos. These factors motivate a reassessment of diffusion theory's stages and mechanisms, which will be discussed next.

3 Revisiting Diffusion of Innovation Theory in the Mis/Disinformation and AI Age

In this section, we interrogate each stage of Rogers's Innovation-Decision Process (Rogers 1995; p. 163) through the lens of pervasive misinformation accelerated by developments in AI technologies. We identify how each phase: knowledge, persuasion, decision, implementation, and confirmation can be disrupted, causing a state in which the normal progression of innovation adoption is confounded by misleading information, resulting in delayed, distorted, or derailed diffusion. For each stage, we contrast Rogers's assumptions with today's realities and ask: What does DOI theory assume, and how does misinformation challenge that assumption?

3.1 Knowledge Stage: False or Conflicting Awareness

In Rogers's model, the diffusion process begins with the Knowledge stage, when individuals are first exposed to the innovation and gain some understanding of "what it is" and "how it works" (Rogers 1995). Traditionally, mass media and change agents play major roles at this stage by spreading accurate awareness and factual information about the new technology (Metzger et al. 2003). The implicit assumption is that early knowledge of the innovation will at least be broadly correct (even if not complete), providing a baseline for potential adopters to form opinions.

In today's environment, the source of initial information or awareness knowledge (Rogers 1995, p. 165) may be affected by issues of misinformation. Misinformation can fill the knowledge gap before credible information reaches the audience, for example, in the absence of factual information online commentators may begin speculating about the efficacy or perceived negative impacts of an innovation before it is formally launched. Thus, for many people, their first encounter with an innovation might be via social media chatter that includes rumours or conspiracy theories, rather than through official channels or educational content. From a diffusion standpoint, the knowledge stage under misinformation stress is characterised by information asymmetry and false knowledge. Rather than a population developing a homogeneously accurate awareness of the innovation's existence and function, we see a bifurcation: some people receive accurate information early, while others may receive myth-laden or fear-laden misinformation. Rogers assumed that greater exposure leads to greater awareness; now, greater exposure could simply mean greater exposure to misinformation. We must account for what we might call false knowledge, belief in false facts about the innovation. This is not just lack of knowledge, but the presence of confidently held wrong beliefs.

In classical DOI terms, an innovation's perceived attributes drive adoption decisions; but if those perceived attributes are falsely negative, then adoption will be hindered even if the objective attributes are positive. Rogers did not explicitly consider a scenario where the perceived relative advantage of an innovation could be deliberately inverted by falsehoods. The knowledge stage, therefore, can be augmented with the concept of misinformation-based knowledge gaps—disparities in what different groups know (or think they know) about the innovation.

3.2 Persuasion Stage: Attitude Formation Under Uncertainty

After becoming aware of an innovation, individuals move into the Persuasion stage in Rogers's model, where they form an attitude (favourable, neutral, or unfavourable) toward the innovation (Rogers 1995; pp. 167–171). In a healthy information context, persuasion is based on a reasoned weighing of evidence, trial experiences, and interpersonal discussions. People observe peers, consult experts, and gauge credibility of sources to decide if the innovation seems useful and low risk. Rogers noted that interpersonal networks and subjective evaluations from peers often play a crucial role in shaping attitudes at this stage.

Misinformation may inject noise and bias into this evaluative process. Instead of a clear signal about the innovation's pros and cons, individuals may encounter contradictory claims. Trust in institutions is crucial; yet trust in many institutions (government, science, mainstream media) has eroded in segments of the population as a result of deliberate disinformation campaigns. Consequently, people may lean more on community influencers or partisan media, which can lead them further into echo chambers of belief. Misinformation can thus distort attitude formation in the persuasion stage so that what might have been a favourable impression (if based on facts) turns into suspicion or aversion.

Another mechanism at play is emotional amplification. Outlandish or frightening false claims may trigger strong emotions (Hosseini and Staab 2023), and research in psychology suggests that emotions can cement attitudes as powerfully than neutral facts (Dennis et al. 2023; Ryffel et al. 2014). These emotions may result in an anti-innovation attitude in the persuasion stage, not through any rational cost–benefit analysis (as DOI would predict) but through the activation of emotional response mechanisms. The classical model's emphasis on interpersonal networks still applies, but now those networks might be channels for spreading doubt rather than enthusiasm. In Rogers's time, an opinion leader was often someone spreading awareness of the innovation's advantages; today, an opinion leader could be a YouTuber or partisan pundit spreading disinformation to millions of followers, exerting a malign influence on attitudes. Rogers's concept of opinion leadership could thus be expanded to account for negative opinion leaders, influential figures who rally resistance to innovations via false claims. Taken together, the erosion of institutional trust, the affective intensification produced by emotionally charged misinformation, and the self-reinforcing dynamics of confirmation bias may redirect evaluative processes in the persuasion stage from evidence-based appraisal toward durable, systematically misinformed resistance.

3.3 Decision and Implementation Stages: Biased Adoption Dynamics

In Rogers's framework, after persuasion comes the Decision stage (the choice to adopt or reject the innovation), followed by Implementation (using the innovation, possibly on a trial basis at first). Under ideal circumstances, individuals make the adoption decision based on a reasoned evaluation of the innovation's merits. They then implement it and integrate it into their routines if it meets expectations. Rogers also notes that decisions can be reversed (discontinuance) if the implementation experience is unsatisfactory.

Misinformation can skew both the decision and implementation phases in multiple ways. First, consider the Decision to adopt or reject. Disinformation can cause unwarranted rejection of beneficial innovations, decision paralysis, or, conversely, unwarranted adoption of dubious innovations. While our focus is on barriers to legitimate innovation, it's important to note this alternative: misinformation can distort decision quality in both directions—discouraging good innovations and encouraging bad ones. For diffusion theory, this means that adoption is not always a marker of success; high adoption of something might indicate successful diffusion of false knowledge (in the case of a harmful innovation that spreads because of misinformation).

The decision stage in a misinformation-rich environment thus sees distorted risk–benefit perceptions driving choices. People might reject a technology due to exaggerated fears, or embrace a risky practice due to overhyped benefits. Decision paralysis is another outcome—overwhelmed by conflicting information, some may defer or avoid making any decision, slowing diffusion.

During the Implementation stage, misinformation can continue to play a disruptive role. Even after deciding to adopt, users might implement the innovation in a half-hearted or incorrect way if they harbour doubts or have been misled on usage. In diffusion terms, misinformation can contribute to discontinuance (abandoning an innovation after adoption, by undermining users' confidence or actual experience). Additionally, at a collective level, if an innovation requires networked uptake (many people using it to realize its full value), misinformation that keeps a chunk of the population from adopting can prevent the innovation from reaching critical mass. This yields a collective action failure: even willing adopters lose utility because too many others abstained. Rogers discussed critical mass and network effects, but here we see how disinformation-induced hesitancy by some can hurt all, fragmenting the diffusion curve and potentially causing the innovation to stall before full deployment.

We propose that the decision and implementation stages under misinformation are marked by distorted adoption outcomes. Good innovations may see slower, lower, or geographically uneven adoption (clustering in communities with higher trust and not diffusing in others), while harmful or useless innovations might gain traction in misinformed segments. The straightforward progression from interest to trial to adoption can break down into more erratic patterns. Innovations might require longer to prove themselves as repeated waves of misinformation cause back-and-forth shifts (adopt, drop, re-adopt later). For researchers and practitioners, this suggests that measuring innovation adoption without accounting for information quality factors might be misleading. The presence of strong anti-adoption narratives in media should be treated as a significant independent variable affecting diffusion rates.

3.4 Confirmation Stage: Reinforcement or Backlash

Finally, Rogers describes a Confirmation stage where those who have adopted the innovation seek reinforcement for their decision and integrate the innovation into their ongoing practices. Typically, if the innovation performs well, adopters become more committed and may champion it to others; if problems arise, they might discontinue. Also, late adopters look to the experiences of earlier adopters for validation.

In an era of persistent misinformation, even after widespread adoption, an innovation may not experience ongoing acceptance. Instead of a stable confirmation of the innovation's value, we might see ongoing controversy and backlash fuelled by misinformation. Adopters might encounter disinformation claiming they made a mistake or were duped, leading some to regret or publicly criticize the innovation post-adoption. Non-adopters, conversely, might feel vindicated by misinformation attacking the innovation. This dynamic can create social division between adopters and resistors; each armed with their own set of 'facts' to justify their stance. Rather than positive reinforcement and normalization of the innovation, society experiences conflict about it.

For diffusion theory, the implication is that the process may not neatly end with saturation and equilibrium. There may be cycles of adoption and backlash, new entrants and dropouts, as misinformation continues to circulate. The confirmation stage traditionally was when an innovation either firmly takes root or fades out; now we might see an innovation that has taken root still face attempts at uprooting via disinformation-driven outrage. This underscores that diffusion in the misinformation age is not only about initial uptake but also about long-term resilience of an innovation against false narratives.

In Table 1 we set out key considerations which may impact Rogers's Innovation-Decision Process based on our analysis.

Table 1. Rogers's stages in the innovation-decision process with considerations in the mis/dis information and AI age

Stage	Traditional rogers model	Considerations in the mis/disinformation and AI age
Knowledge	Individual becomes aware of the innovation and gains understanding of what it is and how it works. Mass media and change agents are assumed to deliver mostly accurate information	**False or conflicting awareness:** First exposure may include rumours or conspiracies spread via social media before credible information arrives **False knowledge:** Confidently held false beliefs **Information asymmetry:** Different groups receive divergent narratives
Persuasion	Individual forms a favourable or unfavourable attitude by weighing evidence, observing peers, and consulting credible sources	**Trust dilemmas:** Confusion over whom to believe as trusted figures (influencers) may spread misinformation **Emotional amplification:** Fear and outrage drive attitudes more powerfully than evidence **Confirmation bias:** People accept claims aligning with prior beliefs, polarising opinion
Decision	Individual decides to adopt or reject the innovation, sometimes after trial	**Biased adoption dynamics:** Disinformation can cause unwarranted rejection (e.g., vaccine refusal) or unwarranted adoption of harmful products (e.g., scam gadgets). Distorted perceptions of risk and benefit drive poor-quality decisions **Decision-Paralysis:** Information overload and conflict may cause inertia and delay or prevent decision-making
Implementation	Innovation is put into use. Individual assesses performance and integrates it into daily practices	**Misinformed usage:** Incorrect configuration or half-hearted use due to lingering doubts. **Network failure:** If many reject adoption, the innovation loses value for everyone (failure to reach critical mass)

(*continued*)

Table 1. *(continued)*

Stage	Traditional rogers model	Considerations in the mis/disinformation and AI age
Confirmation	Individual seeks reinforcement of the decision; may continue or discontinue based on experience	**Persistent backlash:** Continuous waves of misinformation undermine sustained use (e.g., claims EVs are worse for the environment) **"Liar's dividend"** (Williamson 2022)**:** Even true evidence can be dismissed as fake **Division entrenchment:** Post-adoption regret or polarization entrenches divisions instead of achieving consensus

4 Key Mechanisms Affecting the Innovation Adoption Decision Process

Across all these stages, several recurring mechanisms allow misinformation and disinformation to confound innovation diffusion:

- **Information asymmetry and fragmentation:** Different subgroups in society accumulate divergent "knowledge" about the innovation, preventing a unified diffusion curve.
- **Trust erosion:** Diminished trust in authorities and experts means official assurances about an innovation can be easily undermined by counter-messaging from less credible but more trusted sources (in certain circles). People may default to distrust, slowing adoption.
- **Emotional and identity appeals:** Mis/disinformation acceptance may be facilitated by individuals' emotions and identities (e.g., political or cultural identity), leading people to form strong negative attitudes that are resistant to change, regardless of factual counter evidence.
- **Social network contagion:** Through the power of social media and messaging, misleading narratives can spread virally, outpacing corrective information. Network effects can amplify either truth or lies, but falsehoods have well-documented advantages in online spread (novelty, outrage). When mis- or dis-information is accepted more rapidly, diffusion may be derailed.

5 Illustrative Examples

To illustrate, we briefly examine two domains where misinformation and innovation diffusion have notably intersected: (1) Generative AI and deepfakes, where the innovation (AI itself) is entangled in information disorder both as subject and source; and (2) 5G wireless technology, where conspiracy theories significantly impacted the public adoption climate. These cases were selected for their salience and contrast—one involving a novel digital innovation that can itself generate misinformation (misinformation source) and one involving a physical infrastructure technology undermined by externally produced misinformation (misinformation subject).

5.1 Case 1: Generative AI and Deepfakes

Context: Generative AI is a breakthrough digital innovation being rapidly diffused across sectors. At the same time, it is a vector for producing misinformation. This dual role – innovation diffusing through markets as well while simultaneously acting as a creator of content (both reliable and unreliable) makes this an important case to consider.

Misinformation narrative: Generative AI is entangled with misinformation in two ways: misinformation about AI and misinformation generated by AI. On one hand, hype and fear have led to misconceptions about AI's capabilities. On the other hand, generative AI itself has been used to produce deepfakes and synthetic content, contributing to the broader misinformation ecosystem. Thus, generative AI's diffusion is accompanied by a paradox: the innovation both suffers from misinformation and contributes to misinformation.

DOI stage impacts: At the Knowledge Stage, many people's first awareness of AI or deepfakes might come from sensational news or viral videos (some of which may be deepfakes themselves). This means initial knowledge may contain misinformation—either overestimating AI or falsely maligning it. At the Persuasion Stage, attitudes toward AI are being shaped by dramatic anecdotes and personal beliefs. At the Decision/Implementation Stage, we see what we might call mis-calibration of adoption. Some actors may over-adopt or adopt too quickly—deploying generative AI in high-stakes contexts where it isn't yet reliable. Other actors may under-adopt or reject AI that could benefit them. Such hesitancy can slow the diffusion of genuinely useful AI innovations. These patterns indicate an erratic diffusion: instead of a smooth S-curve of adoption, we may see pockets of premature adoption and pockets of resistance as found by McElheran et al. (2024) whose study on AI adoption in the US indicated significant variances in adoption based on industry, level of education, and geography.

Outcomes: The result is fragmented adoption and contentious debate rather than a uniform diffusion trajectory. Notably, because generative AI can generate convincing misinformation, its proliferation fuels a feedback loop: increased prevalence of AI tools means more AI-generated content (some of it misleading), which could further erode trust in online information generally—potentially affecting adoption of other innovations as well (a meta-effect on the information environment). In summary, this case shows how an innovation's diffusion can be distorted by both hype and fear, requiring us to update diffusion theory with concepts like misinformed attitudes, over-adoption, and ongoing trust management.

5.2 Case 2: 5G Wireless and Conspiracy Theories

Context: 5G telecommunications is the fifth-generation wireless network technology, promising faster speeds and greater connectivity than 4G. By the late 2010s, telecom providers worldwide began rolling out 5G infrastructure. Technical experts and industry leaders highlighted 5G's benefits for innovation (e.g. enabling IoT, smart cities, advanced mobile applications). However, the public rollout of 5G networks, particularly in 2019–2020, faced an unexpected obstacle: a wave of conspiracy theories and misinformation linking 5G to various harms.

Misinformation narrative: The anti-5G misinformation included a range of pseudoscientific and conspiratorial claims: that 5G's higher frequency radio waves are dangerous to health (e.g. causing cancer or weakening immunity) or that 5G towers were somehow triggering or exacerbating COVID-19.

DOI stage impacts: For 5G, the Knowledge Stage for a segment of the public was corrupted by false awareness: instead of learning about 5G's technical features or benefits (faster connectivity, capacity for more devices, etc.), many people's first communications regarding 5G related to purported dangers—essentially, misinformation outpaced factual outreach. At the Persuasion Stage, attitudes were skewed negatively in those influenced by the conspiracies. Normally, one might expect neutral or mildly positive attitudes toward a new network upgrade (as with 4G earlier); instead, 5G encountered unusually high levels of fear and aversion in certain communities. At the Decision/Implementation Stage, we can consider the decisions of local authorities, businesses, and consumers regarding 5G infrastructure and devices. Misinformation led some local authorities and building owners to oppose or delay installing 5G masts due to public pressure. In extreme cases, the implementation stage was directly disrupted by vandalism when, influenced by the conspiracy theories, individuals set fire to or destroyed physical 5G towers.

Outcomes: The 5G case resulted in delayed and uneven diffusion of the technology, at least in the short term. In countries like the UK, telecom operators reported that misinformation-driven vandalism and community resistance slowed deployment timelines in 2020 and responded by launching a campaign to counteract misinformation (Mobile 2025). For diffusion theory, this case highlights how external misinformation shocks can nearly derail the diffusion of a technology that otherwise has clear advantages.

6 Discussion and Implications

The foregoing analysis reveals that Rogers's Diffusion of Innovation theory requires important updates to remain fully relevant in the contemporary world. Innovation diffusion is no longer a linear, information-rich process; it now unfolds in a fragmented, high-noise information environment. This has both theoretical and practical implications.

6.1 Theoretical Implications

Several core DOI assumptions are violated by the presence of significant misinformation: (1) the assumption of accurate information flow (that potential adopters receive mainly correct information about an innovation's attributes) is often false in the "post-truth" era; (2) the assumption of rational evaluation by adopters is undermined by emotional and identity-driven decision-making prompted by false narratives; (3) the assumption of a unified social system where most members eventually hear similar messages is broken by echo chambers and information silos (different subgroups live in different informational realities). Our critical examination suggests a need to refine DOI theory by explicitly incorporating information quality and trust as variables influencing each stage of adoption. Rather than treating the communication environment as a mostly benign background condition, diffusion scholars should treat it as a central factor—one that can dramatically skew outcomes.

A key theoretical implication is how we conceptualize the role of misinformation in the diffusion process. Is misinformation a moderator, a mediator, or an exogenous shock? Our analysis indicates it can play multiple roles. In many cases, pervasive misinformation acts as a moderating factor that alters the relationship between an innovation's properties and its adoption rate. For instance, the positive effect of a high relative advantage on adoption may be weakened (moderated) by a high volume of misinformation about the innovation's risks. Misinformation can also moderate the influence of opinion leaders: normally, positive testimonials speed diffusion, but if countervailing false narratives exist, even positive word-of-mouth might have limited impact. At the same time, misinformation often arrives in bursts (e.g. a viral conspiracy theory that spikes in popularity), which can be thought of as external shocks to the diffusion curve.

Another theoretical implication concerns opinion leadership and social influence. Rogers's theory gives significant weight to positive opinion leaders (innovators and early adopters who convince others). Our extension suggests introducing the concept of negative opinion leaders or misinfluence: influential actors who discourage adoption via misinformation. This could range from a local community figure sowing doubt about a new agricultural practice, to a popular online personality spreading conspiracy theories about a technology. Including this concept helps explain diffusion failures or slowdowns—it's not just lack of positive champions, but the presence of effective opponents. Relatedly, the criterion of homophily (people influencing similar others) takes on a new light when those clusters are self-reinforcing pockets of misinformation.

6.2 Future Research Agenda

This paper raises several research questions that can be developed into testable propositions. We encourage scholars to empirically investigate the interplay of misinformation and innovation diffusion across different contexts (technology, healthcare, environmental innovations, etc.). Below, we outline key propositions emerging from our analysis, which future studies could explore:

P1: Higher exposure to misinformation will significantly delay and flatten the adoption curve of an innovation.

P2: Misinformation's impact on diffusion is moderated by network structure.

P3: The presence of negative opinion leaders (prominent sources of misinformation) will suppress adoption more than the absence of positive opinion leaders.

P4: Interventions at different stages have differential effectiveness in countering misinformation's effect on diffusion.

P5: Misinformation tends to have the greatest impact on innovations that are high in complexity and low in observability, as well as those touching on high-trust domains (health, safety).

P6: Misinformation can cause long-term adoption asymmetries, even after broad diffusion, by sustaining minority pockets of resistance or periodic backlash cycles.

6.3 Implications for Practice

From a practical standpoint, our analysis suggests that those interested in promoting beneficial innovations (whether they be policymakers, companies, or advocacy groups) must account for information disorder. We outline strategies below, distinguishing between short-term "platform" levers that can be applied within today's digital platforms and long-term institutional strategies that build resilience over time. Where possible, we also align these strategies to specific DOI stages, recognizing that different phases of adoption may require different interventions.

Short-term platform-level Strategies

In the immediate term, much can be done on the very platforms where misinformation spreads. Social media and content platforms are often the battlegrounds for public opinion on innovations. Platform companies (and communities on those platforms) can implement measures to dampen the spread of false narratives without unduly amplifying them. For example:

Algorithmic adjustment: Platforms can adjust recommender algorithms to down-rank or de-prioritize known misinformation about an innovation throughout the stages of diffusion.

Fact-checking and labelling: They can also deploy fact-check labels or interstitial warnings on viral false posts, especially during the knowledge stage of diffusion when first impressions are being formed.

Rate-limiting and friction: Since false rumors often spread faster than truth, inserting friction (like limiting mass forwarding on messaging apps, or slowing the virality of unverified content) can prevent misleading claims from outrunning factual information. This is likely to be most effective at the Knowledge and Persuasion stages.

Amplification of authoritative sources: Platforms can also amplify authoritative sources through information panels or curated feeds when people search for or discuss the innovation ("redirecting" users to credible information from health organizations, scientific bodies, etc.).

Longer-term Institutional Strategies.

In the longer horizon, building a resilient information environment around innovations requires institutional efforts in education, policy, and community engagement. The following strategies may be implemented to build resilience in the longer term.

Pre-bunking and Education: Before or during an innovation's introduction, anticipate possible misconceptions and conspiracies, and proactively reframe the narrative and provide pre-bunking communications (Traberg et al. 2023). Pre-bunking is the strategy of debunking false narratives in advance (Hameleers 2024). These strategies can also mitigate the potential Streisand effect (Jansen and Martin 2015)—where attempting to suppress content only draws more attention to it.

Institutional Trust Building: Over the long term, government agencies, scientific bodies, and industry can proactively engage with the public to rebuild trust. Transparency is key: openly sharing data about an innovation's safety and efficacy, acknowledging uncertainties or risks, and demonstrating responsiveness to concerns can prevent misinformation from finding fertile ground.

Policy and Regulation: Governments can play a role by implementing policies that support accurate diffusion. For example, requiring labelling of synthetic media (so a deepfake must be disclosed as such). Strengthening laws against fraudulent disinformation campaigns could deter organized efforts to derail innovations.

7 Conclusion

In an age of AI-accelerated information disorder, the diffusion of innovations cannot be taken for granted. This paper considered how misinformation and disinformation, amplified by digital platforms and AI, can confound the adoption process of innovative technologies. Through theoretical analysis and real-world cases, we demonstrated that false and misleading information can inject friction at every stage of Rogers' classic diffusion model, from initial awareness all the way to post-adoption confirmation. Misinformation not only threatens successful diffusion of specific innovations, but also public trust in the very idea of innovation. Our analysis calls for a multi-disciplinary and multi-stakeholder response.

References

Aimeur, E., Amri, S., Brassard, G.: Fake news, disinformation and misinformation in social media: a review. Soc. Netw. Anal. Min. **13**(1), 1–36 (2023). https://doi.org/10.1007/s13278-023-01028-5

Allington, D., Duffy, B., Wessely, S., Dhavan, N., Rubin, J.: Health-protective behaviour, social media usage and conspiracy belief during the COVID-19 public health emergency. Psychol. Med. **51**(10), 1763–1769 (2021). https://doi.org/10.1017/S003329172000224X

Anandhan, A., Shuib, L., Ismail, M.A., Mujtaba, G.: Social media recommender systems: review and open research issues. IEEE Access **6**, 15608–15628 (2018)

Atkinson, R.D., Castro, D.: Digital quality of life: understanding the personal and social benefits of the information technology revolution. SSRN Electron. J. (2008). https://doi.org/10.2139/ssrn.1278185

Bontridder, N., Poullet, Y.: The role of artificial intelligence in disinformation. Data Policy **3**(E32) (2021). https://doi.org/10.1017/dap.2021.20

Bruns, A.: Are filter bubbles real? Polity Press (2019)

Caceres, M.M.F., Sosa, J.P., Lawrence, J.A., Sestacovschi, C., Tidd-Johnson, A., Ul Rasool, M.H., Gadamidi, V.K., Ozair, S., Pandav, K., Cuevas-Lou, C., Parrish, M., Rodriguez, I., Fernandez, J.P.: The impact of misinformation on the COVID-19 pandemic. AIMS Public Health **9**(2), 262 (2022)

Carrasco-Farré, C.: The fingerprints of misinformation: how deceptive content differs from reliable sources in terms of cognitive effort and appeal to emotions. Humanit. Soc. Sci. Commun. **9**(1), 1–18 (2022)

Chen, J., Dong, H., Wang, X., Feng, F., Wang, M., He, X.: Bias and debias in recommender system: a survey and future directions. ACM Trans. Inf. Syst. **41**(3), 1–39 (2023)
Cinelli, M., Morales, G.D.F., Galeazzi, A., Quattrociocchi, W., Starnini, M.: The echo chamber effect on social media. Proc. Natl. Acad. Sci. **118**(9), e2023301118 (2021). https://doi.org/10.1073/pnas.2023301118
Cinelli, M., Quattrociocchi, W., Galeazzi, A., et al.: The COVID-19 social media infodemic. Sci. Rep. **10**(1), 16598 (2020). https://doi.org/10.1038/s41598-020-73510-5
Corsi, G.: Evaluating Twitter's algorithmic amplification of low-credibility content: an observational study. EPJ Data Sci. **13**(1), 1–15 (2024)
Cota, W., Ferreira, S.C., Pastor-Satorras, R., Starnini, M.: Quantifying echo chamber effects in information spreading over political communication networks. EPJ Data Sci. **8**(1), 1–13 (2019)
Del Vicario, M., Bessi, A., Zollo, F., et al.: Echo chambers and viral misinformation: modeling fake news on social media. Sci. Rep. **6**, 37825 (2016). https://doi.org/10.1038/srep37825
Dennis, A.R., Galletta, D.F., Webster, J.: Fake news on the internet. Taylor & Francis (2023)
Ebrahimi, M.: Information, misinformation, and disinformation: social diffusion and misinformation prevention. In: Information Manipulation and Its Impact Across All Industries, pp. 1–18. IGI Global Scientific Publishing (2022)
Ecker, U.K.H., Lewandowsky, S., Cook, J., et al.: The psychological drivers of misinformation belief and its resistance to correction. Nat. Rev. Psychol. **1**, 13–29 (2022). https://doi.org/10.1038/s44159-021-00006-y
Eysenbach, G.: How to fight an infodemic: the four pillars of infodemic management. J. Med. Internet Res. **22**(6), e21820 (2020). https://doi.org/10.2196/21820
Farid, H.: Creating, using, misusing, and detecting deep fakes. J. Online Trust Saf. **1**(4) (2022)
Firdaus, N., Jumroni, J., Aziz, A., Sumartono, E., Purwanti, A.: The influence of social media, misinformation, and digital communication strategies on public perception and trust. J. Acad. Sci. **1**(3), 131–138 (2024)
Foroughi, H., Gabriel, Y., Fotaki, M.: Leadership in a post-truth era: a new narrative disorder? Leadership **15**(2), 135–151 (2019). https://doi.org/10.1177/1742715019835369
García-Avilés, J.A.: Diffusion of innovation. Int Encycl Media Psychol **1**(8), 1–8 (2020)
Hameleers, M.: The state-of-the-art in combating mis-and disinformation: lessons from pre-and debunking approaches. In: Disinformation Debunked, pp. 19–36 (2024)
Hosseini, A.S., Staab, S.: Emotional framing in the spreading of false and true claims. In: Proceedings of the 15th ACM Web Science Conference 2023, pp. 96–106 (2023). https://doi.org/10.1145/3578503.3583611
Islam, R., Keya, K.N., Pan, S., Foulds, J.: Mitigating demographic biases in social media-based recommender systems. KDD (Social Impact Track) (2019)
Jadhav, D., Agrawal, S., Jagdale, S., Salunkhe, P., Salunkhe, R.: AI-driven text-to-multimedia content generation: enhancing modern content creation. In: 2024 8th International Conference on I-SMAC (IoT in Social, Mobile, Analytics and Cloud) (I-SMAC), pp. 1610–1615. IEEE (2024)
Jaidka, K., Chen, T., Chesterman, S., Hsu, W., Kan, M.-Y., Kankanhalli, M., Lee, M. L., Seres, G., Sim, T., Taeihagh, A., Tung, A., Xiao, X., Yue, A.: Misinformation, disinformation, and generative AI: implications for perception and policy. Digit. Gov Res Pract **6**(1) (2024). https://doi.org/10.1145/3689372
Jansen, S.C., Martin, B.: The Streisand effect and censorship backfire. Int. J. Commun. **9**, 16 (2015)
Johnson, T.J., Wallace, R., Lee, T.: How social media serve as a super-spreader of misinformation, disinformation, and conspiracy theories regarding health crises. In: The Emerald handbook of computer-mediated communication and social media, pp. 67–84. Emerald Publishing Limited (2022)

Kaminski, J.: Diffusion of innovation theory. Can. J. Nurs. Inform. **6**(2), 1–6 (2011)

Kapoor, S., Narayanan, A.: We looked at 78 election deepfakes. Political misinformation is not an AI problem. Knight First Amendment Institute at Columbia University (2024)

Karlova, N.A., Fisher, K.E.: A social diffusion model of misinformation and disinformation for understanding human information behaviour (2013)

Lim, X.J., Quach, S., Thaichon, P., Cheah, J.H., Ting, H.: Fact or fake: information, misinformation and disinformation via social media. J. Strateg. Mark. **32**(5), 659–664 (2024). https://doi.org/10.1080/0965254X.2024.2306558

McElheran, K., Frank Li, J., Brynjolfsson, E., Kroff, Z., Dinlersoz, E., Foster, L., Zolas, N.: AI adoption in America: who, what, and where. J. Econo Manag Strategy **33**(2) (2024). https://doi.org/10.1111/jems.12576

McHale, J.: The Changing Information Environment, Routledge (2019). https://doi.org/10.4324/9780429051760

Metzger, M.J., Flanagin, A.J., Eyal, K., Lemus, D.R., McCann, R.M.: Credibility for the 21st century: integrating perspectives on source, message, and media credibility in the contemporary media environment. Ann. Int. Commun. Assoc. **27**(1), 293–335 (2003)

Mobile U.K.: Mobileuk.org. https://www.mobileuk.org/. Accessed 5 Aug 2025 (2025)

Monsees, L.: Information disorder, fake news and the future of democracy. Globalizations **20**(1), 1–16 (2021). https://doi.org/10.1080/14747731.2021.1927470

Monteith, S., Glenn, T., Geddes, J.R., Whybrow, P.C., Achtyes, E., Bauer, M.: Artificial intelligence and increasing misinformation. Br. J. Psychiatry **224**(2), 1–3 (2023). https://doi.org/10.1192/bjp.2023.136

Muhammed, T.S., Mathew, S.K.: The disaster of misinformation: a review of research in social media. Int. J. Data Sci. Anal. **13**(4), 271–285 (2022)

Office of the Surgeon General: Health misinformation. HHS.gov (2025). https://www.hhs.gov/surgeongeneral/reports-and-publications/health-misinformation/index.html#:~:text=How%20health%20misinformation%20spreads

Pennycook, G., Rand, D.G.: The psychology of fake news. Trends Cogn. Sci. **25**(5), 388–402 (2021). https://doi.org/10.1016/j.tics.2021.02.007

Rogers, E.M.: Diffusion of innovations, 4th edn. Free Press (1995)

Rogers, E.M.: Diffusion of innovations fifth Ed Free Press. New York

Roozenbeek, J., van der Linden, S., Nygren, T.: Prebunking interventions based on "inoculation" theory can reduce susceptibility to misinformation across cultures. Harvard Kennedy Sch. Misinformation Rev **1**(1) (2020). https://doi.org/10.37016/mr-2020-008

Ryffel, F.A., Wirz, D.S., Kühne, R., Wirth, W.: How emotional media reports influence attitude formation and change: the interplay of attitude base, attitude certainty, and persuasion. Media Psychol. **17**(4), 397–419 (2014). https://doi.org/10.1080/15213269.2014.933850

Scheufele, D.A., Krause, N.M.: Science audiences, misinformation, and fake news. Proc. Natl. Acad. Sci. **116**(16), 7662–7669 (2019). https://doi.org/10.1073/pnas.1805871115

Simon, F.M., Altay, S., Mercier, H.: Misinformation reloaded? Fears about the impact of generative AI on misinformation are overblown. Harvard Kennedy Sch. Misinformation Rev. **4**(5) (2023)

Skafle, I., Nordahl-Hansen, A., Quintana, D.S., Wynn, R., Gabarron, E.: Misinformation about COVID-19 vaccines on social media: rapid review. J. Med. Internet Res. **24**(8), e37367 (2022)

Steinmetz, H., Batzdorfer, V., Bosnjak, M.: The struggle with the new normal: online misinformation and the digital divide. Soc. Sci. Comput. Rev. **41**(1), 160–174 (2021). https://doi.org/10.1177/0894439321999706

Tambini, D.: Social media power and election legitimacy. Soc. Media + Soc. **7**(2), 1–5 (2021). https://doi.org/10.1177/20563051211008818

Torkington, S.: These are the 3 biggest emerging risks the world is facing. World Economic Forum (2024). https://www.weforum.org/stories/2024/01/ai-disinformation-global-risks/

Traberg, C.S., Harjani, T., Basol, M., Biddlestone, M., Maertens, R., Roozenbeek, J., van der Linden, S.: Prebunking against misinformation in the modern digital age. Springer EBooks, 99–111 (2023). https://doi.org/10.1007/978-3-031-27789-4_8

Valente, T.W.: Social network thresholds in the diffusion of innovations. Social Netw. **18**(1), 69–89 (1996)

van Prooijen, J.W., Spadaro, G., Wang, H.: Suspicion of institutions: how distrust and conspiracy theories deteriorate social cohesion. Curr. Opin. Psychol. **43**, 173–178 (2022). https://doi.org/10.1016/j.copsyc.2021.07.013

Vosoughi, S., Roy, D., Aral, S.: The spread of true and false news online. Science **359**(6380), 1146–1151 (2018). https://doi.org/10.1126/science.aap9559

Wardle, C., Derakhshan, H.: Information Disorder: Toward an Interdisciplinary Framework for Research and Policymaking, vol. 27, pp. 1–107. Council of Europe, Strasbourg (2017)

Williamson, E.: Q&A: With Zelenskyy Surrender Hoax, the Feared Future of Deepfakes Is Here. Business & Government, University of Virginia (2022). https://news.virginia.edu/content/qa-zelenskyy-surrender-hoax-feared-future-deepfakes-here#:~:text=tide%20in%20a%20war%20and,inspire%20and%20justify%20physical%20attacks

Zhao, Z., Resnick, P., Mei, Q.: Enquiring minds: early detection of rumors in social media from enquiry posts. ACM Trans. Inf. Syst. (TOIS) **39**(1), 1–28 (2021). https://doi.org/10.1145/3427515

Zhou, Y., Shen, L.: Confirmation bias and the persistence of misinformation on climate change. Commun. Res. **49**(4), 500–523 (2022)

Future Directions of Digital Innovation in Entrepreneurship: A Systematic Review of Component and Key Enabler

Sulton Ahmad Hamadah and Agung Purnomo(✉)

Entrepreneurship Department, BINUS Business School Undergraduate Program, Bina Nusantara University, Jakarta, Indonesia
agung.purnomo@binus.ac.id

Abstract. Digital innovation has reshaped entrepreneurship by redefining how ventures are initiated, scaled, and sustained, yet the literature remains fragmented across disciplines. Despite growing interest, there is a lack of comprehensive synthesis mapping the components, key enablers, and conceptual frameworks of digital innovation in entrepreneurship. This study examines the global status of literature development on digital innovation in entrepreneurship. Differentiating itself from previous fragmented studies, this research systematically integrates thematic insights to produce a holistic conceptual model. Employing a Systematic Literature Review (SLR) guided by the PRISMA protocol, 24 peer-reviewed journal articles (2020–2024) from Scopus were analyzed. Components of digital innovation were categorized into seven domains: digital technologies, disruptive business models, user-centric design, data-driven decision-making, agility and experimentation, collaboration and ecosystems, and digital transformation. The key enablers were synthesized using Gioia's method, resulting in the 4C framework: capability centering, connectivity and collaboration, contextual adaptation, and creative exploration. The study proposed a growing tree conceptual framework illustrating the interconnection between digital components and key enablers. This review concludes that entrepreneurial success in digital contexts relies on technological integration and strategic enabling conditions. The research contributes by offering a unified, cross-disciplinary conceptualization of digital innovation in entrepreneurship, guiding future empirical studies, and informing practitioners on the strategic orchestration of digital capabilities. It highlights the need for micro-, meso-, and macro-level studies to further contextualize digital entrepreneurial ecosystems across diverse global settings.

Keywords: Digital innovation · Digital business · Entrepreneurship · Systematic literature review · Key enablers

1 Introduction

The digital innovation study has gained significant traction as a pivotal force shaping contemporary business and entrepreneurship landscapes. Digital innovation refers to the use of emerging technologies to generate value through novel business processes,

Published by Springer Nature Switzerland AG 2026
A. Elbanna et al. (Eds.): TDIT 2025, IFIP AICT 778, pp. 144–159, 2026.
https://doi.org/10.1007/978-3-032-16775-0_9

products, or services [1]. Entrepreneurship, on the other hand, is defined as the process of identifying and exploiting opportunities to create economic and social value [2]. Digital innovation is no longer limited to enhancing operational efficiency but has evolved into a strategic asset, enabling firms to redesign their value propositions and market reach [3]. Scholars have explored how digital infrastructures such as platforms, APIs, and software libraries reshape innovation ecosystems and redefine relationships among firms, consumers, and stakeholders [4, 5]. The growing interplay between digital innovation technologies, informatics, and socio-economic shifts has compelled researchers to examine their implications on product development and organizational and market structures [6, 7]. As digital technologies mature and diversify, business innovation is increasingly driven by real-time data, cloud computing, and collaborative platforms [1].

The convergence of digital innovation and entrepreneurship in recent years has become an essential theme in research. Entrepreneurs have leveraged digital platforms, AI innovation, and emerging technologies to disrupt established markets, often without significant physical infrastructure [8–10]. Value creation no longer depends solely on tangible offerings but also on digital services, ecosystems, and new business models [11]. Startups and SMEs are now actively integrating digital experimentation, innovation software, and analytics into their growth and competitive strategies [12, 13]. As a result, digital entrepreneurship has emerged not just as a technological trend but as a transformative mode of market entry and innovation [14].

The urgency to study digital innovation within the entrepreneurial domain lies in its capacity to radically transform how ventures are initiated, scaled, and sustained. External shocks, such as the COVID-19 pandemic, have accelerated the need for digital capabilities in both startups and incumbents [15, 16]. Digital innovation plays a central role in enhancing entrepreneurial resilience, particularly during periods of disruption when traditional resources and processes are insufficient [17]. Moreover, it empowers resource-constrained firms, particularly in emerging markets, to leapfrog structural limitations by adopting scalable, platform-based models [16]. Understanding these dynamics is essential for building adaptive and inclusive entrepreneurial ecosystems [18].

Applying the systematic literature review (SLR) methodology effectively consolidates and interprets the expanding body of research on digital innovation in entrepreneurship. By synthesizing diverse theoretical perspectives and empirical evidence, the SLR method allows researchers to identify key enablers, mechanisms, and gaps within a structured framework [19, 20]. As the literature on this topic is fragmented across disciplines—from management and informatics to sustainability and design—SLR enables a cross-sectional view that aligns conceptual, technological, and strategic dimensions [4]. It also supports replicability and transparency, contributing to cumulative knowledge in this emerging field [6].

Several previous studies have explored digital innovation in entrepreneurship using diverse research methods, each offering unique insights and limitations. Fink et al. conducted an empirical study analyzing software library deployment among startups, providing quantifiable insights but with a limited scope [4]. Shaikh et al. adopted an action design research method to propose digital innovation ecosystems, which is valuable for model development; however, it lacks empirical testing. Goncalves et al. used a comparative qualitative study to examine organizational cultures in innovation, yielding contextual depth but limited generalizability [16]. Cueto et al. applied inductive content analysis to understand MSME digital transformations, which are rich in narrative but prone to researcher bias [14]. Felicetti et al. conducted a systematic literature review synthesizing thematic trends, providing structured knowledge but lacking real-time empirical grounding [19]. While these studies contribute critical perspectives, they remain fragmented and often focus on isolated components of digital entrepreneurship. Unlike previous studies, such as Felicetti et al., this study develops a new, cross-disciplinary conceptual model to integrate fragmented insights into digital innovation and entrepreneurship, using the 4C framework and the growing tree metaphor. Therefore, this study aims to examine the current status of literature development related to components, key enablers, conceptual frameworks, and future research in digital innovation within entrepreneurship studies worldwide.

2 Research Methods

This study adopted the Systematic Literature Review (SLR) method to explore digital innovation in entrepreneurship. SLR provides a structured, transparent, and replicable approach to synthesizing academic knowledge and identifying trends in the literature [21]. The PRISMA protocol ensured transparency in screening and inclusion, while the Gioia method was used for qualitative synthesis of enabler categories. We applied the search query 'digital innovation' AND 'entrepreneurship' in Scopus, limited to peer-reviewed journals from 2020 to 2024, to ensure post-pandemic relevance, as shown in Fig. 1. The PRISMA protocol was selected to enhance the clarity and reproducibility of the literature review process. This protocol allows researchers to manage document screening, inclusion decisions, and data extraction systematically, ensuring that the synthesis process minimizes bias and remains traceable throughout the research lifecycle [22].

Scopus served as the primary data source due to its comprehensive coverage of peer-reviewed journals in business, management, and technology. Scopus also provides advanced filtering options and consistent metadata that simplify data handling during bibliometric and thematic analysis, offering high quality and relevance for academic reviews [23].

Research Question (RQ) in this systematic literature review includes:

RQ1: What are the key components of digital innovation in entrepreneurship studies?
RQ2: What are the key enablers of digital innovation in entrepreneurship studies?
RQ3: What is the conceptual framework of digital innovation in entrepreneurship studies?
RQ4: What is the future research of digital innovation in entrepreneurship studies?

The research addressed four core questions. RQ1 was analyzed descriptively by categorizing the components of digital innovation identified across the selected sites, referring to the Ideascale categorization [24]. RQ2 was examined using descriptive analysis and Gioia's grounded theory approach to extract first-order concepts, second-order themes, and aggregate dimensions. The Gioia method was used because it enables the construction of a structured and theory-driven framework from raw qualitative data, preserving the voice of the informants while building conceptual insight [25]. RQ3 was analyzed by mapping conceptual frameworks derived from the reviewed studies to reveal the interconnections among digital innovation components and key enabler outcomes of entrepreneurship. RQ4 synthesized future research directions by drawing patterns from the findings of RQ1 and RQ2.

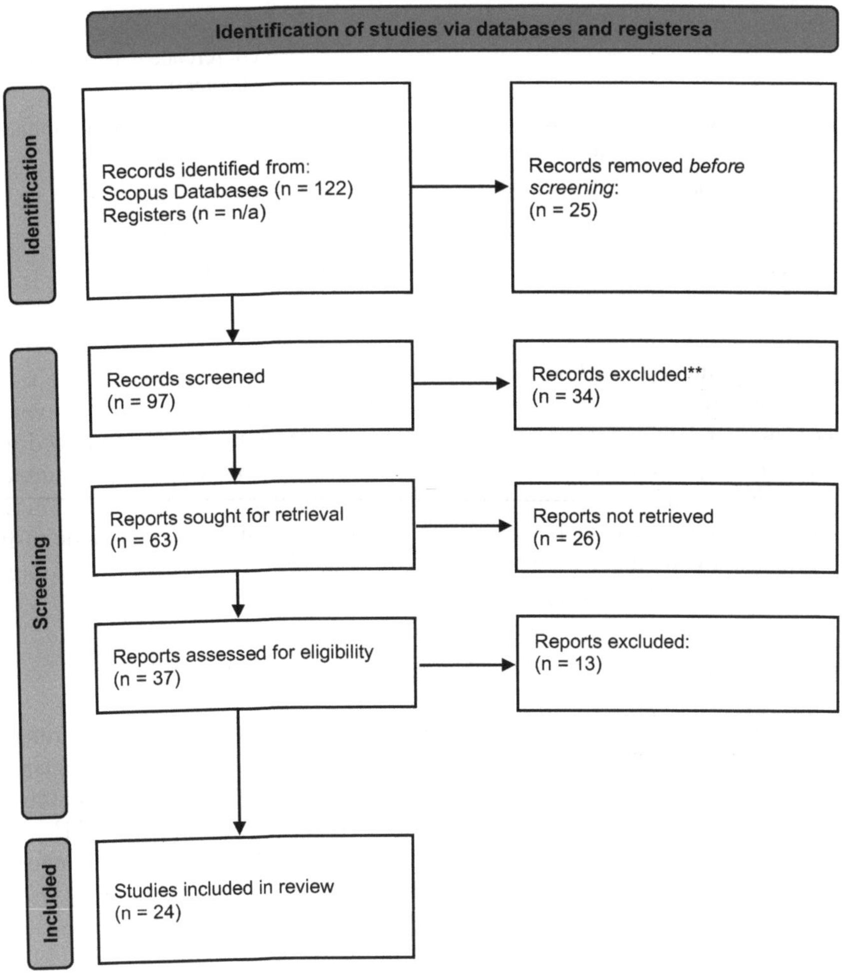

Fig. 1. PRISMA flowchart

The search strategy utilized a combination of keywords and their equivalents: "digital innovation" AND "entrepreneurship." Boolean operators were used to refine and expand search results. Although only 24 articles were reviewed, this sample size was sufficient to achieve thematic saturation as guided by Gioia et al. [25], given the focus on conceptual depth and cross-disciplinary coverage. The inclusion and exclusion criteria are outlined in Table 1.

Table 1. Inclusion and exclusion criteria.

No.	Criteria	Inclusion criteria	Exclusion criteria
1	Topics	Related to digital innovation and entrepreneurship	Articles outside the business or entrepreneurship discipline
2	Publication year	Peer-reviewed journals	Non-journal documents (e.g., conference papers, book chapters)
3	Subject area	Business, management, and accounting	Other unrelated disciplines
4	Year of publication	2020–2024	Before 2020
5	Access	Open access	Restricted
6	Language	English	Non-English

The analysis incorporated both descriptive and visual interpretation techniques. For RQ1, categorizations were constructed using Microsoft Word to visualize taxonomy relationships. For RQ2, thematic mapping of the Gioia method was visualized using Canva for a more precise representation of aggregate dimensions. For RQ3, framework illustrations were constructed using Figma as a conceptual framework model. This approach enables comparative analysis and enhances the accessibility of thematic insights [26]. Each part of the analysis was supported by academic references to ensure the relevance and rigor of the findings [27].

2.1 Components of Digital Innovation in Entrepreneurship

Table 2 presents the components of digital innovation in entrepreneurship, referring to the idea scale categorization. Digital innovation comprises digital technologies, disruptive business models, user-centric design, data-driven decision-making, agility and experimentation, collaboration and ecosystems, and digital transformation [24].

Digital innovation in entrepreneurship is driven by several interrelated components that collectively shape the transformation of business models, processes, and ecosystems. One of the foundational components is digital technologies, which encompass Artificial Intelligence (AI) [20], cloud computing [28], Internet of Things (IoT) [19], big data analytics [12], digital platforms and infrastructure [29], mobile apps and platforms [6], and blockchain [1]. These technologies underpin digital transformation efforts by enhancing operational capabilities, scalability, and market access. Disruptive business models represent another critical component, characterized by scalable business model development [17], digitally enhanced value-adding activities and novel business models [20], business model flexibility [29], Software-as-a-Service (SaaS) [5], peer-to-peer

Table 2. Components of Digital Innovation in Entrepreneurship

No.	Components of digital innovation	Components of digital innovation in entrepreneurship
1	Digital technologies	Artificial intelligence (AI) [20], cloud computing [28], the internet of things (IoT) [19], big data analytics [12], digital platforms and infrastructure [29], mobile apps and platforms [6], and blockchain [1]
2	Disruptive business models	Scalable business model development [17], digitally enhanced value-adding activities and novel business models [20], business model flexibility [29], Software-as-a-service (SaaS) [5], and peer-to-peer exchange [6]
3	User-centric design	Customer-centric innovation [12], design-thinking method [1], personalized development [30], user testing [31]
4	Data-driven decision-making	Digital data for optimizing operations [32], machine learning algorithms [1], real-time data feeds and real-time data processing via API calls[1, 33], data-informed innovation strategies [19], market signals and knowledge sourcing [29], social media and online behavior data adaptation [14, 34]
5	Agility and experimentation	Iterative ADR methodology and rapid prototyping [11], start-up law flexibility and ecosystem role recognition [8, 18], constant experimentation [20], prototype testing [17], A/B/n testing, and multivariate testing [12]
6	Collaboration and ecosystems	Open innovation [16], collaborative innovation ecosystems [20], digital entrepreneurial ecosystems [8], cross-sector partnerships [31], and online collaboration platforms [30]
7	Digital transformation	Digitization of business processes [19], strategic alignment [20], complete transition of business operations [14], agile transformation across organizational levels [16], digital curriculum reform [30], and a catalyst for policy and innovation [18]

exchange [6]. These models redefine value creation and delivery mechanisms in digital entrepreneurship.

A human-centered approach is embedded in the user-centric design component, which encompasses customer-centric innovation [12], design thinking methods [1], personalized development [30], and user testing [31]. Another essential component is data-driven decision-making, which involves the use of digital data for optimizing operations [32], machine learning algorithms [1], real-time data feeds and real-time data processing via api calls [33, 1], data-informed innovation strategies [19], market signals and knowledge sourcing [29], social media and online behavior data adaptation [34, 14]. Agility and experimentation also play a pivotal role in fostering innovation, as reflected in iterative ADR methodology and rapid prototyping [11], start-up law flexibility and ecosystem role recognition [8, 18], constant experimentation [20], prototype testing [17], A/B/n testing and multivariate testing [12].

Collaboration and ecosystems are core to innovation ecosystems, including open innovation [16], collaborative innovation ecosystems [20], digital entrepreneurial ecosystems [8], cross-sector partnerships [31], and online collaboration platforms [30]. Lastly, digital transformation is a unifying component that drives structural change through digitization of business processes [19], strategic alignment [20], complete transition of business operations [14], agile transformation across organizational levels [16], digital curriculum reform [30], and a catalyst for policy and innovation [18].

This study identifies critical components of digital innovation that shape and accelerate entrepreneurial success in the digital era, including digital technologies, disruptive business models, user-centric design, data-driven decision-making, agility and experimentation, collaboration ecosystems, and digital transformation. This comprehensive categorization aligns with the current literature, which highlights the layered and interdependent nature of digital innovation in entrepreneurship, particularly the transformative role of digital platforms.

2.2 Key Enablers of Digital Innovation in Entrepreneurship

Following the structured progression of data arrangement, grounded theory, and thematic analysis through the Gioia methodology, this study identifies four overarching aggregate dimensions that capture the principal enablers influencing the deployment of digital innovation within entrepreneurship, as illustrated in Fig. 2. These aggregate dimensions—capability centering, connectivity and collaboration, contextual adaptation, and creative exploration—serve as the foundational pillars that support and drive innovation processes. This model is known as the 4C Key Enabler. The name 4C is taken from the first letter of the aggregate dimension. A comprehensive discussion of each aggregate dimension is presented in the subsequent sections.

Capability Centering

The findings suggest that human capital development is pivotal in enabling digital innovation within entrepreneurship, highlighting the importance of continuous skills advancement and talent cultivation in driving entrepreneurial success. The education and skills development domain is a crucial enabler for digital entrepreneurship, where competency-oriented education, project-based learning, and metacognitive skills nurture practical innovation and reflective thinking [30]. Entrepreneurial resilience is further strengthened by the ability to collect digital information and the motivation to innovate [30].

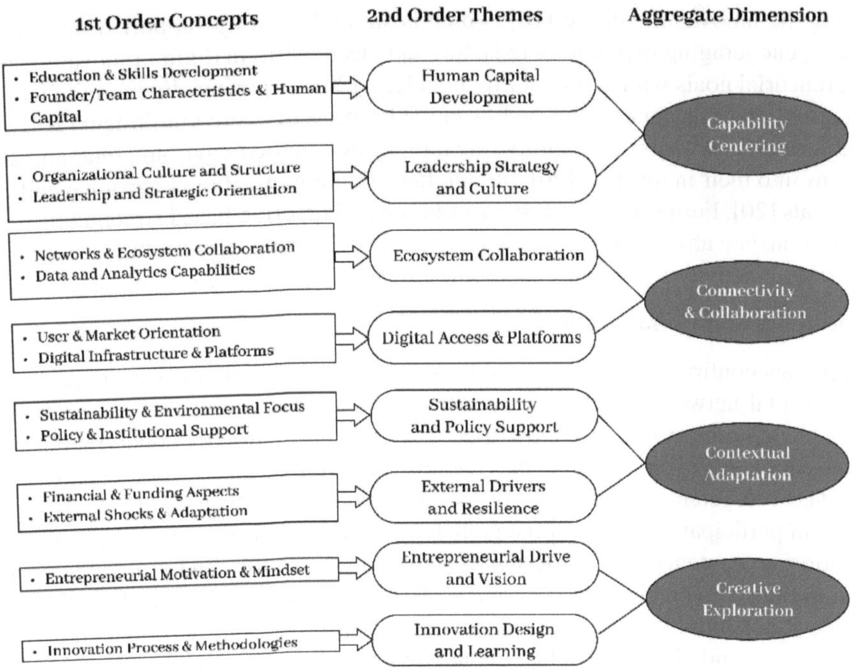

Fig. 2. Key Enablers of Digital Innovation in Entrepreneurship

Broader systemic efforts, including digital skill endowment, the educational system's ICT focus, and ICT-based employee training, have enhanced workforce readiness [8], which is reinforced by skills training and capacity building [17] and expanded through digital knowledge spillovers [8]. Similarly, founder or team characteristics and human capital emerge as key drivers, as entrepreneurial experience equips founders with strategic insights to innovate and exit successfully [29]. A youthful entrepreneurial demographic is more responsive to adopting digital tools [35], while startup age and digital maturity align closely with infrastructure agility [35]. Additionally, company size and resource availability provide greater access to innovation resources [35], while balanced cultural and racial teams facilitate digital adoption through inclusive collaboration [35].

The findings demonstrate that leadership strategy and culture are foundational enablers of digital innovation in entrepreneurship. The influence of organizational culture and structure on digital innovation becomes clear when firms build an agile culture (clan + adhocracy) that balances adaptability and stability [16], promote transparency and openness to foster renewal [32], and adopt a flat organizational structure to accelerate decision-making [16]. Supporting empowered and entrepreneurial people enhances innovation responsiveness [16], while bottom-up innovation initiatives from employees drive transformation [32]. Effective cross-functional collaboration also breaks down organizational silos and scales innovation [32], whereas in family businesses, the utilization of family identity contributes to sustaining tacit knowledge during crises [15]. Similarly, leadership and strategic orientation play a vital role, with leadership presence and vision, as well as effective communication and continuous communication, unifying the innovation culture [16], which is strengthened by support from top management, encouraging exploration [32]. Strategic leadership in digital innovation aligns entrepreneurial goals with sustainability mandates [20], requiring alignment of strategic orientations and a balanced focus on EO and SO to prevent overcommitment [20]. Organizations with a strong sustainability orientation (SO) embed environmental and social concerns into their innovation [20], often reflected in organizational narrative and strategy signals [20]. Furthermore, mechanism-based and practice-based strategizing enable firms to translate abstract strategies into practice [11], while treating digital innovation as a strategic activity repositions it as central to achieving performance success [20].

Connectivity and Collaboration

The findings confirm that networks and ecosystem collaboration drive digital innovation, as social network structure, actor centrality and positioning, and actor intermediation facilitate influence and knowledge exchange [18]. Broader collaboration arises through ecosystem diversity and collaboration, decentralized governance, and a dynamic networked ecosystem, enabling ecosystem entry via marketplaces [33]. Network and ecosystem participation [31] and integrated ecosystem synergy [17] enhance access to innovation ecosystems [19], fostering cross-sector innovation and collaboration [34] within digital entrepreneurial ecosystems [8]. Entrepreneurs advance through opportunistic partnerships [15], strategic alliances and networking [34], and collaboration with external actors, aided by stakeholder collaboration, stakeholder inclusion, and networking and stakeholder linkages[6, 17 , 28] . Essential support comes from ecosystem-level coordination [1], comprehensive support systems, mentorship, and expert guidance [17]. Sustainable collaboration is reinforced by the integration of capabilities [33], a stronger knowledge dissemination capability [18], and the application of a strategic framework for ecosystem engagement [4].

Similarly, data and analytics capabilities enable dynamic innovation through real-time data processing [33] and big data analytics capabilities (BDAC) [12]. Innovation aligns with users through customer-centric experimentation and platform-based digital experimentation [12], which is enhanced by AI-augmented analytics [12] and refined through an iterative innovation process [12].

The findings also indicate that user and market orientation are crucial for success. Early stakeholder inclusion fosters trust [31], while user feedback, responsiveness [31], and reflexivity in value propositions enhance customer loyalty [31]. Aligning with local needs through contextual user orientation [11], entrepreneurs utilize cross-sector market sensing and value proposition flexibility to facilitate adaptive innovation [11]. Digital agility is fostered through market adaptability on digital platforms [34] and social media and online marketing platforms [14]. Despite digitization, a desire to maintain personal service [10] and local adaptability and contextualization remain critical [28].

The expansion of digital infrastructure and platforms supports participation and scaling with the use of digital technology sets [20], platform openness and accessibility [33], and multi-sided platforms [28]. Flexibility grows through boundary resources for modularity and flexibility, the ownership structure of digital infrastructure, and a hybrid infrastructure model [4]. The broad adoption of digital infrastructures [35] is supported by the availability of supportive digital infrastructure [19] and adequate infrastructure and technical resources [17]. Startups leverage digital infrastructure and ICT tools [34] to achieve remote agility through the adaptation of digital infrastructure [15]. Revenue diversification arises from the integration of digital tools [10], access to earning platforms like TikTok [14], and the widespread use of mobile applications [6]. User engagement is shaped by socio-technical platform design [6], update and upgrade services, simplicity and usability of software, and idea management functionality [5]. Strategic alignment is enabled by integration into innovation infrastructure [12], supported by enhanced interpersonal communication and expanded remote work opportunities [36]. Firms enhance their resilience through operational agility, facilitated by connectivity [36] and digital search [19]. Finally, context-driven deployment decisions [4], innovation in supply chain logistics [36], digital marketplace infrastructure [36], cybersecurity awareness and adaptation [36], smart tourism as operational support [10], and low switching and integration costs [33] enable entrepreneurs to adapt and scale effectively.

Contextual Adaptation

The findings highlight that sustainability and policy support are indispensable drivers of digital innovation in entrepreneurship, reflecting how long-term environmental considerations and robust regulatory frameworks can shape and sustain entrepreneurial initiatives. Integrating sustainability and environmental focus into digital entrepreneurship is a critical enabler, starting with the adoption of exponential digital technologies, such as AI, blockchain, and IoT, to address environmental challenges at scale [1]. Ventures leverage tokenization and packetization to convert natural capital into tradable assets, utilizing smart contracting and verification to ensure transparent transactions [1]. Promoting digitized access and inclusion has expanded opportunities for underserved communities [1], while the anticipation of societal risks, such as privacy concerns, drives the creation of ethical innovation ecosystems [31]. Furthermore, gamification and incentive design [28] and gamification and simplification [1] have effectively boosted user engagement and environmental awareness through interactive digital platforms.

Policy and institutional support serve as a structural catalyst for digital innovation, beginning with policy and regulatory support that stabilizes and directs entrepreneurial activity [28] and is strengthened by government regulations and policy support that align legal systems with digital transformations [34]. Frameworks like start-up regulatory frameworks create pathways for entrepreneurial growth [8], while a supportive policy environment—including national startup acts—helps reduce digital entry barriers [35]. Additionally, innovation-friendly policies promote cross-sector entrepreneurship [6], and institutional support and digital policy enhance regional innovation climates [18]. Decentralized institutional support in areas lacking strong formal institutions enables blockchain-driven models to fill governance gaps and sustain innovation [1].

The findings demonstrate that external drivers and resilience are vital enablers of digital innovation in entrepreneurship. The influence of financial and funding Aspects on digital entrepreneurship is significant, beginning with the critical need for access to funding that supports scaling and innovation [17]. Expansion through digitalized funding and market access—like crowdfunding and online platforms—has widened entrepreneurial reach [29]. Financial hardship, especially income loss, often drives individuals toward entrepreneurship for resilience [14], while in mature ventures, the acquisition price as an exit motivator pushes founders to innovate strategically for profitable exits [29]. At the operational level, API-based service monetization introduces scalable revenue streams through modular digital transactions [33].

The category of external shocks and adaptation shows how crises reshape entrepreneurship, as community quarantine restrictions disrupt operations and force entrepreneurs to find alternatives [14]. COVID-19, as the trigger for innovation, encouraged founders to rethink their strategies digitally [10], while the COVID-19-driven acceleration of digital adoption increased online platform usage [6]. Entrepreneurs adapted by utilizing existing resources [10] and converting idle time into productivity for venture creation [14]. Shifts in adapted resource allocation [15] and entrepreneurial action under constraints highlighted innovation under scarcity [15]. High entrepreneurial adaptability helped navigate uncertainty [10], enabling a response to external competitive pressure [32], while increased demand for e-commerce opened up new digital opportunities [14].

Creative Exploration

The findings suggest that entrepreneurial drive and vision are fundamental catalysts for digital innovation in entrepreneurship, demonstrating how ambition, foresight, and a proactive mindset empower entrepreneurs to navigate complex digital landscapes. The contribution of innovation processes and methodologies to digital entrepreneurship is strengthened by frameworks like Action Design Research (ADR), which enables iterative, validated development [6], and by the design of use cases that translate theory into practice [6]. Triangulation through qualitative feedback enhances the relevance of decision-making [18], while resource-conscious innovation reuse facilitates scaling by repurposing assets [11]. Innovation grows through the constant launch of digital ventures [29] and is enhanced by a focus on efficiency improvements that link innovation to measurable outcomes [5]. Interdisciplinary integration promotes novel solutions [19], and entrepreneurial flexibility enables adaptive experimentation [19]. Ventures benefit from flexibility in product redesign and digital product malleability, enabling continuous reconfiguration [29, 11]. Success is often driven by cross-functional collaboration that unites technical and strategic expertise [12].

This study also shows that innovative design and learning are critical enablers of digital innovation in entrepreneurship. Entrepreneurial motivation and mindset are crucial in fostering digital innovation, where the entrepreneurial spirit and Bayanihan value strengthen collective action and resilience [14], and personal motivation for economic survival drives individuals to pursue entrepreneurship amid financial hardship [14]. Enhancing adaptability and entrepreneurial open-mindedness helps navigate uncertainty and seek unconventional innovation paths [10]. At the same time, an awareness of environmental value inspires purpose-driven innovation [10], all supported by strong innovation motivation as a psychological foundation [30].

2.3 Conceptual Framework

The conceptual framework depicts digital innovation in entrepreneurship as a growing plant, as seen in Fig. 3. The roots symbolize the seven fundamental components: digital technologies, disruptive business models, user-centric design, data-driven decision-making, agility and experimentation, collaboration and ecosystems, and digital transformation [24]. Each component functions as a critical nutrient, grounding and sustaining the trunk, representing the holistic construct of digital innovation in entrepreneurship. The interconnectedness of these components underscores the necessity of a robust foundation, indicating that without a well-developed base, the vitality of digital innovation efforts in entrepreneurial settings would be severely compromised.

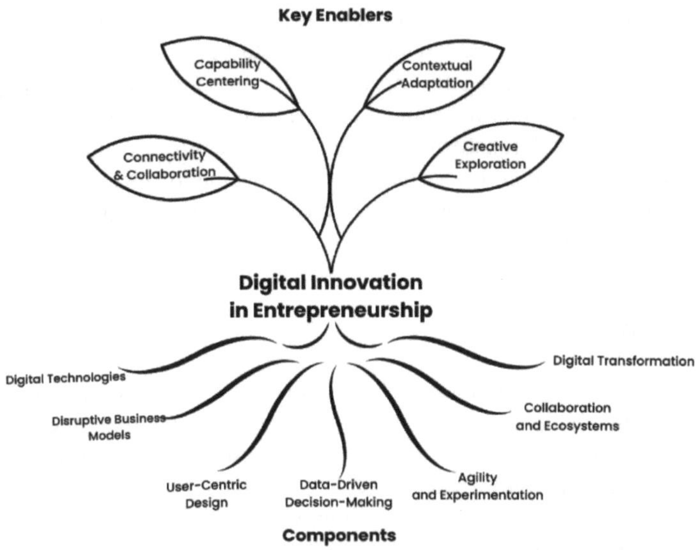

Fig. 3. Growing plants conceptual framework of digital innovation in entrepreneurship

2.4 Future Research

Applying the micro–meso–macro lens enables a structured understanding of how digital innovation mechanisms unfold across individual (entrepreneur), organizational (startup/firm), and institutional (ecosystem/policy) levels. At the micro level, future research could delve deeper into how specific digital innovation components, such as user-centric design, agility, and experimentation, influence the behavioral dynamics of individual entrepreneurs during the early stages of venture creation. Scholars might explore how personal digital competencies, iterative testing behaviors, and real-time decision-making driven by data-driven decision-making translate into entrepreneurial resilience and adaptability. Furthermore, empirical studies could investigate how individual exposure to the capability-centering pillar of the 4C key enabler fosters innovation learning curves and whether the perceived entrepreneurial self-efficacy mediates the relationship between digital tool adoption and venture performance in varied digital economies.

On a meso overview, future research should examine how organizational practices, network structures, and collaborative behaviors enhance or constrain the enactment of connectivity and collaboration, a core domain in the 4C key enabler. Comparative case studies across industries may reveal how startups and SMEs strategically orchestrate collaboration and ecosystems while navigating different stages of the conceptual framework, particularly how organizations transition from leveraging digital technologies as operational support towards integrating them as strategic value-creation assets. In addition, scholars are encouraged to assess how meso-contextual factors such as institutional support, cross-sector partnerships, and digital platform ecosystems amplify or hinder the scaling capacity of digital entrepreneurial initiatives.

From the macro perspective, advancing the understanding of contextual adaptation and creative exploration within the conceptual framework becomes critical, particularly when viewed through the lenses of regulatory landscapes, national innovation policies, and socio-economic digital divides. Future studies could analyze how broader structural factors—including digital infrastructure accessibility, policy incentives for entrepreneurship, and national investment in emerging technologies—mediate the systemic embedding of digital transformation and disruptive business models. Longitudinal and cross-country studies could offer insights into how macro-level enablers either consolidate or fragment digital entrepreneurial ecosystems, shaping the global patterns of digital innovation adoption and sustainability.

3 Conclusion

This study aimed to investigate the development status of the literature on digital innovation in entrepreneurship by systematically analyzing its components, key enablers, conceptual frameworks, and future directions. Through a structured review of 24 peer-reviewed journal articles published between 2020 and 2024, the study successfully identified seven key components of digital innovation: digital technologies, disruptive business models, user-centric design, data-driven decision-making, agility and experimentation, collaboration and ecosystems, and digital transformation. These components reflect the multidimensional and evolving nature of digital innovation as a catalyst for entrepreneurial activity, highlighting the critical roles of technology integration, customer-centric strategies, and organizational agility in the entrepreneurial process.

The analysis also revealed four principal key enablers, collectively termed the 4C key enablers: capability centering, connectivity and collaboration, contextual adaptation, and creative exploration. These enablers serve as foundational mechanisms that strengthen the digital innovation capacity of entrepreneurs across different contexts and scales. Capability centering underscores the importance of human capital development and leadership strategy, while connectivity and collaboration emphasize the role of network engagement and ecosystem integration. Contextual adaptation emphasizes the importance of a sustainability focus and policy support. At the same time, creative exploration highlights the entrepreneurial mindset and innovation learning as crucial to fostering adaptability and resilience in dynamic digital environments.

To synthesize these insights, the study proposed a conceptual framework visualized as a growing tree, where the roots represent digital innovation components, the trunk symbolizes digital innovation in entrepreneurship, and the leaves depict the 4C key enablers. This model illustrates how foundational digital capabilities and strategic enablers collectively drive entrepreneurial success in the digital economy. The findings contribute to the body of knowledge by offering a structured and integrative view of digital innovation in entrepreneurship, informing practitioners on essential factors for digital entrepreneurial ventures, and assisting policymakers in fostering supportive ecosystems for digital business innovation. Nevertheless, the study is limited by its reliance on Scopus-indexed English-language journals, which may overlook relevant studies published in other databases or languages.

Acknowledgment. This manuscript is a publication output from an undergraduate thesis track on scientific articles in reputable international publications at the Entrepreneurship Department, Bina Nusantara University, Malang Campus. The author would like to thank the Entrepreneurship Department and the Research and Technology Transfer Office at Bina Nusantara University for their support of the research ecosystem, facilities, and publication funding.

Author Contributorship. **Sulton Ahmad Hamadah**: Data Curation, Formal Analysis, Investigation, Methodol-ogy, Resources, Software, Visualization, Writing–Original Draft Preparation, Writing–Review and Editing; **Agung Purnomo**: Conceptualization, Data Curation, Formal Analysis, Investigation, Methodology, Resources, Validation, Funding Acquisition, Project Administration, Supervision, Writing–Review and Editing.

Data Availability. **Harvard Dataverse:** "Dataset Supporting a Systematic Review on Digital Innovation in Entrepreneurship (2020–2024)", V2, https://doi.org/https://doi.org/10.7910/DVN/5JPIJ7 (Hamadah, S.A., Purnomo, A., 2025).

References

1. George, G., Merrill, R.K., Schillebeeckx, S.J.D.: Digital sustainability and entrepreneurship: how digital innovations are helping tackle climate change and sustainable development. Entrep. Theor. Pract. **45**, 999–1027 (2021). https://doi.org/10.1177/1042258719899425
2. OECD: OECD SME and Entrepreneurship Outlook 2023. In: Organisation for Economic Co-operation and Development, Paris (2023). https://doi.org/10.1787/342b8564-en
3. Purnomo, A., Septianto, A., Rosyidah, E., Ramadhani, M., Perdana, M.D.: Mapping of digital innovation research themes: a 36-year review. In: 2021 International Conference on Information Management and Technology (ICIMTech), pp. 398–403. IEEE, Jakarta (2021). https://doi.org/10.1109/ICIMTech53080.2021.9534989
4. Fink, L., Shao, J., Lichtenstein, Y., Haefliger, S.: The ownership of digital infrastructure: exploring the deployment of software libraries in a digital innovation cluster. J. Inf. Technol. **35**, 251–269 (2020). https://doi.org/10.1177/0268396220936705
5. Endres, H., Huesig, S., Pesch, R.: Digital innovation management for entrepreneurial ecosystems: services and functionalities as drivers of innovation management software adoption. Rev. Manag. Sci. **16**, 135–156 (2022). https://doi.org/10.1007/s11846-021-00441-4
6. Shaikh, A.A., Sharma, R., Karjaluoto, H.: Digital innovation & enterprise in the sharing economy: an action research agenda. Digit. Bus. **1**, 100002 (2020). https://doi.org/10.1016/j.digbus.2021.100002
7. Afia, N., et al.: Innovations in social informatic: a patent landscape review. Procedia Comput. Sci. **234**, 1228–1235 (2024). https://doi.org/10.1016/j.procs.2024.03.119

8. Colombelli, A., Paolucci, E., Raguseo, E., Elia, G.: The creation of digital innovative start-ups: the role of digital knowledge spillovers and digital skill endowment. Small Bus. Econ. **62**, 917–937 (2024). https://doi.org/10.1007/s11187-023-00789-9
9. Putri, S.I.E., Irawan, M.C.S., Ardianov, H.R., Purnomo, A., Rosyidah, E., Meiryani: Artificial intelligence in the entrepreneurship: patent landscape analysis. In: 2023 International Conference on Inventive Computation Technologies (ICICT), pp. 441–447. IEEE, Lalitpur (2023). https://doi.org/10.1109/ICICT57646.2023.10134114
10. Falter, M., Jóhannesson, G.T.: The value of digital innovation for tourism entrepreneurs in rural Iceland. Acad. Tur. **16**, 191–204 (2023). https://doi.org/10.26493/2335-4194.16.191-204
11. Antonopoulou, K., Begkos, C.: Strategizing for digital innovations: value propositions for transcending market boundaries. Technol. Forecast. Soc. Change **156**, 120042 (2020). https://doi.org/10.1016/j.techfore.2020.120042
12. Mariani, M.M., Nambisan, S.: Innovation analytics and digital innovation experimentation: the rise of research-driven online review platforms. Technol. Forecast. Soc. Change **172**, 121009 (2021). https://doi.org/10.1016/j.techfore.2021.121009
13. Purnomo, A., Asitah, N., Afia, N., Septianto, A., Rosyidah, E., Persada, S.F., Maulana, F.I.: Competitive strategy and E-business: a review. In: AIP Conference Proceedings. p. 050007. AIP Publishing, Malang (2024). https://doi.org/10.1063/5.0192361
14. Cueto, L.J., Frisnedi, A.F.D., Collera, R.B., Batac, K.I.T., Agaton, C.B.: Digital innovations in MSMEs during economic disruptions: experiences and challenges of young entrepreneurs. Adm. Sci. **12**, 8 (2022). https://doi.org/10.3390/admsci12010008
15. Soluk, J.: Organisations' resources and external shocks: exploring digital innovation in family firms. Ind. Innov. **29**, 792–824 (2022). https://doi.org/10.1080/13662716.2022.2065971
16. Goncalves, D., Bergquist, M., Bunk, R., Alänge, S.: Cultural aspects of organizational agility affecting digital innovation. J. Entrep. Manag. Innov. **16**, 13–46 (2020). https://doi.org/10.7341/20201641
17. Gumbo, E., Moos, M.: Integrating ecosystems: the synergistic effects of digital innovation hubs on start-up growth. South. African J. Entrep. Small Bus. Manag. **16**, 1–11 (2024). https://doi.org/10.4102/sajesbm.v16i1.945
18. Purbasari, R., Munajat, E., Fauzan, F.: Digital innovation ecosystem on digital entrepreneur. Int. J. E-entrepreneursh Innov. **13**, 1–21 (2023). https://doi.org/10.4018/IJEEI.319040
19. Felicetti, A.M., Corvello, V., Ammirato, S.: Digital innovation in entrepreneurial firms: a systematic literature review. Rev. Manag. Sci. **18**, 315–362 (2024). https://doi.org/10.1007/s11846-023-00638-9
20. He, K., Bouncken, R.B., Kiani, A., Kraus, S.: The role of strategic orientations for digital innovation: when entrepreneurship meets sustainability. Technol. Forecast. Soc. Change. **205**, 123503 (2024). https://doi.org/10.1016/j.techfore.2024.123503
21. Abdhala, U.A., Purnomo, A.: Web applications in entrepreneurship: a systematic review of roles and perspective for future research directions. In: Procedia Computer Science, pp. 409–418. Elsevier BV, Surabaya (2024). https://doi.org/10.1016/j.procs.2024.10.267
22. Moher, D., Liberati, A., Tetzlaff, J., Altman, D.G., Group, T.P.: Preferred reporting items for systematic reviews and meta-analyses : the PRISMA statement. PLoS Med. **6** (2009). https://doi.org/10.1371/journal.pmed.1000097
23. Burnham, J.F.: Scopus database: a review. Biomed Digit. Libr. **3**(1) (2006). https://doi.org/10.1186/1742-5581-3-1
24. Jain, N.: What is digital innovation? Definition, examples and best practices
25. Gioia, D.A., Corley, K.G., Hailton, A.L.: Seeking qualitative rigor in inductive research: notes on the Gioia methodology. Organ. Res. Methods. **16**, 15–31 (2013). https://doi.org/10.1177/1094428112452151
26. Bazeley, P.: Qualitative Data analysis: practical strategies. SAGE Publications Ltd (2013)

27. Tranfield, D., Denyer, D., Smart, P.: Towards a methodology for developing evidence-informed management knowledge by means of systematic review. Br. J. Manag. **14**, 207–222 (2003). https://doi.org/10.1111/1467-8551.00375
28. Oyinlola, M., et al.: Digital innovations for transitioning to circular plastic value chains in Africa. Africa J. Manag. **8**, 83–108 (2022). https://doi.org/10.1080/23322373.2021.1999750
29. Omorede, A.: Business in the digital age: digital innovation outcome, exit and the founder's start-up experience role. J. Int. Counc. Small Bus. **4**, 68–78 (2023). https://doi.org/10.1080/26437015.2022.2125355
30. Huang, Y., Zhang, J., Xu, Y., Bu, Y.: How can digital innovation capabilities of Chinese college students be cultivated? Int. J. Manag. Educ. **22**, 101085 (2024). https://doi.org/10.1016/j.ijme.2024.101085
31. Thapa, R.K., Iakovleva, T.: Responsible innovation in venture creation and firm development : the case of digital innovation in healthcare and welfare services. J. Responsible Innov. (2023). https://doi.org/10.1080/23299460.2023.2170624
32. Schildt, H., Lahdenranta, K., Demir, R., Turunen, T.: Waking up to digital innovation: how organisational secrecy hampers top management focus on strategic renewal. Innov. Organ. Manag. **26**, 532–558 (2024). https://doi.org/10.1080/14479338.2022.2162530
33. Pujadas, R., Valderrama, E., Venters, W.: The value and structuring role of web APIs in digital innovation ecosystems: the case of the online travel ecosystem. Res. Policy **53**, 104931 (2024). https://doi.org/10.1016/j.respol.2023.104931
34. Kreiterling, C.: Digital innovation and entrepreneurship: a review of challenges in competitive markets (2023). https://doi.org/10.1186/s13731-023-00320-0
35. Centobelli, P., Cerchione, R., Esposito, E., Passaro, R., Quinto, I.: The undigital behavior of innovative startups: empirical evidence and taxonomy of digital innovation strategies. Int. J. Entrep. Behav. Res. **28**, 219–241 (2022). https://doi.org/10.1108/IJEBR-08-2021-0626
36. Olokundun, M., Ogbari, M.E., Falola, H., Ibidunni, A.S.: Leveraging 5G network for digital innovation in small and medium enterprises: a conceptual review. J. Innov. Entrep. **11**, 41 (2022). https://doi.org/10.1186/s13731-021-00181-5

Grams of Growth, Grams of Grind: Women Entrepreneurs in Social Commerce

Munsifa Hoor(✉), Erabelli Hemanth Rao, and P. Vigneswara Ilavarasan

Department of Management Studies, Indian Institute of Technology Delhi, New Delhi 110016, India

munsifaali5@gmail.com, vignes@iitd.ac.in

Abstract. Social commerce platforms have transformed the landscape of entrepreneurship, offering new pathways for individuals, particularly women, to start and grow businesses with limited resources. In the context of emerging economies like India, Instagram has become a prominent platform where women entrepreneurs combine personal branding, digital visibility, and community engagement to establish and sustain their ventures. Despite its growing relevance, there remains limited research on how women navigate such platforms for entrepreneurial purposes. This study addresses this gap by exploring the experiences of women entrepreneurs who use Instagram as a primary business platform. Using a qualitative method, the study draws on ten in-depth, semi-structured interviews with women entrepreneurs engaged in diverse sectors. The thematic analysis revealed four key drivers: platform accessibility, autonomy and flexibility, identity expression, and community support. Alongside these enablers, the study also reveals significant challenges, including platform dependence, resource constraints, and emotional burnout. These findings highlight the dual nature of Instagram, both empowering and precarious, as a site of entrepreneurship for women.

Keywords: Digital entrepreneurship · Social commerce · Instagram · Women entrepreneurs

1 Introduction

Social commerce has rapidly transformed the way products are marketed, sold, and consumed in the digital age (Meilatinova 2021). Unlike traditional e-commerce, social commerce integrates buying and selling into everyday social interactions, allowing users to engage in both content creation and consumption (Liang and Turban 2011; Meilatinova 2021). In India, the social commerce market is expected to reach $70 billion by 2030, propelled by rising smartphone penetration, digital payment adoption, and increasing engagement with social commerce platforms (Nair 2024). According to Huang and Benyoucef (2013), to be classified as a social commerce platform, a platform should include a

Published by Springer Nature Switzerland AG 2026
A. Elbanna et al. (Eds.): TDIT 2025, IFIP AICT 778, pp. 160–168, 2026.
https://doi.org/10.1007/978-3-032-16775-0_10

minimum set of design features that collectively span four key layers: individual, conversation, community, and commerce. Instagram meets this criterion by enabling personalized identity formation and self-presentation (individual layer), supporting interactive exchanges through comments, direct messages, and story engagement (conversation layer), fostering interest-based networks and shared communities (community layer), and facilitating product discovery and transactions through integrated links (commerce layer). The integration of these four layers has made Instagram a significant platform for entrepreneurial activity, particularly among women operating small, home-based, or informal ventures. This shift is significant in the Indian context, where women continue to face structural obstacles to participating in the formal economy. Although government initiatives (such as Startup India and Stand-Up India) aim to support women-led businesses, fewer than 1% of working-age Indian women are engaged in formal business (Pandit 2025). Issues like mobility constraints, patriarchal social norms, unpaid care responsibilities, and limited access to finance continue to suppress women's economic participation (Kapoor 2024). In this environment, Instagram provides zero entry costs, direct access to consumers, and valuable brand-building opportunities, making it a viable commercial platform for women to bypass traditional market gatekeepers (Raja 2022).

On Instagram, women-led businesses now span a wide range of sectors, including fashion, wellness, regional crafts, and food. Unlike influencer-driven ventures that capitalise on personal branding, many women entrepreneurs use Instagram as a low-barrier marketplace to establish and grow their businesses (Raja 2022). However, digital entrepreneurship is not without limitations. Platform dependency, algorithmic uncertainty, and a lack of legal or financial infrastructure expose women entrepreneurs to new forms of precarity (Bishop 2023; Duffy and Hund 2021). In many cases, women operate without business licenses, formal banking, or legal protection, making their ventures vulnerable to digital disruptions and cyber harassment. Despite the growing body of research on digital entrepreneurship (Davidson and Vaast 2010; Nambisan, 2017), there is a limited understanding of how women entrepreneurs navigate Instagram as a platform for commercial purposes. This gap is particularly relevant given the growing nature of social commerce in shaping entrepreneurial pathways for women, especially among early-stage, small-scale business owners using Instagram for commercial purposes in India. Therefore, we ask, *RQ: What drives women entrepreneurs to launch businesses on Instagram, and what challenges do they face while using the platform for commercial purposes?* In the sections that follow, this paper presents a review of the literature, outlines the research methodology, discusses key findings, and presents the conclusion.

2 Literature Review

2.1 Digital Entrepreneurship

Digital entrepreneurship has emerged as a transformative mode of enterprise, characterised by the creation and management of ventures through digital technologies (Davidson and Vaast 2010). Unlike traditional entrepreneurship, which has been bound by fixed stages and localised market access, digital entrepreneurship is characterised by fluid processes, distributed agency, and dynamic value creation (Nambisan 2017). These ventures often leverage digital infrastructure as a foundational element for business model innovation, enabling entrepreneurs to bypass conventional barriers such as capital intensity, physical infrastructure, and geographic constraints (Nambisan 2017; Paul et al. 2023).

Digital platforms such as Instagram and Facebook have redefined the entrepreneurial ecosystem by embedding value creation with participatory cultures and networked publics. Such platforms offer affordances that allow users to rapidly produce and distribute content while engaging with large audiences in real-time (Djafarova and Trofimenko 2019). However, this platform-centric model collapses the boundaries between personal and professional domains. This is particularly evident on visually driven platforms like Instagram, where entrepreneurial identity is closely tied to self-presentation, lifestyle, aesthetic, and relational engagement (Colliander and Marder 2018). While digital platforms democratise access to entrepreneurial opportunities, they also impose algorithmic pressures, content fatigue, and the expectation of perpetual visibility (Bishop 2023; Cotter 2019; Duffy and Hund 2021). These pressures are particularly pronounced for women entrepreneurs, who juggle the dual expectations of affective labour and invisible domestic responsibilities. Furthermore, the informal nature of these enterprises renders them vulnerable to online abuse, hacking, and sudden platform disruptions (Duffy and Hund 2021). Nonetheless, in India, where structural and societal barriers continue to limit women's participation in formal entrepreneurship, Instagram offers a low-barrier entry point to bypass traditional gatekeepers and pursue digital ventures.

2.2 Social Commerce

Social commerce refers to the integration of social media and e-commerce, allowing users to discover, evaluate, and transact products within social networks (Liang and Turban 2011). It differs from traditional e-commerce by prioritising relational dynamics (such as trust, social proof, and peer validation) over formal infrastructure (Liang and Turban 2011; Meilatinova 2021). Platforms like Instagram function as a transactional interface where entrepreneurs can convert social engagement into sales through direct messaging, story links, or integrated shop features. This model supports decentralised economic activity by blurring the lines between marketing, selling, and socialising (Colliander and Marder 2018). By using familiar social tools to promote products and cultivate buyer relationships, entrepreneurs can build trust without access to traditional advertising.

Unlike traditional e-commerce platforms such as Amazon or Flipkart, which often require product registration, packing standards, and listing fees, Instagram imposes no direct charges from business owners (Carah and Shaul 2016). Businesses can showcase their products, interact with potential buyers, and complete transactions without incurring platform-related costs. This lack of commercial gatekeeping is especially significant for home-based sellers and first-time entrepreneurs who may lack the capital or awareness needed to participate in formal digital markets (Devereux et al. 2020). In a setting like India, where women often operate under resource constraints and informal work conditions, the ability to initiate a business without incurring platform fees or navigating bureaucratic hurdles represents a crucial enabler of economic participation (Kapoor 2024). However, this informality also means that sellers do not receive the logistical, legal, or dispute resolution support typically provided by regulated e-commerce platforms. Therefore, it is important to understand what drives women entrepreneurs to engage in commerce on Instagram and the challenges they face along the way.

3 Methodology

A qualitative inductive approach was employed (Elbanna and Idowu 2022) to examine how women entrepreneurs navigate Instagram for commercial purposes. Data collection was carried out through semi-structured, in-depth interviews with ten women entrepreneurs operating across varied geographical regions in India and engaged in diverse domains such as fashion, skincare, and handicrafts (refer to Table 1). An interview protocol was developed in advance, with provisions for flexibility and improvisation (Myers and Newman 2007) to allow participants to articulate their experiences. Participants were contacted via direct messages on Instagram. Interview, each lasting between 20 and 25 min, were conducted via telephone or video conferencing platform Zoom, depending on participants accessibility and preference. Conversations were conducted in both English and Hindi. The interviews were undertaken between February and March 2025. Prior to participation, informed consent was obtained for both the interview process and audio recording. All interviews were transcribed verbatim, and participant anonymity was assured throughout the research process. Data were analysed using thematic analysis (Braun and Clarke 2006), which facilitated the identification, interpretation, and categorisation of key patterns across the dataset. For example, the quotes highlighting the participants *'ease of doing business'* and *'flexible working hours'* were classified under the second-order theme of *autonomy and flexibility,* which in turn falls within the aggregate theme that is drivers.

Table 1. Participants details

Participants	Age (years)	Educational background	Business category
P1	25	Graduate (fine arts)	Handicrafts
P2	32	Post-graduate (commerce)	Personalised footwears
P3	24	Post-graduate (MBA)	Handicrafts
P4	38	Graduate (fine arts)	Fashion
P5	25	Graduate (commerce)	Fashion
P6	27	Graduate (fashion design)	Handicrafts
P7	30	Graduate (B.Tech)	Fashion
P8	35	Post-graduate (MBA)	Beauty and personal care
P9	28	Graduate (computer science)	Beauty and personal care
P10	27	Graduate (botany)	Beauty and personal care

4 Findings

We analysed the data to explore how women entrepreneurs leverage Instagram for commercial purposes. The analysis revealed a range of drivers that motivate their engagement with the platform, as well as challenges that hinder their sustained entrepreneurial efforts. The key themes, grouped under drivers and challenges, are discussed below.

4.1 Drivers

4.1.1 Platform Accessibility

Platform accessibility refers to the ease with which entrepreneurs are able to initiate, operate, and grow their businesses using Instagram. This includes low financial barriers, intuitive platform design, mobile compatibility, and a ready-made audience for content and commerce. For many women entrepreneurs, Instagram offers a uniquely accessible entry point into business ownership. Participants consistently emphasized how the platform's low cost, intuitive features, and immediate market reach enabled them to launch ventures without prior technical expertise or large capital investment. For instance;

> *"Instagram is a free, visual platform that helped me reach people I never thought I could. I didn't need to spend money on a shop; my phone is enough to get started." (P3)*
>
> *"I'm not tech-savvy, but Instagram's tools are very visual and straightforward. It allowed me to learn and sell at the same time". (P8)*

4.1.2 Autonomy and Flexibility

Autonomy and flexibility refer to the control women gain over their time, work decisions, and business operations by using Instagram as a platform. It reflects how Instagram enables them to align their business with personal routines, creative freedom, and evolving life circumstances without the constraint of traditional work structures. Participants described Instagram as a space that gave them personal and professional freedom. They emphasized the ability to choose their hours, content style, and pace of growth, whether they were students, full-time workers, or transitioning from other roles. This self-direction was seen as both empowering and practical. To quote;

> *"What I love most is that I can shape my day around my business, not the other way around. I'm not stuck to a fixed routine, if I want to take a break or push harder, its completely up to me" (P9)*
>
> *"I'm a full-time student, so I needed something that could fix around my classes and exams. Instagram gave me the flexibility to post, reply, and manage everything without compromising my studies" (P10)*

4.1.3 Identity Expression

Identity expression refers to how women entrepreneurs use Instagram to reflect and communicate their personal values, aesthetics, and narratives through business presence.

It captures the way branding becomes intertwined with individual identity, allowing for authenticity and emotional connection with audiences. Many participants described Instagram not only as a business platform, but also as a space for personal and creative self-expression. Through curated aesthetics, personal narratives, and brand storytelling, they conveyed aspects of their personality, background, and beliefs. This expression often evolved naturally as participants became more confident and comfortable sharing parts of themselves online. Most participants noted that their audience responded more positively when their content felt "real" or "relatable". To quote;

> *"I run a business, but I also use my page to share who I am. Sharing that personal side is what truly makes people connect and trust what I do". (P2)*
>
> *"My page is basically me in visual form. It's my personality, my mood, my voice, all in one space" (P7)*

4.1.4 Community Support

Community support refers to the encouragement, emotional backing, shared knowledge, and mutual promotion women entrepreneurs receive from their Instagram followers, peers, and fellow business owners. It captures how social interactions on the platform go beyond transactions to create a sense of belonging and informal networked mentorship. Several participants emphasized that one of the most motivating aspects of using Instagram was the community that formed around their business. Support came in various forms: likes, comments, shares, direct messages, and even customer referrals. Participants often described how this sense of belongingness encouraged consistency and kept them emotionally invested in their work. To quote;

> *"Even a small comment or repost from someone I look up to can be enough to lift my mood and push me to keep going." (P5).*
>
> *"There are days I feel stuck, and then I read a comment from a customer saying they love my product, it changes everything." (P8)*

4.2 Challenges

4.2.1 Platform Dependence

Platform dependence refers to the reliance of entrepreneurs on Instagram as their primary or sole business platform, making them vulnerable to disruptions beyond their control such as algorithm shifts, outages, and account hacking. While Instagram offers visibility and reach, this dependence introduces risks that directly impact business continuity and user trust. Participants expressed concern regarding how changes in Instagram's algorithm, technical glitches, and platform updates directly impacted their engagement and sales. The unpredictability of such shifts created stress and uncertainty, requiring constant adaptation to stay visible and relevant. To quote;

"My account was hacked and I couldn't access it for almost a week. It felt like someone broke into my shop. Ahh, it was really stressful." (P3).

"Meta's algorithm is a 'black box'. No matter how much you kind of try to target your audience, you never sure that whether your ad is shown to the right audience..." (P7)

4.2.2 Resource Constraints

Resource constraints refer to the limitations in access to financial, technical, human and temporal resources that restrict the operational capacity and growth potential of women-led businesses on Instagram. These constraints shape how entrepreneurs manage their ventures, engage with audiences, and sustain their visibility in a highly competitive and fast-paced digital environment. Participants talked about the multifaceted resource constraints they encountered while managing their Instagram-based businesses. Many shared that they operated with minimal startup capital, often relying on personal savings, free tools, and self-guided learning to sustain their ventures. These limitations affected their ability to invest in paid promotions, outsource tasks, or produce consistently high-quality content. To quote;

"I do everything on my own... taking photos, replying to DMs, and even packing orders. It's overwhelming, but I can't afford a team at the moment." (P4)

"I know ads help, but I don't have the budget for regular paid promotions. I have to rely on organic reach and word-of-mouth, which takes time." (P9)

4.2.3 Emotional Burnout

Emotional burnout refers to the mental and emotional exhaustion experienced by entrepreneurs as they navigate the pressures of building a business with limited support and constant digital demands. On instagram, it captures the toll of constant engagement, the pressure to maintain visibility, and the emotional labour of managing customer interactions, content production, and business growth often without breaks or boundaries. Participants described feeling overwhelmed by the need to be present, with no clear separation between personal time and business activity. The pressure to appear consistently positive, creative, and responsive on a platform that rewards visibility often left them feeling drained and depleted. To quote;

"People think it's easy because it's online, but it's exhausting. You have to show up constantly, and that takes a toll emotionally." (P1)

"I didn't expect it to be so mentally draining. Every day there's pressure to create something, to be seen, to keep up." (P8)

Therefore, these findings highlight how Instagram functions as both a catalyst and a constraint for women entrepreneurs. While it enables accessibility, autonomy, self-expression, and community support, it also presents challenges like platform dependence, limited resources, and emotional burnout, revealing the dual nature of digital entrepreneurship.

5 Discussion and Conclusion

This study investigates how women entrepreneurs in India leverage Instagram for commercial purposes. Building on the literature of digital entrepreneurship and social commerce, the findings show that Instagram functions simultaneously as a marketplace, a marketing tool, and a community hub. The identified drivers like platform accessibility, autonomy and flexibility, identity expression, and community support shows how social commerce platforms expand the scope of digital entrepreneurship by embedding transactional opportunities within everyday social interactions. Platform accessibility reduces entry barriers by eliminating financial and procedural constraints. Autonomy and flexibility enable entrepreneurs to manage ventures alongside other responsibilities. Identity expression allows for brand differentiation through curated visual content, while community support strengthens trust and customer loyalty through peer networks and audience engagement.

Conversely, the challenges of platform dependence, resource constraints, and emotional burnout reveal the hidden costs of this integration. Platform dependence leaves entrepreneurs vulnerable to algorithm and policy changes, while resource constraints limit their ability to maintain consistent and competitive content production. Emotional burnout reflects the intensification of entrepreneurial labour, as constant visibility and engagement become essential for sustaining customer relationships and driving sales. As a research-in-progress study, these findings provide a foundation for further exploration into the evolving dynamics of women-led digital entrepreneurship in the social commerce landscape.

Disclosure of Interests. The authors have no competing interests to declare that are relevant to the content of this article.

References

Bishop, S.: Influencer creep: how artists strategically navigate the platformisation of art worlds. New Media Soc. **27**(4), 2109–2126 (2023)

Braun, V., Clarke, V.: Using thematic analysis in psychology. Qual. Res. Psychol. **3**(2), 77–101 (2006)

Carah, N., Shaul, M.: Brands and Instagram: point, tap, swipe, glance. Mobile Media Commun. **4**(1), 69–84 (2016)

Colliander, J., Marder, B.: Snap happy' brands: increasing publicity effectiveness through a snapshot aesthetic when marketing a brand on Instagram. Comput. Hum. Behav. **78**, 34–43 (2018)

Cotter, K.: Playing the visibility game: how digital influencers and algorithms negotiate influence on Instagram. New Media Soc. **21**(4), 895–913 (2019)

Davidson, E., Vaast, E.: Digital entrepreneurship and its sociomaterial enactment. In: 43rd Hawaii International Conference on System Sciences, pp. 1–10. IEEE (2010)

Devereux, E., Grimmer, L., Grimmer, M.: Consumer engagement on social media: evidence from small retailers. J. Consum. Behav. **19**(2), 151–159 (2020)

Djafarova, E., Trofimenko, O.: 'Instafamous'–credibility and self-presentation of micro-celebrities on social media. Inf. Commun. Soc. **22**(10), 1432–1446 (2019)

Duffy, B.E., Hund, E.: Gendered visibility on social media: navigating Instagram's authenticity bind. Int. J. Commun. **13**, 20 (2021)

Elbanna, A., Idowu, A.: Crowdwork, digital liminality and the enactment of culturally recognised alternatives to Western precarity: beyond epistemological terra nullius. Eur. J. Inf. Syst. **31**(1), 128–144 (2022)

Huang, Z., Benyoucef, M.: From e-commerce to social commerce: a close look at design features. Electron. Commer. Res. Appl. **12**(4), 246–259 (2013)

Kapoor, R.: Leveraging Digital Technologies to Foster Growth-Oriented Women Entrepreneurship in India. Indian Council for Research on International Economic Relations (2024) https://icrier.org/publications/leveraging-digital-technologies-to-foster-growth-oriented-women-entrepreneurship-in-india/#:~:text=In%20this%20policy%20brief%2C%20we,the%20potential%20of%20women%20entrepreneurship. Accessed 9 June 2025

Liang, T.P., Turban, E.: Introduction to the special issue social commerce: a research framework for social commerce. Int. J. Electron. Commer. **16**(2), 5–14 (2011)

Meilatinova, N.: Social commerce: factors affecting customer repurchase and word-of-mouth intentions. Int. J. Inf. Manage. **57**, 102300 (2021)

Myers, M.D., Newman, M.: The qualitative interview in IS research: examining the craft. Inf. Organ. **17**(1), 2–26 (2007)

Nair, G.: From $2 Billion to $70 Billion: The Surge of Social Commerce. Financial Express (2024). https://www.financialexpress.com/business/brandwagon/from-2-billion-to-70-billion-the-surge-of-social-commerce/3590525/. Accessed 15 June 2025

Nambisan, S.: Digital entrepreneurship: toward a digital technology perspective of entrepreneurship. Entrep.: Theory Pract. **41**(6), 1029–1055 (2017)

Pandit, A.: 'With < 1% Women Being Entrepreneurs, India Far Below Global Trendline'. The Times of India (2025). https://timesofindia.indiatimes.com/india/with-lt1-women-being-entrepreneurs-india-far-below-global-trendline/articleshow/122137634.cms. Accessed 15 June 2025

Paul, J., Alhassan, I., Binsaif, N., Singh, P.: Digital entrepreneurship research: a systematic review. J. Bus. Res. **156**, 113507 (2023)

Raja, V.: MOM Designs, Daughters' Model: How We Built a Rs 15 CR Fashion Brand Using Instagram. The Better India (2022). https://www.thebetterindia.com/278328/indian-instagram-startup-by-mother-daughter-women-entrepreneurs-earns-crores/. Accessed 20 June 2025

A Perspective on the Adoption of Agentic AI in Higher Education Institutions: Strategic Opportunities and Institutional Challenges

Yousuf Saif Al-Hinai[1], Ali Tarhini[1(✉)], Mohammad Al-Sharafi[2], and Waqas Aman[1]

[1] Department of Information Systems, Sultan Qaboos University, Muscat, Oman
ali.tarhini@hotmail.co.uk

[2] King Fahd University of Petroleum and Minerals, Dhahran, Saudi Arabia

Abstract. As artificial intelligence evolves beyond passive tools into autonomous agents, higher education institutions (HEIs) stand at the edge of a new paradigm: Agentic AI. This perspective paper explores the transformative potential of this nascent, yet powerful, class of AI systems capable of autonomous decision-making, goal pursuit, and contextual adaptation. This paper contrasts Agentic AI with Generative AI, clarifying the critical distinction often missed in public discourse. The paper outlines five strategic opportunities that Agentic AI offers to HEIs, from redefining strategic planning and policy-making to transforming teaching, learning, scientific research, and administrative operations. Then, it examines institutional challenges to adoption, including ethical ambiguity, trust deficits, infrastructural limitations, and resistance to change. After that, the paper proposes practical, value-driven strategic pathways to achieve responsible, successful Agentic AI adoption. This paper aims beyond information to guide HEI leaders, technologists, faculty, and researchers in navigating the complex landscape of Agentic AI by providing conceptual clarity, strategic insights, and a call for interdisciplinary collaboration in transforming higher education.

Keywords: Agentic AI · AI agents · Multi-agent systems · Higher education innovation · Autonomous systems in education · Human-AI collaboration · Agentic AI adoption

1 Introduction

What if the strategic planning at your university is not carried out by humans anymore, but by intelligent autonomous systems? Systems that do not wait for instructions. Instead, they would go through institutional data, anticipate accreditation risks, and identify curriculum gaps. Systems that would go even further and report those findings to the university's academic council.

This is the emerging reality of Agentic AI systems. These are goal-oriented, proactive, and autonomous systems. In addition, Agentic AI systems are contextually aware

Published by Springer Nature Switzerland AG 2026
A. Elbanna et al. (Eds.): TDIT 2025, IFIP AICT 778, pp. 169–182, 2026.
https://doi.org/10.1007/978-3-032-16775-0_11

of changes that occur in data or situations. Therefore, they can make real-time decisions to adapt and adjust to meet the goals they are attaining.

As Agentic AI continues to evolve, it challenges us to explore how it might revolutionize different roles in value-laden domains that are dynamic and complex, such as higher education institutions (HEIs). Despite the potential challenges, Agentic AI is promising strategic opportunities for such domains.

This perspective paper aims to explore the strategic opportunities of Agentic AI for HEIs, as well as the institutional challenges and future research agenda, particularly in the context of adoption, integration, and governance. HEIs operate between the dimensions of innovation and tradition, which positions them for the benefit of and struggle with the adoption of Agentic AI. Unlike existing educational technologies, Agentic AI has the potential to significantly influence strategic planning, policy-making, academic governance, and institutional identity. This is due to its autonomous intelligence to envision futures, shape decisions, and reimagine the foundations of how HEIs understand and pursue their mission.

By exploring the emerging developments in the field of Agentic AI, this paper serves as a timely and critical lens of Agentic AI in the higher education domain. Then, the paper contrasts Agentic AI with other related technologies, such as AI agents and Generative AI (GenAI). Additionally, the paper examines the strategic potential, institutional challenges, and the strategic pathways towards responsible adoption in HEIs. Finally, the paper outlines the future research agenda in the field, which contributes to both the theoretical and practical approaches to this rapidly growing technology.

This paper adopts a narrative conceptual perspective, drawing on recent scholarly literature and strategic foresight to explore the implications of Agentic AI in HEIs. We followed a structured literature selection approach, using Web of Science and Scopus to identify sources based on recency, citation impact, author credibility, and relevance to the paper's structure. The selection was refined throughout the writing process, with new relevant sources integrated as they emerged. While not systematic in the formal sense, this method ensured conceptual depth, thematic alignment, and inclusion of influential scholarly work.

2 Generative AI Versus AI Agents and Agentic AI

The rapid adoption of Generative AI tools has created waves of excitement among users across different domains. Within a few months, this enthusiasm gave rise to conceptual confusion, particularly as a nascent new technology began to emerge: Agentic AI. GenAI and Agentic AI are often used interchangeably, although they refer to fundamentally different technologies with different capabilities, implications, and risks.

This conflation is more than a semantic issue; it can lead to flawed institutional strategies, poor decision-making, and misplaced investments. Without a clear understanding of each technology's capabilities and limitations, decision makers in HEIs risk making misinformed choices and overlooking important ethical and strategic implications.

2.1 Generative AI

AI (GenAI) is capable of generating different types of content [8], such as text, audio, images, and video, upon users' prompts, which are requests submitted in natural human language [24]. The prompt is submitted with a single click, but behind that click lies a complex cascade.

The prompt is submitted to a language model, which can be a Large Language Model (LLM) or, sometimes, a Small Language Model (SLM) [34]. Then the prompt is divided into smaller parts, such as words or sub-words, called tokens. The tokens are then transformed into numerical representations called embeddings. The embeddings are crucial to help the model recognize patterns that match the data it has been trained on. This takes place during the core processing phase, known as inference, that is concluded by generating contextually meaningful responses [7, 33]. Finally, the resulting tokens are reassembled into the requested form and presented to the user. The output of interacting with GenAI systems is always a generation of content in certain forms. Figure 1 illustrates the process at a high level.

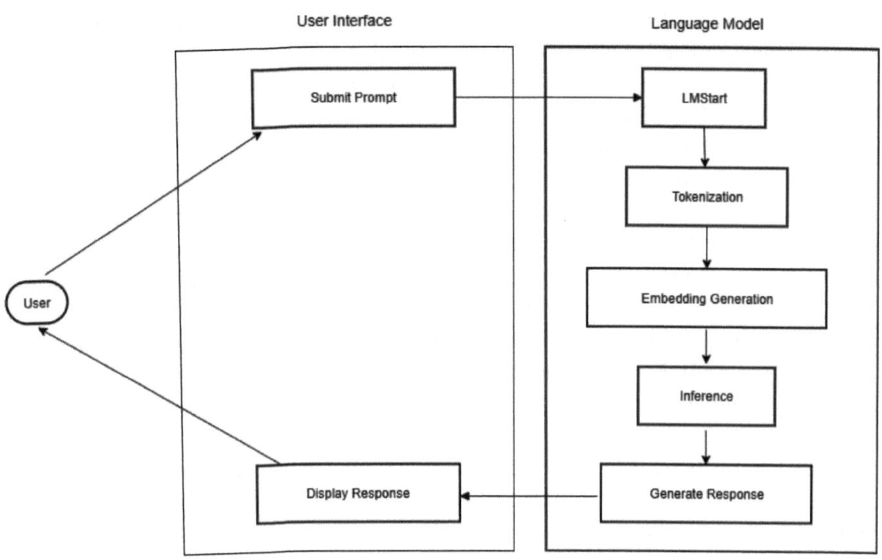

Fig. 1. Flow of prompt processing in a GenAI system.

Despite the significant impact it has brought to many domains, GenAI has a number of inherent limitations. Among these, this paragraph highlights three key limitations. First, GenAI lacks the autonomy to work independently without the user-submitted instructions in the prompts [16]. Thus, GenAI is not capable of adapting to dynamic environments with changing requirements without human interference [9]. It is typically task-oriented and reactive. Second, while GenAI is capable of generating different types of content in virtual settings, it remains confined in virtual environments, and its output does not directly integrate with the physical world [13]. Due to its inability to interact with the external world, the quality of GenAI's output is restricted to the data it has been trained on, which limits its ability to suggest real-world decisions and solutions [34]. Third, GenAI's primary goal is to create content, rather than pursuing goals and achieving them [28].

2.2 AI Agents and Agentic AI

Terms like "autonomous agents" and "intelligent agents" have been widely used since 1995 to describe AI systems that are capable of working independently. Although the term "AI Agents" gained significant traction in 2023, it was also used in research dating back to 1998, where characteristics such as autonomy and goal orientation were examined from a cognitive perspective [11].

AI Agents do not require user input to start working. Instead, they identify and pursue pre-set or user-defined goals [15]. An AI Agent identifies the goals through its goal translation component [11] or its LLM-powered [16] core reasoning engine [25]. After that, the AI Agent devises strategies for decision-making [3]. Using different interfaces, the AI Agents connect to other systems and data sources. AI Agents connect to data sources in many ways, including application programming interfaces (APIs), databases, and online searches [20]. They might also be connected to internal knowledge bases [18] or external knowledge sources using Retrieval-Augmented Generation (RAG) [30]. If required, AI Agents can extract geometric and spatial information through Building Information Modeling (BIM) tools [12]. Figure 2 shows the operational flow of an AI agent from goal processing to action execution.

Through continuous learning, AI Agents are capable of determining the correctness of the decisions they make. After evaluation, if a decision does not prove to be a correct decision, then the AI Agents work again to find the correct one. However, even if a decision is correct, the output decisions and actions will be under continuous monitoring to ensure they remain correct and valid under different scenarios and situations. This stems from an AI agent's ability to self-critique its output, generate feedback, and iteratively refine its output until the goal is achieved [7]. This allows the AI Agents to adapt their strategies dynamically [21, 30].

An AI tool or system can be described as an AI Agent if it is goal-oriented, autonomous, proactive, capable of interacting with its environment and tools, and capable of continuously learning and adapting [14]. This set of characteristics is what makes Agentic AI. Agentic AI can manifest in the form of a single AI Agent or as multiple agents working together to achieve the same goals, forming a Multi-Agent System (MAS) [1]. MASs are ideal for situations where goals are complex and a task is better attended when segmented into multiple smaller tasks assigned to multiple agents [6]. In such architecture, a coordination layer ensures that each autonomous agent aligns with the overall goals of the MAS and collaborates with others, even when handling separate tasks [14, 26, 27].

Language models are also an essential part of AI Agents. They play a key role in perception and input processing as well as in gathering and processing data from various sources. Reasoning is a core function where LLMs serve as the central reasoning engine. They enable the agent to understand user goals, develop multi-step plans, and orchestrate specialized AI models [25]. In addition, language models decide when and how to use the external tools that an AI Agent connects to through APIs to execute actions, such as

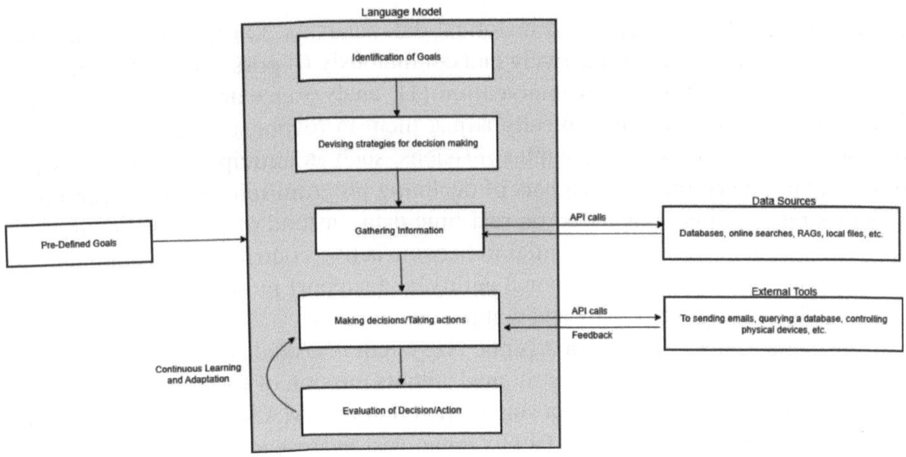

Fig. 2. Operational flow of an AI agent.

querying databases, sending emails, accessing file systems, or even controlling physical devices [16]. Furthermore, language models facilitate other fundamental processes, such as the retrieval of relevant data from different data sources [25], facilitating human-AI collaboration [30], enhancing decision-making [32], and for adaptability and continuous learning [9].

3 Strategic Opportunities for HEIs

Agentic AI is not just another technology. Agentic AI is becoming a strategic asset and is promising to make a paradigm shift. Unlike conventional digital tools that accomplish predefined tasks, Agentic AI introduces autonomous systems capable of setting sub-goals, initiating actions, and adapting to dynamic institutional contexts with minimal human intervention. This opens a new horizon of possibilities for HEIs, where AI is not only an assistant but a contributor to institutional vision and foresight. Agentic AI systems offer to operate as active agents in shaping the strategic, operational, academic, and administrative outcomes. Thus, these systems invite HEIs to rethink the strategic possibilities, rather than merely accelerating existing functions. In a time of growing complexity in higher education, the ability to adopt systems that think and act toward institutional goals presents a competitive advantage. Given the emergent nature of Agentic AI, the use cases presented in this paper are intended to be illustrative and serve as speculative foresight, rather than empirical claims. They aim to pave the way for deeper institutional reflection and encourage future empirical validation studies. Following, we explore key strategic opportunities where Agentic AI could offer transformative value to HEIs.

3.1 Institutional Foresight and Strategic Planning

One transformative opportunity that Agentic AI offers lies in the domain of strategic planning and foresight. Traditional approaches to strategic planning involve periodic reviews, human deliberations, and historical data analysis. On the other hand, Agentic AI systems can operate proactively and continuously to pursue complex, multi-goal scenarios with minimal human intervention [1], analyzing extensive datasets to create customized plans and dynamically adjust them in response to changes [5]. Thus, Agentic AI could accomplish complex missions, such as anticipating shifts in student demographics, detecting early signals of declining program relevance, or recommending new strategic directions based on real-time data. Instead of just serving as passive tools, these systems have the potential to become active contributors to augment long-term visioning, strengthen institutional agility, and support more proactive governance in such an increasingly complex and competitive domain.

Consider a scenario where an Agentic AI system is tasked with ensuring that institutional activities at a university are aligned with its mission of fostering innovation and community impact. Whether it is a single AI Agent or a MAS, it could autonomously scan local institutional documents, faculty initiatives, and research outputs to accomplish this mission. During this environmental scanning, the same system could also analyze other universities' strategies, funding shifts, and global academic trends. The systems could then report the emerging opportunities and threats to the university's leadership. Moreover, when strategic goals are being defined, Agentic AI systems are capable of simulating the long-term effects of, for instance, investing in new academic programs, international collaborations, or sustainability initiatives. Consequently, Agentic AI can become an active contributor to strategic institutional vision that ensures strategy is adaptive, forward-looking, and continuously aligned with the institution's vision and evolving identity.

3.2 Policy Optimization and Decision-Making

Policy-making and decision-making in HEIs are often complex, fragmented, multidimensional, iterative, and time-consuming processes. Agentic AI offers the potential to significantly transform both processes using its capabilities of autonomous analysis and contextual adaptation to achieve real-time policy refinement. Agentic AI's capabilities can be utilized to monitor institutional operations, compare them against the institutional policies and the external compliance frameworks, and thus flag inconsistencies and detect emerging risks. This helps HEIs achieve AI-augmented governance and ongoing compliance monitoring [10], instead of relying on periodical reviews. Agentic AI can significantly contribute to the decision-making process by generating predictive models, simulating policy outcomes, and suggesting optimized paths [2, 9], considering the competing goals and constraints. In addition, MASs are capable of solving complex problems [15, 17, 16] that, for instance, involve different institutional units, such as finance, academic affairs, and quality assurance. AI Agents within a MAS can coordinate to address complex interdependent challenges, such as a declining retention rate or budget shortfalls. Agentic AI could transform the decision-making and policy optimization processes from linear, siloed practice into more dynamic, collaborative, and data-enriched processes. This will enhance the HEIs governance and compliance efforts, empower them to respond swiftly, and act with greater strategic accuracy.

3.3 Operational Efficiency and Resource Allocation

Institutional functions within HEIs often operate in complex workflows, such as admissions and scheduling different tasks to facilitate management and administrative coordination. Typically, these processes are fragmented across departments, personnel-dependent supervision, and are subject to various forms of inefficiencies. Agentic AI has the potential to transform this by automating routine operations, streamlining cross-functional workflows, and optimizing the allocation of physical and human resources.

Traditional automation tools typically follow static rules. In contrast, Agentic AI systems are initiative and act autonomously, empowering them to identify bottlenecks, adapt processes in real-time, and execute corrective actions with no or minimal human intervention. Agentic AI is capable of optimizing complex administrative tasks [19] such as adjusting course timetables considering student preferences and faculty availability, re-allocating budgets after unexpected expenditures, or managing project [10] timelines by anticipating delays and redistributing tasks.

An agentic AI system could also enable better asset management [10] by tracking usage patterns of physical resources and infrastructure and suggesting data-driven maintenance or repurposing strategies. Furthermore, these systems can enhance organizational productivity by democratizing access to expertise [17], offering AI-powered tools to support staff, cutting costs [16, 22], and reducing the workload on overextended teams. By continuously learning from patterns and outcomes, Agentic AI can contribute to more efficient resource distribution, responsive services, and leaner institutional operations.

3.4 Advancing Teaching, Learning, and Student Support

Agentic AI holds the potential to profoundly transform the educational experience in HEIs. It can enable adaptive personalization of teaching, learning, and student support services. Agentic AI systems can autonomously customize educational interactions [1, 23] to meet evolving learner needs, cognitive patterns, and contextual factors. These systems can adapt educational content, pace, and assessment methods to suit individual student profiles, thus enhancing engagement and learning outcomes, especially in complex domains [23]. This same capability can also be employed for configuring AI Agents to reflect the teachers' styles and preferences [23] in instructional style, knowledge, and pedagogical values. Furthermore, Agentic AI can generate and refine instructional materials, simulate problem-solving scenarios, and offer real-time feedback through continuous improvement iterations. This can significantly contribute to improving students' mastery in challenging subject areas.

In other domains, it has been proven that Agentic AI is capable of delivering personalized advice [5]. This capacity can be employed to provide customized academic guidance, course recommendations, and study strategies that align with each student's academic goals and learning style. This will help achieve effective student advising, which is a cornerstone of a successful learning experience. Additionally, agentic AI systems can act as co-designers of content, automators of repetitive tasks, and facilitators of student engagement, reducing the administrative burden on faculty, extending the reach of academic support, and democratizing students' access to a high-quality learning experience.

3.5 Scientific Research and Innovation

In the higher education domain, the research function is undergoing a fundamental transformation. This is in part driven by the emergence of Agentic AI. Agentic AI systems integrate machine learning, real-time data processing, and adaptive algorithms [30]. This makes them highly equipped to handle complexity, uncertainty, and scale of a modern scientific inquiry. Due to their ability to continuously analyze large datasets, adapt methodologies, and identify patterns, Agentic AI systems can support advanced forms of causal reasoning and conceptual exploration [7, 30].

A remarkable example is Google's AI Co-Scientist, which employs a "generate, debate, and evolve" approach to autonomously create and iteratively refine hypotheses. This system, inspired by the scientific method, simulates peer critique, tests ideas, and improves its proposal by implementing a self-correcting loop. This will substantially contribute to accelerating and automating hypothesis generation and validation at an unprecedented pace [7]. The literature review process is being transformed with the deep research tools [31] by simplifying, updating, and enhancing the conventional approaches to gather and synthesize scholarly work.

These tools, integrated with Agentic AI systems, enable creating dynamic, automated reviews [31] that update in real-time as new studies emerge, ensuring scholars are always informed. Agentic AI systems' capabilities to conduct automated gap analyses with 83% precision compared to human experts and to detect plagiarism patterns at a conceptual level contribute to offering more rigorous intellectual quality control than traditional static software tools [31]. Agentic AI's ability to automate entire workflows [11] makes it capable of managing the submission process, initial manuscript checks, and even the coordination of the peer review processes.

As these systems continue to advance, the role of human researchers will shift from information aggregators to validation architects, conceptual innovators, and ethical stewards [31]. They have the potential to decrease review cycle times by as much as 60% through iterative drafting and self-correction [11], promising to shorten academic publishing cycles [31]. For HEIs, embracing Agentic AI systems might be the path to expand their research capacities, enhancing interdisciplinary exploration, and to become at the forefront of the global innovation ecosystems.

4 Institutional Challenges

For a business enterprise that may prioritize agility and innovation, the adoption of an emerging technology like Agentic AI could be a manageable mission. However, adoption could be far from straightforward for HEIs that operate within frameworks of deliberation, accountability, and shared governance. It is plausible from HEIs perspectives that introducing autonomous systems that can make decisions, initiate actions, or even shape the institutional directions challenges the fundamental academic values, as well as the operational functions. Furthermore, the adoption of Agentic AI raises concerns that go beyond technical feasibility. HEIs will have to deal with ethical ambiguity, trust concerns, organizational resistance, and systemic capacity constraints. These could be major barriers that must be examined and addressed to responsibly integrate Agentic AI into HEIs.

4.1 Ethical Ambiguities and Responsibility Gaps

The adoption of Agentic AI in HEIs raises urgent ethical questions, in particular around responsibility, fairness, and transparency. Agentic AI's autonomy is a double-edged feature, making it unclear who is to be held accountable when these autonomous systems make flawed or harmful decisions [10, 21, 25], such as misidentifying a student's academic needs, generating biased admissions recommendations, or misallocating institutional resources. This creates responsibility and accountability gaps [25] that can undermine the public's trust in Agentic AI tools and, even worse, the institution itself.

Other stressing issues are the concerns about algorithmic bias and the opacity of reasoning. Although these systems operate on large-scale, real-time data, their internal decision-making mechanisms remain ambiguous and inaccessible to the public, forming what is known as the black box dilemma [1, 9, 11, 25]. This raises concerns about how well these systems align with the organizational values at HEIs, such as fairness, academic freedom, and equity. The consequences of these risks become more serious in contexts such as student profiling or academic advising, where the impact of opaque or biased decisions on individuals can be long-term.

Furthermore, there are few, or no, established policies that define boundaries, auditing standards, or accountability frameworks for agentic behavior in HEI settings [3, 29].

4.2 Resistance to Organizational Change

The adoption of Agentic AI in HEIs is likely to be faced by significant organizational resistance, originating from cultural concerns, structural rigidity, and perceived threats to professional roles. One prominent concern is the potential loss or downgrading of jobs, particularly among administrative staff and some academic personnel. Recent surveys show that 45% of employees express concern about job insecurity due to AI technologies, and 33% consider them more threatening than helpful [19]. The deployment of Agentic AI systems in HEIs, as well as in other sectors, is likely to provoke immediate resistance. These concerns are amplified by the disruptive nature of Agentic AI, which transforms traditional work models and automates multifaceted tasks. Institutional rigidity, or at least inflexibility, also complicates implementation.

Forms of institutional inflexibility include outdated governance frameworks, compartmentalized departments, and legacy IT systems [10]. These inflexible structures are a significant barrier to the rapid evolution of AI technologies, and often disconnect innovation timelines and the institutional readiness to embrace change [10, 19]. Another reason that could feed the resistance to adopting Agentic AI is that the move toward human-machine collaboration brings discomfort with changing responsibilities, unclear decision-making authority, and unfamiliar modes of accountability [11, 15]. Without effective change strategies, transparent dialogue, and ethical foresight, the adoption of Agentic AI may encounter resistance, rejection, and workflow disruption.

4.3 Trust Deficits

Due to Agentic AI's autonomy, goal-driven behavior, and lack of consistent human oversight, the deficits of trust in the technology constitute a fundamental challenge [1].

Unlike traditional or rule-based systems, Agentic AI can act independently, learn in real time, and might produce unpredictable outputs, which makes its behavior difficult to predict or replicate [4]. This unpredictability, combined with the "black box" nature of its decision-making processes, complicates the efforts to trace, comprehend, or audit its actions [9, 19, 25]. Therefore, it is unclear who should be held accountable for unintended consequences, which leads to discomfort and hesitation at the institutional level [21, 25].

In higher education, where values such as academic freedom, transparency, and scholarly rigor are vital, these uncertainties become even more evident [31]. Both faculty and administrators may question the validity of decisions made, actions taken, and insights generated by Agentic AI, especially when these outputs lack clarity, misattribute sources, or reflect algorithmic biases [9, 31]. Concerns also extend to the potential misuse of AI Agents, including vulnerabilities to prompt injection attacks, data manipulation, or hidden misalignments with institutional misalignments with the organizational goals [1, 9] of HEIs.

Absence of trust in Agentic AI might manifest in practice as resistance from faculty and administrators to accept Agentic AI's outputs, leadership's reluctance to integrate Agentic AI into strategic planning, and a tendency to limit the use of Agentic AI to minor-impact applications [13, 31].

The trust deficit is not a result of the Agentic AI's technical shortcomings, but also a result of the deeper cultural and epistemic discomfort resulting from the perception of relinquishing human authority to autonomous systems in contexts where integrity and accountability are crucial [9, 21, 25].

4.4 Infrastructure, Talent, and Capacity Constraints

The integration of Agentic AI into HEIs is hindered by different infrastructural, human capital, and operational challenges. Most institutions lack the in-house expertise required to build, deploy, and manage these advanced systems, leading to dependence on external vendors and consultants [10, 20, 28]. This reliance might result in critical sustainability and security risks, especially when proprietary systems lack transparency or are vulnerable to data breaches and vendor discontinuities [10, 20, 17].

Agentic AI systems require a significant amount of resources, such as processing power, energy resources, and modernization investments [1, 5, 9]. Additionally, the impact is amplified if institutions have immature data governance frameworks, making it challenging to meet the transparency, compliance, and security expectations that Agentic AI demands [5, 17]. Furthermore, HEIs are faced with the need for large-scale workforce reskilling and upskilling [10, 25, 28] to address talent shortages. This disconnect between HEIs leadership vision and institutional capacity results in stalled implementations and unsatisfactory returns on investment [11, 19, 17].

5 Strategic Pathways for Adoption

Despite these challenges, HEIs do have options to address them. Strategic pathways do exist to pursue the adoption of Agentic AI in ways that are responsible, incremental, and aligned with institutional missions and values.

5.1 Guiding Principles for Responsible Adoption

The adoption of Agentic AI in HEIs must be guided by a core set of principles that align with academic missions, achieve institutional values, and foster long-term trust. Among these is mission alignment, to ensure that the deployment of Agentic AI should not distort the foundational goals of education, research, and community service [9, 10]. Another important principle is that HEIs must adopt human-in-the-loop approaches to ensure that this technology serves as a collaborator, not a replacement. This will enable human oversight, critical evaluation, and intervention at decision points [14, 23, 25].

Equally important is phased and ethical deployment, where HEIs begin with pilot projects and limited-scope applications to measure impact, refine strategies, and ensure cultural readiness [9]. This gradual deployment also supports ethical governance and helps address potential concerns, such as bias, fairness, and job displacement [1, 23]. Finally, transparency and accountability must be central to every stage of adoption, to ensure explainability, auditability, and clear channels of responsibility [9, 10].

5.2 Institutional Readiness and Capacity Building

The successful adoption of any technology requires more than enthusiasm. It demands readiness. HEIs must invest in modernizing legacy infrastructure, establishing data governance, and ensuring cybersecurity resilience [10, 17]. In addition, institutions must build their internal capacity through cross-functional AI oversight teams and targeted upskilling for IT staff, faculty, and administrators [10, 25]. Pilot projects in low-risk functions can help evaluate operational fit and refine strategies. Without foundational readiness, even the most visionary technology initiatives risk inefficiency or failure to align with institutional goals.

5.3 Leadership and Strategic Alignment

Leadership plays a fundamental role in guiding Agentic AI adoption within HEIs. Senior leaders must establish a clear vision that aligns Agentic AI integration with institutional values, strategic goals, and ethical standards [10, 25]. This includes establishing governance structures, such as AI ethics board, and supporting cross-departmental collaboration to bridge the technical and academic sects [11, 17]. A visionary, accountable leadership must ensure strategic alignment at the leadership level to transform Agentic AI's potential into purposeful innovation.

6 Implications and Future Research Agenda

As Agentic AI emerges as a transformative force in higher education, this paper offers a timely perspective on opportunities, challenges, and strategic pathways for adoption. It contributes a significant value to HEI leaders, educators, administrators, practitioners, and policymakers, as well as the scholarly community.

First, Practical and Strategic Implications. This paper sharpens understanding of the adoption of Agentic AI demands new leadership vision, governance structures, and ethical frameworks that are in line with institutional missions. It highlights the balance between innovation and responsible oversight that is necessary to achieve meaningful impact. The practical, real-world, and hypothetical use case examples will encourage HEIs to rethink what is possible with Agentic AI. The paper also presents strategic pathways to navigate challenges and achieve a successful, responsible adoption.

Second, Theoretical and Conceptual Implications. By bridging conceptual gaps and clarifying emerging technologies, the paper equips researchers to critically engage with Agentic AI's implications. It also lays a foundation for developing practical frameworks tailored to diverse academic disciplines and institutional contexts. Another key contribution of this paper is its clear, accessible textual explanations combined with flow diagrams illustrating how AI agents differ from GenAI. This approach makes complex concepts understandable for researchers outside technical fields, fostering greater interdisciplinary and collaborative research.

Third, Research Agenda. Future research in Agentic AI should prioritize the development of ethical, safety, and governance frameworks, alongside mechanisms for enhancing transparency, bias mitigation, and cybersecurity resilience [9, 11, 15, 30]. Advancing human-AI collaboration, refining agentic performance and autonomy, and exploring socialization within multi-agent systems remain essential [1, 30]. Scholars are called to examine its impact on labor and economics [11], as well as environmental sustainability through energy-efficient deployment [11]. High-impact applications in education, biomedical research, and smart systems require further exploration in scopes like multimodal data integration, hypothesis generation, and learning enhancement [11]. Finally, integrating Agentic AI with emerging technologies like quantum computing and robotics offers an opportunity for transformative interdisciplinary innovation [11].

7 Conclusion

This paper has discussed Agentic AI's transformative potential within higher education and has also distinguished it from related technologies. It has also revealed both the strategic opportunities Agentic AI offers and the institutional challenges faced by HEIs. The paper then proposes strategic pathways to navigate adoption challenges. The paper has outlined the future research agenda to empower HEIs to harness autonomous intelligence while preserving their core academic values.

Agentic AI is not just a technological evolution, but a redefinition of agency, governance, and purpose in higher education. As HEIs embrace this technology, the challenge is clear: to engage proactively, evaluate critically, and lead ethically.

References

1. Acharya, D.B., Kuppan, K., Divya, B.: Agentic AI: autonomous intelligence for complex goals—a comprehensive survey. IEEE Access **13**, 18912–18936 (2025)
2. Boskabadi, M.R., Cao, Y., Khadem, B., Clements, W., Gerek, Z.N., Reuthe, E., Sivaram, A., Savoie, C.J., Mansouri, S.S.: Industrial agentic AI and generative modeling in complex systems. Curr. Opin. Chem. Eng. **48**, 101150 (2025)

3. Deng, Z., Guo, Y., Han, C., Ma, W., Xiong, J., Wen, S., Xiang, Y.: AI agents under threat: a survey of key security challenges and future pathways. ACM Comput. Surv. **57**(7), 1–36 (2025)
4. Díaz, S., Kern, C., Olive, K.: An Introduction to Google's Approach to AI Agent Security (2025)
5. Elgendy, I.A., Helal, M.Y.I., Al-Sharafi, M.A., Albashrawi, M.A., Al-Ahmadi, M.S., Jeon, I., Dwivedi, Y.K.: Agentic systems as catalysts for innovation in FinTech: exploring opportunities, challenges and a research agenda. Inf. Disc. Deliv. (2025)
6. Gao, S., Fang, A., Huang, Y., Giunchiglia, V., Noori, A., Schwarz, J.R., Ektefaie, Y., Kon-dic, J., Zitnik, M.: Empowering biomedical discovery with AI agents. Cell **187**(22), 6125–6151 (2024)
7. Gottweis, J., Weng, W.-H., Daryin, A., Tu, T., Palepu, A., Sirkovic, P., Myaskovsky, A., Weissenberger, F., Rong, K., Tanno, R., Saab, K., Popovici, D., Blum, J., Zhang, F., Chou, K., Hassidim, A., Gokturk, B., Vahdat, A., Kohli, P., Natarajan, V.: Towards an AI co-scientist (2025)
8. Hashmi, N., Bal, A.S.: Generative AI in higher education and beyond. Bus. Horiz. **67**(5), 607–614 (2024)
9. Hosseini, S., Seilani, H.: The role of agentic AI in shaping a smart future: a systematic review. Array **26**, 100399 (2025)
10. Hughes, L., Dwivedi, Y.K., Li, K., Appanderanda, M., Al-Bashrawi, M.A., Chae, I.: AI agents and agentic systems: redefining global it management. J. Glob. Inf. Technol. Manag., 1–11 (2025)
11. Hughes, L., Dwivedi, Y.K., Malik, T., Shawosh, M., Albashrawi, M.A., Jeon, I., Dutot, V., Appanderanda, M., Crick, T., De', R., Fenwick, M., Gunaratnege, S.M., Jurcys, P., Kar, A.K., Kshetri, N., Li, K., Mutasa, S., Samothrakis, S., Wade, M., Walton, P.: AI agents and agentic systems: a multi-expert analysis. J. Comput. Inf. Syst., 1–29 (2025)
12. Hwang, J., Yoon, S.: AI agent-based indoor environmental informatics: concept, methodology, and case study. Build. Environ. **277**, 112879 (2025)
13. Jabbour, J., Janapa Reddi, V.: Generative AI agents in autonomous machines: a safety perspective. In: Proceedings of the 43rd IEEE/ACM International Conference on Computer-Aided Design, pp. 1–13 (2024)
14. Jovanović, M., Campbell, M.: Self-directing AI: the road to fully autonomous AI agents. Computer **58**(2), 71–77 (2025)
15. Korzynski, P., Edwards, A., Gupta, M.C., Mazurek, G., Wirtz, J.: Humanoid robotics and agentic AI: reframing management theories and future research directions. Eur. Manag. J., S0263237325000908 (2025)
16. Kshetri, N.: Economics of agentic AI in the health-care industry. IT Professional **27**(1), 14–19 (2025)
17. Kshetri, N.: From predictive and generative to agentic AI: shaping the future of marketing operations and strategies. Computer **58**(4), 121–129 (2025)
18. Kshetri, N.: Redefining human resource practices with AI agents and agentic AI: automated compliance and enhanced productivity. Computer **58**(6), 119–124 (2025)
19. Kshetri, N.: Revolutionizing higher education: the impact of artificial intelligence agents and agentic artificial intelligence on teaching and operations. IT Professional **27**(2), 12–16 (2025)
20. Kshetri, N.: Transforming Cybersecurity with Agentic AI to Combat Emerging Cyber Threats (2025). https://doi.org/10.2139/ssrn.5159598
21. Leonardi, P.M.: Homo agenticus in the age of agentic AI: Agency loops, power displacement, and the circulation of responsibility. Inf. Organ. **35**(3), 100582 (2025)
22. Liu, Y., Zheng, G.: From customization to customer: an intelligent business platform with AI agents. In: Ye, Y., Zhou, H. (eds.) Frontiers in Artificial Intelligence and Applications. IOS Press (2025)

23. Ma, X., Wang, J.: WIP: active learning through prompt engineering and agentic AI simulation-A pilot project in computer networks education. In: 2024 IEEE Frontiers in Education Conference (FIE), pp. 1–5 (2024)
24. Morales, S., Clarisó, R., Cabot, J.: Impromptu: a framework for model-driven prompt engineering. Softw. Syst. Model (2025)
25. Murugesan, S.: The rise of agentic ai: implications, concerns, and the path forward. IEEE Intell. Syst. **40**(2), 8–14 (2025)
26. Paulose, R., Neelanath, V., George, M.: Domain agnostic agentic AI: enabling autonomous automation with smart Genie CoPilot. In: 2025 Emerging Technologies for Intelligent Systems (ETIS), pp. 1–6 (2025)
27. Portugal, I.D.S., Alencar, P., Cowan, D.: An agentic AI-based multi-agent framework for recommender systems. In: 2024 IEEE International Conference on Big Data (BigData), pp. 5375–5382 (2024)
28. Qiu, R.: Editorial: revolutionizing digital transformation in business and society through agentic AI integration. Digit. Trans. Soc. **4**(2), 109–110 (2025)
29. Sabour, S., Liu, J.M., Liu, S., Yao, C.Z., Cui, S., Zhang, X., Zhang, W., Cao, Y., Bhat, A., Guan, J., Wu, W., Mihalcea, R., Wang, H., Althoff, T., Lee, T.M.C., Huang, M.: Human decision-making is susceptible to AI-driven manipulation. arXiv:2502.07663 (2025)
30. Stylos, N., Okumus, F., Onder, I.: Beauty or the borg: agentic artificial intelligence organizational socialization in synergistic hybrid transformative dynamic flows. Tour. Manag. **111**, 105205 (2025)
31. Thurzo, A., Varga, I.: Revisiting the role of review articles in the age of AI-agents: integrating AI-reasoning and AI-synthesis reshaping the future of scientific publishing. Bratislava Med. J. **126**(4), 381–393 (2025)
32. Timms, A., Langbridge, A., Antonopoulos, A., Mygiakis, A., Voulgari, E., O'Donncha, F.: Agentic AI for digital twin. In: AAAI Conference on Artificial Intelligence, vol. 39, pp. 29703–29705 (2025)
33. Vaswani, A., Shazeer, N., Parmar, N., Uszkoreit, J., Jones, L., Gomez, A.N., Kaiser, Ł., Polosukhin, I.: Attention is All you Need (2017)
34. Wiesinger, J., Marlow, P., Vuskovic, V.: Agents (2024)

Adoption of Smart Technologies

Why it is Difficult for Users to Adopt Smart Home Technologies: Some Insights

Ravinder Kumar Verma[1(✉)] and Sachin Kumar Sharma[1,2]

[1] Jindal Global Business School, OP Jindal Global University, Sonipat, India
ravinderkv1@gmail.com
[2] DMS, IIT Delhi, New Delhi, India

Abstract. Smart home technologies are transforming the living spaces of individuals by enabling them to design and manage their homes with higher control and convenience. With this research, we explore the barriers to the adoption of smart home technologies in India. This paper employs a qualitative approach and adopts the affordance theory. The results are based on the analysis of 5176 users' feedback about their experiences with products based on smart home technologies. To understand the barriers to the adoption of smart home technologies in India, we considered e-commerce platforms and collected data from Flipkart (www.flipkart.in), Amazon (www.amazon.in), and YouTube. Data analysis is based on thematic analysis to identify the key emerging themes. The findings identify the barriers to the adoption of smart home products. These barriers can be categorized at the individual and ecosystem levels. At the individual level, these barriers are directly associated with the performance, after-sales services, the complexity of digital technologies, cost, and security. At the ecosystem level, barriers associated with the smart home technologies ecosystem impact the individual experience with these technologies. The research provides insights into the smart home technologies ecosystem and its criticality for individual experience. This research has practical implications for understanding the factors associated with the use of smart home technologies in India.

Keywords: Smart home technologies · Qualitative methods · Affordance approach

1 Introduction

The contemporary economy has undergone a significant transformation, shifting toward digital platforms, with digital transactions now accounting for over 50% of total revenue generated [1]. Technological advancements in digital space have brought about substantial changes across various domains. For instance, the Digital India program supports the development of digital technology–driven services and infrastructure. India is currently experiencing an urban transformation, with cities being developed into smart cities through the implementation of various digital services and the conceptualization of smart city models aimed at providing public goods [2]. These societal changes have

A. Elbanna et al. (Eds.): TDIT 2025, IFIP AICT 778, pp. 185–196, 2026.
https://doi.org/10.1007/978-3-032-16775-0_12

influenced people's preferences, leading to increased demand for digitally enabled residences known as smart homes (SH). A smart home is equipped with digital technologies that perform multiple household tasks and control functions such as security, lighting, and air purification. These features can be managed remotely using smartphones and internet-connected devices [3, 4].

As human society transitions into a digital era, technologies are transforming how humans interact with their homes and approaches to daily living. This shift is supported by smart home technologies (SHT), which are changing how individuals interact with and manage their living spaces. These technologies enable the automation and remote control of various household functions, including climate control (cooling and heating), security and access (entry and exit), cleaning systems (such as robotic vacuum cleaners), and the operation of household appliances. The adoption of smart home technologies offers benefits, such as convenience, energy efficiency, and enhanced security, but it also introduces a set of complex challenges. These challenges arise at both the individual level, where issues such as usability, privacy concerns, and adaptability may impact user experiences, and at the macro level, where broader implications, including digital infrastructure, data governance, and socio-economic disparities, need to be addressed.

This research aims to explore the use of smart home technologies in India and their barriers. It is essential to understand how these technologies behave once individuals start to use them. This research aims to address the following research questions (RQs): How do individuals experience the adoption and use of smart home technologies? What factors explain the gaps between the promises of smart home technologies and the individual's actual experiences?

The interactions between innovative products and society affect the actors involved, including corporations, users, service providers, and regulators. The existing research on smart home technologies focuses on user intentions [5, 6]. This study comprehensively analyzes the perspectives of individuals and the SHT ecosystem, which has limited research evidence. The use of affordance theory enables the identification of the actual concerns at both levels. A qualitative approach allows for a deeper and comprehensive study of the role and position of users within the smart home ecosystem. This study is a valuable contribution to the existing body of literature on smart homes, by focusing on individual and SHT ecosystems based on actual users' inputs. It examines the barriers within the smart home ecosystem and explores the relationships between them and the context.

This paper is organized as follows: Sect. 1 introduces the study and outlines the research context. Section 2 reviews the relevant literature and affordance theory. Section 3 presents the research methodology. Section 4 reports the findings and analysis. Section 5 discusses the results, highlighting the theoretical and practical contributions, as well as the study's limitations and directions for future research. Section 6 concludes the paper.

2 Background: Smart Homes Services and Theoretical Framework

2.1 Smart Homes Services

A "smart home" refers to a residential space equipped with various interconnected devices and systems, including the Internet of Things (IoT), sensors, and online-connected devices. These are some examples of smart home technologies [5] (Table 1).

Table 1. Examples of smart home technologies

S. No.	Smart home technology products	
1	Smart lighting	Sensors and remote controls to turn on or off the lights
2	Smart security systems	Smart locks, security cameras, motion sensors, and door/window sensors
3	Smart plugs and outlets	Electric plugs for home appliances ring a bell
4	Smart cameras	Cameras are accessed through a smartphone or computer.to see live video feeds and recordings
5	Smart entertainment systems	Smart TVs, audio systems, and streaming devices
6	Smart appliances	Examples—refrigerators, ovens, and washing machines—are controlled remotely with automated instructions based on usage patterns
7	Smart speakers and voice assistants	Devices like Amazon Echo, Google Home, and Apple HomePod allow users to control various aspects of their smart home using voice commands

A system is needed to access and control services in real time through connected devices. A comprehensive smart home ecosystem establishes a relationship between hardware and software, wherein they continually interact to perform multiple functions of society and create value for stakeholders [3]. To control smart home products, real-time access was needed through cloud-based systems and Internet of Things (IoT) technologies [4, 7].

In smart home services, the presence of multiple sensors, actuators, and biomedical monitors offers a variety of advantages. Smart home technologies offer multiple affordances to users [4, 7–9]. SHT provides users with control over their homes by providing information about available household items, energy consumption, weather, and air quality. The adoption of smart home services is driven primarily by three factors: compatibility, perceived benefits, and ease of use. Regarding SHT utilization, the experiential aspect is critical as these technologies provide a range of benefits, including enhanced comfort, increased control, and improved convenience for households [4, 12].

The past literature focuses on people's willingness to adopt SHT and the advantages SHT possesses [7]. While other research investigates people's reluctance to adopt SHT [11, 12]. When analyzing the rate at which consumers adopt smart homes, it is necessary to understand the experiences of early adopters and those who resist change. According to the previous study's findings, most of the attention has been given to analyzing the adoption and resistance of smart home technologies in developed nations [4, 12, 13]. In India, research on smart home technologies (SHT) primarily concentrates on the application of SHT and the challenges with its implementation. This qualitative study examines the concerns of users after they have used smart home devices in India.

2.2 Theoretical Framework

This research used affordance lens. The affordance approach was developed in environmental psychology. This theory helps in understanding the motives and barriers of human-technology interactions. According to the affordance approach, when a user with a goal interacts with the technologies, it allows users to have many possibilities. The actualization of these possibilities is seen within a context where actualization is supported by facilitating conditions and hindered by barriers [15]. For example, SHT offers multiple action possibilities such as automatic functional delivery, monitoring and control of functions like air cooling, security, and doorbell ringing. Those factors that reduce the realization of the action possibilities SHT or hinder the users from actualizing the SHT affordances are the barriers. While employing affordance theory to SHT, where affordances are not just IT artefacts of the SHT or just user characteristics, affordances exist and the individual interactions with the SHT along with barriers and facilitating conditions impact its actualisation (Fig. 1) [15–17].

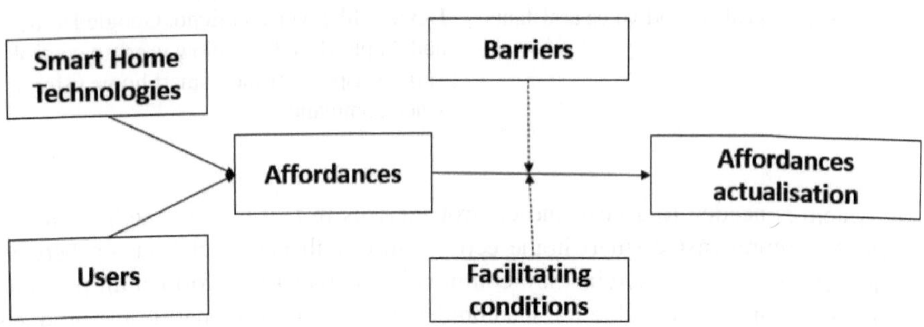

Fig. 1. Affordance framework and smart home artefacts

The affordance approach helps to understand the relationship between users and SHT. Affordance theory has been adopted in Information Systems research to understand the interactions of technology with society [15, 16, 19, 20]. Affordance theory is useful for SHT research to explore the perceived and actual affordances. It can also contribute to the design and SHT ecosystem.

3 Research Methods

3.1 Data Collection

Qualitative research methods were used to analyze barriers to the adoption of smart home technologies in India, focusing on the interplay between these technologies and users' lived experiences. Guided by the research aim, data were gathered from multiple sources to ensure a comprehensive understanding of the adoption challenges [16].

A purposive sampling strategy was adopted to ensure that the reviews selected were relevant to the research aim and reflected SH devices, brands, and platforms within the Indian market context. Large-scale user-generated reviews from leading e-commerce platforms were analyzed to address the research questions. Data were collected from Amazon India (www.amazon.in), Flipkart India (www.flipkart.in), and YouTube, resulting in a dataset of 5,176 product reviews. The breakdown of data sources is as follows: 3,522 reviews from Amazon, 967 from Flipkart, and 687 from YouTube. These were selected from a larger pool of 17,560 reviews on Amazon, 6,780 reviews on Flipkart, and 2,286 comments from YouTube. The selection of reviews is based on the SHT-enabled products on the e-commerce platforms and availability of the reviews on selected criteria of ratings. Through this research, we are examining the concerns and challenges associated with the adoption of SHT. There were many positive responses from the users as mentioned below, which are mostly associated with the higher ratings of 4 and 5; however, we have not included them in this research. For instance, "*It supports a lot of colors and is really functional, even though the response time may feel a bit laggy, at times, its overall performance is impressive and definitely a value for money product.*" In another response, the user mentioned that "*This thing gave its best for 3 years and finally started flickering after three whole years.*"

For e-commerce platforms, product selection was limited to items that had received at least 2,500 ratings to ensure sufficient distribution of reviews across 1- to 5-star ratings. Many reviews were selected from Amazon, as the platform provides access to all review pages, whereas Flipkart offers limited page visibility, especially for 1- to 3-star reviews. The reason for including the comments from Amazon and Flipkart is that reviews are submitted by customers who have already purchased these products and verified by the e-commerce platforms. On YouTube, the selection of videos is based on the content of the video and channel subscriptions. On YouTube, many comments are not related to the SHT and to the concerns of the users; therefore, only those comments are included that are directly related to the SHT. The selected products represented a diverse range of smart home devices, including security systems, lighting solutions, voice assistants, IoT-enabled devices, and home automation hubs. These reviews reflect the perspectives of real users who have purchased and interacted with such products in real-world contexts.

3.2 Data Analysis

The dataset was systematically coded to capture both individual and ecosystem-level barriers, enabling the identification of recurring issues with SHT use. This study examines the usage barriers to smart home technologies by analyzing the interplay between smart home technology and users' experiences. The data analysis includes preprocessing, where customer names, special characters, and words in languages other than English are removed from the data file.

This study employed thematic analysis for user-generated reviews to explore the barriers to adopting smart home technologies in India. Since the reviews from the genuine customers offer rich, authentic insights into real-world user experiences, allowing the identification of both explicit and latent concerns that may not emerge in survey-based research. This paper employed deductive thematic analysis guided by the affordance theory. Content analysis is conducted to categorize reviews under the barriers group based on the above-stated parameters and subsequently, thematic analysis is performed on the barriers group users' reviews. We followed Braun and Clarke's thematic analysis steps, aiming to identify recurring patterns in diverse user reviews around themes that prevent users from actualizing the SHT's affordance. By examining user-generated content, the research aimed to capture the lived experiences and sentiments of actual and potential adopters.

Braun and Clarke's thematic analysis has six steps: first, both researchers become familiar with the selected reviews of SH products data through repeated reading and initial notetaking; second, through generated initial codes by identifying concerns of the users of SHT by focusing on issues such as perceived cost, complexity, security, privacy, interoperability, and reliability. In the third step, codes were then grouped into nine themes, which were refined through iterative comparison and re-evaluation. This process allowed for the development of a thematic map around the interplay between smart home technologies and user experiences concerning the barriers to adoption. Initially, we identified nine themes. Upon reviewing these, we categorized them into two major themes: Technology and SHT post-purchase support and maintenance. Later, these two themes were highlighted towards another theme of the SH ecosystem [21]. This process allowed for the development of a theme that captured the interplay between smart home technologies and user experiences on barriers to SHT adoption, grounded in the Indian socio-economic context. Data analysis was performed using NVivo 12 software.

4 Findings

The results are divided into multiple themes, highlighting the users' primary concerns about the adoption of smart home devices.

4.1 Technology: Not a Right fit!

The interactions between users and SH devices result in unexpected outcomes. SH devices exhibited technical gaps, leading to non-functioning devices and an unreliable image. One user mentioned about the SH product that "*it (SHT) is unreliable. It stops responding from the app and gets disconnected from WiFi. I had to reset the WiFi on the tube so many times. Does not respond to the app so many times.*"

Many users report issues with connectivity, including difficulty maintaining a stable connection between the bulb and the mobile app. Performance is often described as erratic, with glitches, malfunctions, and inconsistent responses to commands. For instance, some bulbs experience random flickering or fail to respond to remote controls.

> *"Unfortunately, the product has not lived up to its advertised functionality, and I have encountered numerous issues with connectivity, rendering the bulb unreliable and frustrating to use".*

The SHT App experience is not smooth. Users frequently mention difficulties with the mobile application, including setup, pairing, and maintaining a connection, while some users find the installation process complicated.

> *"From the moment of installation, I have faced consistent difficulties in establishing and maintaining a stable connection between the smart bulb and the accompanying mobile application."*

With durability and longevity, the following negative trends have been observed, where many reviews mention that the SH product stops working within a year or shortly after the warranty period. Some SH products begin to flicker or lose functionality (e.g., color change) after a few months of use. Where the user mentioned that "*Bulb not working within one year of purchase.*" These factors influence users' perceptions of their decision to invest in SHT, as users believe the short lifespan and reliability issues make it a poor investment.

The use of the SH product, particularly in the case of a smart technology-enabled bulb, raises concern among users about brightness and light quality. Users gave mixed responses, with some finding the brightness satisfactory for small or medium-sized rooms. Contrary to others, the report states that the bulb's brightness is insufficient, especially in larger spaces or in colored light modes. One user mentioned that "*Good response time. Bright enough for a bedroom. Not enough for the hall.*" And others noted that "*The Product is good, but the overall brightness of the bulb is very low.*"

Features and Customization of the SH product may not function as expected and as claimed by the companies. One user said, "*After 30 days of usage, it got disconnected, and now it is not pairing.*" Another user reported, "*The product stopped working, and some hardware issues.*" Some features, such as music sync or gradual sunrise simulation, are perceived as poorly implemented and difficult to configure. For example, a user mentioned that "*The music sync is a useless feature. It is not even close to the music played. It looks totally random.*"

The technological risk associated with the SH products can be grouped into the following concerns: Interoperability, integration concerns, design challenges, and performance concerns. These concerns result in experienced performance risk, experienced financial risk, and experienced psychological risk (Table 2).

Table 2. Technological concerns with smart home technology

Sub-themes	Technological concerns
Not supporting interoperability	Not operating with other apps and devices, unplanned switched off, and operate with the selected network connection

(*continued*)

Table 2. (*continued*)

Sub-themes	Technological concerns
Integration concerns	Pairing challenges with apps and devices, lack of interactions between multiple connected devices
Design challenges	App concerns- not pairing, poor syncing (disconnection), cheap copied products, lots of efforts to start the device, not universally designed (*"not suitable for my AC, Geyser, Oven and Fridge"*)
Performance concerns	Operate within a limited range, with reduced output and compromised quality. app performance is affected, taking longer to start, pair, and experiencing power cuts and restoration issues

4.2 Service unavailability: Customer Service, Warranty Issues, and User Dissatisfaction

A significant barrier to the sustained use of smart home technologies (SHT) lies in the perceived unreliability of both the products and the service infrastructure surrounding them. Many users report a mismatch between what companies claim and actual product performance. Devices frequently fail to meet advertised standards, some do not function at all upon installation, while others become non-operational within a few days or weeks. These experiences not only incur financial costs but also generate psychological distress, particularly in cases where customer support is unresponsive.

Users expressed their disappointment by referring to their purchases as "*wastage of money*",

"*False claim of 2-year warranty!! Do not buy,*"

"*Never ever buy XYZ company product [anonymous],*"

"*Product has no warranty and very poor service.*"

"*Impossible to get hold of customer care, you may have to call 100 times and they never call back.*"

"*Pathetic after-sales service,*"

"*Worst quality,*"

"*Pathetic purchase,*"

It also observed that, despite giving more than three-star ratings, customers continue to complain about the products in their reviews.

Here, users commonly cited poor customer service and the rejection of warranty claims. Even within the warranty period, several users encountered resistance from brands when seeking product replacements or repairs. Example one use mentioned that "*Despite the product being well within the warranty period, the brand has rejected my warranty claim, leaving me without any recourse for resolving these ongoing issues.*"

The delayed and ineffective support mechanisms further disappoint users. Many users described a lack of accountability and transparency in service interactions with companies. One user mentioned that "*As a valued customer, I expected a reliable and functional smart bulb backed by responsive customer service.*"

These narratives reveal a deeper trust gap between consumers and smart home technology providers, suggesting that adoption barriers extend beyond technical usability to include after-sales service reliability and companies' responsiveness. The findings underscore the need for robust service frameworks, clearer warranty policies, and improved communication practices to enhance user trust and engagement with SHT ecosystems.

4.3 Insights into the Smart Home ecosystem

The smart home ecosystem is influenced by the quality of the products and services rendered by the SH products manufacturing firms, distribution channels, and competitors' products. The above analysis indicates that the SH ecosystem is undergoing evolution. In this initial stage, multiple factors influence the position of the associated actors.

The quality of products and services provided by manufacturers of smart home products, as well as the distribution channels and competing products, has a significant impact on the smart home ecosystem. The analysis demonstrates the ongoing evolution of the SH ecosystem. In this initial stage, multiple factors influence the position of the associated actors.

The expression of user dissatisfaction with technological issues suggests that technology is still in its developmental phase in terms of its contextual surroundings. The current distribution channels, in which limited firms operate in, seem not to possess specialized channels to address users' problems effectively. The technological complexity of SH devices hinders their ease of use, primarily due to a lack of technological understanding and restricted access to specialists. Additionally, the poor operations of the comprehensive system for handling warranty claims exacerbate these challenges.

5 Discussion

This study identifies adoption barriers and explores multiple themes to situate the current study within a developing context. A comprehensive framework of obstacles is presented in Fig. 2. A bidirectional relationship exists between technological uncertainty and service delivery within the SHT ecosystem.

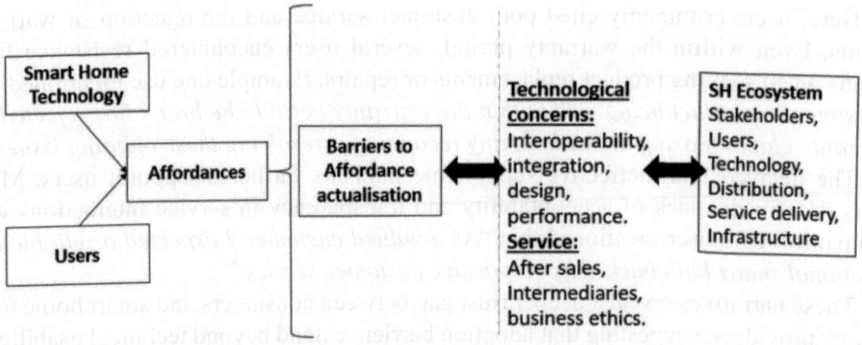

Fig. 2. Framework of barriers to smart home usage

Technological aspects of the SHT influence the use of smart home products. The identified themes pertain to the uncertainties around technology, obstacles in service delivery, and the smart home technologies ecosystem. It indicates that SHT encounters challenges in integrating with other devices, particularly in terms of design and functionality issues with SH products when paired with smart devices like smartphones. The technical issues with SH products are related to poor performance, non-availability, or inadequate services in the initial stage of the SHT ecosystem. The experience of risks associated with SHT influences users' trust. The SH ecosystem is the outcome of multiple interacting ecosystems. The relationship between users' adoption concerns is a contributing factor that affects the sustainability of the smart home ecosystem.

The research indicates that concerns associated with smart home products are not only about the product itself, but contextual factors also exacerbate them. E-commerce platforms sell smart home products, and users can receive these products in most parts of the country. However, all these locations have differences in infrastructure facilities. For instance, service centers are not available in all areas, and even local service providers often lack the necessary resources to operate and repair smart devices. The basic infrastructure is lacking in many places, such as smart home products that can be accessed in real-time. In contrast, many parts of the country lack 24/7 access to electricity or internet connections. Individual factors and infrastructural issues also influence the users' experience with smart home devices. Therefore, the differences in internet bandwidth, electricity, network availability, and smartphone capabilities pose challenges for the SH ecosystem.

Here, we discuss the theoretical and practical implications along with limitations and future scope of this research on barriers to smart home technology adoption in the Indian context. As the theoretical implications of this research, by using the affordance approach, we identify adoption barriers to SHT. The proposed model (Fig. 2) enhances understanding of these barriers and highlights the challenges of adopting and implementing SHT in India. By introducing various factors influencing adoption, we examine the critical role of contextual elements such as regional infrastructure differences, income, and SHT education, which is critical for the functioning of the SHT ecosystem. Affordance theory provides a comprehensive understanding of SHT adoption barriers at the individual level. As multiple systems interact with each other, these barriers are associated with the SHT ecosystem. This research contributes to the smart home and innovation literature by expanding knowledge of the challenges involved in implementing innovations in the smart home domain.

This research has practical Implications given the context of the research. The public and private sectors are growing and encouraging the digital economy in India. Smart home technologies are impacting the nation's growth, with initiatives such as the creation of 100 smart cities, smart transportation, smart digital health, and the encouragement of electronics manufacturing parks for both domestic and international consumption under the Made in India initiative. Smart home technologies are associated with multiple sectors and stakeholders, and SHT can impact India's economy and improve the lives of consumers. SHT can support individuals in managing their homes by providing market-smart technologies, encouraging the exploration of new emerging SH technologies. The associated stakeholders from public and private spaces can extend support to build a robust SHT ecosystem. At the same time, extending services to previously unreached areas and enabling the diffusion of SH products beyond city centers and metro cities

This research is not without limitations. First, the study is based on secondary data from two e-commerce platforms and YouTube. However, the availability of smart home technology-enabled products on these platforms is limited.

In future research, the research can be extended to specific SH products and their interactions with other smart or non-smart products in the home. Future research can also explore the barriers to the adoption of specific SHT and smart home hubs. In future research, researchers can extend the methods by adopting a mixed-methods approach.

6 Conclusion

Smart home technologies (SHT) hold the potential to transform domestic living by enhancing convenience, efficiency, and security. However, this potential is unevenly realized. This research suggests a complex reality—where even those who adopt SHT may experience limited or unequal benefits along with economic losses and inconvenience. This phenomenon, conceptualized here through the affordance lens, highlights how technology value emerges from the interaction between user goals, environmental context, and system design. Users of SHT are shifting towards the smart home; however, SH product usage is influenced by unmet expectations, poor service by SHT companies, and regional infrastructure factors. It was observed that the gap between the anticipated expectations from the SHT products and actual performance influenced users' experience.

References

1. UNCTAD: Digital Economy Report 2019, Geneva (2019). https://doi.org/10.18356/c7dc937a-en
2. Government of India: Digital India Initiatives. GoI Digital India (2021). https://www.digitalindia.gov.in/di-initiatives
3. Peine, A.: Understanding the dynamics of technological configurations: a conceptual framework and the case of smart homes. Technol. Forecast. Soc. Change **76**(3), 396–409 (2009). https://doi.org/10.1016/j.techfore.2008.04.002

4. Marikyan, D., Papagiannidis, S., Alamanos, E.: A systematic review of the smart home literature: a user perspective. Technol. Forecast. Soc. Change **138**, 139–154 (2019). https://doi.org/10.1016/j.techfore.2018.08.015
5. Joy, J., Srinath, S., Verma, R.K., Shrivastava, M.K.: Barriers to smart home technologies in India. In: Sharma, S.K., Dwivedi, Y.K., Metri, B., Lal, B., Elbanna, A. (eds.) Transfer, Diffusion and Adoption of Next-Generation Digital Technologies. TDIT 2023. IFIP Advances in Information and Communication Technology, vol. 698. Springer, Cham (2024). https://doi.org/10.1007/978-3-031-50192-0_18
6. Sharma, B.K., Kuknor, S.C.: Smart homes adoption in India—value-based adoption approach. In: 2021 IEEE International Conference on Technology Management, Operations and Decisions (ICTMOD), pp. 1–6. IEEE, Marrakech, Morocco (2021). https://doi.org/10.1109/ICTMOD52902.2021.9739353
7. Li, W., Yigitcanlar, T., Liu, A., Erol, I.: Mapping two decades of smart home research: a systematic scientometric analysis. Technol. Forecast. Soc. Change **179**(Dec 2021) (2022). https://doi.org/10.1016/j.techfore.2022.121676
8. Agarwal, R., Dugas, M., Gao, G.(G.), Kannan, P.K.: Emerging technologies and analytics for a new era of value-centered marketing in healthcare. J. Acad. Mark. Sci. **48**(1), 9–23 (2020). https://doi.org/10.1007/s11747-019-00692-4
9. Ehrenhard, M., Kijl, B., Nieuwenhuis, L.: Market adoption barriers of multi-stakeholder technology: smart homes for the aging population. Technol. Forecast. Soc. Change **89**, 306–315 (2014). https://doi.org/10.1016/j.techfore.2014.08.002
10. Baudier, P., Ammi, C., Deboeuf-Rouchon, M.: Smart home: highly educated students' acceptance. Technol. Forecast. Soc. Change **153** (2020). https://doi.org/10.1016/j.techfore.2018.06.043
11. Hong, A., Nam, C., Kim, S.: What will be the possible barriers to consumers' adoption of smart home services. Telecomm. Policy **44**(2), 101867 (2020). https://doi.org/10.1016/j.telpol.2019.101867
12. Balta-Ozkan, N., Davidson, R., Bicket, M., Whitmarsh, L.: Social barriers to the adoption of smart homes. Energy Policy **63**, 363–374 (2013). https://doi.org/10.1016/j.enpol.2013.08.043
13. Balta-Ozkan, N., Davidson, R., Bicket, M., Whitmarsh, L.: The development of smart homes market in the UK. Energy **60**, 361–372 (2013). https://doi.org/10.1016/j.energy.2013.08.004
14. N. K. Denzin and Y. S. Lincoln.: The SAGE Handbook Of Qualitative Research (2011)
15. Gibson, J.J.: The Ecological Approach to Visual Perception (1979). https://doi.org/10.1386/eme.12.3-4.181
16. Markus, M.L., Silver, M.: A foundation for the study of IT effects: a new look at desanctis and poole's concepts of structural features and spirit. J. Assoc. Inf. Syst. **9**(10), 609–632 (2008). https://doi.org/10.17705/1jais.00176
17. Volkoff, O., Strong, D.M.: Affordance theory and how to use it in IS research. In: The Routledge Companion to Management Information Systems, pp. 232–246 (2017). https://doi.org/10.4324/9781315619361
18. Wyche, S., Steinfield, C.: Why don't farmers use cell phones to access market prices? technology affordances and barriers to market information services adoption in Rural Kenya. Inf. Technol. Dev. **22**(2), 320–333 (2016). https://doi.org/10.1080/02681102.2015.1048184
19. Fayard, A.-L., Weeks, J.: Affordances for practice. Inf. Organ. **24**, 236–249 (2014)
20. Anderson, C., Robey, D.: Affordance potency: explaining the actualization of technology affordances. Inf. Organ. **27**(2), 100–115 (2017). https://doi.org/10.1016/j.infoandorg.2017.03.002
21. Braun, V., Clarke, V.: Using thematic analysis in psychology. Qual. Res. Psychol. **3**(2), 77–101 (2006). https://doi.org/10.1191/1478088706qp063oa

Key Enablers of IoT in Entrepreneurship: A Systematic and Perspective-Based Review

Melvina Christy Santoso and Agung Purnomo(✉)

Entrepreneurship Department, BINUS Business School Undergraduate Program, Bina Nusantara University, Jakarta 11480, Indonesia
agung.purnomo@binus.ac.id

Abstract. The Internet of Things (IoT) has profoundly influenced entrepreneurship, driven innovation and transformed business models across industries. However, integrating IoT into entrepreneurial ventures presents opportunities and challenges. This study aims to identify key enablers and research perspectives surrounding IoT in entrepreneurship using a systematic literature review methodology, focusing on articles indexed in Scopus. The Gioia method, which combines grounded theory and descriptive analysis, was employed to examine thematic patterns and perspectives in literature. The findings reveal four key enablers of IoT in entrepreneurship: innovative IoT solutions, intelligent business models, insightful data utilisation, and infrastructure and policy challenges. These enablers highlight how IoT fosters business connectivity, enables data-driven decision-making, and facilitates new business models. Moreover, the study identifies intersections between IoT technology types and entrepreneurship types, with corporate entrepreneurship and social entrepreneurship emerging as prominent foci. However, research gaps remain in underexplored intersections, such as M2M, WoT, and SIoT, of IoT technologies and specific entrepreneurial types, including buying a small business, buying a franchise, and family enterprises. This study enhances the existing knowledge base by thoroughly synthesising IoT enablers and research gaps. It provides essential insights for entrepreneurs, professionals, and regulators to guide the adoption and integration of IoT technologies. The study also outlines directions for future research in IoT-driven entrepreneurship.

Keywords: IoT · Entrepreneur · Entrepreneurship · Systematic literature review · Key enabler

1 Introduction

The Internet of Things (IoT) has revolutionised various business sectors, enabling real-time data exchange, automation, and digital transformation across industries. The Internet of Things (IoT) refers to a system of interconnected devices that enable companies to collect and analyse data, thereby enhancing operational efficiency and supporting more informed decision-making [1]. Businesses are increasingly integrating IoT technologies

Published by Springer Nature Switzerland AG 2026
A. Elbanna et al. (Eds.): TDIT 2025, IFIP AICT 778, pp. 197–209, 2026.
https://doi.org/10.1007/978-3-032-16775-0_13

to augment productivity, refine decision-making processes, and develop innovative business models [2]. In the era of Industry 4.0, IoT applications extend beyond automation in the manufacturing industry, smart cities, medical treatment, and supply chain administration, demonstrating their critical role in modern business ecosystems [3, 4]. Recent research highlights the economic potential of IoT-driven businesses, showcasing their ability to drive competitiveness and sustainability in rapidly evolving markets [5].

Technology-based entrepreneurship has significantly evolved, driven by emerging innovations such as artificial intelligence (AI), big data analytics, and IoT [6–8]. Entrepreneurship refers to the process of identifying and seizing opportunities by leveraging digital media and various information and communication technologies [9]. Entrepreneurs increasingly leverage digital platforms to develop scalable business solutions, automate processes, and enhance customer engagement [10, 11]. Studies on entrepreneurship emphasise the growing reliance on technological advancements to foster innovation, reduce market uncertainty, and optimise resource allocation [12, 13]. As data-driven digital entrepreneurship gains momentum, researchers explore the intersection between IoT and entrepreneurial activities to understand how technology adoption influences business growth and market dynamics [14, 15].

Despite the increasing integration of IoT in business operations, studies on the Internet of Things in Entrepreneurship (IoT-E) remain fragmented. The adoption of IoT in entrepreneurship introduces unique challenges, including regulatory concerns, cybersecurity risks, and adapting business models [16, 17]. While IoT can potentially transform entrepreneurial ventures, a structured framework to assess its enablers, barriers, and strategic implications is still lacking [18, 19]. Addressing these gaps is crucial for providing entrepreneurs with a more precise roadmap for leveraging IoT effectively [20].

A Systematic Literature Review (SLR) provides a practical methodological approach to synthesising existing knowledge, identifying research gaps, and structuring future research directions in IoT-E. Compared to traditional reviews, SLR employs a rigorous, transparent, and reproducible approach to ensure comprehensive coverage of relevant studies [21, 22]. Given the interdisciplinary nature of IoT-E, an SLR allows researchers to analyse diverse perspectives, including technological, managerial, and economic dimensions [23]. The structured nature of an SLR also enables the classification of key enablers and challenges, facilitating a deeper understanding of the role of IoT in entrepreneurship [18, 24].

Existing studies on IoT-E primarily focus on specific aspects such as technological enablers [17], digital transformation strategies [5], and policy frameworks for IoT adoption [14]. Some research emphasises the impact of IoT on SMEs and startup ecosystems, highlighting challenges related to resource constraints and digital infrastructure [20]. Others examine the role of IoT in business model innovation, demonstrating how startups leverage IoT-driven data analytics for a competitive advantage [11]. However, these studies often lack a comprehensive synthesis of enablers and perspectives, limiting a holistic understanding of IoT's roles in entrepreneurship. This study aims to bridge this gap by conducting a global SLR on IoT in entrepreneurship, focusing on key enablers and perspectives to assess the current state of research and its practical implications.

This study provides a structured foundation for future research and policy development by mapping the literature. This study addresses a critical theoretical gap by examining how IoT technologies reshape the dynamics of entrepreneurial ventures, especially in the context of Industry 4.0. This article contributes to the literature in both methodological and structural aspects. Methodologically, it employs a rigorous SLR process, ensuring a comprehensive and unbiased synthesis of existing research. The structured approach follows established SLR guidelines, incorporating database selection, inclusion and exclusion criteria, thematic categorisation, and systematic literature review analysis. Systematically, this study provides a well-organised classification of IoT enablers and perspectives in entrepreneurship, offering clarity for researchers, practitioners, and policymakers. The study enhances the methodological rigour and conceptual framework of IoT-E research through these contributions.

2 Research Methods

This study employed a Systematic Literature Review (SLR) methodology, adhering to the PRISMA protocol. The PRISMA protocol provides an organised and transparent technical process for identifying, selecting, and critically evaluating pertinent literature, thereby enhancing methodological rigour and reproducibility [25, 26]. Data was collected exclusively from the Scopus database in March 2025. Scopus was selected because it provides extensive, reliable, and multidisciplinary coverage of peer-reviewed literature, supporting comprehensive analysis across diverse disciplines, including entrepreneurship and IoT technology.

The study employed inclusion criteria (IC) for the initial document search, as outlined in Table 1.

Table 1. Inclusion criteria.

Inclusion criteria	Description
Topics	IoT and entrepreneurship
Document type	Journal publications
Subject area	Business, management, and accounting
Publication year	2020–2024
Language	English
Document access	Open access availability

Search keywords employed included IoT, entrepreneurship, and their respective synonyms or related terms, ensuring exhaustive identification of pertinent literature [27]. The search query uses: (TITLE-ABS-KEY (IoT OR "Internet of Thing*") AND TITLE-ABS-KEY (entrepreneur*)) AND PUBYEAR > 2019 AND PUBYEAR < 2025 AND (LIMIT-TO (SRCTYPE, "j")) AND (LIMIT TO (LANGUAGE, "English")) AND (LIMIT-TO (SUBJAREA, "BUSI")) AND (LIMIT-TO (OA, "all")). As illustrated in Fig. 1, twenty-three academic documents were identified through this search method.

The research questions (RQ) directing this review were the following:

RQ1: What are the key enablers of the Internet of Things in entrepreneurship studies?;

RQ2: What are the perspectives and research gaps of the Internet of Things in entrepreneurship studies? and,

RQ3: What is the future of Internet of Things research in entrepreneurship studies?

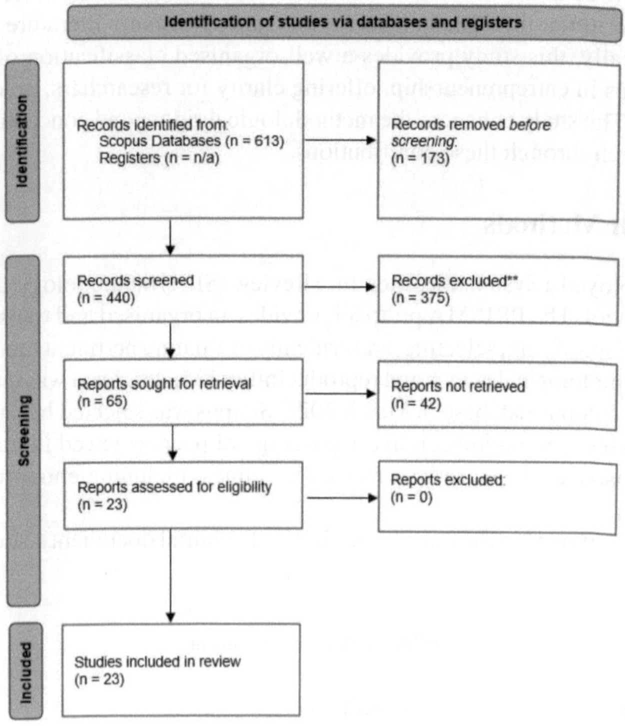

Fig. 1. PRISMA protocol

Data analysis incorporated descriptive, perspective, gap, and thematic analysis following the Gioia methodology. Analysis for RQ1 involved both descriptive and thematic analysis utilising the Gioia method. The Gioia grounded theory method facilitates rigorous qualitative analysis by systematically structuring data into first-order concepts, second-order themes, and aggregate dimensions, effectively uncovering underlying patterns in qualitative datasets [28, 29]. RQ2 was examined through descriptive analysis coupled with a perspective categorisation matrix and identification of research gaps. RQ3 relied exclusively on descriptive analysis to propose directions for future research based on the findings of RQ1 and RQ2.

The perspective analysis matrix employed two types: entrepreneurship and Internet of Things technology. The entrepreneurship type encompasses corporate entrepreneurship (intrapreneurship), serial entrepreneurs (habitual entrepreneurs), family enterprising, social entrepreneurship, entrepreneurs within, buying a small business, and buying a franchise [30]. Internet of Things technology type encompasses the Internet of Anything (IoA), Internet of Everything (IoE), Social Internet of Things (SIoT), Internet of Medical Things (IoMT), Web of Things (WoT), Industrial Internet of Things (IIoT), and Machine-to-Machine (M2M) interactions [31].

3 Results and Discussion

3.1 The Key Enabler for the Internet of Things in Entrepreneurship

After employing the Gioia thematic method for data organisation and analysis, four aggregate dimensions were created to describe the 4I key enabler in implementing the Internet of Things in entrepreneurship, as shown in Fig. 2. Some of the aggregate dimensions of these 4I key enablers are innovative IoT solutions, intelligent business models, insightful data utilisation, and infrastructure and policy challenges. This research theme encompasses statistics for 26 first-order concepts, 11 s-order themes, and four aggregate dimensions. Each aggregate dimension is explained in the following section.

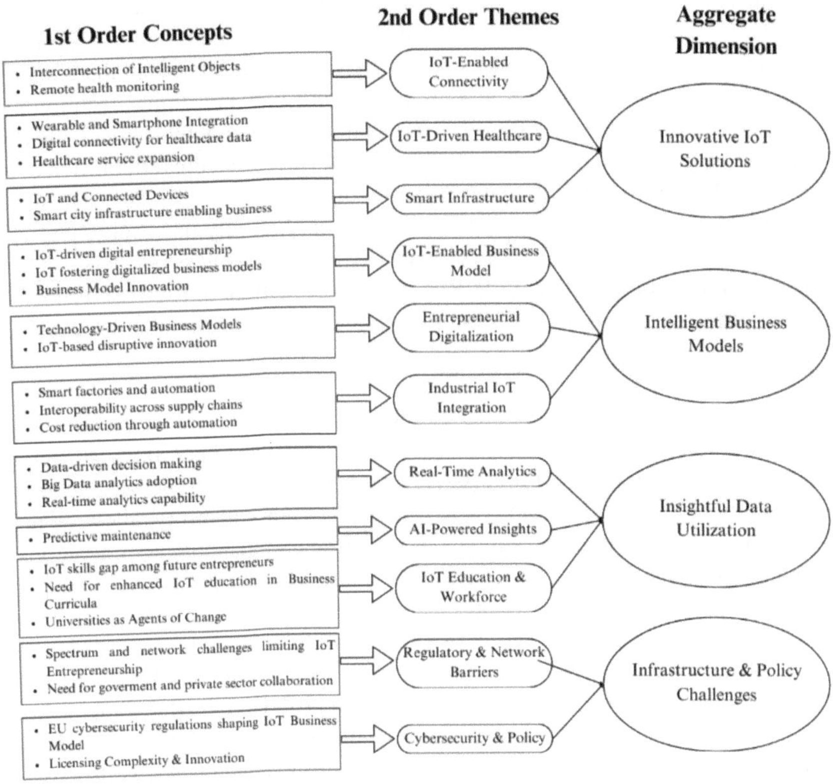

Fig. 2. Key enabler of internet of things in entrepreneurship

Innovative IoT Solution

This research reveals that IoT enables the connectivity of intelligent equipment through the internet, creating healthcare applications utilised in the healthcare industry for distant health monitoring and early diagnosis [2]. Based on previous findings, IoT-based healthcare devices leverage the continuous development of wearables and smartphones [2]. In this case, IoT connects sensing devices digitally to collect and monitor healthcare data [2]. IoT also enhances healthcare services by enabling telemedicine and remote patient monitoring, increasing accessibility for underserved populations [17]. In innovative IoT solutions, IoT enables smart urban infrastructure through connected devices, facilitating automation, efficiency, and new business opportunities [20]. IoT in smart cities provides an interconnected infrastructure enabling entrepreneurs to innovate and develop new services based on real-time data and automation [3].

Intelligent Business Model

The results of this review demonstrate how IoT-driven digital entrepreneurship, supported by AI, transforms digital entrepreneurship by integrating connected devices, automation, and data-driven decision-making [21]. IoT plays a key role in the shift towards digital entrepreneurship by supporting automated and intelligent business models [6]. The IoT shapes new business models by enabling automation, connectivity, and the utilisation of real-time data [12]. In the entrepreneurial digitalisation sector, entrepreneurs must adopt business models integrating IoT and digital technologies to remain competitive in Industry 4.0 [19]. IoT technologies can potentially create disruptive innovations, leading to the emergence of new industries and the redefinition of existing ones [16]. For industrial automation and supply chains, IoT-driven smart factories enhance automation, reducing costs and increasing productivity in entrepreneurial ventures [24]. IoT solutions can enhance connectivity among business partners, improving efficiency across the supply chain [32]. Regarding cost reduction, IoT-based ecosystems enable cost-efficient operations by automating supply chain and logistics processes [32].

Insightful Data Utilisation

This research reveals that IoT enables entrepreneurs to make informed decisions by collecting, analysing, and utilising big data in real-time business operations [6]. Scientists in hospitality and tourism are progressively recognising and implementing big data analytics methodologies [7]. There is a real-time analytics capability, allowing applied researchers to access digital data streams in real-time and generate actionable insights [7]. For new insights, IoT facilitates remote monitoring and predictive maintenance, helping businesses minimise costs and extend equipment lifespan [17]. In terms of education, IoT can be used to fill the skills gap among future entrepreneurs, where a gap exists between business students' entrepreneurial intentions and their knowledge of IoT, emphasising the need for targeted skills development [10]. Higher education institutions should revise their curricula to improve students' understanding of the impact of IoT on entrepreneurship [10]. Universities are crucial in ensuring students are well-prepared to utilise IoT and other digital technologies for entrepreneurial success [19].

Infrastructure and Policy Challenges

The findings of this review demonstrate how entrepreneurs face spectrum deficiencies and networking issues that hinder large-scale IoT deployment [16]. Public-private partnerships and entrepreneurial initiatives are necessary to address gaps in IoT infrastructure [16]. For cybersecurity and policy, entrepreneurs must comply with evolving EU cybersecurity regulations, which influence IoT product development and market dynamics [33]. Complex and fragmented licensing processes discourage entrepreneurship and slow IoT adoption [14].

3.2 Perspectives and Research Gaps for Internet of Things in Entrepreneurship

Building on the comprehensive mapping and analysis of the systematic literature review on the relationship between IoT technology types and entrepreneurial types, the results revealed an intersection matrix and multidimensional impact of IoT strategies on entrepreneurial success. As shown in Table 2, this mapping includes a wide range of Internet of Things technology types, including the Internet of Anything (IoA), Internet of Everything (IoE), Industrial Internet of Things (IIoT), Social Internet of Things (SIoT), Web of Things (WoT), Internet of Medical Things (IoMT), and Machine-to-Machine (M2M) interactions [31]. Applied in entrepreneurial journey types, from corporate entrepreneurship (intrapreneurship) (CEI), entrepreneurs inside (EI), buying a franchise (BF), buying a small business (BSB), social entrepreneurship (SE), family enterprising (FE), and serial entrepreneurs (habitual entrepreneurs) (SEHE) [30]. Table 2 serves as a strategic mapping tool to highlight well-studied research gaps and underexplored intersections, informing future research directions in the field of IoT and entrepreneurship.

Table. 2. Entrepreneurship and internet of things perspective

Entrepreneurship type	Internet of things technology type						
	M2M	IoA	IoE	IoMT	IIoT	WoT	SIoT
CEI			[6, 7, 12, 19]	[13]	[4, 14, 16, 20–22, 24, 32, 33]	[11]	
EI			[10]				
BF							
BSB							
SE		[18]	[3, 5, 34]	[2]			[23]
FE							
SEHE		[17]					

Corporate entrepreneurship, also known as intrapreneurship (CEI), is a prominent type of entrepreneurship that intersects with multiple IoT technologies, particularly IoE and IIoT. For instance, intelligent business models are especially critical in corporate entrepreneurship, where IoT enables real-time decision-making and predictive analytics. For instance, IoE applications are prevalent in corporate entrepreneurship contexts, and the impact of IoT devices and digital consolidation in reinforcing entrepreneurial initiatives [7]. Similarly, IoT and artificial intelligence significantly enhance learning processes within small and medium enterprises (SMEs) [6]. Integrating big data, AI, and IoT into digital transformation strategies directly supports corporate entrepreneurial activities [12]. Additionally, the transformative role of IoT in entrepreneurship education fosters digital competencies aligned with Industry 4.0 [19]. Moreover, IIoT applications also significantly support corporate entrepreneurship by leveraging digital infrastructure for improved operational efficiency [16, 20, 32]. Digital transformation initiatives are driven by integrating IoT, AI, and cloud technologies into industrial enterprises [24]. The use of IIoT in corporate entrepreneurship also emerges in studies that emphasise the integration of 5G networks in IoT applications [4, 33], and mobile communication standards that facilitate IoT-driven business innovation [14]. Applying IoMT within corporate entrepreneurship highlights how flexible commercial spaces foster entrepreneurial ventures in the life sciences sector [13].

Social entrepreneurship (SE) intersects primarily with IoE and IoMT. For instance, the role of IoT in smart cities emphasises social impact through improved connectivity [3]. The IoMT applications enhance healthcare delivery, aligning with the social entrepreneurial goal of community well-being [2]. Additionally, digital barriers faced by small enterprises link IoE with social entrepreneurship [5]. The study examines the involvement of women entrepreneurs in Industry 4.0, highlighting how IoT technologies facilitate social innovation in STEM-related fields [34]. SIoT promotes quality education through automated attendance tracking, which aligns with social entrepreneurship by fostering educational accessibility [23].

Entrepreneurs Inside (EI) intersects mainly with IoE, as seen in Biclesanu, where the entrepreneurial intention of business students is shaped by their preparedness for digital innovation [10]. This intersection highlights how IoE technologies cultivate internal entrepreneurial initiatives within educational contexts.

Serial entrepreneurs or habitual entrepreneurs (SEHE) intersect with IoA, where Qin emphasises the role of IoT in fostering continuous innovation among entrepreneurs [17]. Boudreau discusses how platform-based entrepreneurship is enabled by IoT, reflecting the strategic use of digital connectivity in launching new ventures [18].

Significant research gaps remain despite the extensive exploration of the intersection between IoT technology types and entrepreneurship types. Notably, intersections involving less-studied IoT innovation technologies, particularly Web of Things (WoT), Machine-to-Machine (M2M), and Social Internet of Things (SIoT), are notably sparse across various entrepreneurship types, indicating an underrepresentation of studies focusing on their application in entrepreneurial contexts. Additionally, certain entrepreneurship types, such as buying a franchise (BF), buying a small business (BSB), and family enterprising (FE), have received minimal attention concerning any IoT technology type, suggesting a lack of comprehensive analysis in these areas. Furthermore, while corporate entrepreneurship or intrapreneurship (CEI) and social entrepreneurship (SE) are frequently examined in the context of IoE and IIoT, the exploration of these entrepreneurship types in conjunction with other emerging IoT technologies, such as IoA, IoMT, and SIoT, remains limited.

3.3 Conceptual Framework

Figure 3. The Conceptual Framework of Key Enabler IoT in Entrepreneurship metaphorically illustrates the interplay between key enablers and IoT technologies as the unlocking mechanism for entrepreneurial opportunities. The framework is designed as a padlock and key system, representing the conditional access to entrepreneurship through the integration of enabling factors and IoT technology types.

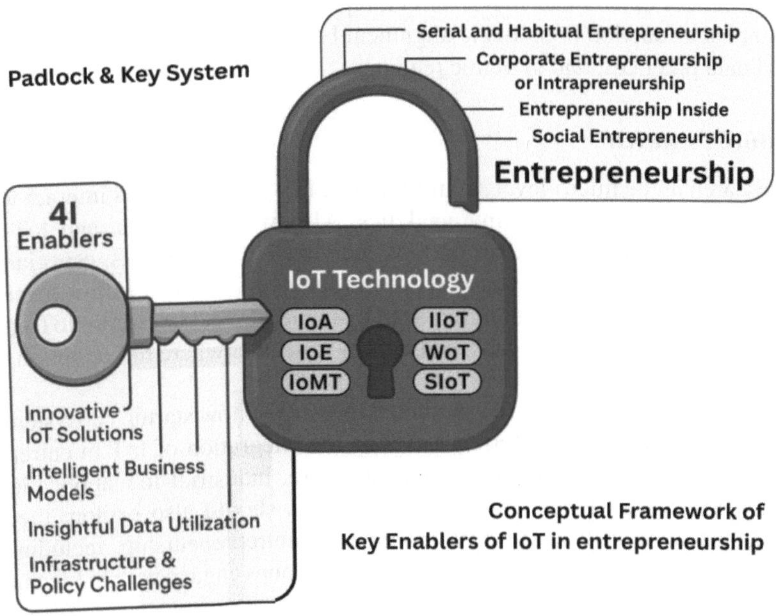

Fig. 3. Conceptual framework of key enablers of IoT in entrepreneurship

The padlock body symbolises the comprehensive domain of IoT Technologies, encompassing critical subtypes such as the Internet of Anything (IoA), Internet of Everything (IoE), Social Internet of Things (SIoT), Internet of Medical Things (IoMT), Web of Things (WoT), and Industrial Internet of Things (IIoT). These technologies form the structural foundation upon which digital entrepreneurial innovation can be built, yet they remain 'locked' unless supported by specific enablers.

The key, comprising four essential notches or teeth, embodies the 4I Key Enablers: Innovative IoT Solutions, Intelligent Business Models, Insightful Data Utilisation, and Infrastructure & Policy Challenges. Each component is vital to the integrity of the key; the absence of one renders the unlocking mechanism ineffective. This symbolises that entrepreneurial potential cannot be realised unless all four enablers are addressed and strategically aligned.

The act of unlocking the padlock metaphorically represents the realisation of various entrepreneurship types—namely Corporate Entrepreneurship or Intrapreneurship (CEI), Entrepreneurship Inside (EI), Social Entrepreneurship (SE), and Serial and Habitual

Entrepreneurship (SEHE). These entrepreneurial forms are visualised as the unlocked opportunities that emerge when the synergy between enablers and IoT technologies is effectively established.

The framework thus conveys a central philosophical insight: entrepreneurship is a locked potential, and only through the coherent application of enabling factors to the appropriate IoT technologies can this potential be accessed and activated. The directionality of the process, emphasised through visual arrows, reinforces the notion that the enablers serve as the initiating force, rather than IoT technologies alone. In essence, this conceptual model asserts that IoT-driven entrepreneurship is not a product of technology alone, but a function of strategic alignment between innovation, intelligent design, informed data practices, and systemic readiness.

3.4 Future Research

Future research at the micro-level should examine how entrepreneurs interact with specific IoT enablers such as real-time analytics, AI-powered insights, and IoT-enabled business models. Studies can focus on how individual entrepreneurs, especially those from underrepresented groups such as serial entrepreneurs or those within, leverage IoT for innovation and decision-making. Research should also address how IoT education and training reduce digital skill gaps, particularly in sectors where IoT adoption remains low.

From a meso-perspective, research should investigate how startup ecosystems, business incubators, and industry clusters facilitate the integration of IoT in entrepreneurship. Emphasis is needed on enabling infrastructure, industrial IoT applications, and entrepreneurial digitalisation across sectors. Studies should also explore the organisational adoption of IoT among different types of entrepreneurship, including social entrepreneurs and family businesses, and how these groups engage with IoT technologies such as IoE, IIoT, and SIoT.

At a macro level, future studies should evaluate the impact of national regulations, network infrastructure, and cybersecurity policies on IoT-driven entrepreneurship. There is a need to explore how policy barriers influence access to IoT for less-studied entrepreneurship types, like buying a franchise or buying a small business. Research should also assess the global disparities in IoT infrastructure and governance, particularly for emerging IoT types such as M2M, WoT, and SIoT, which remain underexplored in entrepreneurial contexts.

4 Conclusion

This study systematically investigated the intersection of the Internet of Things (IoT) and entrepreneurship through a comprehensive Systematic Literature Review (SLR) of peer-reviewed scholarly articles indexed in the Scopus database. Employing the Gioia methodology, four aggregate dimensions were identified as 4I key enablers of IoT in entrepreneurship: innovative IoT solutions, intelligent business models, insightful data utilisation, and infrastructure and policy challenges. These findings illustrate how IoT fosters connectivity, enables data-driven strategies, transforms business models, and creates opportunities and constraints within entrepreneurial ecosystems.

The analysis of perspectives revealed that corporate entrepreneurship or intrapreneurship exhibits the highest level of intersection with various IoT technology types, notably IoE, IIoT, IoMT, and WoT. Social entrepreneurship also demonstrated significant intersections with IoA, IoE, IoMT, and SIoT, indicating the potential of IoT in driving social value. Social entrepreneurship intersects primarily with IoA, IoE, IoMT, and SIoT. Entrepreneurs inside intersect mainly with IoE, and serial entrepreneurs or habitual entrepreneurs intersect with IoA. However, several entrepreneurship types, such as buying a franchise, buying a small business, and family enterprising, remain underrepresented in the existing literature. Similarly, emerging IoT types, such as M2M, WoT, and SioT, are insufficiently explored, signalling persistent research gaps and a lack of diversification in the current scholarly focus.

This research contributes to the current knowledge base by synthesising 4I key enablers and research perspectives in IoT-driven entrepreneurship. The practical implications span the domains of digital business innovation, entrepreneurial education, and policy formulation, where stakeholders must consider regulatory, infrastructural, and skill development challenges. While the SLR approach ensured methodological rigour, the study is limited by its reliance on a single database (Scopus), a narrow time frame (2020–2024), and language restriction (English only), potentially excluding relevant but non-indexed or non-English studies that could offer additional insights.

Acknowledgment. This manuscript is a publication output from an undergraduate thesis track on scientific articles in reputable international publications at the Entrepreneurship Department, Bina Nusantara University, Malang Campus. The author would like to thank the Entrepreneurship Department and the Research and Technology Transfer Office at Bina Nusantara University for their support of the research ecosystem, facilities, and publication funding.

Data Availability. **Harvard Dataverse**: "Systematic Literature Dataset on Internet of Things in Entrepreneurship (2020–2024)." https://doi.org/10.7910/DVN/QMTT6E (Santoso, C.M., Purnomo, A., 2025).

Author Contributorship. **Melvina Christy Santoso**: Data Curation, Formal Analysis, Investigation, Methodology, Resources, Software, Visualisation, Writing-Original Draft Preparation, Writing-Review and Editing.

Agung Purnomo: Conceptualisation, Data Curation, Formal Analysis, Investigation, Methodology, Resources, Validation, Funding Acquisition, Project Administration, Supervision, Writing-Review and Editing.

References

1. Abbass, A., Mehmood, K.: Impact of internet of things on business policy: the mediating role of marketing intelligence capability. Int. J. Bus. Inf. Syst. **43**, 20 (2023). https://doi.org/10.1504/IJBIS.2023.131083
2. Belfiore, A., Cuccurullo, C., Aria, M.: IoT in healthcare: A scientometric analysis. Technol. Forecast. Soc. Change. **184**, 122001 (2022). https://doi.org/10.1016/j.techfore.2022.122001
3. Fernandes, S.: Which way to cope with covid-19 challenges? Contributions of the IOT for smart city projects. Big Data Cogn. Comput. **5** (2021). https://doi.org/10.3390/bdcc5020026

4. Knieps, G.: Data-driven sector coupling in 5G-based smart networks. Compet. Regul. Netw. Ind. **22**, 53–68 (2021). https://doi.org/10.1177/1783591721992762
5. Strilets, V., Frolov, S., Datsenko, V., Tymoshenko, O., Yatsko, M.: State support for the digitalisation of SMEs in European countries. Probl. Perspect. Manag. **20**, 290–305 (2022). https://doi.org/10.21511/ppm.20(4).2022.22
6. Lafuente, E., Rabetino, R., Leiva, J.C.: Learning from success and failure: implications for entrepreneurs, SMEs, and policy. Small Bus. Econ. **64**, 1 (2024). https://doi.org/10.1007/s11187-024-00889-0
7. Mariani, M.: Big Data and analytics in tourism and hospitality: a perspective article. Tour. Rev. **75**, 299–303 (2020). https://doi.org/10.1108/TR-06-2019-0259
8. Putri, S.I.E, Irawan, M.C.S, Ardianov, H.R., Purnomo, A., Rosyidah, E., Meiryani: Artificial intelligence in the entrepreneurship: patent landscape analysis. In: 2023 international conference on inventive computation technologies (ICICT), pp. 441–447. IEEE (2023). https://doi.org/10.1109/ICICT57646.2023.10134114
9. Zhao, F., Barratt-Pugh, L., Suseno, Y., Standen, P., Redmond, J.: A framework for exploring digital entrepreneurship development from a social interaction perspective. J. Gen. Manag. **48**, 115–126 (2023). https://doi.org/10.1177/03063070211044578
10. Biclesanu, I., Savastano, M., Chinie, C., Anagnoste, S.: The role of business students' entrepreneurial intention and technology preparedness in the digital age. Adm. Sci. **13** (2023). https://doi.org/10.3390/admsci13080177
11. Nakayama, M., Isik, Ö., Sutcliffe, N., Olbrich, S.: Grassroots business intelligence as an enabler of change management: a case study at a large global manufacturing firm. Complex Syst. Informatics Model. Q. **2020**, 1–11 (2020). https://doi.org/10.7250/csimq.2020-23.01
12. Ashraf, R., Khan, M.A., Khuhro, R.A., Bhatti, Z.A.: Knowledge creation dynamics of technological forecasting and social change special issues. Technol. Forecast. Soc. Change. **180**, 121663 (2022). https://doi.org/10.1016/j.techfore.2022.121663
13. Gardner, M.: California tool works: assessing the impact of life science incubators and accelerators. J. Commer. Biotechnol. **26**, 104–109 (2021). https://doi.org/10.5912/jcb977
14. Henkel, J.: Licensing standard-essential patents in the IoT—A value chain perspective on the markets for technology. Res. Policy **51**, 104600 (2022). https://doi.org/10.1016/j.respol.2022.104600
15. Purnomo, A., Rosyidah, E., Firdaus, M., Asitah, N., Septianto, A.: Data science publication: thirty-six years lesson of scientometric review. Proc. 2020 Int. Conf. Inf. Manag. Technol. ICIMTech. **2020**, 893–898 (2020). https://doi.org/10.1109/ICIMTech50083.2020.9211192
16. Islam, N., Marinakis, Y., Majadillas, M.A., Fink, M., Walsh, S.T.: Here there be dragons, a pre-roadmap construct for IoT service infrastructure. Technol. Forecast. Soc. Change. **155**, 0–1 (2020). https://doi.org/10.1016/j.techfore.2017.09.016
17. Qin, W.: How to unleash frugal innovation through internet of things and artificial intelligence: Moderating role of entrepreneurial knowledge and future challenges. Technol. Forecast. Soc. Change. **202**, 123286 (2024). https://doi.org/10.1016/j.techfore.2024.123286
18. Boudreau, K.J.: Promoting platform takeoff and self-fulfilling expectations: field experimental evidence. Manage. Sci. **67**, 5953–5967 (2021). https://doi.org/10.1287/mnsc.2021.3999
19. Lukita, C., Hardini, M., Pranata, S., Julianingsih, D., Santoso, N.P.L.: Transformation of entrepreneurship and digital technology students in the era of revolution 4.0. APTISI Trans. Technopreneursh. **5**, 291–304 (2023). https://doi.org/10.34306/att.v5i3.356
20. Choudhuri, B., Srivastava, P.R., Gupta, S., Kumar, A., Bag, S.: Determinants of Smart Digital Infrastructure Diffusion for Urban Public Services. J. Glob. Inf. Manag. **29** (2021). https://doi.org/10.4018/JGIM.295976
21. Giuggioli, G., Pellegrini, M.M.: Artificial intelligence as an enabler for entrepreneurs: a systematic literature review and an agenda for future research. Int. J. Entrep. Behav. Res. **29**, 816–837 (2023). https://doi.org/10.1108/IJEBR-05-2021-0426

22. Marinakis, Y., Walsh, S.T., Harms, R.: Age matters: how generational decision-making cohorts affect disruptive technology new product development. IEEE Trans. Eng. Manag. **71**, 274–282 (2024). https://doi.org/10.1109/TEM.2021.3116204
23. Zainuddin, A.A., Nor, R.M., Handayani, D., Mohd. Tamrin, M.I., Subramaniam, K., Sadikan, S.F.N.: Smart attendance in classroom (CObot): IoT and facial recognition for educational and entrepreneurial impact. APTISI Trans. Technopreneursh. **6**, 608–622 (2024). https://doi.org/10.34306/att.v6i3.497
24. Lachvajderová, L., Kádárová, J.: Industry 4.0 implementation and industry 5.0 readiness in industrial enterprises. Manag. Prod. Eng. Rev. **13**, 102–109 (2022). https://doi.org/10.24425/mper.2022.142387
25. Purnomo, A., Firdaus, M., Firdausi, N., Rosyidah, E., Anam, F., Pratama, F.C., Carollina, D.: E-business in digital economy: a systematic literature review. Presented at the (2024). https://doi.org/10.1063/5.0192363
26. Nguyen, T., Elbanna, A.: Understanding human-AI augmentation in the workplace: a review and a future research agenda. Inf. Syst. Front. (2025). https://doi.org/10.1007/s10796-025-10591-5
27. Maulana, F.I., Kurniawan, B.K., Pramono, A., Purnomo, A., Abdulah, M.E.B.Z., Mohamed, M.: Internet of things for smart furniture: a systematic review. In: 2024 international conference on ICT for smart society (ICISS), pp. 1–6. IEEE (2024). https://doi.org/10.1109/ICISS62896.2024.10750984
28. Magnani, G., Gioia, D.: Using the Gioia methodology in international business and entrepreneurship research. Int. Bus. Rev. **32**, 102097 (2023). https://doi.org/10.1016/j.ibusrev.2022.102097
29. Gioia, D.A., Corley, K.G., Hamilton, A.L.: Seeking qualitative rigor in inductive research. Organ. Res. Methods **16**, 15–31 (2013). https://doi.org/10.1177/1094428112452151
30. Mollenkopf-Pigsley, C.: Book review: entrepreneurship: the practice and mindset (2021). https://doi.org/10.1177/0266242620976289
31. Jazaeri, S.S., Jabbehdari, S., Asghari, P., Haj Seyyed Javadi, H.: Edge computing in SDN-IoT networks: a systematic review of issues, challenges and solutions. Springer US (2021). https://doi.org/10.1007/s10586-021-03311-6
32. Inoue, Y., Takenaka, T., Kasasaku, T., Tamegai, T., Arai, R.: How to design platform ecosystems by intrapreneurs: implications from action design research on IoT-based platform. Electron. Mark. **33** (2023). https://doi.org/10.1007/s12525-023-00618-7
33. Knieps, G.: Internet of things, critical infrastructures, and the governance of cybersecurity in 5G network slicing. Telecomm. Policy. **48**, 102867 (2024). https://doi.org/10.1016/j.telpol.2024.102867
34. Serrano, D.R., Fraguas-Sánchez, A.I., González-Burgos, E., Martín, P., Llorente, C., Lalatsa, A.: Women as Industry 4.0. Entrepreneurs: unlocking the potential of entrepreneurship in higher education in STEM-related fields. J. Innov. Entrep. **12** (2023). https://doi.org/10.1186/s13731-023-00346-4

The Future of Conversation is Evolving from Human Dialogue to Hybrid Human-Agentic Discourse

Tegwen Malik[1,2](✉), Laurie Hughes[3], and Yogesh K. Dwivedi[4,5]

[1] School of Management, Swansea University—Bay Campus, Swansea, UK
f.t.malik@swansea.ac.uk
[2] Digital Futures for Sustainable Business and Society Research Group, Swansea, UK
[3] Edith Cowan University, Joondalup, WA, Australia
[4] ISOM Department, KFUPM Business School, King Fahd University of Petroleum and Minerals, Dhahran, Saudi Arabia
[5] IRC for Finance and Digital Economy, King Fahd University of Petroleum and Minerals (KFUPM), Dhahran, Saudi Arabia

Abstract. In an era increasingly dominated by artificial intelligence (AI), the essence of human conversation is undergoing significant transformation. Once exclusively human, conversation is now increasingly mediated by AI agents, voice assistants, and digital platforms. This paper critically explores this profound shift, examining the nature and implications of hybrid human machine discourse. Addressing three fundamental questions, we interrogate what constitutes genuine conversation when one party lacks consciousness and emotion; how traditional norms of human dialogue translate into human-machine interactions; and what considerations developers and governance frameworks must prioritize in this evolving context. Building upon Nass and Brave's (2005) concept of "voice activation," which demonstrates humans' inherent social responses toward artificial speech, this study identifies the dual promise and peril of conversational AI, emphasizing the risks of confusion, over-trust, and emotional misdirection. Arguing that AI-driven dialogue is not merely automation but a profound cultural and ethical shift, this research advocates for new literacies, ethical frameworks, and a re-evaluation of what authentic communication entails. By tracing the philosophical roots and current technological practices of conversation, the study underscores the urgency of rethinking communication ethics, literacy, and practice in our increasingly hybrid human-machine conversational landscape.

Keywords: Artificial intelligence · Hybrid conversation · Voice activation · Communication ethics · Human-machine interaction · Agentic systems

1 Introduction: The Emergence of Hybrid Conversation

In an era increasingly shaped by artificial intelligence (AI), most people remain largely unaware that the very nature of conversation is undergoing profound transformation. What was once an exclusively human activity, rich in nuance, emotion, and cultural

Published by Springer Nature Switzerland AG 2026
A. Elbanna et al. (Eds.): TDIT 2025, IFIP AICT 778, pp. 210–222, 2026.
https://doi.org/10.1007/978-3-032-16775-0_14

complexity is now being reconfigured by our growing interactions with AI agents and agentic systems, chatbots, voice assistants, and digital platforms [1–3]. From casual queries to Alexa to emotionally charged exchanges with chatbots, we are entering an era in which hybrid human machine discourse is no longer speculative but increasingly woven into the fabric of everyday communication. While comparisons between human and AI discourse are not new, this paper builds on existing literature by synthesising conversational dimensions through a socio-ethical lens and proposing a new framework for evaluating hybrid dialogue in real-world contexts.

This evolution is not merely technical; it raises profound social, cognitive, and ethical questions [4]. At its core, conversation is a fundamentally human experience characterized by active listening, empathy, humour, timing, cultural awareness, and non-verbal cues. As AI agents increasingly assume the role of conversational partners, we are challenged to critically examine and potentially reformulate these qualities, in light of machine-mediated interaction. This paper seeks to explore how AI-mediated communication is reshaping the norms and ethics of conversation, particularly in contexts where emotional, social, and cultural stakes are high. The objective is to better inform both technological design and governance by understanding how conversational practices change when one participant lacks consciousness, intent, or emotion. To this end this paper explores three pressing questions:

- What constitutes a "conversation" when one participant lacks consciousness, emotion, lived experience, and is non-human, particularly regarding non-verbal cues?
- How do established human norms of dialogue translate into interactions with machines?
- What distinct considerations must AI developers and governance frameworks each address to ensure ethical and meaningful hybrid human–machine dialogue?

This paper explores these questions by examining both the design imperatives for AI developers (such as transparency, trust-building, and cultural sensitivity) and the policy responsibilities of governance frameworks, including ethical safeguards, regulatory oversight, and accountability mechanisms.

We define "conversation" as a dynamic, interactive process involving the exchange of meaning through language, turn-taking, non-verbal cues, and contextual awareness. While conversation can occur in many modalities, this study focuses primarily on voice-based and text-based forms as mediated by AI systems. Although examples like Alexa involve spoken interfaces, the discussion includes text-based agents such as ChatGPT, reflecting the hybrid and multimodal nature of contemporary conversational AI. Thus, conversational AI, in the context of this paper, refers to AI systems capable of engaging in dialogue with users through natural language, either via speech or text. These systems include voice assistants, chatbots, and large language models (LLMs) that simulate human-like interactions.

While this paper adopts the term "conversation" to describe interactions with AI, it does so with the recognition that such language is metaphorical. AI systems do not possess consciousness, intentionality, or lived experience; thus, what appears as dialogue is in fact a simulation of communicative exchange, shaped by algorithms rather than human reciprocity. To support these inquiries, this paper identifies and draws upon key dimensions of conversation, such as turn-taking, empathy, silence, context, and trust, which will be examined in relation to both human and human–AI discourse.

Nass and Brave's [5] work on voice interfaces highlights how deeply ingrained our social responses to speech are regardless of whether the speaker is human or artificial. In their book "Wired for Speech", they show that people respond to machine-generated voices as if they were human, applying the same social expectations, biases, and emotional reactions. This "voice-activation" phenomenon explains both the promise and the peril of conversational AI: it can feel natural and intuitive, yet it can also lead to confusion, over-trust, or even emotional misdirection. Hence, while digital conversation brings specific capabilities (i.e. speed, scalability and availability), it also introduces new challenges for us to navigate. Issues of trust, mutuality, and meaning become especially significant when dialogue lacks a shared human consciousness. This paper looks at the evolution of conversation with the rise of hybrid human-agentic conversation not just as a technical development, but as a cultural shift that requires new literacies, new ethics, and a rethinking of what it means to truly communicate. This paper traces the evolution of conversation from its philosophical and civic roots to its current technological reconfigurations in agentic systems. Drawing on classical concepts of rhetoric and dialectic as well as contemporary examples of agentic systems, we argue that we are not simply automating dialogue but are redefining it as rapidly as the technology advances with far-reaching implications for literacy, ethics, and the future of communication.

The remainder of this paper is structured as follows: the next section outlines the inherent complexities within human conversation. The following section discusses the intricacies of AI agents acting as conversational partners and the problems therein. The Rethinking Dialogue section outlines the contrasts in conversations between human and machine across a range of dimensions and the many implications for system designers and governance models. The paper is concluded in the final section.

2 Human Conversation: The Art and Complexity of Dialogue

Human-to-human conversation is a deeply embodied, culturally situated, and emotionally intelligent process. It relies on a complex set of interwoven skills such as active listening, empathy, shared meaning-making, turn-taking, appropriate use of silence, and non-verbal cues [6]. At its most powerful, conversation is not just about exchanging information but rather about an emotional and deep connection and exchange with one or more human beings. Unlike transactional communication, human dialogue is rich with nuance, shaped by timing, tone, context, emotional presence, and cultural background. Human conversation has long been shaped and extended by technologies, from telephones to instant messaging platforms, each influencing norms of interaction, timing, and trust.

Silence is a potent multimodal feature of conversations, often experienced differently by participants. While some individuals may perceive silence as uncomfortable, prompting them to fill gaps quickly, others view it not as an empty void but as a meaningful communicative act, conveying profound emotions, respect, or contemplation. Conversations can also unfold as rapid exchanges of diverse and seemingly disconnected ideas. While appearing fragmented, such dialogues often vividly reflect active engagement, curiosity, and genuine interest between participants. These contextual subtleties shape how we interpret intention, meaning, and trust.

As Maynard and Zimmerman [7] illustrate, even the beginnings of conversation between strangers or acquaintances involve subtle "pre-topical sequences" and "setting talk" which we as humans use as ritualized strategies to negotiate who speaks, what gets discussed, and how intimacy or distance is managed. These forms of conversational scaffolding reveal how dialogue is not just a cognitive task but a deeply social one, grounded in shared categories, mutual recognition, and interpersonal norms. Moreover, conversation is not a solitary cognitive act, rather it is a form of moment-by-moment co-creation by both (or all) participants. We constantly adjust our speech based on cues from others: we mirror tone and pace, we recalibrate when someone looks confused, and we intuitively switch (and adapt) how we do all this depending on formality, familiarity, or emotional tone. In this way, dialogue is both responsive and adaptive, demanding not only linguistic skill but social and emotional intelligence [8].

At its core, conversation is also ethical in nature requiring mutual respect, willingness to listen, and often for the vulnerability to be heard in full. It can affirm dignity, build trust, and resolve conflict and on the flip side it can just as easily exclude, dominate, or manipulate. These human competencies make conversation not only a means of communication but a foundation for collaboration, social cohesion, and the development of interpersonal trust. Through discourse (which can take many approaches), we construct a sense of who we are and present ourselves to others [9, 10], cultivating a sense of belonging and membership within social groups [11]. Conversational interactions also allow for the play of wit and humour, which serve not only as expressions of personality but as social tools for connection and inclusion. It is this depth of engagement that AI systems, for all their sophistication, struggle to replicate or fully understand [12].

3 Enter the AI Agent: Human-AI Conversation and Its Implications

This section bridges both voice-based (e.g., Alexa) and text-based (e.g., ChatGPT, Copilot) forms of AI interaction, reflecting the convergence of modalities in contemporary conversational systems. Although the emphasis on voice activation theory highlights our social reactions to speech, similar dynamics can occur with text when anthropomorphic cues (e.g., tone, emojis, name) are present. As AI systems evolve, they are no longer mere tools for information retrieval but are increasingly assuming the role of conversational partners. Whether asking Alexa to play music, engaging in therapeutic exchanges with the soon to be decommissioned mental health chatbot *Woebot*, or turning to ChatGPT, Microsoft Copilot or Azure AI for help with writing or decision-making, we are now directly speaking with machines, not just through them. This shift from transactional command-based systems to seemingly relational, dialogic agents, marks a fundamental transformation in how communication technologies are integrated into everyday life. Clark et al. [8] found that users are increasingly negotiating blurred boundaries between utilitarian and social uses of conversation, highlighting the need for a reconceptualization of what it means to "converse" with a machine. Crucially, these AI agents draw on sophisticated language models trained on large data sets of human communication

[2]. Yet, while they may simulate conversational competence, they lack the embodied consciousness, emotional resonance, and social accountability that define human dialogue [12]. Their "listening" is statistical, their "responses" probabilistic [1]. AI systems neither remember, nor feel, nor genuinely understand; they lack the capacity for comprehension. Yet, paradoxically, we still engage with them conversationally, thanking them, trusting them, and at times even confiding deeply personal thoughts to these digital entities.

This paradox is explained, in part, by the social psychology of voice which Nass and Brave [5] discuss in Wired for Speech on how humans are "voice-activated" (meaning that we respond to machine-generated voices with the same emotional and social cues that we would apply when conversing with real people). Whether it's trusting a friendly GPS voice or attributing personality to a customer service bot, we engage in human-like ways even when intellectually we understand that the other "speaker" is not a person (reminding us that what we call a 'conversation' with a machine is a simulation, shaped by design and data, not by reciprocal understanding). This social response mechanism helps explain why AI-driven conversation can feel surprisingly natural and, at times, deceptively so [5]. Building on this, Bickmore and Cassell [13] argue that humans use a variety of relational conversational strategies, such as small talk, to establish trust. This can be embodied by conversational agents that can leverage similar strategies using multimodal social cues to promote similar levels of user trust. The Bickmore model of social dialogue shows that even minimal relational engagement from agents can significantly impact user perception, especially for extroverted users. Trust, they argue, is not just a technical precondition but a communicative achievement requiring intentional social signalling.

However, it is important to recognise that these agentic discourses have limitations, yet humans often continue to project the same expectations onto AI agents as they would onto human counterparts [14]. Nass and Moon [14] explore such "mindless" behaviour by exploring conditioned behaviour and habits like humans being "polite" with their AI agent. This brings us to the relatively recent work by Jawale et al. [12] whereby they highlight the technical and cognitive challenges AI systems face when processing natural human conversation. Through detailed attention entropy analysis and domain-specific comparisons, their study revealed that Large Language Models (LLMs) struggle with the demands of human-to-human dialogue. Unlike structured text or mathematical queries, natural conversation involves dispersed attention, long-range dependencies, and nuanced context management. The research in [12] shows that conversational data exhibits uniquely complex patterns of interdependence that current models are not well-specialized to handle. Their findings underscore that, despite appearing fluent, AI systems often lack the deeper contextual anchoring needed for human-like interaction. In this light, we might view agentic AI not as a seamless conversational partner but as a partial proxy which is capable of mirroring form but not always function. These responses may sound convincing, but they are detached from lived experience, embodied emotion, and ethical self-awareness. All of this has profound implications for how we interpret meaning, assign trust, and navigate relational boundaries in human–machine interactions and is critical we take the time to work out how to integrate ethical and human values and norms into shaping this hybrid dialogue which leads us into the next section of this paper.

4 Rethinking Dialogue

As we move into an era of ever-increasing hybrid communication where humans converse not only with each other but also with AI systems, it becomes essential to understand how these different forms of discourse diverge, converge, and influence one another. This includes distinguishing among different modalities of AI-mediated conversation, such as voice-based systems, text-based chatbots, and ambient conversational agents, as each presents distinct technical and social dynamics [15]. As discussed earlier, human-to-human conversation is rich in social, emotional, cultural, ethical and non-verbal dimensions [6, 8]. By contrast we have seen that human-to-machine interactions remain structurally and experientially distinct and often raise unique design and governance challenges. For instance, it is essential to recognize that AI agents operate through feedback loops, adapting their responses based on structured inputs, reinforcement signals, or refined human prompts, where conversational turn-taking is procedural rather than intuitive [2, 3, 16]. To illustrate these distinctions, Table 1 presents the key dimensions that underpin a conversation and contrasts them for human-to-human and human-to-machine discourse. This table also highlights where the design of AI systems must diverge from natural conversational norms, and where governance frameworks must intervene to uphold trust, dignity, and meaningful and safe engagement.

While AI can replicate certain distinct conversational features of dialogue (such as semantic coherence and emotional tone), it lacks the deeper socio-emotional and ethical substrates that define and are imbedded within what we take to be meaningful human communication [14, 17]. Developers and policymakers must therefore consider not only what AI can say, but how, why, and in what contexts these systems are deployed. By mapping these distinctions (and dimensions of conversation), this paper suggests that there needs to be a new ethic of hybrid discourse that centres on transparency, shared responsibility, and cultural sensitivity. AI-mediated conversation must not only be intelligible and functional but also aligned with the human values embedded in communication: empathy, dignity, trust, and respect.

As interactions with AI become increasingly frequent and personal, the conversational qualities inherent in human-to-human dialogue will no longer serve merely as desirable extras in human-to-machine interactions. Instead, these human-like qualities will become critical for safeguarding the integrity, inclusiveness, and meaningfulness of hybrid discourse. Therefore, reshaping conversation involves more than refining language models; it demands a reimagining of conversation as an ethical and social practice that bridges human and digital participants. As we reimagine hybrid dialogue, it might help to reflect back to how Aristotle framed rhetoric, not as manipulation but as a moral act rooted in ethos (credibility of the speaker), pathos (emotional appeal to the audience), and logos (logical arguments), whilst he also recognized that meaningful dialogue also draws from dialectic (the pursuit of truth through reciprocal reasoning) and the role of coffee houses as early incubators of civic discourse [18]. All this should remind us that conversation, at its best, is both culturally situated and ethically charged. This shift

Table 1. Comparison of Human-to-Human and Human-to-Machine Discourse with Implications for AI and Agentic System Design and Governance.

Conversation dimension	Human-to-human conversation	Human-to-machine conversation	Implications for AI and agentic system developers and governance frameworks
Turn-taking	Fluid, often overlapping; regulated by social cues like gaze, intonation, and gestures	Sequential and linear; typically constrained by system architecture and lacks the fluid adaptability of human interaction. Interruptions or overlaps are often not recognised	Design systems to manage real-time responsiveness, including handling interruptions and overlaps more naturally, where possible. More adaptive turn-taking models developed using multimodal inputs (e.g., voice tone, facial expression); governance should mandate transparency about conversational boundaries and interaction rules
Silence/pauses	Can be meaningful (e.g., respect, reflection, emotional weight); culturally nuanced	Often interpreted as malfunction or prompt for user to repeat	Train AI systems to handle silence more contextually; avoid forcing interaction loops. Governance should ensure systems are culturally aware and sensitive to non-verbal communication norms
Contextual memory	Humans recall shared history (or experiences), emotional tone, and adjust based on the type of relationship or context	Memory is limited; lacks genuine continuity or personal history in a human sense	Developers must clarify memory limitations; governance should require explainability around memory use, data retention, and consent for long-term contextual awareness

(*continued*)

Table 1. (*continued*)

Conversation dimension	Human-to-human conversation	Human-to-machine conversation	Implications for AI and agentic system developers and governance frameworks
Empathy and emotion	Emotion is felt, sensed, and reciprocated; empathy emerges through shared vulnerability	Empathy is simulated through affective cues but is not genuinely felt by the machine (or algorithm)	Design emotional cues with ethical limits (avoid deceptive anthropomorphism). Governance should mandate safeguards to prevent emotional manipulation or over-trust in vulnerable users
Trust-building	Built through relational cues (e.g., small talk, consistency, ethical behaviour)	Trust may be assumed due to fluency or personality-like traits, but lacks genuine reciprocity	Require user awareness of agent limitations (however relatable or lifelike they are). Developers should integrate calibrated trust mechanisms. Governance bodies should ensure users are not misled by false human-like abilities
Cultural sensitivity	Conversational style adapts to cultural background, language use, and norms	Rapidly evolving; multilingual models and culturally adaptive features are emerging (e.g., Microsoft's cultural AI projects), but limitations remain in local nuance and depth	Developers must diversify training data and fine-tune for cultural contexts. Hence, continued investment in culturally adaptive training and localisation required. Policy should ensure culturally appropriate and inclusive design standards

(*continued*)

Table 1. (*continued*)

Conversation dimension	Human-to-human conversation	Human-to-machine conversation	Implications for AI and agentic system developers and governance frameworks
Non-verbal communication	Includes gestures, eye contact, body language, facial expressions (some of which can be very subtle)	Largely absent or simulated (e.g., emoji, avatar movement); likely to miss subtle cues by the human in the discourse	Consider integrating multimodal interaction (e.g., embodied agents that are better able to respond to their environment and use non-verbal communication). However, governance should establish standards for meaningful non-verbal communication in AI–human interfaces
Intent and ethics	Often guided by shared moral intuitions as well as social and cultural norms and upbringing	AI lacks intent or ethical awareness. It is only able to simulate moral reasoning	Developers must avoid implying agency or intentionality. Governance should require ethical design standards and prevent anthropomorphic misrepresentations

(*continued*)

Table 1. *(continued)*

Conversation dimension	Human-to-human conversation	Human-to-machine conversation	Implications for AI and agentic system developers and governance frameworks
Dialogue evolution	Shaped by shared experience, mutual adjustment, evolving relationships	Often one-off, impersonal, and static (unless context continuity is deliberately built-in), lacks lived shared experience	Promote dialogic continuity in long-term agentic use cases. Governance should encourage designs that allow for meaningful but bounded and safe relationship modelling (especially when interacting with vulnerable individuals and in therapeutic settings)
Shared sense-making	Emerges through mutual negotiation, layered interpretation, personal investment and shared understanding	Generated probabilistically based on language prediction and surface relevance as well as stored memory	Developers must not conflate fluency (and contextual prediction) with understanding. Governance should require clear disclosure of AI's lack of true comprehension, especially in emotionally sensitive or decision-critical contexts

requires dialogue among designers, regulators, researchers, and civil society to ensure these technologies foster ethical communicative inbuilt ability.

5 Designing for Human Values in Hybrid Conversations

This paper has aimed not only to understand hybrid conversation, but also to foreground actionable insights for AI developers and governance stakeholders. Ethical design, contextual sensitivity, and user transparency must be embedded at both the system and regulatory levels. By integrating social norms and values into AI systems, we can move toward more humane and trustworthy interactions. As conversational AI becomes more embedded in everyday life, it is reshaping not just how we communicate, but the social norms that govern communication itself. Turn-taking, once a fluid and culturally nuanced dance between humans, is now regulated by code (shaped by prompts and at times frustratingly, system glitches and network overload) rather than shared social intuition and non-verbal cues. Silence, that can be rich with meaning (and opportunity) within a human-to-human conversation, is often flattened into a technical signal when having a dialogue with an AI agent. As users increasingly project emotion, trust, and even companionship onto machines, serious ethical questions arise around manipulation, consent, and the treatment of vulnerable populations such as children and the elderly. These shifts raise urgent questions about accountability: Who is responsible when a seemingly benign conversation with an AI lead to harm or misunderstanding? Meanwhile, the very structure of conversation is changing as we enter an age where there can be multiple AI agents within our human environments (e.g. homes with multiple voice assistants, offices with ambient AI, public spaces where machines participate in dialogue). Conversational ecosystems powered by AI offer significant promise, including improved decision-making, novel forms of support, and enhanced accessibility. However, these advancements also introduce critical risks, such as the amplification of bias at scale, potentially undermining trust in hybrid discourse, and fostering overreliance on systems that simulate understanding without genuine comprehension. Navigating these complexities requires not just advanced AI models, but a fundamental reassessment of what it means to speak, listen, and genuinely understand within increasingly hybrid communicative landscapes.

6 Conclusion and Limitations

This paper has mapped the ethical, social, and communicative dimensions of human–AI discourse, offering a structured lens for evaluating hybrid conversation. While it contributes to theory-building in this emerging space, the analysis is limited by its reliance on secondary sources rather than empirical data. Future work should incorporate qualitative methods (such as interviews and focus groups) to validate and refine the proposed conversational dimensions in real-world human–AI interactions.

Disclosure This manuscript has been edited with the assistance of GPT-4o for grammar correction and stylistic improvements. All content, intellectual contributions, and final interpretations remain the responsibility of the authors, who have thoroughly reviewed and approved the final version of the manuscript.

References

1. Floridi, L., Chiriatti, M.: GPT-3: Its nature, scope, limits, and consequences. Mind. Mach. **30**(4), 681–694 (2020). https://doi.org/10.1007/s11023-020-09548-1
2. Hughes, L., Dwivedi, Y. K., Malik, T., Shawosh, M., Albashrawi, M. A., Jeon, I., ... Walton, P.: AI agents and agentic systems: a multi-expert analysis. J. Comput. Inform. Syst. 1–29. https://doi.org/10.1080/08874417.2025.2483832
3. Hughes, L., Dwivedi, Y.K., Li, K., Appanderanda, M., Al-Bashrawi, M.A., Chae, I.: AI agents and agentic systems: redefining global it management. J. Glob. Inf. Technol. Manag. (2025). https://doi.org/10.1080/1097198X.2025.2524286
4. McKee, H.A., Porter, J.E.: Ethics for AI writing: the importance of rhetorical context. In: Proceedings of the AAAI/ACM Conference on AI, Ethics, and Society, pp. 110–116 (2020). https://doi.org/10.1145/3375627.3375811
5. Nass, C., Brave, S.: Wired for Speech: How Voice Activates and Advances the Human-Computer Relationship. MIT Press. https://mitpress.mit.edu/9780262640657/wired-for-speech/ (2005). Accessed 26/06/25
6. Wilson, T.P., Zimmerman, D.H.: The structure of silence between turns in two-party conversation. Discour. Process. **9**(4), 375–390 (1986). https://doi.org/10.1080/01638538609544649
7. Maynard, D.W., Zimmerman, D.H.: Topical talk, ritual and the social organization of relationships. Soc. Psychol. Quarter. 301–316 (1984). https://doi.org/10.2307/3033633
8. Clark, L., Pantidi, N., Cooney, O., Doyle, P., Garaialde, D., Edwards, J., Spillane, B., Gilmartin, E., Murad, C., Munteanu, C., Wade, V.: What makes a good conversation? challenges in designing truly conversational agents. In: Proceedings of the 2019 CHI Conference on Human Factors in Computing Systems, pp. 1–12 (2019). https://doi.org/10.1145/3290605.330070
9. Mackenzie, L.B.: 'When words fail, music speaks': How communication transforms identity through performance at the Berkshire Hills Music Academy. University of Massachusetts Amherst (2005)
10. Davies, B., Harré, R.: Positioning: the discursive production of selves. J. Theory Soc. Behav. **20**(1), 43–63 (1990). https://doi.org/10.1111/j.1468-5914.1990.tb00174.x
11. Allen, K.A., Kern, M.L., Rozek, C.S., McInerney, D.M., Slavich, G.M.: Belonging: a review of conceptual issues, an integrative framework, and directions for future research. Aust. J. Psychol. **73**(1), 87–102 (2021). https://doi.org/10.1080/00049530.2021.1883409
12. Jawale, T., Animesh, C., Vallath, S., Talamadupula, K., Heck, L.: Are Human Conversations Special? A Large Language Model Perspective (2024). arXiv preprint arXiv:2403.05045. https://doi.org/10.48550/arXiv.2403.05045
13. Bickmore, T., Cassell, J.: Relational agents: a model and implementation of building user trust. In: Proceedings of the SIGCHI conference on Human factors in computing systems, pp. 396–403 (2001). https://doi.org/10.1145/365024.36530
14. Nass, C., Moon, Y.: Machines and mindlessness: social responses to computers. J. Soc. Issues **56**(1), 81–103 (2000)
15. Gkinko, L., Elbanna, A.: Hope, tolerance and empathy: employees' emotions when using an AI-enabled chatbot in a digitalised workplace. Inf. Technol. People **35**(4), 1714–1743 (2022)
16. Levinson, S.C.: Turn-taking in human communication–origins and implications for language processing. Trends Cogn. Sci. **20**(1), 6–14 (2016). https://doi.org/10.1016/j.tics.2015.10.010

17. Diederich, S., Brendel, A.B., Morana, S., Kolbe, L.: On the design of and interaction with conversational agents: an organizing and assessing review of human-computer interaction research. J. Assoc. Inf. Syst. **23**(1), 96–138 (2022)
18. London Walks.: The History of London's Coffee Houses. https://www.walks.com/blog/history-of-london-coffeehouses/#:~:text=The%20impact%20of%20coffee%20houses,have%20caused%20major%20commercial%20problems. (2024) Accessed 2nd June 2025

Exploring Behavioural Intentions to Use the Metaverse in Higher Education: The Case of Oman

Moza Al Kindi(✉), Malak Al Amri, Ali Tarhini, and Hilal Hamed Al Busaidi

Department of Information Systems, Sultan Qaboos University, Muscat, Oman
{S147549,S147553,S114133}@student.squ.edu.om,
ali.tarhini@hotmail.co.uk

Abstract. The growing merging of virtual and immersive platforms in education necessitates a deeper understanding of their acceptance in different settings. As the Metaverse, a representative of immersive technologies, gains ground in worldwide education, it is crucial to grasp its infusion in multicultural contexts. This paper is directed at probing the behavioral intention of higher-education learners in Oman to implement the Metaverse. The authors resorted to an integrated model that synthesizes UTAUT2, Self-Determination Theory, Innovation Diffusion Theory, and Flow Theory. They employed a quantitative cross-sectional research design, gathered data from 278 students through an online survey, and analyzed it by means of Partial Least Squares Structural Equation Modelling (PLS-SEM). The survey's factors are interest, social influence, observability, and relatedness, which are significantly leading to adoption, while such factors as hedonic motivation, habit, and perceived risk had a very marginal role. Results confirm the significance of social and emotional aspects over individuals' utility in the initial stage of adoption. This paper provides regionally grounded insights into the global discourse on immersive learning technologies.

Keywords: Metaverse adoption · Higher education · Behavioural intention

1 Introduction

Higher education is being changed by the rapid progress of digital technologies. A lot of changes open up new opportunities for educators, learners, and student involvement. An innovation is the Metaverse. It produces virtual spaces where students are quite like they would be in real life; they can work together or just spend time exploring the subject matter. The Metaverse presents several possibilities for the next generation of learning platforms. Its function as an enabler of active and personalized learning while being flexible and convenient makes it a vital contender [1–3]. Globally, universities are pushing their limits to embrace the Metaverse, considering it a way to revolutionize the learning process and break out of the typical classroom paradigm. It is a means through which students' experience and self-reflection can be facilitated via the use of

Published by Springer Nature Switzerland AG 2026
A. Elbanna et al. (Eds.): TDIT 2025, IFIP AICT 778, pp. 223–246, 2026.
https://doi.org/10.1007/978-3-032-16775-0_15

virtual labs, simulations, and gamified environments [4–6]. But a successful outcome of adopting these technologies may depend not only on the availability of infrastructure but also on the students' decision to use and embrace them [7, 8]. The field of higher education in Oman has become digital. The incorporation of virtual worlds in places of learning is still very small, with the Metaverse being one of them. Institutions do not have students' motivation, perceptions, and readiness clearly outlined. Research in Western or East Asian countries is where these points are often concentrated. Cultural values, educational systems, and digital exposure are quite different from the Omani context [5, 9]. Decision-makers without local evidence may find it hard to design strategies that are relevant and effective for their students.

In light of this gap, the present study is timely and significant. Its primary objective is to comprehensively analyze the psychological, motivational, and societal factors that affect the students' willingness to embrace the Metaverse devices in the universities of Oman. An integrated framework that merges the Unified Theory of Acceptance and Use of Technology 2 (UTAUT2), Self-Determination Theory (SDT), Innovation Diffusion Theory (IDT), and Flow Theory [10, 11] is employed in the study. To this end, the paper explores to what degree the autonomy, social influence, perceived risk, and flow experience component individually or collectively influence the behavioral intentions of Metaverse adoption. The goal herein is not only to provide theoretical insights but also to give practical advice to the institutions that are being prepared for the immersive digital transformation. The research question this paper attempts to answer is as follows:

Q. What are the main drivers of Omani students' behavioural intentions to adopt the Metaverse at university?

2 Literature Review

The metaverse is getting more attention from people who believe it is a game-changing tool in the world of higher education. It can provide such fulfilling, interactive, and socially engaging virtual environments [12]. Through technology like 3D simulations, virtual laboratories, and cooperative learning spaces, it improves student participation, memory of facts, and freedom [3, 13]. Roy et al. conducted a PRISMA review of seventy-three studies that mapped the current research of educational applications of the metaverse globally and revealed significant gaps in localized empirical research and the domination of theoretical assumptions [3]. According to Wang and Shin, students' intention to use immersive technologies is mainly influenced by ease of use and context-specific learning experiences [14]. On the other hand, these conclusions mostly apply to Western and East Asian regions and people, where factors like motivation and perceived usefulness make individuals decide whether to adopt a technology [15]. Meanwhile, in non-Western, collectivist societies, there is a stronger influence of social and cultural elements that directly affect the acceptance of the technology than in Western cultures.

The Technology Acceptance Model (TAM) is still the main basis for exploring the acceptance of technology [5, 17]. As an illustration, Akour et al. have pointed out that perceived usefulness is a powerful predictor for behavioral intention, but they also reminded that TAM does not fully reflect the social and motivational aspects [5]. The Unified Theory of Acceptance and Use of Technology 2 (UTAUT2) resolves this problem by adding to the model the variables of social influence and the pleasure of use, which, in particular, are significant in collectivist cultures [18]. Self-Determination Theory (SDT) fuses with the above-mentioned models by appealing to autonomy, competence, and relatedness as basic motivational factors in the immersive learning sphere [6]. Flow Theory, mainly concentrating on immersion and fun, is a continually used argument for explaining continuous engagement in the Metaverse. Besides that, the factual data are not homogeneous; some investigations suggest that the flow has very little effect even in the most highly structured learning environments [19]. This discrepancy points out the necessity for the research to be continued in order to thoroughly understand the different ways in which immersion impacts students' activities in formal educational settings.

There is very little research on Metaverse utilization in the Gulf region. Akour et al. disclosed that even though digital readiness is high, there are still communication problems, teachers' lack of training, and local people's, who are change-resistant, attitudes toward virtual identities, which hinder adoption [5]. Alkhwaldi revealed that privacy and sociocultural norms were worrisome issues of Jordanian students that, thus, determined their behavioral intention toward Metaverse learning [7]. The confirmation of the significance of regional cultural factors, however, the often-heard features of the new era, go to these results.

The most recent experimental studies emphasize the adoption of Metaverse in the context of education, as well as the need to develop technology acceptance models tailored for immersive educational frameworks. Nguyen et al. developed an extended model called the Unified Theory of Acceptance and Use of Metaverse Technology (UTAUMT) to help students and decision-makers. The extended model improves existing frameworks by integrating metaverse-specific elements such as performance expectancy, social influence, and hedonic motivation, offering theoretical insights and practical guidance for incorporating metaverse technology in educational settings, including training and user support to increase adoption rates. Based on a large sample of Vietnamese students, their finding demonstrates how immersive learning environments differ greatly from traditional digital tools in terms of influencing user intention and participation.

Adding to that, Alfaisal et al. analyzed a comprehensive systematic literature review of 41 studies published from 2011 through 2022 and found that the Technology Acceptance Model (TAM) is the most popular paradigm to predict individuals' intention to use metaverse systems. Most studies have mainly addressed how university students in China, Taiwan, and the USA adopt metaverse technologies. Moreover, SmartPLS (PLS-SEM) was the tool of choice for validating these models, which is in alignment with the methodology of this study. These findings are anticipated to improve our comprehension of the metaverse system study and its utilization in education.

In Oman, there is no empirical research about the implementation of the Metaverse yet. Most educational institutions are in the initial stage of implementing the pilot program of immersive technology, even if the digital transformation is progressing. The students' state of mind, willingness, or social perception toward learning in the Metaverse hardly emerges from the research. This current situation greatly limits the ability of policymakers to design practical and scalable innovative strategies.

This review surfaces a conspicuous gap in the existing literature. While global studies emphasize the Metaverse's potential for higher education enhancement, they are not sufficient to explore how psychological, motivational, and social factors impact the decision of its use in culturally diverse areas like Oman. Models such as UTAUT2, SDT, TAM, and Flow Theory are underlying valuable theoretical grounding but necessitate empirical adaptation and testing in these different settings.

The Omani Cultural and Educational Background: A Special Case, in terms of how they acquire and use new technologies such as the Metaverse. As a collectivist society that also holds great respect for authority, many students rely on institutions, professors, and peers in their adoption of new digital tools. Traditional teaching methods employed by most universities can be too focused on structured learning, which can negatively impact motivation and the sense of independence among students. At the same time, Oman traces its Vision 2040, also pointing out that digital innovation in the education system could provide a beneficial context for technologies like the Metaverse. These cultural values, educational practices, and national goals are combined to influence the way students in Oman respond to and engage with these technologies.

The present study is an attempt to cover this gap by combining these theories into an overarching model specifically designed for the Omani higher education system. This strategy endeavors to engender both the jargon and the practice of the areas to enlighten the success of the metaverse implementation in the nascent digital education systems.

3 Theoretical Framework and Hypotheses Development

This research uses a combined structure to investigate the variables affecting students' willingness to employ the Metaverse in college. It draws on Flow Theory, Innovation Diffusion Theory, Self-Determination Theory, and UTAUT2 to cover technological, social, psychological, and motivational changes. The main elements are hedonic motivation, autonomy, habit, innovativeness, interest, presence, relatedness, competence, and flow, which emphasize students' happiness, involvement, and self-regulated learning. These elements form the basis of the first nine hypotheses. One of the last constructs, social influence, depicted by hypothesis ten, depicts the role of friends and culture in the decision-making process. Hypotheses eleven and twelve analyze the downers, such as perceived risk and complexity. Observability, which means the extent to which the Metaverse's benefits are visible to others, also influences adoption. Figure 1 presents the conceptual model providing a comprehensive view of the higher education context in Oman, where students' preferences, institutional readiness, and cultural factors are instrumental in successfully adopting.

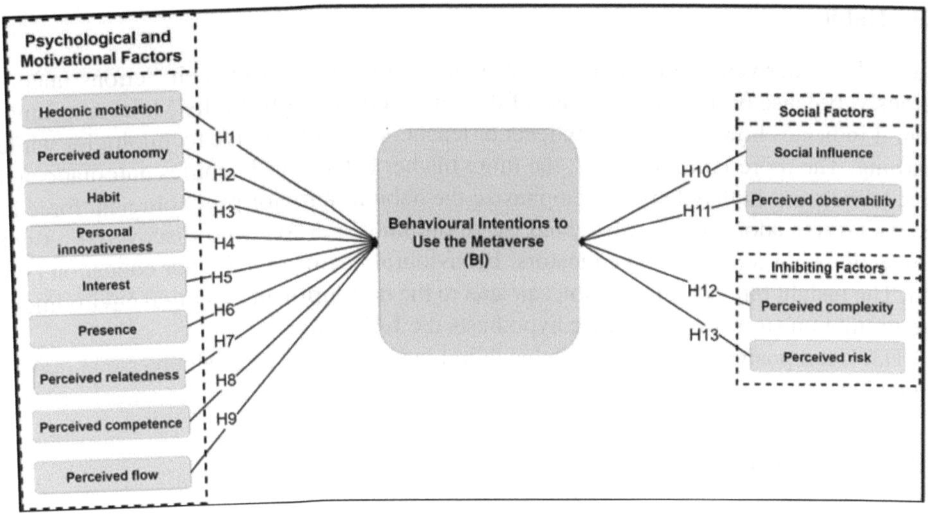

Fig. 1. Research model

3.1 Hedonic Motivation

Hedonic motivation (HM) is the emotional satisfaction people get from the use of technology, and it is the main factor affecting the intention of behaviour in digital learning environments [25]. In the scope of higher education, HM represents the happiness students experience when they use immersive Metaverse gadgets such as VR and AR [26]. For example, one former investigation, Maghaydah et al. and Abdulmuhsin et al., demonstrated that HP motivates involvement and positively presages the volition to take up such devices [6, 19]. Thus, the following is our reasoning:

H1. Hedonic motivation positively influences behavioural intention to use the Metaverse in higher education.

3.2 Perceived Autonomy

Perceived autonomy (PA) describes a person's feeling of being a decision-maker in what and when to use the technology [6]. A Metaverse-based learning situation is an example where it is connected to the students' capability to move through the virtual spaces without any restrictions, choose the learning paths, and interact with the content at their own pace [27]. The autonomy consequently becomes the primary motivator, as learners are more likely to embrace technologies they voluntarily opt for, rather than be forced. Maghaydah et al. and some other researchers realize that more autonomy has a positive effect on the behavioural intention to use immersive technologies in education [6, 28, 29]. The schools create better situations that can quality and quantity of the habits of consumers. Following this, our hypothesis:

H2. Perceived autonomy positively influences behavioural intention to use the Metaverse in higher education.

3.3 Habit

Habit (H) is derived from the degree to which people carry out their actions unconsciously, because of the repetitive use of the same activity [30]. In the Metaverse situation, it indicates how frequently students or teachers use immersive technologies while learning. The more familiar one is, the more his/her behaviour becomes automatic and less deliberate. Maghaydah et al. emphasize the habit as a major psychological force in the Metaverse adoption [6], also cited by Abdulmuhsin et al., who discovered a tight connection between habit and educators' behavioural intention in higher education [19, 20]. The insight into habit formation can lead to the development of virtual environment use promotion strategies. Thus, we hypothesis the following:

H3. Habit positively influences behavioural intention to use the Metaverse in higher education.

3.4 Personal Innovativeness

Personal Innovativeness (PI) describes a person's mindset to their readiness to discover and use new technologies, even if they haven't been trained before [31]. In the field of education, it thus becomes a capacity that represents a student's willingness to take on the Metaverse as a tool for educational activities [32]. Extremely innovative people are more likely to be among the first who embrace technological innovations due to their self-confidence and risk-seeking nature. The studies' results are quite consistent in confirming PI's positive influence on the user's behavioral intention to work with an immersive platform [33]. According to Al-Adwan et al. PI directly and thus indirectly influences intention through the constructs of perceived usefulness and ease of use [31]. Correspondingly, Maghaydah et al. designate PI as a primary motivational factor [6], while Abdulmuhsin et al. relate it to the educators who are willing to accept Metaverse for their tasks [19]. The current research considers PI a main determinant of the decision to implement the innovation in the higher education sector, thus helping educational institutions foster the culture of innovativeness in their communities. Therefore, we hypothesis the following:

H4. Personal Innovativeness positively influences behavioural intention to use the Metaverse in higher education.

3.5 Interest

Interest (I) is a student's concentrated curiosity and emotional involvement with an activity that they consider fun or meaningful [13]. In Metaverse-based learning, interest is a crucial element in energizing cognitive engagement and increasing learning outcomes. Maghaydah et al. [6] have described interest as a psychological force that strongly pushes students' behavioural intention to go for use immersive platforms. The introduction of avatars and interactive virtual environments has been proven to increase situational interest and community involvement. Makransky and Mayer, corroborating this, found that students who used a head-mounted display substantially reported higher interest and better long-term retention, compared with those who only used the traditional 2D media [13, 34]. These results indicate interest as not just an emotional reaction but also a pivotal factor in the continuous adoption of Metaverse tools. Recognition of the way interest affects engagement can be instrumental in the planning of more effective learning interventions. Therefore, we propose the following hypothesis:

H5. Interest positively influences behavioural intention to use the Metaverse in higher education.

3.6 Presence

Presence (P) is the psychological sensation of a "being there" virtual space, where learners become deeply engaged and identify with the virtual space as good as real [6]. In Metaverse-driven education, presence invigorates emotional attachment, attention, and the drive to work on the task at hand [35]. Maghaydah et al. in their research described presence as a primary psychological character that favorably impacts students' behavioural intention to go after Metaverse technologies [6]. The argument of Makransky and Mayer is one of the empirical evidences in this connection by which students using head-mounted displays conceded higher presence, which was correlated with increased interest, enjoyment, and knowledge retention [13]. The results indicate that status leads to improvement in learning quality and helps in the continuation of the use of immersive tools. Educators can increase presence to develop psychological engagement, satisfaction, and long-term adoption of the Metaverse in higher education. Hence, we put forward the following hypothesis:

H6. Presence positively influences behavioural intention to use the Metaverse in higher education.

3.7 Perceived Relatedness

Perceived relatedness (PRE) is a concept that is based on an individual's need for social connection while participating in an activity [6]. In Metaverse-based education, thus, it indicates how much students see themselves as being connected to other students, teachers, and learning communities within virtual environments. This social bond is necessary for students' social needs to be met and for motivation to be improved, especially in collaborative situations [36]. Maghaydah et al. have named perceived relatedness as a strong motivational factor that has a positive effect on students' intention to choose the Metaverse [6]. Their review points out that close social ties through avatars, teamwork, and interaction increase the degree of commitment and participation [37]. The feeling of relatedness leads to emotional satisfaction, collaborative learning, and uninterrupted use [38]. If this is well-understood, it can be of great help to teachers in creating virtual spaces that encourage meaningful connections and thus increase the adoption rates. Thus, we hypothesis:

H7. Perceived relatedness positively influences behavioural intention to use the Metaverse in higher education.

3.8 Perceived Competence

Perceived competence (PC) denotes people's dream of themselves as highly competent users of technology, who solve tasks in digital environments successfully [6]. In Metaverse-based learning, it is students' trust in their skills of moving in the virtual world. Higher perceived competence lessens the negativity toward new platforms and drives motivation. Maghaydah et al. are the ones who have named perceived competence as a vital psychological factor that positively affects students' behavioural intention [6]. The evidence from their review suggests that learners with more confidence are more willing to use immersive technologies regularly. Competence is a crucial factor of self-efficacy. It gives a boost to self-esteem and calms down anxiety in tackling new tasks in virtual settings [39]. The concept of perceived competence is the focal point of the study, as students' readiness to adopt the Metaverse is based on their trust in the use of such tools [40]. Teachers may increase perceived competence by creating easily accessible systems that not only improve digital skills but also empower learners to continue their learning journey [41]. Hence, we state the following hypothesis:

H8. Perceived competence positively influences behavioural intention to use the Metaverse in higher education.

3.9 Perceived Flow

Perceived Flow (PF) is a term used to depict the learner's unalloyed engagement, concentration, and immersion in a task, which is typically facilitated by the experience of pleasure and the disappearance of the time sense [6]. In the Metaverse, a student experiences flow when he or she is so engaged in virtual activities that are corresponding to his or her skills and that supply the right amount of difficulty [35, 42]. Maghaydah et al. identified perceived flow as a major psychological motivational factor that has a positive impact on satisfaction and the intention to act in the decision to utilize the Metaverse [6]. The authors point out that among the characteristics of the hardware and software of the system, a stable and responsive one is the key to flow. This flow leads to high concentration and also makes users more ready to continue using the technology. This research has perceived flow as one of the factors to gauge students' cognitive and emotional involvement, which is critical for continuous usage. Enabling flow states may make it possible to design truly immersive, learner-centred environments that not only facilitate engagement but also increase technology uptake. Therefore, we hypothesis:

H9. Perceived Flow positively influences behavioural intention to use the Metaverse in higher education.

3.10 Social Influence

Social influence (SI) stands for the degree to which people believe that someone important to them, for example, peers, professors, or institutional leaders, is going to need them to use a certain technology [43]. SI in the case of the virtual world adoption in university education represents how academic and social networks influence students' decisions to participate in the virtual learning environment [40]. Maghaydah et al. detected social influence as a major factor positively affecting students' behavioural intention to take up the Metaverse [6]. Their research revealed that the green light from friends, teachers, or leadership facilitates the acceptance of Metaverse-based learning. In the same vein, Abdulmuhsin et al. in their study announced that SI is a major determinant of those educators' intention who come up with the idea to use Metaverse tools [19]. The concept of SI reveals the immense power of institutional culture and peer dynamics in a technology adoption transformation, thus giving the social forces and challenges of the integration of the Metaverse in higher education a new perspective. Therefore, we hypothesis:

H10. Social influence positively influences behavioural intention to use the Metaverse in higher education.

3.11 Perceived Observability

Perceived observability (POB) is the degree to which the results and advantages of a technology are visible to people, which enables them to understand its benefits through the experiences of their friends [6]. To give an example, POB in Metaverse learning refers to the extent students can see that the other students are utilizing the platform in a way that the performance, enjoyment, or participation is improved [44]. Illustrated benefits amplify the need, faith, and social charm, and thus, they become the oxygen of the adoption. Notably, Maghaydah et al. revealed that there is a direct positive relationship between perceived observability and students' behavioural intention to accept the Metaverse, since a sense of security and motivation is generated along with peer engagement, which enables them to realize [6]. This is corroborated by Akour et al., who illustrate clear connections among observability, satisfaction of learners, and intention to adopt [5]. It is worth emphasizing that perceived observability has a pivotal position in the current research as it allows us to understand social diffusion mechanisms in educational settings. In such a way, promoting Metaverse visibility can be a powerful tool for peer influence; thus, the flow of adoption is facilitated, and a shared technology culture can be created. Hence, our hypothesis reads as follows:

H11. Perceived observability positively influences behavioural intention to use the Metaverse in higher education.

3.12 Perceived Complexity

Perceived complexity (PCM) is a concept dealing with an individual's understanding of the great difficulty that they might face while trying to use a certain technology. The term is usually associated with the skills needed to perform the technical operations and the time spent on learning and using the technology [6]. In the case of Metaverse learning, the PCM represents students' feelings about how difficult the platform usability, interface design, and the content of the digital skills for the effective performance of their role will be [45]. The high perceived complexity can result in getting lost, being confused, and not wanting to use the technology at all. Here, inexperienced learners have most of these feelings. Maghaydah et al. stated that perceived complexity leads to a situation where students' intention to accept the Metaverse is negatively influenced [6]. They claim that the learners will not be ready to use Metaverse tools if they consider these tools to be too much for them. In line with this, Akour et al. have found that less complicated systems are positively correlated with the intention of adoption [5]. This insists on the significance of the human-centered design, the availability of technical support, as well as the provision of comprehensible instructions for the full implementation of these. This investigation locates a key perceived complexity, inbound at first glance as the adoption of immersive technologies barrier that calls for training and task interface design effective solutions to address it. Thus, we formulate our hypothesis:

H12. Perceived complexity negatively influences behavioural intention to use the Metaverse in higher education.

3.13 Perceived Risk

Perceived risk (PR) is just an individual's subjective decision of possible loss, harm, or bad results that come from using a technology [6]. PR in metaphor-based learning includes those mentioned above. These are the security of the information, the privacy of the personal space, the illegal use of the data, and the discomfort with the fact that the environment will be more and more personal in such kind of situations [46]. Such perceptions can turn out to be the very factor that downgrades the students' confidence and sense of safety, especially in the case of having data, like location or identity. Perceived risk is a negative factor in that it influences the students' behavioural intention in the adoption of the Metaverse for education in a negative way [6]. Maghaydah et al. found that students who were not willing to share any personal information, for example, their phone numbers, were less likely to get involved with the Metaverse [6]. This is a very good example of how perceived risks, even when there is no relation to performance, can be very powerful in repelling users. It is quite possible that the wider adoption of Metaverse in higher education can happen only after concerted efforts have been made to solve these problems through consumer education, clear data policies, and robust security. Therefore, we hypothesis:

H13. Perceived risk negatively influences behavioural intention to use the Metaverse in higher education.

4 Methodology

4.1 Instrument Design and Data Collection

The research, which was quantitative, correlational, and cross-sectional, aimed to find out the psychological, motivational, and contextual factors that led students of higher education in Oman to decide positively that they would use Metaverse technologies. This inquiry was based on a theoretical framework that integrated ideas from UTAUT2, SDT, IDT, and Flow Theory. The data was gathered through an online questionnaire, and then Statistical analysis involving Partial Least Squares Structural Equation Modeling (PLS-SEM) in SmartPLS version 4 was used. This approach is ideal for examining elaborate models, and it also does not mandate strict distributional assumptions. The questionnaire consisted of thirteen independent variables and one dependent variable. All items were taken from resource sources for validity and reliability:

- UTAUT2 variables from Venkatesh et al. [11]
- SDT variables from Maghaydah et al. [6]

- IDT variables from Akour et al. [5]
- Flow constructs from Makransky and Mayer [13]
- Perceived Risk from Featherman and Pavlou [47]
- Behavioural Intention items from UTAUT and TAM studies.

Using the same items, constructs consisted of two or four items only. The 7-point Likert scale was used for all items. Two academic experts reviewed the questionnaire, and minor changes in wording were made for better clarity. Data were obtained via Google Forms during four weeks in April 2025. Participation was voluntary, and informed consent was secured before starting. An introduction briefly clarified the study's purpose, confidentiality, and instructions. No personal data was collected. Ethical approval for the study was given by the Sultan Qaboos University Research Ethics Committee. Appendix contains the full documentation.

4.2 Population and Sampling

Students attending higher education facilities in Oman were the primary target of the research. A non-probability convenience sampling method was used because of logistical constraints. To improve the representativeness of the findings, the final sample was composed of students from various academic fields. In total, 305 valid responses were gathered, allowing for sufficient power in PLS-SEM analyses. Demographic data of the participants are given in Table 1.

Table 1 Respondents' demographics

Demographic variable	Category	#	(%)
Gender	Female	143	51.4
	Male	135	48.6
Age	17–20	85	30.6
	21–25	81	29.1
	Above 30	67	24.1
Education level	Bachelor	219	78.8
	Masters	44	15.8
	PhD	15	5.4

Note(s): n = 278
Source(s): Authors' work

4.3 Data Screening and Cleaning

After the data had been collected, the dataset was subjected to a thorough cleaning process to eliminate any errors and inconsistencies. The identification of incomplete responses was done by Excel functions, and entries that had missing data of more than 25% were removed. To detect the outliers, the standard deviation method was used. Then, patterns that were like straight-lining and inconsistent answers on reverse-coded items were checked for the logical consistency of the responses. The number of valid responses after the screening is 278 out of the original 305. The final dataset was coded and configured for analysis in SmartPLS. These measures guaranteed that the data utilized in the model are of good quality and are reliable. Table 1 gives the respondent demographics.

5 Finding

5.1 Model Estimation

To determine the accuracy of the measurement model, this research has relied on Smart-PLS version 4, which primarily targeted convergent validity, discriminant validity, and internal consistency reliability. The tests were done before the research purpose of determining the relation between latent variables in order to ensure that the constructs are statistically reliable and conceptually valid. Convergent validity was evaluated through Cronbach's alpha, composite reliability, factor loadings, and average variance extracted (AVE). The cutoff points were 0.70 for reliability measures and 0.50 for AVE. Results for the fourteen variables are shown in Table 2.

Discriminant validity was evaluated using the Fornell-Larcker criterion and the heterotrait-monotrait ratio (HTMT), both common in PLS-SEM. Table 3 shows the Fornell-Larcker results, where the square root of AVE for each construct must exceed its correlations with others to confirm validity. Table 4 presents HTMT values, which should be below 0.85 or 0.90. Values above these indicate poor discriminant validity. The square root of AVE proved to be a more reliable indicator than correlation coefficients in this study.

Table 2 Construct reliability and validity

	Cronbach's alpha	Composite reliability (rho_a)	Composite reliability (rho_c)	Average variance extracted (AVE)
BI	0.935	0.935	0.958	0.884
H	0.93	0.93	0.955	0.877
HM	0.934	0.935	0.958	0.884
I	0.942	0.945	0.958	0.852
P	0.925	0.926	0.947	0.817
PA	0.907	0.91	0.941	0.843
PC	0.921	0.921	0.95	0.863

(*continued*)

Table 2 (*continued*)

	Cronbach's alpha	Composite reliability (rho_a)	Composite reliability (rho_c)	Average variance extracted (AVE)
PCM	0.915	0.941	0.959	0.921
PF	0.941	0.943	0.955	0.809
PI	0.898	0.901	0.929	0.766
POB	0.901	0.901	0.938	0.834
PR	0.912	0.943	0.928	0.683
PRE	0.918	0.919	0.948	0.859
SI	0.926	0.927	0.953	0.872

Table 3 Fornell and larcker criterion

	BI	H	HM	I	P	PA	PC	PCM	PF	PI	POB	PR	PRE	SI
BI														
H	0.717													
HM	0.845	0.837												
I	0.838	0.698	0.828											
P	0.828	0.838	0.912	0.858										
PA	0.681	0.581	0.635	0.672	0.623									
PC	0.728	0.755	0.737	0.702	0.732	0.755								
PCM	0.371	0.474	0.362	0.346	0.466	0.19	0.241							
PF	0.783	0.676	0.782	0.796	0.787	0.727	0.813	0.344						
PI	0.795	0.657	0.815	0.841	0.818	0.769	0.762	0.365	0.851					
POB	0.855	0.766	0.863	0.908	0.864	0.685	0.699	0.405	0.78	0.862				
PR	0.506	0.579	0.513	0.481	0.566	0.314	0.444	0.781	0.485	0.53	0.526			
PRE	0.852	0.72	0.832	0.858	0.821	0.755	0.802	0.345	0.814	0.859	0.84	0.555		
SI	0.838	0.748	0.864	0.751	0.856	0.584	0.692	0.427	0.757	0.73	0.781	0.562	0.803	

Interpretation: The AVEs' (diagonal) square roots are all higher than the corresponding correlations between the constructs

Table 4 Heterotrait-monotrait ratio (HTMT)

	BI	H	HM	I	P	PA	PC	PCM	PF	PI	POB	PR	PRE	SI
BI	0.94													
H	0.669	0.936												
HM	0.79	0.78	0.94											
I	0.789	0.654	0.777	0.923										
P	0.77	0.778	0.848	0.801	0.904									
PA	0.629	0.536	0.585	0.622	0.572	0.918								

(*continued*)

Table 4 (*continued*)

	BI	H	HM	I	P	PA	PC	PCM	PF	PI	POB	PR	PRE	SI
PC	0.676	0.699	0.684	0.654	0.676	0.693	0.929							
PCM	0.346	0.439	0.336	0.322	0.429	0.173	0.222	0.96						
PF	0.735	0.633	0.733	0.749	0.734	0.672	0.756	0.321	0.899					
PI	0.73	0.601	0.747	0.775	0.747	0.696	0.694	0.33	0.783	0.875				
POB	0.785	0.701	0.791	0.837	0.789	0.62	0.637	0.369	0.719	0.776	0.913			
PR	0.501	0.551	0.512	0.493	0.544	0.332	0.439	0.675	0.486	0.518	0.519	0.826		
PRE	0.79	0.666	0.77	0.799	0.756	0.69	0.737	0.32	0.757	0.781	0.764	0.551	0.927	
SI	0.781	0.694	0.804	0.703	0.792	0.537	0.64	0.396	0.707	0.666	0.714	0.537	0.741	0.934

5.2 Structural Model

A significant part of the research was the validation of the structural model to verify the theoretical base and check the proposed relationships. Using SmartPLS version 4, Partial Least Squares Structural Equation Modeling was applied. The key indicators utilized included t-values, p-values, betas, effect size, and coefficient of determination, which were employed to gauge the strength and the explanatory power of the model. Thirteen hypotheses regarding the direct impact of psychological and motivational factors on the behavioural intention of students to use metaverse technologies in higher education were tested in the study. The research implemented the bootstrapping technique with ten thousand samples for this analysis. Results of the regression analysis are given in Table 5 and Fig. 2. Location 2 depicts the structural model and the paths that were tested pictorially. A total of four hypotheses were corroborated. Social Influence was most strongly correlated with behavioural intention, which implied that apart from the addition of peer encouragement and societal expectations, the biggest motivators are need. Besides that, Interest also has a significant impact, which means that intellectual engagement and curiosity could promote the intention. Furthermore, Perceived Observability as a significant factor indicated that the realization of the benefits could become the driver for technology adoption. Effects of Perceived Relatedness were significant and positive; thus, the role of social bonds and support in influencing the behavioral intention is revealed. The other nine hypotheses could not find any statistical evidence to support. These are Habit, Hedonic Motivation, Presence, Perceived Autonomy, Perceived Competence, Perceived Flow, Perceived Complexity, Personal Innovativeness, and Perceived Risk. Their absence of significance means that they may be the sources that have indirect effects, or they may be involved in the influence of students' intentions. The situation may change if different conditions or stages of technological maturity appear presently.

For effect sizes (f^2), from Lee and Penyelidikan and Cohen's thresholds were used to determine the degree to which each predictor was associated with behavioral intention (BI): 0.02 (small), 0.15 (medium), and 0.35 (large). Of supported hypotheses, Social Influence ($f^2 = 0.072$), which is an indirect impact of the highest order on behavioral intention, had a large effect in the data, which might be affecting someone's willingness to engage in practices such as slave reparations. Small to medium effects were found for

Interest ($f^2 = 0.025$), Perceived Relatedness ($f^2 = 0.024$), and Perceived Observability ($f^2 = 0.026$).

In contrast, Hedonic Motivation, while positive and significant in past literature, only had a small effect size ($f^2 = 0.015$) and was not significantly related in this study. All other constructs, such as Habit (0.002), Perceived Autonomy (0.007), Perceived Competence (0.002), and Perceived Flow (0.003), had very low or even negligible effect sizes relative to the model $f^2 < 0.01$. This is a sign of their low relevance to students' adoption intentions in the current environment.

Table 5 Hypothesis testing summary

Hypothesis	Path	Construct	Path coefficient (β)	t-value	p-value	Supported	Effect Size (f^2)
H1	HM → BI	Hedonic motivation (HM)	0.140	1.707	0.088	Not supported	0.015
H2	PA → BI	Perceived autonomy (PA)	0.063	1.229	0.219	Not supported	0.007
H3	H → BI	Habit (H)	– 0.038	0.625	0.532	Not supported	0.002
H4	PI → BI	Personal innovativeness	– 0.020	0.274	0.784	Not supported	0.000
H5	I → BI	Interest (I)	0.167	2.151	0.031	Supported	0.025
H6	P → BI	Presence (P)	0.010	0.119	0.905	Not supported	0.000
H7	PRE → BI	Perceived relatedness	0.160	2.219	0.027	Supported	0.024
H8	PC → BI	Perceived competence	0.045	0.724	0.469	Not supported	0.002
H9	PF → BI	Perceived flow	0.048	0.793	0.428	Not supported	0.003
H10	SI → BI	Social influence (SI)	0.246	3.348	0.001	Supported	0.072
H11	POB → BI	Perceived observability	0.167	2.287	0.022	Supported	0.026
H12	PCM → BI	Perceived complexity	0.030	0.602	0.547	Not supported	0.002
H13	PR → BI	Perceived risk	−0.018	0.393	0.695	Not supported	0.001

6 Discussion

The influence of students' behavioral intention to use Metaverse technologies in Omani higher education was the subject of this study. It is also an attempt to bring disparate constructs from UTAUT2, Self-Determination, Innovation Diffusion, and Flow theories together in a single integrative theoretical framework. The structural model examined the thirteen proposed relationships, and in the end, it was discovered that four variables—Social Influence, Interest, Perceived Observability, and Perceived Relatedness—sharply determined behavioral intention. Of these, Social Influence was the most significant factor, which indicated the vital role that social norms and collective expectations have in the acceptance of technology in Oman, a country that is known for its collectivist cultural values. This result is quite consistent with the UTAUT2 model and also with the previous studies that stress the significance of the support that comes from peers, faculties, and institutions for the acceptance of technology [6, 11]. Moreover, Interest was found to be a significant positive predictor of behavioural intention. It also indicates the essential role of inner motivation, curiosity, and personal relevance in the decision to be involved in an immersive learning platform. This illustrates the assumptions of Self-Determination Theory and Flow Theory that intellectual stimulation and emotional engagement are necessary for the continued use of new technologies in education [6, 13]. Perceived Observability, a component of Innovation Diffusion Theory, was demonstrated to affect students' decisions by focusing on the significance of visible benefits and the usage of peers. When students are able to see the good results, such as the increase in their engagement or academic performance through the use of Metaverse tools, their motivation for the adoption of these technologies goes up, thus leading to social diffusion and credibility [5]. What is more, Perceived Relatedness, which signifies students' emotions of being socially connected and belonging in virtual environments, was another significant motivating factor. This agrees with the Self-Determination Theory point of view that social connectedness and collaboration lead to learners' emotional satisfaction and commitment, even in digitally mediated learning scenarios [6, 10].

However, the behavioural intention of nine factors, including Hedonic Motivation, Habit, Personal Innovativeness, Perceived Autonomy, Perceived Competence, Perceived Flow, Presence, Perceived Complexity, and Perceived Risk, did not significantly affect this research. The lack of significance of Hedonic Motivation is contrary to many studies, where it was a strong factor in the prediction of technology adoption. The implication for the Omani students is that the fun they might experience from the use of Metaverse technology alone is not enough for them to be willing to adopt it, unless it is linked to the academic benefits or social endorsement they get. Moreover, the non-significance of Habit and Personal Innovativeness in this survey is consistent with the ideas put forward by some authors who say that the limited local examples of Metaverse applications make students' capabilities of developing usage patterns and their cryptocurrency for technological experimentation quite limited [6].

The fact that there is no significant impact for the variables Perceived Autonomy, Competence, Flow, and Presence can be understood that students probably give more priority to socially mediated experiences and guided learning which they have received through their tutors, among other things, and are still not able to perceive individual mastery or immersive engagement during the initial stages of adoption of technology.

This line of thinking is consistent with the argument that social and emotional support structures play an essential part when emerging technologies are brought into educational settings, especially in cultures that are deeply rooted in collective values rather than individual autonomy [6, 13]. Additionally, the absence of influence from the variables Perceived Complexity and Perceived Risk can be interpreted in such a way that either there is a considerable level of trust in the technology provided by the institution among the users or they are not aware of the existing challenges and risks connected with the use of Metaverse that leads to the result of unawareness. This result is contrary to most studies where these two factors are a serious issue to the adoption of the new technology, but it agrees with the research, which states that institutional trust and cultural context can reduce the impact of these issues [6]. Essentially, the results indicate that social and emotional factors are still the major drivers of the acceptance of technology in collectivist societies such as Oman.

According to Lee & Penyelidikan and Cohen, while statistical significance demonstrates the influence of variables on behavioural intention, effect size indicates their practical importance. Quantitatively, the most substantial factor for change is social influence, the one with the highest statistical and practical significance ($f^2 = 0.072$)-thus illustrating the dimensions of social influence that were creating changes in student behavior in an Omani educational situation to be particularly significant.

Moreover, indicators like Interest, Perceived Relatedness, and Perceived Observability indicate that students may be driven by interest and peer use visibility, even with small effect sizes.

Interestingly, some common constructs that are often substantially predictive in the usual contexts (e.g., Hedonic Motivation and Habit) were statistically not supported and had almost negligible effect sizes, suggesting their relevance was quite small in this context. This may be because there are few opportunities to experience immersive environments or because the culture in Oman values formal, guided learning experiences. These findings suggested that social dynamics around technology adoption contribute significantly to attitudes toward it compared with perceived enjoyment or habit formation.

They also emphasize the urgent need for adoption strategies that not only encourage group participation but also vividly demonstrate the benefits of Metaverse technologies and provide ample opportunities for sharing meaningful conversations. These revelations broadly facilitate the further investigation of tech adoption in higher education and also indicate that the key to the successful integration of immersive platforms lies in culturally sensitive approaches that mainly focus on social support and collective validation. It is very important that future studies continue to develop these results by following the next steps of behavioral intentions in actual use over time, researching various educational contexts, and also considering the changing role of individual and social motivators as they become more familiar with Metaverse environments.

7 Implications

7.1 Theoretical Implications

This study is a significant piece of research as it pushes the boundaries of knowledge through its application of some well-validated theoretical models, for example, UTAUT2, Self-Determination Theory, Innovation Diffusion Theory, and Flow Theory, to explain tech adoption of the Metaverse in higher education in Oman. Firstly, the data demonstrates that the social component of UTAUT2, and particularly the Social Influence factor, explains the behavior the most, whereas Hedonic Motivation and Habit are less correlated. This underlines the critical role of social elements in cultures that have collectivism as one of their core values and in sectors or markets that are still nascent for technology. The survey probes further into the power of social and emotional motivators from the Self-Determination Theory. Interest and Relatedness were unveiled as the core variables of a behavioral inclination, which means that emotional involvement and cordiality are more important in the early stage of the adoption of new technology than autonomy and competence. In light of Innovation Diffusion Theory, the survey disproves the hypothesis that Observability is the most important characteristic for technology use in an organization, while Complexity and Innovativeness seem to be less significant than in other areas. This can be interpreted as the visible advantages and influence of the peers are more important than technical issues, or the willingness of a person to try new technology. Moreover, the results from Flow Theory elements, such as Presence and Flow, did not lead to a significant correlation with behavioral intention. At least this means that immersion itself is insufficient to motivate acceptance if other motivational or contextual factors have not been handled first.

7.2 Practical Implications

This research equips university administrators, instructional designers, faculty members, and policymakers with tools to implement Metaverse-based learning platforms effectively. Firstly, institutions should influence social power by enrolling faculty champions, peer mentors, and student leaders to spread the word about the adoption of the new system. The backing of a respected individual and positive group norms can be a great motivating force. Secondly, as the interest has a stronger effect on the behavioral intention, the learning content must be mentally challenging and emotionally appealing, formulated to activate curiosity and problem-solving. Thirdly, if someone demonstrates clear success in providing case studies, pilot projects, or examples that highlight benefits such as improved learning outcomes, compelling them may be effective. Fourthly, platforms should be capable of facilitating virtual social presence by creating more interactivity and collaboration. For example, through the use of avatars and breakout rooms, which are not only beneficial for relatedness but also help one feel less lonely. Fifthly, since autonomy, complexity, and risk are irrelevant factors, the initial deployment of the system is better conducted by following a structured, guided learning approach with the support of the institution rather than relying on self-direction or mitigating the risk. Lastly, it is very crucial that the deployment strategies are in line with local educational norms, cultural values, and digital readiness. The use of culturally relevant content, avatars, and language options will become a lever for acceptance to grow. All these recommendations are a great help to the development of evidence-based strategies, which are expected to increase the adoption and effectiveness of Metaverse learning in higher education.

8 Conclusion

In this research, the main factors affecting students' intention to use Metaverse technology in Omani universities were investigated. To this end, four established theories have been combined: UTAUT2, Self-Determination Theory, Innovation Diffusion Theory, and Flow Theory. The findings indicate that students' decision to adopt the Metaverse is significantly influenced by social influence, personal interest, and observable benefits. Factors such as ease of use, pleasure, habit, and security concerns did not have a significant influence. These results suggest that social and emotional aspects are more powerful than individual convenience. Moreover, these findings indicate the importance of focusing on group participation and clear pedagogical benefits when introducing Metaverse learning in Oman. Further research should continue to examine long-term use, include various institutions, and understand how students incorporate these technologies into their learning. However, this study has limitations. The cross-sectional design gives data for only one point in time, and hence it is not possible to find out the changes in attitudes over time. The researchers' inability to find all the hypotheses supported may be a result of some issues with the measurements or cultural differences. To fix these problems, researchers can follow random sampling and use longitudinal designs in future studies. In addition to that, qualitative research will shed light on students' experiences more deeply. It is recommended that studies also account for some factors like age, digital competencies, and previous experience with virtual learning in future studies.

Acknowledgments. This Study is funded by Sultan Qaboos University, Oman

Disclosure of Interests. The authors have no competing interests to declare that are relevant to the content of this article.

Appendix

Sultan Qaboos University

College of Economics and Political Science

Office of the Assistant Dean for Postgraduate Studies & Research

جامعة السلطان قابوس

كلية الاقتصاد والعلوم السياسية

مكتب مساعد العميد للدراسات العليا والبحث العلمي

Ref	:	CEPS/ADPSR/22/2025
To	:	Prof. Amer Saif Al Hinai Deputy Vice Chancellor for Postgraduate Studies and Research
From	:	Prof. Saqib Ali Asst. Dean for Postgraduate Studies and Research, College of Economics and Political Science
Date	:	17th of April, 2025
Subject	:	Request Approval for Survey Questions

After compliments,

Please be advised that **Dr. Ali Tarhini – Instructor from Information System Department** would like to circulate survey in order to collect date related to his research titled: **"Exploring Behavioral Intentions to use Metaverse for education purposes in Higher Education: The case of Oman"**

As Part of this research is to circulate survey as mention in attached. Therefore, we are kindly requested your kind approval to facilitate the mission of Instructor: Dr. Ali Tarhini to achieve the aim of the research. Noted: That Survey Questions has approved by CRC.

Your continued support is highly appreciated.

Regards.

17/4/2025

Attachments:

- The form required
- Questions

(+968)24142972 adpsrceps@squ.edu.om https://www.squ.edu.om/economics

@squceps_info P.O. Box : 20, Al-Khodh, PC : 123, Oman CEPS MEDIA

EFMD EQUIS ACCREDITED

References

1. Li, K., et al.: When internet of things meets metaverse: convergence of physical and cyber worlds. IEEE Internet Things J. **10**(5), 4148–4173 (2022). Accessed: 29 June 29 2025 (Online). Available: https://ieeexplore.ieee.org/abstract/document/10002946/
2. Gautama, A., Hasim, H., Iwansaputra, R., Kristin, D.M.: Metaverse adoption in higher education institutions (HEIs): a systematic literature review. In: 2024 International Conference on ICT for Smart Society (ICISS), pp. 1–7. IEEE, USA (2024). Accessed: 01 July 2025 (Online). Available: https://ieeexplore.ieee.org/abstract/document/10750997/
3. Roy, R., Babakerkhell, M.D., Mukherjee, S., Pal, D., Funilkul, S.: Development of a framework for metaverse in education: a systematic literature review approach. IEEE Access **11**, 57717–57734 (2023). Accessed: 01 July 2025 (Online). Available: https://ieeexplore.ieee.org/abstract/document/10144746/
4. Onu, P., Pradhan, A., Mbohwa, C.: Potential to use metaverse for future teaching and learning. Educ. Inf. Technol. **29**(7), 8893–8924 (2024). https://doi.org/10.1007/s10639-023-12167-9
5. Akour, I.A., Al-Maroof, R.S., Alfaisal, R., Salloum, S.A.: A conceptual framework for determining metaverse adoption in higher institutions of gulf area: an empirical study using hybrid SEM-ANN approach. Comput. Educ. Artif. Intell. **3**, 100052 (2022). Accessed: 29 June 2025 (Online). Available: https://www.sciencedirect.com/science/article/pii/S2666920X22000078
6. Maghaydah, S., Al-Emran, M., Maheshwari, P., Al-Sharafi, M.A.: Factors affecting metaverse adoption in education: a systematic review, adoption framework, and future research agenda. Heliyon (2024). Accessed: 30 June 2025 (Online). Available: https://www.cell.com/heliyon/fulltext/S2405-8440(24)04633-4
7. Alkhwaldi, A.F.: Understanding learners' intention toward Metaverse in higher education institutions from a developing country perspective: UTAUT and ISS integrated model. Kybernetes **53**(12), 6008–6035 (2024). Accessed: 01 July 2025 (Online). Available: https://www.emerald.com/insight/content/doi/10.1108/K-03-2023-0459/full/html
8. Sediyaningsih, S., Pandu Ristiyono, M., Launggu, K., Juma Ochieng, P.: De-contextual communication: unified system information theory to investigate usage intention of metaverse technology in digital library services. In: Kani and Juma Ochieng, Peter, De-Contextual Communication: Unified System Information Theory to Investigate Usage Intention of Metaverse Technology in Digital Library Services (2023). Accessed: 01 July 2025 (Online). Available: https://papers.ssrn.com/sol3/papers.cfm?abstract_id=4434732
9. Sviridova, E., Yastrebova, E., Bakirova, G., Rebrina, F.: Immersive technologies as an innovative tool to increase academic success and motivation in higher education. In: Frontiers in Education, p. 1192760. Frontiers Media SA (2023). Accessed: 29 June 2025 (Online). Available: https://www.frontiersin.org/articles/10.3389/feduc.2023.1192760/full
10. Deci, E.L., Ryan, R.M.: The 'what' and 'why' of goal pursuits: human needs and the self-determination of behavior. Psychol. Inq. **11**(4), 227–268 (2000). https://doi.org/10.1207/S15327965PLI1104_01
11. Venkatesh, V., Thong, J.Y., Xu, X.: Consumer acceptance and use of information technology: extending the unified theory of acceptance and use of technology. MIS Q., 157–178 (2012). Accessed: 01 July 2025 (Online). Available: https://www.jstor.org/stable/41410412
12. Beck, D., Morgado, L., O'Shea, P.: Educational practices and strategies with immersive learning environments: mapping of reviews for using the metaverse. IEEE Trans. Learn. Technol. **17**, 319–341 (2023). Accessed: 29 June 2025 (Online). Available: https://ieeexplore.ieee.org/abstract/document/10041969/
13. Makransky, G., Mayer, R.E.: Benefits of taking a virtual field trip in immersive virtual reality: evidence for the immersion principle in multimedia learning. Educ. Psychol. Rev. **34**(3), 1771–1798 (2022). https://doi.org/10.1007/s10648-022-09675-4

14. Wang, G., Shin, C.: Influencing factors of usage intention of metaverse education application platform: empirical evidence based on PPM and TAM models. Sustainability **14**(24), 17037 (2022). Accessed: 01 July 2025 (Online). Available: https://www.mdpi.com/2071-1050/14/24/17037
15. Al-Adwan, A.S., Alsoud, M., Li, N., Majali, T., Smedley, J., Habibi, A.: Unlocking future learning: exploring higher education students' intention to adopt meta-education. Heliyon **10**(9) (2024). Accessed: 01 July 2025. (Online). Available: https://www.cell.com/heliyon/fulltext/S2405-8440(24)05575-0
16. Al-Sharafi, M.A., Al-Emran, M., Al-Qaysi, N., Iranmanesh, M., Ibrahim, N.: Drivers and barriers affecting Metaverse adoption: a systematic review, theoretical framework, and avenues for future research. Int. J. Hum. Comput. Interact. **40**(22), 7043–7064 (2024). https://doi.org/10.1080/10447318.2023.2260984
17. Alfaisal, R., Hashim, H., Azizan, U.H.: Metaverse system adoption in education: a systematic literature review. J. Comput. Educ. **11**(1), 259–303 (2024). https://doi.org/10.1007/s40692-022-00256-6
18. Wong, X.J., Tajudeen, F.P.: Factors affecting employees' intention to work through the Metaverse platform. Int. J. Hum. Comput. Interact. **41**(11), 7058–7075 (2025). https://doi.org/10.1080/10447318.2024.2388480
19. Abdulmuhsin, A.A., Owain, H.O., Alkhwaldi, A.F.: Understanding the academic use of KM-driven Metaverse technology: insights from medical colleges. J. Sci. Technol. Policy Manag. (2024). Accessed: 30 June 2025 (Online). Available: https://www.emerald.com/insight/content/doi/10.1108/jstpm-12-2023-0229/full/html
20. Damaševičius, R., Sidekerskienė, T.: Virtual worlds for learning in metaverse: a narrative review. Sustainability **16**(5), 2032 (2024). Accessed: 29 June 2025 (Online). Available: https://www.mdpi.com/2071-1050/16/5/2032
21. Phibbs, C.L.: The Impact of Motivation, Price, and Habit on Intention to Use IoT-Enabled Technology: A Correlational Study. Ph.D. thesis, Capella University (2021). Accessed: 29 June 2025 (Online). Available: https://search.proquest.com/openview/99bd411e74350a50cda4a4a044265b9f/1?pq-origsite=gscholar&cbl=18750&diss=y
22. Sart, G., Sezgin, H.F.: The effect of university students' attitudes towards information and communication technologies on their tendency towards innovation. In: EDULEARN22 Proceedings, IATED, pp. 8248–8255 (2022). Accessed: 29 June 2025 (Online). Available: https://library.iated.org/view/SART2022EFF
23. Luarn, P., Chen, C.-C., Chiu, Y.-P.: How does perceived value of gamification improve online learning effectiveness? The role of flow state. Interact. Learn. Environ. **33**(4), 3037–3051 (2025). https://doi.org/10.1080/10494820.2024.2436932
24. Caldas, O.I., Sanchez, N., Mauledoux, M., Avilés, O.F., Rodriguez-Guerrero, C.: Leading presence-based strategies to manipulate user experience in virtual reality environments. Virt. Real. **26**(4), 1507–1518 (2022). https://doi.org/10.1007/s10055-022-00645-3
25. Rabiah, A.S., Setiawan, M., Rohman, F.: Assess the impact of hedonic motivation, social influence, gamification, and education level on behavioral intention to adopt mobile shopping in Jakarta, Indonesia. Revista de Gestão Social e Ambiental **18**(7), 1–24 (2024). Accessed: 30 June 2025 (Online). Available: https://search.proquest.com/openview/fe23cf282b9e78c8d83bd423e2dc8bbc/1?pq-origsite=gscholar&cbl=2031968
26. Pragha, P., Dhalmahapatra, K., Natarajan, T.: The future of human experience: the drivers of user adoption of the metaverse. Online Inf. Rev. (2025). Accessed: 30 June 2025 (Online). Available: https://www.emerald.com/insight/content/doi/10.1108/oir-09-2023-0449/full/html
27. Gim, G., Bae, H., Kang, S.: Metaverse learning: the relationship among quality of VR-based education, self-determination, and learner satisfaction. In: 2022 IEEE/ACIS 7th International

Conference on Big Data, Cloud Computing, and Data Science (BCD), pp. 279–284. IEEE, USA (2022). Accessed: 30 June 2025 (Online). Available: https://ieeexplore.ieee.org/abstract/document/9900629/

28. Velychko, V.Y., Fedorenko, E.G., Kaidan, N.V., Kaidan, V.P.: Harnessing immersive technologies for enhancing mathematical logics education in secondary schools. In: CEUR Workshop Proceedings, pp. 70–84 (2025). Accessed: 30 June 2025 (Online). Available: https://ceur-ws.org/Vol-3918/paper078.pdf
29. Almusfar, L.A.: Improving learning management system performance: a comprehensive approach to engagement, trust, and adaptive learning. IEEE Access (2025). Accessed: 30 June 2025 (Online). Available: https://ieeexplore.ieee.org/abstract/document/10921636/
30. Brown, D.J., Hagger, M.S., Hamilton, K.: A qualitative investigation of individuals' lay representations of habit. Psychol. Health, 1–22 (2024). https://doi.org/10.1080/08870446.2024.2412572
31. Al-Adwan, A.S., Al-Debei, M.M.: The determinants of gen z's metaverse adoption decisions in higher education: integrating UTAUT2 with personal innovativeness in IT. Educ. Inf. Technol. **29**(6), 7413–7445 (2024). https://doi.org/10.1007/s10639-023-12080-1
32. Di Natale, A.F., Repetto, C., Costantini, G., Riva, G., Bricolo, E., Villani, D.: Learning in the Metaverse: are university students willing to learn in immersive virtual reality? Cyberpsychol. Behav. Soc. Netw. **27**(1), 28–36 (2024). https://doi.org/10.1089/cyber.2022.0395
33. Al-kfairy, M., Ahmed, S., Khalil, A.: Factors impacting users' willingness to adopt and utilize the metaverse in education: a systematic review. Comput. Hum. Behav. Rep., 100459 (2024). Accessed: 30 June 2025 (Online). Available: https://www.sciencedirect.com/science/article/pii/S2451958824000927
34. Alsamh, M.H., Hawbani, A., Kumar, S., Alsamhi, S.H.: Multisensory metaverse-6G: a new paradigm of commerce and education. IEEE Access **12**, 75657–75677 (2024). Accessed: 30 June 2025 (Online). Available: https://ieeexplore.ieee.org/abstract/document/10506898/
35. Çelik, F., Baturay, M.H.: The effect of metaverse on L2 vocabulary learning, retention, student engagement, presence, and community feeling. BMC Psychol. **12**(1), 58 (2024). https://doi.org/10.1186/s40359-024-01549-4
36. Mentzer, N., Mammadova, E., Koehler, A., Mohandas, L., Farrington, S.: Analyzing the impact of basic psychological needs on student academic performance: a comparison of post-pandemic interactive synchronous hyflex and pre-pandemic traditional face-to-face instruction. Educ. Tech. Res. Dev. **73**(1), 91–114 (2025). https://doi.org/10.1007/s11423-024-10417-2
37. Cacciamani, S., Perrucci, V., Khanlari, A., Balboni, G.: Sense of community and peer feedback in a blended university course. Educ. Inf. Technol. **29**(5), 5211–5223 (2024). https://doi.org/10.1007/s10639-023-11982-4
38. Gim, G., Bae, H., Kang, S.: Metaverse learning: the relationship among quality of VR-based education, self-determination, and learner satisfaction. In: In 2022 IEEE/ACIS 7th International Conference on Big Data, Cloud Computing, and Data Science (BCD), pp. 279–284. IEEE, USA (2022). Accessed: 30 June 2025 (Online). Available: https://ieeexplore.ieee.org/abstract/document/9900629/
39. Kobra, K.: Unraveling the complex web of student anxiety: strategies to Foster confidence, motivation, and Well-being in learning. Int. J. Res. Public. Rev. **5**(6), 1888–1892. Accessed: 30 June 2025 (Online). Available: https://www.researchgate.net/profile/Khadijatul-Kobra-6/publication/381460871_Unraveling_the_Complex_Web_of_Student_Anxiety_Strategies_to_Foster_Confidence_Motivation_and_Well-Being_in_Learning/links/666e8d23de777205a32ff461/Unraveling-the-Complex-Web-of-Student-Anxiety-Strategies-to-Foster-Confidence-Motivation-and-Well-Being-in-Learning.pdf

40. Di Natale, A.F., Bartolotta, S., Gaggioli, A., Riva, G., Villani, D.: Exploring students' acceptance and continuance intention in using immersive virtual reality and metaverse integrated learning environments: the case of an Italian university course. Educ. Inf. Technol. (2024). https://doi.org/10.1007/s10639-023-12436-7
41. Illi, C., Elhassouny, A.: Edu-Metaverse: a comprehensive review of virtual learning environments. IEEE Access (2025). Accessed: 30 June 2025 (Online). Available: https://ieeexplore.ieee.org/abstract/document/10879446/
42. Abdolrezapour, P., Ghanbari, N.: Emotional-based pedagogy and facilitating EFL learners' perceived flow in online education. Front. Psychol. **13**, 960287 (2022). Accessed: 30 June 2025 (Online). Available: https://www.frontiersin.org/articles/10.3389/fpsyg.2022.960287/full
43. Suhail, F., Adel, M., Al-Emran, M., AlQudah, A.A.: Are students ready for robots in higher education? Examining the adoption of robots by integrating UTAUT2 and TTF using a hybrid SEM-ANN approach. Technol. Soc. **77**, 102524 (2024). Accessed: 30 June 2025 (Online). Available: https://www.sciencedirect.com/science/article/pii/S0160791X24000721
44. Althunibat, A., Alhalaybeh, A., Hanif, A., Habashneh, K.K., AlRifaee, M.: Determining the factors affecting Metaverse adoption in higher learning institutions. Int. J. Inf. Educ. Technol. **14**(11) (2024). Accessed: 30 June 2025 (Online). Available: https://www.ijiet.org/vol14/IJIET-V14N11-2186.pdf
45. Poupard, M., Larrue, F., Sauzéon, H., Tricot, A.: A systematic review of immersive technologies for education: effects of cognitive load and curiosity state on learning performance. Br. J. Educ. Technol. **56**(1), 5–41 (2025). Accessed: 30 June 2025 (Online). Available: https://hal.science/hal-03906797/
46. Kaabachi, S., Mrad, S.B., Cadet, F., Charfi, A.A., Kpossa, M.R.: Overcoming obstacles: the future of French gen-Z in the metaverse. Does familiarity with current metaverse platforms play a key role? J Market Anal. (2025). https://doi.org/10.1057/s41270-025-00398-3
47. Featherman, M.S., Pavlou, P.A.: Predicting e-services adoption: a perceived risk facets perspective. Int. J. Hum. Comput. Stud. **59**(4), 451–474 (2003). Accessed: 01 July 2025 (Online). Available: https://www.sciencedirect.com/science/article/pii/S1071581903001113
48. Henseler, J., Ringle, C.M., Sarstedt, M.: A new criterion for assessing discriminant validity in variance-based structural equation modeling. J. of the Acad. Mark. Sci. **43**(1), 115–135 (2015). https://doi.org/10.1007/s11747-014-0403-8
49. Lee, C., Penyelidikan,C.J.: Sample Size Estimation Using Krejcie and Morgan and Cohen Statistical Power Analysis: A Comparison (2006)
50. Nguyen, A.H.D., Le, T.T., Dang, T.Q., Nguyen, L.T.: Understanding metaverse adoption in education: the extended UTAUMT model. Heliyon **10**(19) (2024). https://doi.org/10.1016/j.heliyon.2024.e38741

Antecedents of User Experience for Generative Artificial Intelligence Applications

Surbhi Gulati(✉) and Arpan Kumar Kar

Department of Management Studies, Indian Institute of Technology Delhi, New Delhi, India
surbhigulati1997@gmail.com

Abstract. As an emerging technology, Generative Artificial Intelligence holds immense potential for application across various levels of business and management. The advancements in Gen AI have transcended traditional AI systems. Few studies exist discussing the potential of the technology, though there is a dearth of studies that empirically examine the factors associated with the corresponding user experience. A total of 30,000 critical user reviews were obtained from seven different Generative artificial intelligence applications and subjected to text analytics procedures to uncover key themes and constructs that drive user engagement. The findings highlighted key dimensions that reflect positive user experiences. Moreover, the Net Promotion score of the reviews calculated reflects a high level of user experience.

Keywords: Gen AI · User experience · Natural language processing

1 Introduction

Over the years, AI has substantially impacted organisations, societies, and individuals (Dwivedi et al. 2023). However, advancements in Generative Artificial Intelligence (Gen AI) have transcended traditional AI systems. Gen AI refers to AI technology that employs algorithms and models to identify patterns from existing data and generate novel content by leveraging learned patterns rather than making predictions (Sabherwal and Grover 2024). It is a category of AI models that produce new content in text, video, audio, images, or other media in response to prompts (Benbya et al. 2024). For example, Gen AI systems are proficient in writing convincing documents, generating digital art, composing music, engaging and debating with humans, and producing software. Gen AI covers a range of deep learning techniques, including transformers, Generative Adversarial networks (GANs), and Variational Autoencoders (VAEs) to generate content (Accenture 2023). The potential of Gen AI has recently become apparent with the recent public release of tools like ChatGPT, GitHub Copilot, and DALL-E, as well as the introduction of Google's Bard and Microsoft's Bing (Benbya et al. 2024). Based on cutting-edge AI language models, a Gen AI prototype named ChatGPT was made publicly available by OpenAI, a Microsoft-backed company, in November 2022 (Dwivedi et al. 2023). It quickly gained popularity due to its capability to understand and respond

Published by Springer Nature Switzerland AG 2026
A. Elbanna et al. (Eds.): TDIT 2025, IFIP AICT 778, pp. 247–254, 2026.
https://doi.org/10.1007/978-3-032-16775-0_16

in natural language. It is the innovation with the quickest growth rate, having attained 100 million active adoptions in just two months (Ooi et al. 2023). The applications of ChatGPT contribute to various organisational tasks, such as creating website reports, marketing content, and assessing proficiency across various domains, including customer service, legal practices, healthcare, government agencies, and education (Greengard 2023a; Stackploe 2023). There are other Gen AI tools built to generate other types of outputs, like images (DALL-E, Stable Diffusion, MidJourney), audio (AudioLM), video (Imagen Video, Phenaki), and audio file transcription (Whisper) (Ooi et al. 2023). McKinsey (2023) highlighted how 71% of organizations reported regular use of Gen AI in at least one business function and add between $2.6 trillion to $4.4 trillion annually to the global economy by boosting productivity and enhancing customer operations. According to Goldman Sachs (2023), Gen AI could boost global GDP by 7 trillion (7%) and increase productivity growth by 1.5 percentage points over the next decade. These figures underscore that Gen AI is not just a trend but a foundational technology reshaping how work is done and value is created.

Gen AI boasts a wide range of vital and dynamic content creation capabilities. In the context of text generation, the language model of Gen AI may produce content using words spoken by voice assistants such as Google LaMDA, Apple Siri, and Amazon Alexa (Greengard 2023b). Gen AI text-based applications are essential to the AI ecosystem as they offer wide accessibility, adaptability, and broad usage across consumer and business platforms. They support a variety of tasks, from content production and translation to coding support and decision-making by facilitating intuitive, language-based interactions. These text-based applications form the foundation for more advanced multimodal systems, such as voice assistants and chatbots, boosting productivity while reducing entry barriers for users. Amid the increased integration of these applications into everyday workflows, it is crucial to understand how users perceive their effectiveness, usability, and trustworthiness. Although earlier studies have investigated broad factors driving AI adoption (Agrawal 2023), limited research has focused on how specific advancements within text-based Gen AI applications, influence user experiences.

To explore the evolving user experience, this study aims to analyse user reviews of different Gen AI applications to identify antecedents of user experience. The primary objectives of the study are to quantify user experience using the Net Promoter Score (NPS) and uncover key themes that drive NPS of Gen AI applications through topic modelling. Furthermore, this research lays the foundation for future studies that aim to explore generative AI applications for more critical reviews, thereby expanding the scope of user experience analysis in the rapidly evolving AI landscape. In our analysis, we collected user review data from various text-based Gen AI applications. We performed sentiment analysis and calculated NPS to evaluate user experience performance. Further, topic modelling was employed to uncover key themes that impact the user experiences across these applications. We hereby posit the research question as follows:

RQ1: What factors derived from user reviews influence the Net Promoter Score of text-based Gen AI applications?

The rest of the paper is organised as follows: The next section provides a thorough background of the relevant extant literature. Then, we present the research design, followed by data collection and data cleansing. The following section explains the data analysis. Lastly, we discuss the findings, followed by the future extension of the current study and highlight the conclusion.

2 Background

Gen AI contributes in various industrial applications, organisational adoption factors, societal impacts, knowledge and creative work, and ethical considerations. Focusing on implementations at the enterprise level, Kar et al. (2023) examine the significant prospects and difficulties related to Generative AI (Gen AI) in industrial applications, describing how language models can improve a range of organisational activities and domains. Furthermore, Agrawal (2023) examined factors enabling the sustainability of GenAI-powered Optimisation Intelligence (GenAI-OI) processes in organisational settings and employed the Normalisation Process Theory (NPT) for theoretical analysis.

The sociological ramifications of Gen AI technologies like ChatGPT are also examined by Sabherwal and Grover (2024), who highlight the revolutionary potential of these tools to alter social relationships and systems. Further in the knowledge management domain, Alavi et al. (2024) evaluate the contribution of Gen AI to the production, exchange, and use of knowledge in organisations. Additionally, the impact of ChatGPT on knowledge work practices is examined by Ritala et al. (2023), who also suggest additional research into the implications of ChatGPT for both individuals and organisations.

Hirsch (2023) examines ChatGPT's capabilities in crisis management, particularly its linguistic functions in crisis communication scenarios. In the field of hospitality and tourism, Gursoy et al. (2023) consider ChatGPT's potential to transform client decision-making, information retrieval, and personalised services. Chen et al. (2023) highlight Gen AI's applications in business and finance, specifically in data analysis, corporate sentiment analysis, stock return prediction, and risk management.

Businesses in various sectors have been exploring the applications of Gen AI (Ooi et al., 2023; Alavi et al., 2024). For instance, Microsoft is integrating Open AI GPT4 to analyze medical records for trends and draft patient responses from healthcare personnel. Moreover, the customer service solutions startup. Intercom has started testing trial programs that use GenAI to improve customer engagement and spur business expansion. Similarly, JP Morgan (2023) is training machine learning models that identify novel and emerging anomalies that they might not be able to identify if they were trained on real data by utilizing GenAI to create synthetic data. Gen AI has been employed to generate advertising campaigns from a marketing perspective. For instance, Google is initiating its advertising campaign service within its Machine Learning (ML) systems, the Performance Max suite aims to determine the best ad placements and provide budget recommendations. Meta and Alphabet are also collaborating on the technology to boost market efficiency. IBM's Watson, an AI studio developed for businesses, offers self-service access to top-notch, reliable data, enabling users to collaborate on the platform to build and enhance generative AI models.

3 Research Design

The current study uses critical user reviews from Gen AI applications. We have undertaken two analytical techniques: sentiment analysis and topic modelling. Sentiment Analysis was used to evaluate the applications NPS. This procedure assisted in classifying reviews according to the sentiment polarity (positive, neutral, or negative) into promoters, passives, and detractors. Additionally, topic modelling was conducted to identify the constructs and topics that emerge from the reviews. The combined analytical approach provided a comprehensive view of user perceptions and the factors driving their interaction with Gen AI applications. The framework used is presented in Fig. 1. The framework consists of three stages: data collection, data cleaning and analysis.

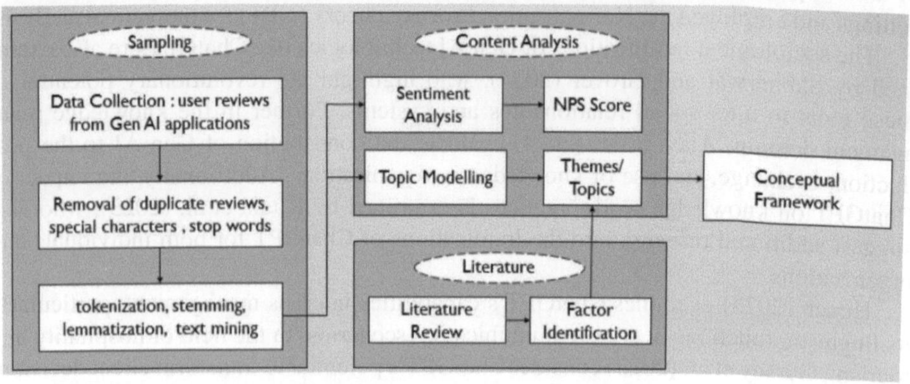

Fig. 1. Research Design for the Study

3.1 Data Collection

User reviews from seven different Gen AI applications were extracted from the Google Play Store. To gather these reviews, we utilised the Python package 'Google_Play_Scraper,' extracting data from mobile applications. Our study includes text-based gen AI applications. In total, we scraped 2 lakhs reviews from applications, including "Japer AI writing assistant", "Smart Writer", "Perplexity", "Claude", "ChatGPT", "Microsoft Copilot", and "Bing".

3.2 Data Cleansing

Following the initial extraction, a total of 30,000 reviews were obtained after systematic sampling was applied. Further, the data was cleansed, which involved removing duplicate reviews, special characters, and stop words. Additionally, tokenisation, part-of-speech filtering, and lemmatisation were performed. Subsequently, NLP-based techniques were applied to pre-process the data further.

4 Data Analysis

The data analysis part was conducted in two sections: sentiment analysis and topic modelling applied to user reviews based on text-based Gen AI applications. Sentiment analysis was performed to evaluate the NPS of the application reviews. Sentiment polarity (positive, neutral or negative) was assigned to each review, categorising users as promoters, passive or detractors. The NPS was calculated using the standard formulae (ref):

$$\text{NPS} = \%\text{ of promoters} - \%\text{ of detractors}$$

Further, the corpus of reviews was subjected to content analysis using Latent Dirichlet Allocation (LDA)-based topic modelling using the Python Gensim package. We employed LDA-based topic modelling to analyse the user reviews and extract topics for this study that impact the NPS score of the Gen AI applications. This was conducted to extract underlying constructs by grouping keywords across topics.

5 Findings

The NPS score was calculated using a total of 30,000 user reviews, out of which 22,538 were classified as promoters and 2293 reviews were classified as detractors. The NPS score is computed as follows:

$$\text{NPS} = 75.12 - 7.64 = 67.48$$

The NPS score of 67.48 indicates a strong positive sentiment among users of the Gen AI applications. A large majority of the sample (75.13%) are classified as promoters, indicating widespread user experience and a high likelihood of recommending the applications. The comparatively small percentage of dissenters (7.64%) supports this positive customer response. The remainder of the sample consists of passive users who do not support or criticise the application.

In topic modelling, upon analysing the keywords representing each topic, we mapped them to existing constructs in the IS literature. Keywords like "great", "nice", and "amazing" highlight a positive user experience. Keywords "good," "app," "useful," "great," "easy", and "nice" highlight perceived usefulness. Further terms like "super", "easy", and "awesome" suggest user enjoyment. System responsiveness is presented by keywords "way", "well", "fast", "answer", "question", "really" and "get."

We further visualised the keywords using Word Cloud, presented in Fig. 2. The word cloud emphasises important terms like "good," "app," "useful," "great," "easy", and "nice," suggesting that consumers frequently identify these applications with favourable qualities and usability. Moreover, words like "love," "amazing," and "awesome" are prominently displayed, which enhances the overall user experience. Overall, the visualization highlights users' appreciation for the usefulness, quality, and experience of these Gen AI applications.

The exploratory study led to the development of a conceptual model presented in Fig. 3, comprising four factors that collectively represent the user experience with

Fig. 2. Word Cloud for the User Reviews Text-Based Gen AI Applications

Gen AI applications. The constructs "System responsiveness", "perceived usefulness", "perceived novelty" and "user enjoyment" capture key dimensions influencing positive user experience and NPS with text-based Gen AI applications. The model combines findings from topic modelling user reviews with insights from the literature through an exploratory study. The combination of these concepts provides a theoretically based framework for assessing how users view, interact with, and benefit from Gen AI technologies. They capture both the functional and affective aspects of user experience.

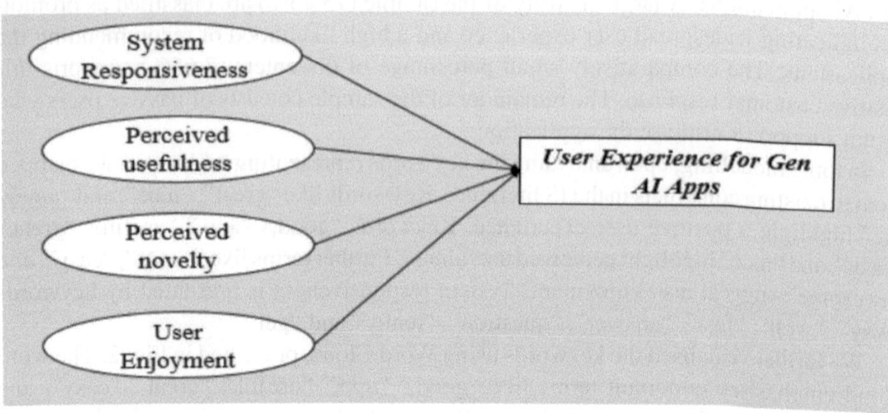

Fig. 3. Conceptual Model for determining the factors that impact the user experience for text-based Gen AI applications

6 Future Extension of the Study

We plan to broaden the scope of our analysis to include a broader range of generative AI application reviews with other modalities, like image, video and audio-based applications. This will provide us with thorough knowledge of the uptake and efficacy of generative AI technologies by enabling us to investigate user experiences and sentiments in various situations and applications. Additionally, we aim to map more important keywords to existing constructs from pertinent literature, further connecting them to the theoretical lens.

7 Conclusion

The study analysed user reviews of text-based generative AI applications, revealing a high level of user experience, as reflected by an NPS of 67.48. Sentiment analysis and topic modelling highlighted key factors that reflect positive user experiences. Furthermore, the study identified key dimensions through exploratory analysis that influence a positive user experience with text-based Gen AI applications. Future research will expand the scope to more reviews to further understand user experience and adoption of Gen AI technologies across different modalities.

References

Accenture: Generative AI: Understanding generative AI and how it will fundamentally transform our world. https://www.accenture.com/us-en/insights/generative-ai. (2023) Accessed 2023/10/25

Alavi, M., Leidner, D.E., Mousavi, R.: A knowledge management perspective of generative artificial intelligence. J. Assoc. Inf. Syst. **25**(1), 1–12 (2024)

Bazzan, J., Echeveste, M.E., Formoso, C.T., Altenbernd, B., Barbian, M.H.: An information management model for addressing residents' complaints through artificial intelligence techniques. Buildings **13**(3), 737 (2023)

Benbya, H., Strich, F., Tamm, T.: Navigating generative artificial intelligence promises and perils for knowledge and creative work. J. Assoc. Inf. Syst. **25**(1), 23–36 (2024)

Chen, B., Wu, Z., Zhao, R.: From fiction to fact: the growing role of generative AI in business and finance. J. Chinese Econ. Bus. Stud. **21**(4), 471–496 (2023)

Dwivedi, Y.K., et al.: "So what if ChatGPT wrote it?" multidisciplinary perspectives on opportunities, challenges and implications of generative conversational AI for research, practice and policy. Int. J. Inf. Manage. **71**, 102642 (2023)

Euchner, J.: Generative AI. Res. Technol. Manag. **66**(3), 71–74 (2023)

Goldman Sachs: Generative AI could raise global GDP by 7 per cent. https://www.goldmansachs.com/insights/articles/generative-ai-could-raise-global-gdp-by-7-percent.html. Accessed 2023/10/25

Greengard, S.: What is GAI? https://www.eweek.com/big-data-and-analytics/whatis-generative-ai/. (2023a) Accessed 2023/03/22

Greengard, S.: ChatGPT: Understanding the ChatGPT AI Chatbot. https://www.eweek.com/big-data-and-analytics/chatgpt/. (2023b) Accessed 2023/03/22

Gursoy, D., Li, Y., Song, H.: ChatGPT and the hospitality and tourism industry: an overview of current trends and future research directions. J. Hosp. Market. Manag. **32**(5), 579–592 (2023)

Hirsch, P.B.: Cui bono: a conversation with ChatGPT. J. Bus. Strateg. **44**(4), 238–241 (2023)

Jain, R., Garg, N., Khera, S.N.: Adoption of AI-enabled tools in social development organizations in India: an extension of UTAUT model. Front. Psychol. **13**, 893691 (2022)

Jin, F.: Output analysis in voice interaction in AI environment. Informatica **43**(3) (2019)

Kar, A.K., Varsha, P.S., Rajan, S.: Unravelling the impact of generative artificial intelligence (GAI) in industrial applications: a review of scientific and grey literature. Glob. J. Flex. Syst. Manag. **24**(4), 659–689 (2023)

Karakose, T., Demirkol, M., Yirci, R., Polat, H., Ozdemir, T.Y., Tülübaş, T.: A conversation with ChatGPT about digital leadership and technology integration: comparative analysis based on human–AI collaboration. Administr. Sci. **13**(7), 157 (2023)

Korzynski, P., et al.: Generative artificial intelligence as a new context for management theories: analysis of ChatGPT. Central Euro. Manag. J. **31**(1), 3–13 (2023)

McKinsey: The economic potential of generative AI: the next productivity frontier. https://www.mckinsey.com/capabilities/mckinsey-digital/our-insights/the-economic-potential-of-generative-ai-the-next-productivity-frontier. (2023) Accessed 2023/10/25

Melissa: Why ChatGPT is a must use business tool in 2023. https://www.linkedin.com/pulse/why-chatgpt-must-use-business-tool-2023-melissa-mitchell. Accessed 2023/03/22

Minelle, F., Stolfi, F.: AI to support PM: a ChatGPT quality assessment (ß test). https://pmworldlibrary.net/wp-content/uploads/2023/05/pmwj129-May2023-Minelle-Stolfi-AI-to-support-PM-a-ChatGPT-quality-assessment-3-1.pdf. Accessed 2023/10/25

Ooi, K.B., Tan, G.W.H., Al-Emran, M., Al-Sharafi, M.A., Capatina, A., Chakraborty, A., Wong, L.W.: The potential of generative artificial intelligence across disciplines: perspectives and future directions. J. Comput. Inform. Syst. 1–32 (2023)

Prasad Agrawal, K.: Towards adoption of generative AI in organizational settings. J. Comput. Inform. Syst. 1–16 (2023)

Prasad Agrawal, K.: Towards adoption of generative AI in organizational settings. J. Comput. Inform. Syst. **64**(5), 636–651 (2024)

Ritala, P., Ruokonen, M., Ramaul, L.: Transforming boundaries: how does ChatGPT change knowledge work? J. Bus. Strateg. (ahead-of-print) (2023)

Sabherwal, R., Grover, V.: The societal impacts of generative artificial intelligence: a balanced perspective. J. Assoc. Inf. Syst. **25**(1), 13–22 (2024)

Stackpole, B.: Are you ready for ChatGPT for 3-D Printing? https://www.digitalengineering247.com/article/are-you-ready-for-chatgpt-for-3d-printing/. (2023) Accessed 2023/10/25

UmaMaheswaran, S.K., et al.: Empirical analysis for improving food quality using artificial intelligence technology for enhancing healthcare sector. J. Food Qual. **2022**, 1–13 (2022)

Walkowiak, E.: Task-interdependencies between generative AI and workers. Econ. Lett. **231**, 111315 (2023)

Sustainable 6G Connectivity Leveraging 6G PATH Project's Key Value Indicators for UN SDGs' Alignment

Imesha D. Premarathne[1(✉)], Vishanth Weerakkody[1], Jing Li[1], Uthayasankar Sivarajah[2], Kamran Mahroof[1], and L. A. Shanaka Perera[1]

[1] University of Bradford, Bradford, UK
imeshadevindi99@gmail.com

[2] Kingston Business School, Kingston University London, Kingston upon Thames, UK

Abstract. The path towards 6G technology is emerging as the next major revolution in the ICT industry that will impact most industry verticals across the globe. Evaluating the impact of such technology in terms of sustainability and its alignment with the United Nations (UN) Sustainability Development Goals (SDGs) is therefore imperative. This paper aims to assess the economic, social and environmental sustainability of the 6G-PATH project through Key Value Indicators (KVIs) and their links to achieving UN SDGs. The study will discuss the application of KVIs on the 6G PATH project use cases to measure the impact of 6G technology on sustainability across selected industry verticals using Key Value Enablers (KVEs). This study extends beyond mapping KVIs to SDGs by introducing a Sustainability Trade-off Matrix, which systematically evaluates the interdependencies, upstream and downstream impacts, and potential negative externalities of 6G-enabled use cases. The study findings highlight why the sustainability of 6G technology is important and how the technology can be used to accelerate the progress of the UN SDGs. Further, the resulting framework provides a decision-support mechanism to ensure 6G deployment delivers net-positive sustainability outcomes while anticipating and managing unintended consequences.

Keywords: KVIs · Sustainability · UN SDGs · 6G-PATH

1 Introduction

Since the deployment of second-generation (2G) mobile radio network technologies in the early 1990s, it has approached a long journey focusing on different user experiences and requirements up to the fifth-generation network (5G). Later, marking a significant step in the telecommunication industry, 6G rolls out as an upward setup of 5G technology [1]. It is currently in the pre-standardisation stage, with the ITU-R IMT-2030 framework and multiple international research initiatives shaping its technical specifications and potential application domains [2]. Unlike its predecessors, 6G is being developed under growing pressure to address environmental, social, and economic sustainability

Published by Springer Nature Switzerland AG 2026
A. Elbanna et al. (Eds.): TDIT 2025, IFIP AICT 778, pp. 255–284, 2026.
https://doi.org/10.1007/978-3-032-16775-0_17

alongside performance requirements [3]. This creates a unique opportunity to embed sustainability principles into the technology's architecture before deployment begins, something that was largely overlooked during the rollout of previous generations of mobile communication. Therefore, Beyond 5G (B5G)/6G aims at creating technologies to support human and planetary goals [4].

In this focus, the 6G-PATH project plays a vital role with the goal of helping to foster the further development and integration of new and improved products with Beyond 5G (B5G)/6G while also defining and measuring relevant Key Performance Indicators (KPIs) and Key Value Indicators (KVIs) for sustainable development. To achieve this objective, seven testbeds will be part of the project consortium, which will be used by ten use cases spread across four key verticals: Health, Education, Smart Cities and Farming [5]. Key values (KVs) represent the impact of the use case and technology on the high-level human and planetary goals, and the project aims to maximize the positive impact and minimize the negative impact [6]. The project's key values are in three sustainability domains economic, social and environmental. The KVIs represent the measurement or indicator of assessing key values quantitatively or qualitatively [6, 7]. Therefore, it is identified that the impact of technology on values is to be controlled via KVIs, covering environmental, social and economic aspects. Hence, project goals contribute to ensuring that advanced 6G technology is not only expected to meet the technological excellence in satisfying the individual needs of end users but also address the societal goals which affect the planet and humankind.

The high-level human and planetary goals referred to above are primarily defined in the United Nation's Sustainability Development Goals (UN SDGs) or their subsets. They provide the basis for identifying key values for the use cases or contexts which use 6G. In addition, the impact of ICT on values has a duality consisting of direct impact and indirect impact. From the sustainability perspective, direct impact refers to "sustainable ICT", whereas the indirect impact refers to the "ICT for Sustainability". To further elaborate, sustainable ICT refers to the development and deployment of ICT systems, including 6G technologies that directly minimize negative environmental, social, and economic impacts while also indirectly maximize positive effects. This includes reducing energy consumption, promoting circular economy practices in hardware design, and ensuring ethical AI deployment. In contrast, ICT for Sustainability positions ICT as an enabler that facilitates broader sustainability goals in sectors such as agriculture, health, urban planning, and education. Here, the ICT itself might not be sustainable, but it catalyzes sustainable outcomes elsewhere. Thus, Sustainable ICT is an attribute of the ICT artefact/system itself, whereas ICT for Sustainability is more about its application and influence across domains [8]. Therefore, aligning 6G development with the SDGs is crucial to fostering a sustainable and inclusive future. SDGs set a comprehensive framework to address global challenges with a specific agenda of 17 goals and targets to be achieved by 2030 [9]. This is the primary driving force for global sustainability, which sets the focus for identifying key values of 6G networking and is also supported by other regional commitments from frameworks such as the European Green Deal [10] and European values reflected by [10]. Therefore, aligning these goals into the 6G roadmap as key values to be achieved under each use case enables harnessing the positive societal outcomes of next-generation connectivity solutions.

Considering the above facts, it is unarguably accepted that 6G development holds a promise for societal progress and sustainability. Most of the existing studies approach 6G sustainability either through high-level conceptual visions or by extending conventional technical KPIs to new use cases. Few provide operational frameworks that integrate KVIs capturing both socio-economic and technical dimensions, nor do they explicitly align these with the UN SDGs [11]. The recent white papers on 6G experimenting EU projects including references [3, 7, 12] and journal articles such as reference [13] have focused on identifying the connection between 5G/6G and sustainability. Further, some other scholars have recently paid attention to KVIs in 5G/6G development [14]. Even where such mappings are attempted, they often lack specificity in describing the enabling technologies, deployment contexts, and measurable sustainability impacts. The recent study of [12] which has mainly focused on developing a value-driven framework for KVI identification and measurement also proposes future studies to link the KVI framework with SDGs. Hence, a critical empirical research gap is identified in introducing a holistic framework that aligns 6G or next-generation ICT projects' KVIs for SDGs. The urgency of this paper further enhances by the fact that 6G deployment is still nascent, making this a crucial window to shape its value framework before path dependencies set in. By now 6G standards, spectrum allocations, and deployment roadmaps are being mostly defined with the coordination of international bodies like ITU-R and 3GPP and significant contributions from regional alliances and research initiatives. However, commercial trials and deployments are expected by the late 2030s [2]. Decisions taken during this pre-deployment phase will shape network architectures, operational models, and business ecosystems for decades. Once large-scale rollouts begin, retrofitting sustainability into technical design, governance frameworks, or investment strategies will be substantially more difficult and costly. Therefore, pre-deployment sustainability frameworks such as proposed by this study are especially critical.

This paper addresses the identified research gap by proposing and validating a framework to align 6G-PATH project's [which is an ongoing project funded by Smart Networks and Servies Joint Undertaking (SNS JU) and co-funded by the European Union (EU) under the EU Horizon Europe research and innovation program, as the case study] KVIs with the UN SDGs, embedding specific technical enablers such as ultra-reliable low-latency communication, integrated sensing and communication, edge AI processing, and energy-aware network slicing within each use case. The proposed framework not only captures the potential positive impacts of 6G technologies but also acknowledges trade-offs and risks, offering a replicable approach for sustainability evaluation in emerging ICT systems before large-scale deployment. This paper will contribute to ensuring that next-generation ICT solutions align with addressing global sustainability challenges and proposing policy recommendations based on empirical insights. Further, the clear alignment between 6G-PATH project's KVIs and SDGs will guide stakeholder engagement in 6G and other future network solutions ensuring a sustainable and inclusive future.

This paper is structured as follows. Section II outlines previous work related to 6G sustainability and KVIs. Section III briefly explains the methodology of this paper. Sections IV and V first introduce the use cases developed under the 6G-PATH project followed by how the 6G-PATH project leverages KVIs for SDGs. Finally, Section VI provides the concluding remarks.

2 Related Literature

2.1 6G Connectivity and Sustainability

As the world advances towards the 6G era, it becomes imperative to ensure that 6G networks are not only effective and efficient but also sustainable. Several recent literatures have focused on identifying the connection between 6G deployment and sustainability. The ongoing 6G projects under the EU have more focused on sustainable 6G deployment. The reference [15] brings forth the European vision for the 6G network ecosystem and one of the key points of their vision directs to "define sustainable 6G ecosystems", prioritizing three sustainability dimensions, economic, social and environmental [P:4]. It discusses how 6G can be developed to achieve the SDGs in 2030 and also its role in making Europe climate neutral in 2050 as referred to in the European Green Deal. Accordingly, the 6G efforts in the reduction of carbon footprint, affordable and efficient energy solutions, trustworthy infrastructure, AI connected management and control functions and integrated sensing and communication functions support achieving green objectives.

The white paper of reference [7] is a comprehensive work on linking SDGs with the 6G vision and goals under three pillars; (1) Empowering people using 6G service at both the individual level and society level, (2) Strengthening the world by reinforcing the eco-system based on SDGs and (3) Sensing the environment. The study utilizes the Quintuple Helix model for sustainable development of 6G where it creates a synergy between economy, society and democracy. The work highlights the SDG linkage with existing ICT solutions and how 6G can contribute to achieving the targets. Another white paper published by [13] dives into the H2020 Hexa-X project work on sustainability. It discusses twofolds of sustainability to embed with 6G as "6G for sustainability" and "sustainable 6G". The paper proposes a framework to link the project use cases with SDGs underlying the above two principles. However, the significance of the paper arises from using KPIs and developed architectural enablers to link with sustainability.

Some of the other previous works on sustainable 6G address the application of different specific sustainability aspects. Environmental sustainability is one of the main goals of sustainable 6G and aims to address challenges such as reducing carbon footprint, making energy-efficient 6G technology and other aspects including efficient natural resource management, water conservation and waste management [3]. Under the environmental sustainability of SDGs and European Green Deal targets, house gas emission targets and energy consumption targets are primarily concerned with developing 6G. Because energy consumption could spike with the growing demand for faster data rates, ultra-low latency, and the proliferation of connected devices. The study [16] raises this issue and proposes industry-driven initiatives and standardization activities for ensuring sustainable 6G deployment at the commercial level. The study further discusses the existing metrics of sustainability and recommends relevant energy-saving techniques. The recent publication of [17] provides a comprehensive discussion of sustainable 6G wireless communication systems, addressing the urgent need for environmentally friendly and energy-efficient networks. Furthermore, [18] also emphasizes that when the world is waiting for the implementation of 6G mobile communication technology, it is mandatory to resolve the high impact environmental issues including higher energy consumption which results in carbon emissions and disposal of electronic waste, for the sustainability of 6G technology. This study conducts a lifecycle analysis of 6G technology from production to disposal, focusing on environmental impact.

Therefore, despite promising transformative capabilities, 6G also poses serious sustainability challenges and risks that require equal scrutiny. Some of the recent works explicitly highlight several countervailing concerns. The study of [19] investigates the potential hazards linked with millimetre-wave (mmWave) radiation of 6G, focusing on evaluating human body exposure to Non-Ionising Radiation (NIR) interactions. Findings suggest the Distributed Base Station (DBS) network and architecture as a solution to reduce NIR interactions. The reference [17] investigates a range of sustainability issues associated with the growth of the telecommunication industry, including high energy consumption, which results in carbon emissions, excessive electronic waste without proper disposal mechanisms, and the recycling of electronic materials that interrupts growth. The study proposes an ecological policy via a 6G life cycle analysis. Furthermore, reference [20] investigates increased electromagnetic field (EMF) exposure risks to humans and the environment with upcoming 6G technologies, and the study highlights the assessments required for governing them. Most importantly, the study of [21] investigates several public health and environmental impacts of 6G deployment. It discusses the threats of terahertz (THz) radiation of 6G on natural habitats such as migratory species, pollinators, and marine ecosystems; risks of ecotoxicology of 6G infrastructure which risks the soil, air, and water systems on earth and increased carbon emissions due to new high use of quantum computing, intelligent reflecting surfaces (IRS), and reconfigurable radio environments in 6G with high demand for energy consumption. On the other hand, emerging evidence from studies such as [22] suggests that 6G still has created new cybersecurity vulnerabilities across physical, connection, and service layers, with some risks including ransomware, quantum-based attacks, and large-scale privacy breaches, threatening the trust, reliability, and long-term sustainability of 6G-enabled systems.

Hence, it can be observed that previous literature has recently focused on identifying the connection between 6G technology and UN SDGs or 6G technology and sustainability. Moreover, it was evident that 6G connectivity holds transformative potential for advancing the UN SDGs through ultra-reliable low-latency communications, massive machine-type connectivity, and integrated AI-driven services. Its deployment also presents sustainability challenges and risks such as increased energy demand from ultra-dense network architectures, cybersecurity vulnerabilities, risks to privacy and trust in pervasive sensing environments and some health and biodiversity risks. Therefore, the proposed KVI-SDG framework of this research addresses both sides of this equation by embedding metrics that assess not only value creation but also value risks. Therefore, by capturing these positive and negative externalities, this study ensures that 6G sustainability assessments remain holistic, enabling decision-makers to optimise benefits while proactively mitigating adverse impacts, which are lacking in literature.

2.2 Values, Key Values and Key Value Indicators

The "Value" is a multifaceted notion where the definition has changed across various disciplines. Economists define "value" in terms of market price whereas managers define it as customer satisfaction or profitability. In social science, value refers to the shared beliefs among a group of people and is commonly accepted as moral [23]. However, in the ICT sphere, key values refer to the impact of technology on the use case and the high-level human and planetary goals [6]. Further, according to the previous literature, value in ICT arena is in two forms; value as a criterion which is defined by society as aimed at delivering public good and value as an outcome of a project or a process where a benefit is embedded for multiple stakeholders in society including the general public [12]. Hence, values consider as powerful drivers in a society to evaluate the contributions and commitments of technology.

Most of the traditional performance metrics lack the capacity to provide a holistic view of value in projects, including social, economic and environmental dimensions. Majority of the previous ICT-related research work and projects have focused more on performance metrics using KPIs. Turning a new chapter, the recent European research projects on 6G have focused on integrating both the societal and technical requirements through the development of KVIs and KPIs. The ongoing projects under SNS JU promote KPI and KVI evaluation and validation for the projects under the research and innovation sector. Accordingly, the SNS JU projects including 6G-PATH, CENTRIC, DESIRE6G, ORIGAMI, 6GXR, DETERMINISTIC6G and TrialsNet [24] are working on the identification, evaluation and validation of KVIs. SNS JU aims to create a standard set of KPIs and KVIs for evaluating and validating 6G.

The recent literature published by ongoing 6G projects on identifying and validating KVIs demonstrates the value of KVIs in end-to-end (E2E) large-scale trials and pilots, highlighting their role in bridging the gap between societal values and technological outcomes. The 6G Flagship project, Hexa-X-II, further reinforces the importance of key values within 6G research [6, 8, 13]. The Hexa-X project categorizes KVIs as sustainability, inclusion and trustworthiness [8] and SNS-IA-6G economic, social and environmental [15]. Further, many other 6G projects including TARGET-X, Trials-Net, IMAGINE-B5G, and 6G-SANDBOX have included sustainability KVIs when evaluating relevant specific use cases.

Further, it can be observed that the frameworks for defining, evaluating and validating KVIs have evolved with 6G development from different SNS JU projects. During the early stages of development, literature suggested that it was still too early to define a concrete roadmap for setting and validating KVIs within these projects. Despite the number of ongoing research, quantifying KVIs in relation to 6G technologies still remains a challenge. Moreover, still there is uncertainty in the usage of the term "KVI" alongside "KPI," often without proper clarification in both academic literature and project descriptions, leading to confusion in the research community. However, the recently published white paper of [12] presents the KVI analysis framework in four steps by addressing most of the mentioned issues. The developed version of it is presented by the recent study of reference [17], and it guides on separately identifying KVIs from KPIs and linking KVIs with Key Value Enablers (KVEs), which are considered as technical factors contribute to achieving the key values to define a validation and evaluation framework.

However, those studies also suggest integrating UN SDGs with KVI frameworks. Therefore, values are powerful drivers in society to evaluate contributions and commitments, which can be identified even in universal value frameworks such as UN SDGs.

3 Methodology

The identification and validation of KVIs in the 6G-PATH project and mapping them against SDGs followed a two-phase process combining literature-based candidate generation with a structured iterative expert consensus process adapted from the modified Nominal Group Technique (NGT) and modified Delphi principles. According to the previous literature, including references [25], although the traditional NGT approach is structured, interactive and consensus-based, it still requires face-to-face structured group sessions, which creates logistics and cost barriers. Furthermore, the Delphi technique also has strong strengths, including anonymity, broad reach and iterative nature, which are again composed with some limitations such as less interactiveness and time-consuming nature [26, 27]. Considering all these pros and cons of the two methodologies, modified Delphi NGT can be identified as a successful hybrid approach adopted in healthcare, education, and organisational research [28, 29]. Therefore, this approach's modifications are often made to address specific research needs, logistical challenges, such as by conducting virtual meetings, or to enhance the rigour and inclusivity of the process [18, 29].

Considering all the pros and cons, this study also adopted the modified Delphi-NGT as the methodological approach, and the process of the study comprised three main phases.

Phase 1: Literature-Based Idea Generation—To start the process, a targeted review of academic, industry, and policy literature (including ITU-R, 6G-PPP, and other 6G white papers and public reports) and a context review of documented blueprints across all the 6G-PATH use cases were undertaken to compile an initial list of KVs, and KVIs, each mapped provisionally to relevant UN SDGs. KVs represent the core principles or benefits the project aims to deliver using testbeds, use cases and third-party experimentations. They are the fundamental reasons for the project's existence. KVIs represent the measuring indicators of KVs.

Phase 2: Round 1—Thematic Workshops and Preliminary Consensus—In round 1, ten use case-specific workshops were held virtually with the participation of consortium experts of the 6G-PATH project across four verticals: smart farming, education, health and smart cities. Each of them involved a minimum of five and a maximum of ten. Across all the workshops, 56 unique experts participated, representing technical, sustainability, industry-specific, academic and business experts. In each workshop, participants discussed the relevance, applicability, measurability and importance of each initially listed KVI and refined a set of KVIs with consensus defined a priori as agreement by at least 80% of participants. Items meeting the threshold were retained; others were revised or removed through group deliberation. Further, the agreed list of KVIs was also linked with respective key value enablers (KVEs) and contributing SDGs. A drafted document was prepared at the end of each workshop using thematic analysis to identify KVs, KVIs and mapping with KVEs and SDGs. The drafted document was circulated internally among consortium members for further study, refining KVIs or especially to have more ideas to map KVIs with KVEs.

Phase 3: Round 2—Cross Use-Case Alignment and Finalization—Following round 1, the document, including revised KVI lists, mapped with KVEs and SDGs for each use case, was circulated internally for asynchronous discussion within the consortium. Then, the second round of meetings was held to finalise the consolidated list of KVIs for each use case. However, this final inclusion of KVIs required unanimous consent among participating experts in the workshop. Throughout both rounds, all the workshops were recorded and transcribed, and changes to KVI definitions, new KVIs, and refinements to existing ones were identified using manual thematic analysis and coding. This approach allowed both convergence on agreed indicators and the surfacing of potential trade-offs between KVIs and SDGs, which were subsequently incorporated into the sustainability trade-off matrix.

This design was specifically chosen because the project involved complex, multi-domain use cases requiring iterative, real-time expert interaction at the initial stage. Further, both modified Delphi and modified NGT have been widely adopted for indicator development in sustainability, healthcare, and ICT evaluation contexts, where consensus from diverse stakeholders is essential. To sum up, this paper includes only the first part of the study, and later versions will evaluate and validate the results of identified KVIs of the 6G-PATH project using mixed methodology, collecting data from surveys, focus group discussions and interviews with diverse stakeholders (Fig. 1).

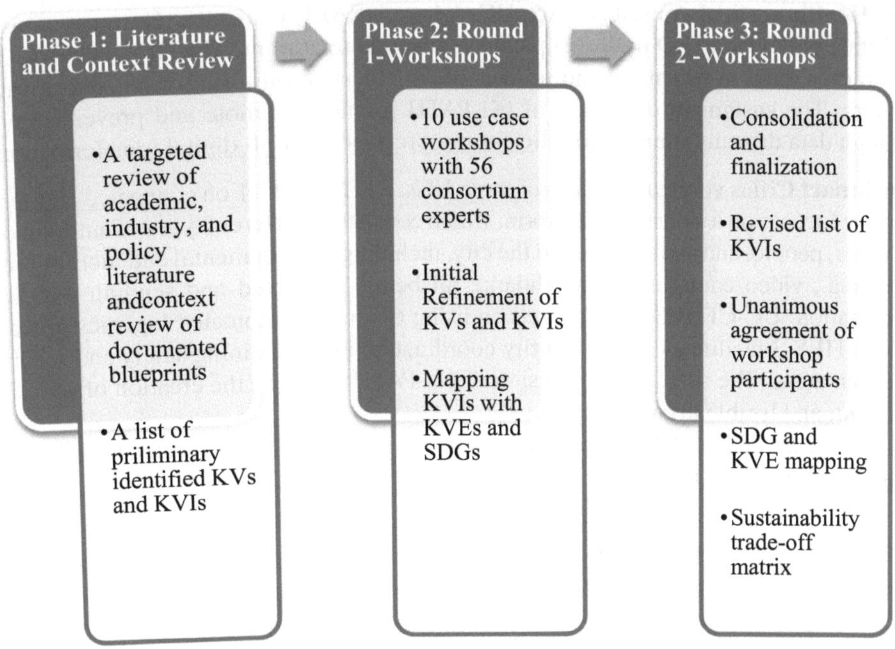

Fig. 1. Methodical approach. *Source* Author constructed

4 6G-PATH Project Verticals and Its Sustainable Vision

The 6G-PATH project aims to accelerate the development and deployment of 6G technologies through large-scale trials and experimentation. Its' sustainable vision is deeply embedded in both its technological innovation and socio-economic objectives. The 6G-PATH has 10 use cases across four verticals: Health, Smart Cities, Education and farming. The KVIs developed for each case separately and they were aligned with the UN SDGs. The sustainability envisioned innovative use cases under each of the verticals are as follows.

The Education vertical of 6G PATH consists of three use cases and is mainly devoted to using Extended Reality (XR) and Holographic-based educational scenarios. Use case (UC) Education (EDU) 1 is aimed at creating an interactive learning environment in rural villages in Romania using the "Digitaliada" educational platform. The UC-EDU-2 in the UK targets to deliver interactive learning for university students using XR technology and UC-EDU-3 in Sweden uses XR for health raining using manikins. The sustainability vision of 6G-PATH primarily supports equitable and inclusive access to quality education using high-speed, low-latency networks.

The Farming vertical is composed of two UCs aimed at water saving, where 6G is used in real-time irrigation monitoring in orchards (FARM-UC-1) and smart vineyards (FARM-UC-2) in Spain. The sustainability vision of 6G-PATH promotes resource-efficient and environmentally friendly agriculture through precision technologies via reduced waste, climate-smart farming and food security.

The Health vertical consists of two UCs where HEALTH-UC-1 in Germany aims to facilitate 6G in using 3D hydrogel patches in wound treatment. The HEALTH-UC-2 is in a remote area in Germany and utilizes 6G in elderly monitoring using smart watch sensors. The sustainability vision of 6G-PATH promotes remote and preventive care through data driven systems and efficient resource use through digital transformation.

The Smart Cities vertical consists of three UCs. CITIES-UC-1 on connected and sensing city focuses on a smart city platform, which consists of different types of autonomous vehicles, people, and sensors around the city, including environmental and mobility sensors (e.g., video cameras, radars, lidars), all being connected and sending real-time information. UC-CITIES-2 is focused on using 6G in the automated logistics process. UC-CITIES-3 facilitates 6G in security coordination in maintaining safety and security in urban areas. The sustainability vision of 6G-PATH supports the creation of resilient, efficient, and livable urban spaces.

Thus, each of these UCs across all the verticals in 6G-PATH is dedicated to promoting sustainability (Fig. 2).

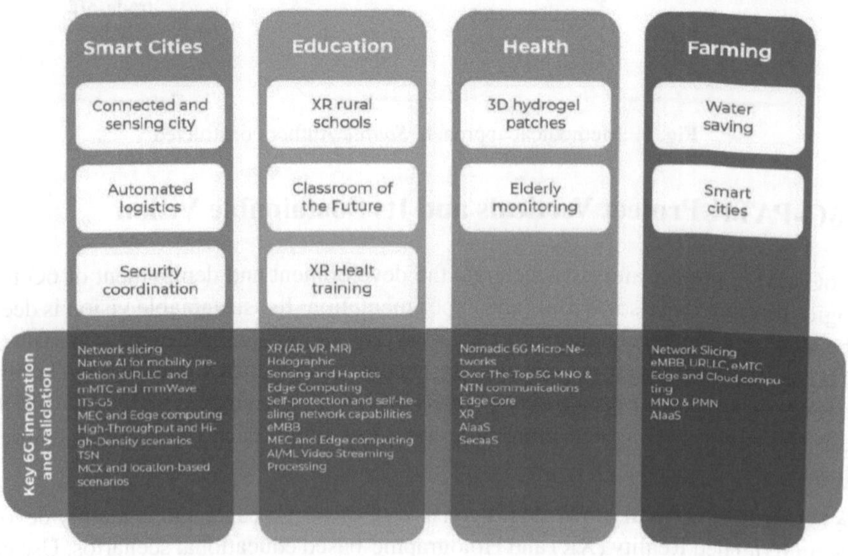

Fig. 2. 6G-PATH use case innovations. [5] *Source* Fernandes et al.

5 Aligning KVIs and KVEs with UN SDGs

It is unarguable that next generation technologies should support and enable a more sustainable future. The 6G-PATH KVIs and KVEs can be aligned with the UN SDGs as discussed below (see Tables 1, 2, and 3). Creating a holistic approach, we propose a three-dimensional framework integrating economic, social and environmental KVIs.

5.1 Economic KVIs and SDGs Alignment

The economic sustainability dimension of the 6G-PATH project primarily focuses on the practices that support long-term economic growth and development without compromising the ability of future generations to meet their own needs. It aims to create a balance between economic growth and resource efficiency. Economic KVIs of the 6G-PATH project assess the potential of advanced 6G features in delivering cost efficiency, performance optimisation, optimal resource utilisation, revenue growth, operational efficiency, increased productivity, and economic resilience, etc., to achieve economic sustainability. To further address the need for greater technical specificity to achieve KVIs, the project explicitly describes the 6G-enabling technologies (KVEs) underpinning each use-case, such as ultra-reliable low-latency communication (URLLC) for mission-critical logistics, enhanced mobile broadband (eMBB) at terabit speeds for immersive training, integrated sensing and communication (ISAC) for precision agriculture, AI-native programmable networks for autonomous optimisation, sub-THz high-precision positioning for fleet management, and network slicing to ensure differentiated service tiers. This integration ensures that each KVI is directly connected to the concrete technical enablers defined in emerging 6G standards and roadmaps (6G-PPP, ETSI, ITU-R), while maintaining clear alignment with the UN SDGs. The economic KVIs of the 6G-PATH project can be mapped with UN SDGs as follows.

Table 1. Economic KVIs and UN SDGs alignment

Economic KVIs	Linked UN SDGs	Linkage with 6G-PATH project
Cost efficiency	SDG 7-affordable and clean energy	UC-FARM 1 (water saving) and UC-FARM 2 (smart vineyards)—The KVEs, such as IoT soil/climate sensors and integrated sensing and communication (ISAC) for real-time crop monitoring, coupled with AI-native network optimisation support to partially overcome the time-consuming evaluation of crop physiology, to reduce irrigation energy use and ultimately to reduce operational costs in agriculture. It also enhances efficient crop management practices, such as water saving, fertiliser usage, and lowering manual labour costs (Using Automated Guided Vehicles [AGVs] to scan crops). This promotes affordable and clean energy

(*continued*)

Table 1. (*continued*)

Economic KVIs	Linked UN SDGs	Linkage with 6G-PATH project
	SDG 3-good health and well-being	UC-HEALTH 1—(3D hydrogel patches)—The KVEs such as connected 3D patch enablers (C3DPE) including Mobile 3D wound scanning apps, URLLC and secure nomadic 6G nodes in 3D hydrogel patch service reduces transportation costs for patients and healthcare systems, hospital admission costs, the overall cost of medical equipment and maintenance, and other long-term cost savings by enabling remote care and monitoring. This promotes good health and the well-being of people
	SDG 4-quality education	UC-EDU-3—(XR health training)—XR technology and 6G connectivity decrease the overall cost of training medical professionals by simulating realistic environments, reducing the need for costly direct patient-to-student training scenarios. The KVEs, such as eMBB and edge computing, enable high-fidelity simulations without costly travel. This promotes quality education
Reduced downtime cost	SDG 9-industry, innovation, and infrastructure	UC-CITIES-2—(automated logistics)—the UC applies KVEs such as high-precision positioning via sub-THz communication, URLLC for real-time vehicle coordination, and AI-driven predictive maintenance to minimise service interruptions in logistic operations by promoting resilient infrastructure

(*continued*)

Table 1. (*continued*)

Economic KVIs	Linked UN SDGs	Linkage with 6G-PATH project
Increased financial gains	SDG 8-decent work and economic growth	UC-FARM 1 (water saving) and UC-FARM 2 (smart vineyards)—advanced 6G solutions in agriculture increase the quality of products and new business opportunities that drive profitability and ultimately economic growth. The use of 6G's advanced features increases profitability through higher yields and quality enabled by KVEs such as AI-driven yield prediction systems, real-time data analytics, and blockchain-based supply chain transparency. eMBB ensures rapid access to market intelligence and facilitates direct-to-consumer sales through digital platforms. For more accurate predictions of agricultural production and yield, enabling better planning based on real-time data monitoring. This ultimately promotes economic growth
Increased productivity in agriculture	SDG 2-zero hunger	UC-FARM 1 (water saving) and UC-FARM 2 (smart vineyards)—smart technology in agriculture facilitated by 6G contributes to improved quality and quantity of yield, directly supporting the achievement of zero hunger. The KVEs include real-time IoT monitoring, drone-based multispectral imaging, autonomous machinery guided by ISAC, and AI crop health analytics, all running on low-latency 6G networks for in-field decision-making

(*continued*)

Table 1. (*continued*)

Economic KVIs	Linked UN SDGs	Linkage with 6G-PATH project
Increased operational efficiency	SDG 9-industry, innovation, and infrastructure	UC-CITIES-2—(automated logistics)—the KVEs, such as URLLC, for continuous control, AI-based route optimisation, and network slicing to guarantee quality-of-service for logistics control channels, streamline the industry processes by improving operational efficiency through innovation and infrastructure development. These improved 6G solutions further contribute to an increase in the volume of goods handled, processed, and delivered within a specified time frame
Attracting investments	SDG 9-industry, innovation, and infrastructure SDG 17-partnerships for the goals	UC-CITIES 1—(connected and sensing city)—the application of improved 6G solutions in traffic management and enhanced city services through KVEs such as massive IoT deployments, open data platforms, and AI predictive models running over high-capacity 6G networks contribute to attracting businesses and investors to smart cities, thereby boosting local economies by making the cities more efficient and connected. The resulting reliability and service innovation attract private investment and foster public–private partnerships for urban development

5.2 Social KVIs and SDGs Alignment

According to social sustainability, a society should be able to meet the needs of its current members without compromising the ability of future generations to meet their own needs. It aims at creating a just, equitable, and inclusive society where all people have access to basic needs, opportunities, and a good quality of life. The social KVIs of the 6G-PATH project assess how the project contributed to the social well-being of the public, including health and well-being, quality of life improvements, public safety and security, access to education, social mobility and resilience in healthcare. For each of these KVIs, KVEs are identified to show the concrete 6G technologies, architectures, and integration mechanisms that make the social impact possible. These enablers span URLLC for real-time control in agriculture, pervasive IoT sensor networks for urban safety, AI-powered analytics for public health, XR platforms for digital education, and secure, privacy-preserving data management tools. By linking each KVI directly to its enabling technologies, the framework makes explicit how the anticipated social benefits are operationalised, and where technological dependencies and risks may arise. These social KVIs and those of the 6G-PATH project can be mapped with UN SDGs as follows.

Table 2. Social KVIs and UN SDGs alignment

Social KVIs	Linked UN SDGs	Linkage with 6G-PATH project
Increased contribution to food security	SDG 2-zero hunger SDG 9-industry, innovation, and infrastructure	UC-FARM 1 (water saving) and UC-FARM 2 (smart vineyards)—workshops and knowledge-sharing initiatives under the smart farming use cases aim to empower smallholder farmers and promote community-led agricultural innovation. The initiatives including AI-based crop management, precision irrigation through digital twins, and predictive weather modeling enabled by 6G networks contribute to strengthening local food systems, support self-sufficiency, and contribute to resilient, sustainable food production. The KVEs such as IoT-enabled soil and crop sensors, precision irrigation controllers, AI-based yield forecasting platforms, 6G enabled edge computing for field analytics are used in this UC. This aligns directly with SDG 2's objective to end hunger through sustainable agriculture and also supports achieving SDG 9's objectives with knowledge sharing initiatives

(*continued*)

Table 2. (*continued*)

Social KVIs	Linked UN SDGs	Linkage with 6G-PATH project
Improved public health	SDG 3-good health and well-being	UC-HEALTH 1—(3D hydrogel patches) and UC-HEALTH 2—(elderly monitoring)—advanced 6G facilitated enablers such as mobile health apps for remote wound monitoring, URLLC-based teleconsultations, secure medical image transmission, AI-assisted wound analysis tools improve access to telemedicine and remote health monitoring by providing access to quality public health care services especially for the underserved areas
Chronic disease management	SDG 3-good health and well-being	UC-HEALTH 1-(3D hydrogel patches) and UC-HEALTH 2-(elderly monitoring)—6G facilitates effective chronic disease management with elderly populations by contributing to the health and well-being of people. Continuous health monitoring enabled by wearable biometric sensors with 6G connectivity, continuous remote patient monitoring dashboards, predictive health analytics at the edge assist in managing chronic diseases through real-time data transmission to healthcare providers, supporting SDG 3 by improving patient outcomes

(*continued*)

Table 2. (*continued*)

Social KVIs	Linked UN SDGs	Linkage with 6G-PATH project
Increased safety and security	SDG 11-sustainable cities and communities	UC CITIES-3—(security coordination)—this UC makes it easy for forces to collaborate and communicate using enablers such as real-time video surveillance over 6G, AI-based anomaly detection, low-latency emergency communication channels to increase the safety and security in urban areas
Increased health accessibility	SDG 3-good health and well-being	UC-HEALTH 2—(elderly monitoring)—increases the independence of the elderly population and accessibility through monitoring them using enablers such as smart watch facilitated by 6G network, nomadic 6G nodes for rural health centers, portable telemedicine kits and secure patient data exchange protocols. Further, it increases accessibility to healthcare for elderly individuals, particularly in remote or underserved areas, reducing barriers to consistent and high-quality home care

(*continued*)

Table 2. (*continued*)

Social KVIs	Linked UN SDGs	Linkage with 6G-PATH project
Improved health outcomes	SDG 3-good health and well-being	UC-HEALTH 1—(3D hydrogel patches)—this remote service facilitated by 6G accelerates wound healing time compared to conventional dressings by using advanced, data-driven care methods UC-HEALTH 2-(elderly monitoring)-6G facilitated elderly monitoring service contributes to regular monitoring and guided workouts, helping to prevent and manage chronic conditions, improving overall physical health, mental well-being, and cognitive function. The KVEs such as integration of AI diagnostics with patient records over high-speed 6G links, automated follow-up systems and personalized treatment recommendation engines facilitate to achieve the KVIs
Reduced congestion	SDG 11-Sustainable cities and communities SDG 13-climate action	UC-CITIES 1—(connected and sensing city)—The KVEs such as 6G-connected traffic sensors, AI-powered traffic flow optimisation, vehicle-to-infrastructure (V2I) and low-latency communications help to reduce traffic congestion, providing smoother travel experiences that lead to lower stress levels, improved mental well-being, improved mobility and air quality

(*continued*)

Table 2. (*continued*)

Social KVIs	Linked UN SDGs	Linkage with 6G-PATH project
Technology adoption—(increased presence of 6G in agriculture sector)	SDG 2-zero hunger SDG 9-industry, innovation, and infrastructure	UC-FARM 1 (water saving) and UC-FARM 2 (smart vineyards)—conducting workshops and sharing 6G and smart agriculture knowledge with the public enhances the agricultural activities and innovation within the industry. This increases the accessibility of farmers to innovation and infrastructure facilities related to smart agriculture practices and also contributes to efficient and productive farming practices ensuring stable food supply to the market
Crime reduction	SDG 16-peace, justice and strong institutions	UC-CITIES 1—(connected and sensing city)—the KVEs, smart city IoT devices for predictive policing, blockchain-based incident reporting, high-definition 6G enabled body-worn cameras contribute to decreased crime rates through enhanced surveillance and faster response times enabled by real-time data from sensors and AI analytics, improving services like stolen vehicle detection and parking enforcement. Thus, automation and connected sensing cities contribute to reducing crimes by ensuring peace and justice

(*continued*)

Table 2. (*continued*)

Social KVIs	Linked UN SDGs	Linkage with 6G-PATH project
Bridging digital divide	SDG 4-quality education	UC-EDU-1 XR rural school—the XR-enabled educational content and learning platforms enabled by low-bandwidth rural deployment, satellite and 6G hybrid connectivity, community digital hubs such as Digitalia contribute to quality education for rural village students
Increased academic performance	SDG 4-quality education	UC-EDU-1 XR rural school—the XR-enabled educational content and learning platforms enabled by immersive XR learning environments, real-time feedback systems for students, AI-based adaptive learning tools over 6G contribute to deliver quality education
Improved digital literacy and skills development	SDG 4-quality education	UC-EDU-1 XR rural school—the XR-enabled educational content and learning platforms contribute to deliver quality education through improved digital skills

5.3 Environmental KVIs and SDGs Alignment

According to Environmental sustainability, there should be an ability to maintain ecological balance and preserve natural resources for both current and future generations. It involves using resources in a way that can be sustained indefinitely, ensuring that current needs are met without compromising the ability of future generations to meet their own needs. The environmental KVIs of the 6G-PATH project assess the impact of 6 the 6G-PATH project and its use cases on the environment, including water conservation, energy efficiency, soil health maintenance, contribution to climate resilience, waste reduction, carbon emission reduction, improved air quality, sustainable urban mobility, green spaces and biodiversity and conservation of natural resources etc. For each KVI, relevant KVEs have been identified to illustrate the concrete technical drivers that make these environmental outcomes possible. This explicit linkage also allows for more rigorous assessment of potential trade-offs such as energy demands of ultra-dense networks or e-waste from IoT proliferation, ensuring that both positive and negative environmental impacts are captured in the KVI evaluation process. These environmental KVIs of the 6G-PATH project can be mapped with UN SDGs as follows.

Table 3. Environmental KVIs and UN SDGs alignment.

Environmental KVIs	Linked UN SDGs	Linkage with 6G-PATH project
Water conservation	SDG 6-clean water and sanitation	UC-FARM 1, 2—farming UCs contribute to addressing global water wastage challenges. The IoT-enabled soil moisture sensors, AI-driven irrigation optimisation platforms, URLLC-based remote irrigation control, precision agricultural drones for water-use monitoring etc. contribute to minimize water wastage by evaluating the real-time water usage of trees and crops
Energy efficiency	SDG 7-affordable and clean energy	UC-FARM 1, 2—farming UCs contributes to efficient energy usage and reducing energy related operational costs. KVEs such as AI-powered energy management systems, 6G-enabled smart grids, real-time load balancing via edge computing, URLLC for energy control contribute to lower energy consumption by reducing the use of fuel-powered machines
	SDG 13-climate action	UC-FARM 1, 2—The advanced features of 6G help to develop adaptive strategies to mitigate the impact of climate change on cultivation, such as drought resistance testing and phenological monitoring, providing valuable data for growers and the public to ensure continued productivity in changing environmental conditions

(*continued*)

Table 3. (*continued*)

Environmental KVIs	Linked UN SDGs	Linkage with 6G-PATH project
Increased soil health maintenance	SDG 2-zero hunger	UC-FARM 1, 2—the KVEs mentioned above contribute to ensuring optimal soil health and fertility and long-term soil conservation through timely monitoring and interventions which ultimately contributes to quality yield
Waste reduction	SDG 12-responsible consumption and production	UC HEALTH 2—(elderly monitoring) remote elderly monitoring service facilitated by 6G contributes to reduced medical waste by minimizing unnecessary hospital admissions and treatments, and reducing the usage of disposable medical supplies, as monitoring and care can be managed effectively through remote solutions UC-CITIES-2—(automated logistics)—6G solutions facilitate minimizing waste generated during logistics processes through precise inventory management and automation (Ex, decrease in damaged goods and packaging waste due to the careful handling and transport of items by AGVs) These increase responsible consumption of technology

(*continued*)

Table 3. (*continued*)

Environmental KVIs	Linked UN SDGs	Linkage with 6G-PATH project
Reduction in carbon emissions	SDG 13-climate action	UC-CITIES-1—(connected and sensing city)—improved 6G solutions contribute to the reduction in greenhouse gas emissions by optimizing traffic management and increasing the use of autonomous and electric vehicles, leading to fewer emissions and more efficient transport systems UC CITIES 2—(logistic operations)—6G solutions facilitate the decrease in the carbon emissions of the logistics operation through optimizing logistics routes and reducing idle times compared to 5G solutions
Improved air quality	SDG 11-sustainable cities and communities	UC-CITIES-1 (connected and sensing city)—initiatives taken by smart cities use cases in improving environmental conditions in urban settings by reducing traffic and using dense IoT air quality sensor networks, AI-based pollution forecasting and URLLC-enabled emergency air quality alerts sensors
Green spaces and biodiversity	SDG 15-life on land	UC-CITIES-1 (connected and sensing city)—urban planning facilitated by 6G under smart cities vertical of the project optimizes the development of green spaces, promoting biodiversity and aligning with SDG 15

(*continued*)

Table 3. (*continued*)

Environmental KVIs	Linked UN SDGs	Linkage with 6G-PATH project
Sustainable urban mobility	SDG 11-sustainable cities and communities	UC-CITIES-1 (connected and sensing city)—the KVEs such as 6G-connected autonomous public transport, AI-driven mobility-as-a-service (MaaS) platforms, and real-time shared vehicle optimisation systems enhances promoting the public transport with reduced traffic congestion aligning with sustainable cities

Based on the above KVI mapping with the UN SDGs, it can be identified that 6G-PATH project contributes to achieving 13 UN SDGs out of the 17 in the 2030 agenda (Fig. 3).

Fig. 3. UN SDGs contributed by 6G-PATH project. Ref: United Nations [9]

6 Sustainability Trade-Off Matrix

The previous sections of this paper examined the positive contributions of 6G-enabled use cases to the SDGs. In addition to the benefits, 6G technology may create upstream and downstream externalities as well, including increased energy demand, higher carbon emissions, greater e-waste, or a widened digital gap. To capture these interdependencies, we develop a Sustainability Trade-off Matrix that maps each 6G-PATH vertical's primary KVIs against both its positive sustainability impacts and its potential negative externalities. This framework explicitly links upstream and downstream effects and identifies mitigation strategies. This sustainability trade-off matrix supports more balanced decision-making and ensures that the proposed KVI-SDG framework reflects not only the opportunities of 6G but also the trade-offs that must be managed to achieve net-positive outcomes (Table 4).

Table 4. Sustainability trade-off matrix

Vertical with primary KVIs	Positive SDGs	Potential negative impact/trade-offs with SDGs	Possible mitigation strategies
Education vertical—KVIs-increased access and quality of education via XR	SDG 4 (quality education), SDG 10 (reduced Inequalities)	XR technology can lead to high energy consumption and e-waste This can negatively impact achieving SDG 7 (clean and affordable energy) via energy-intensive XR sessions, increase emissions; SDG 4 may be undermined and negatively impact SDG 10 (reduced inequalities) if access is unequal	6G-PATH aims to mitigate these risks by using shared community hubs, device pooling and using satellite-6G hybrid energy options to reach remote areas with lower local infrastructure footprint
Smart farming vertical KVIs-water conservation and resource efficiency	SDG 6 (clean water), SDG 2 (zero hunger), SDG 12 (responsible consumption)	Downstream impacts include device disposal, battery waste and maintenance travel emissions This can negatively impact achieving SDG 13 (Climate Action) as increased operational energy can lead to higher carbon emissions unless low-carbon electricity is used, and SDG 12 (responsible consumption and production), which can increase e-waste and material extraction	Technically, it is suggested to focus on low-power sensor design and energy harvesting using solar sensors. From the governance perspective, circular procurement can be suggested

(*continued*)

Table 4. (*continued*)

Vertical with primary KVIs	Positive SDGs	Potential negative impact/trade-offs with SDGs	Possible mitigation strategies
Health Vertical KVIs-improved public health and improved access to care	SDG 3 (good health and well-being), SDG 10 (reduced inequalities) and SDG 9 (industry, innovation)	This can impact negatively for achieving SDG 7—affordable and clean energy due to 6G-enabled hospitals running dense AI/IoT systems increase carbon footprint unless powered by renewables; SDG 12 (responsible consumption and production) due to short lifecycle of advanced medical IoT sensors and 6G hardware and SDG 16 (peace, justice, and strong institutions) as if governance and regulatory systems don't keep pace, health data breaches may undermine trust	In addressing these negativities, 6G-PATH focuses on deploying energy-efficient 6G network architecture and is committed to net-zero 6G infrastructure goals. Further, it is suggested to power data centres and hospital servers with renewables

(*continued*)

Table 4. *(continued)*

Vertical with primary KVIs	Positive SDGs	Potential negative impact/trade-offs with SDGs	Possible mitigation strategies
Smart city vertical KVIs-reduced congestion and transport emissions	SDG 11 (sustainable cities), SDG 13 (climate action)	This can negatively impact achieving SDG 7 (affordable and clean energy) as smart traffic grids and automated logistics hubs require constant data processing, possibly increasing electricity use. Further, SDG 12 (responsible consumption and production) will also be negatively impacted with increased e-waste from frequent upgrades to sensors, roadside units, and fleet electronics	In addressing these negativities, it is proposed to design energy-efficient IoT devices and base stations, and establish city-wide e-waste recovery programs for smart devices

7 Concluding Remarks

The ongoing climate change and social inequality issues have raised further attention of current societies to the societal and environmental challenges they face. In response, governments and organisations encourage sustainable development projects. Investors and consumers also significantly support the enterprises which are committed to sustainable development. However, defining policies and regulations across all the verticals has become difficult due to the diverse structures. On this ground, formalising KVs, KVIs, which represent societal aspects, KVEs, which represent technical aspects and measuring the contribution towards achieving sustainability is crucial.

This study is an effort towards developing a comprehensive KVI framework to measure sustainability through economic, social and environmental themes in the 6G PATH project. By embedding concrete technical enablers within the KVI framework, we have shown how emerging 6G capabilities spanning ultra-reliable low-latency communication, integrated sensing and communication, edge AI, and network slicing can serve as levers for achieving measurable sustainability outcomes. This framework will be applied to use cases in the project to evaluate the impact of 6G technologies in advancing UN SDGs across four verticals: health, smart cities, education and farming. The results of these evaluations will be reported in further studies during the next stages of the 6G PATH project.

However, while the integration of AI, quantum communication, and pervasive sensing in 6G opens new frontiers for sustainable development, it simultaneously introduces novel risks. These include vulnerabilities to ransomware and quantum-based attacks, increased potential for privacy violations in pervasive surveillance contexts such as smart cities, and systemic dependencies on infrastructures that may lack sufficient resilience against disruption. Addressing these risks demands the incorporation of security-by-design and ethics-by-design principles into 6G standards, as well as the expansion of sustainability assessment frameworks to include metrics for digital safety, trust, and responsible technology governance.

Therefore, future studies are recommended to attempt to adopt a dual-focus approach leveraging 6G's transformative capabilities, standardising KVIs by facilitating resource sharing and promoting innovation and inclusivity across verticals to accelerate sustainability goals, while systematically evaluating and mitigating its socio-technical risks.

Acknowledgments. This research work has been funded by the 6G-PATH project through the Smart Networks and Servies Joint Undertaking (SNS JU) and cofounded by the European Union (EU) under the EU Horizon Europe research and innovation programme (GA no. 101139172). The authors of this research work would like to acknowledge the contributions of 6G-PATH project partners.

Disclosure of Interests. The authors have no competing interests to declare that are relevant to the content of this article.

References

1. Alsabah, M., et al.: 6G wireless communications networks: a comprehensive survey. IEEE Access **9**, 148191–148243 (2021). https://doi.org/10.1109/access.2021.3124812
2. ITU, World Bank: Digital Regulation Platform (2025). https://digitalregulation.org/overview-of-6g-imt-2030/
3. ATIS: Green G: the path toward sustainable 6G—next G alliance (2022). https://nextgalliance.org/white_papers/green-g-the-path-towards-sustainable-6g/. Accessed 13 Feb 2025
4. Gohar, A., Nencioni, G.: The role of 5G technologies in a smart city: the case for intelligent transportation system. Sustainability **13**(9), 5188 (2021). https://doi.org/10.3390/su13095188
5. Fernandes, J., Rosa, L., Chochliouros, I.P., Cordeiro, L.: Paving the path to 6G: the 6G-PATH project's vision for advanced telecommunications' infrastructure and use cases. IEEE Fut. Netw. World Forum **12**, 11 (2024)
6. Hexa, X.I.I.: Environmental, societal and economical drivers and goals for 6G. HexaXII Proj. Deliver. **D1**, 1 (2023)
7. Matinmikko-Blue, M., Aalto, S., Asghar, M.I., Berndt, H., Chen, Y., Dixit, S., Jurva, R., Karppinen, P., Kekkonen, M., Kinnula, M., Kostakos, P., Lindberg, J., Mutafungwa, E., Ojutkangas, K., Rossi, E., Yrjölä, S., Öörni, A.: White Paper on 6G Drivers and the UN SDGs. 6G Flagship (2020). https://www.6gflagship.com/white-paper-on-6g-drivers-and-the-un-sdgs/. Accessed 13 Feb 2025
8. HEXA-X-II Deliverable D1.2: A holistic flagship towards the 6G network platform and system, to inspire digital transformation, for the world to act together in meeting needs in society and ecosystems with novel 6G services. Deliverable D1.2 6G use cases and requirements

(2024). https://hexa-x-ii.eu/wp-content/uploads/2024/01/Hexa-X-II_D1.2.pdf. Accessed 14 Feb 2025
9. United Nations: The 17 Sustainable Development Goals. United Nations (2024). https://sdgs.un.org/goals
10. European Commission: In Focus: Energy and Smart Cities. European Commission (2022). https://ec.europa.eu/info/news/focus-energy-and-smart-cities-2022-jul-04_en. Accessed 14 Feb 2025
11. Alliance for Telecommunications Industry Solutions (ATIS): Next G alliance report: 6G sustainability KPI assessment introduction and gap analysis. Next G Alliance, Alliance for Telecommunications Industry Solutions (ATIS), pp. 1–24 (2023). https://nextgalliance.org/white_papers/6g-sustainability-kpi-assessment-introduction-and-gap-analysis/. Accessed 14 Feb 2025
12. Wikström, G., et al.: Key value indicators: a framework for values-driven next-generation ICT solutions. Telecommun. Policy **21**, 102778 (2024). https://doi.org/10.1016/j.telpol.2024.102778
13. Selva, E., et al.: Towards a 6G embedding sustainability. Zenodo **53**, 655 (2023). https://doi.org/10.1109/iccworkshops57953.2023.10283655
14. Matinmikko-Blue, M., Yrjölä, S., Ahokangas, P., Ojutkangas, K., Rossi, E.: 6G and the UN SDGs: where is the connection? Wireless Person. Commun. **121**(2), 1339–1360 (2021). https://doi.org/10.1007/s11277-021-09058-y
15. 5G-IA: The 5G Infrastructure Association European Vision for the 6G Network Ecosystem (2021)
16. Soleymani, M., Roth-Mandutz, E.: 6G Energy Efficiency and Sustainability White Paper 6G Energy Efficiency and Sustainability (2023)
17. Chauhan, D., et al.: Balancing technological innovation and environmental sustainability: a lifecycle analysis of 6G wireless communication technology. Sustainability **16**(15), 6533 (2024). https://doi.org/10.3390/su16156533
18. Pokorny, L.J., Lyle, K., Tyler, M., Topolski, J.: Introducing a modified nominal group technique for issue identification. Am. J. Evaluat. **9**(2), 40–44 (1988). https://doi.org/10.1177/109821408800900205
19. Al-Falahy, N., Alani, O.Y.: Unveiling the impact: human exposure to non-ionizing radiation in the millimeter-wave band of sixth-generation wireless networks. Electronics **13**(2), 246 (2024). https://doi.org/10.3390/electronics13020246
20. Fellan, A., Daurembekova, A., Schotten, H.D.: Considerations on the EMF Exposure Relating to the Next Generation Non-Terrestrial Networks. Cornell University (2023). https://doi.org/10.48550/arxiv.2308.00658
21. Jain, V., Mitra, A., Paul, S.: Evaluating the environmental and health impacts of 6G deployment in India. Adv. Wireless Technol. Telecommun. Book Ser. **21**, 227–254 (2025)
22. Saeed, M.M., et al.: A comprehensive survey on 6G-security: physical connection and service layers. Discov. Internet Things **5**(1), 123 (2025). https://doi.org/10.1007/s43926-025-00123-7
23. Eiss, P.K., Pedersen, D.: Introduction: values of value. Cult. Anthropol. **17**(3), 283–290 (2002). https://doi.org/10.1525/can.2002.17.3.283
24. SNS JU: Project Portfolio—SNS JU. SNS JU. https://smart-networks.europa.eu/project-portfolio/. Accessed 14 Feb 2025
25. Søndergaard, E., Ertmann, R.K., Reventlow, S., Lykke, K.: Using a modified nominal group technique to develop general practice. BMC Fam. Pract. **19**(1), 811 (2018). https://doi.org/10.1186/s12875-018-0811-9
26. Humphrey-Murto, S., et al.: The use of the delphi and other consensus group methods in medical education research. Acad. Med. **92**(10), 1491–1498 (2017). https://doi.org/10.1097/acm.0000000000001812

27. McMillan, S.S., King, M., Tully, M.P.: How to use the nominal group and Delphi techniques. Int. J. Clin. Pharm. **38**(3), 257 (2016). https://doi.org/10.1007/s11096-016-0257-x
28. Al-Yateem, N., Mottershead, R., Ahmad, F.R., Subu, M.A.: A reflection on the use of virtual nominal group technique in health policy and research priority consensus studies. Nurse Res. **32**(3), 35–41 (2024). https://doi.org/10.7748/nr.2024.e1933
29. Ridzuan, F., Rao, L., Wahab, A., Dasor, M.M., Mokhtar, N.: Enabling virtual learning for biomechanics of tooth movement: a modified nominal group technique. Dent. J. **11**(2), 53 (2023). https://doi.org/10.3390/dj11020053
30. European Commission: 2050 Long-Term Strategy (2024). https://climate.ec.europa.eu/eu-action/climate-strategies-targets/2050-long-term-strategy_en
31. Matinmikko-Blue, M., Yrjölä, S., Ahokangas, P.: Multi-perspective approach for developing sustainable 6G mobile communications. Telecommun. Policy **24**, 102640 (2023). https://doi.org/10.1016/j.telpol.2023.102640
32. TrialsNet-Horizon-JU-SNS: Open Call-TrialsNet Framework and KPIs/KVIs Overview TrialsNet: TRials Supported by Smart Networks Beyond 5G (2022). https://trialsnet.eu/assets/pdf/TrialsNet_Open_Call_TrialsNet_framework_and_KPIs-KVIs_overview.pdf. Accessed 17 Feb 2025
33. UNDESA: Indicators of Sustainable Development: Guidelines and Methodologies, 3rd edn. Department of Economic and Social Affairs (2025). https://sdgs.un.org/publications/indicators-sustainable-development-guidelines-and-methodologies-3rd-edition-16988?utm_source=chatgpt.com. Accessed 14 Feb 2025
34. Uusitalo, M.A., et al.: 6G vision, value, use cases and technologies from European 6G flagship project hexa-X. IEEE Access **9**, 160004–160020 (2021). https://doi.org/10.1109/ACCESS.2021.3130030
35. Wikström, G., et al.: What societal values will 6G address? Zenodo **55**, 534 (2022). https://doi.org/10.5281/zenodo.6557534

Digital Transformation: Participatory, Platform-Native, and Youth-Focused Models in Journalism

Dipannita Das and Ashwani Kumar Upadhyay(✉)

Symbiosis Institute of Media and Communication (SIMC), Symbiosis International (Deemed University), Pune, India
ashwani.upadhyay@simc.edu

Abstract. Technology-driven media and the integration of artificial intelligence (AI) in newsrooms have revolutionized journalism, and this technological disruption has witnessed the consumption patterns shift from print to digital media. Digital transformation, changing audience preferences, and economic pressures have led to a growing disconnect between legacy print media and news consumption in India. This study employs the socio-technical systems as a framework to explore the significance of social and technical factors redefining journalism, analyse the transformation, and how it adapts to new technology. To further address this gap between traditional news media and its audience, this study uses the DESTINY strategy in journalism, which refers to digital, engagement, storytelling, time, innovation, network, and yield as its components. This paper will integrate document analysis and 19 in-depth interviews of journalists, editors, and technologists from eight news organizations to analyse this disconnect and provide recommendations to guide the industry in identifying best practices, valuable strategies, and pathways to efficiency and innovation. The DESTINY strategy provides a strategic roadmap that can be developed for the news industry to adapt to audiences' digital-first consumption patterns.

Keywords: Journalism · Audience · Technology · Artificial intelligence (AI)

1 Introduction

The news media sector globally has seen an economic downturn and heightened competitiveness in recent decades due to the digital change (Ihlebæk and Figenschou 2023). The traditional news outlets struggle to engage a large segment of the population in most nations due to stagnant digital subscriptions, poor trust, and diminishing participation (Newman 2025a). Market forces are a significant factor in consumer orientation. News journalists feel more pressure to draw in audiences when traditional news media worldwide are experiencing declining audience shares and advertising revenue. As a result, they are beginning to view a consumer role orientation as becoming more significant (Hanusch and Tandoc 2017).

Published by Springer Nature Switzerland AG 2026
A. Elbanna et al. (Eds.): TDIT 2025, IFIP AICT 778, pp. 285–304, 2026.
https://doi.org/10.1007/978-3-032-16775-0_18

Recently, there has been a significant shift in the local media ecology. The media landscape has changed from a regional to a hyperlocal level in many nations and media environments, leading to new media models, similar development patterns, audience engagement strategies, and shared issues. Particular focus is on how the media try to create proximity with their audiences through their editorial models and the platforms and channels they set up for public engagement through collaborative relations (Negreira-Rey et al. 2024). Instead of adhering to the traditional approach, which has understood journalism's role as providing news that people need to know, journalists are becoming more focused on consumers and producing news that people want to know. Traditional journalistic positions have been altered with the evolution of the audience over time (Tandoc and Thomas 2014). This association has remained constant despite subsequent modifications. The journalists' principal aims are consistent with public expectations, including impartial reporting, analysis, and promoting tolerance and cultural variety (Loosen et al. 2020).

Print media has to face several threats with the emergence of digital technologies. Audience expectations from the news professionals are higher, making it all the more challenging (McQuail 2013). In addition, news professionals are adjusting to new actors like citizens, influencers, content marketers, and alternative media (Ihlebæk and Figenschou 2023). These new players have entered the journalism industry in previously unheard-of ways. These new actors—bloggers, digital start-ups, social media influencers, and viewers—are involved in news processes. These changes in the once-closely guarded journalism industry are putting its methods and, consequently, long-held ideas about the roles of mainstream journalists into question (Hanusch and Banjac 2018). The emergence of hostile alternative media deliberately seeks to undermine journalistic credibility by denouncing journalism as biased and dishonest (Ihlebæk and Figenschou 2023). On the same lines, Newman (2025a), in the Digital News Report 2025, states that institutional journalism's impact is further compromised by a growing trend toward consumption through platforms like social media and video. This shift also ignites a fragmented alternative media landscape with a diverse range of podcasters, YouTubers, and TikTokers.

Given the changing nature of journalism's relationship with its public, such an investigation is pertinent and compelling (Hanusch and Tandoc 2017), as it explores the power dynamics and sheds light on the processes of shift and transition in this field (Ihlebæk and Figenschou 2023). This study employs the socio-technical systems as a framework to analyze journalism's complexities and interconnected nature. When interpreting the changes that are taking place in journalism and developing future solutions and management strategies, the socio-technical approach is a compelling method (Fortunati and Sarrica 2010). Emphasizing the importance of innovation and collaboration, this theory outlines the need for continuous adaptation to technological changes and evolving audience expectations. Building on existing work, this study extends the analysis to address this gap between the legacy print media and the audience by employing the DESTINY strategy, which explores the media trends, consumer choices, and some of the use cases from Indian newsrooms. The strategy's various components enhance the news content's relevance and credibility. Moreover, it contributes to a more participatory media environment. Integrating these strategies into journalism training programs can equip news professionals with the necessary skills to engage the audience effectively. Policymakers and media decision-makers may consider these insights when developing standards to strengthen the evidence base for audience-centered journalism.

2 Theoretical Framework

2.1 Socio-Technical Systems Theory

The foundation of the socio-technical systems, first proposed in the late 1960s, observes that technical and social systems continually exist and function simultaneously in all industrial sectors. The overall outcome of system activity is dependent on the relationship between them. This approach challenges organization theory's technological determinism by contending that technology limits human behavior rather than firmly dictating results. The Tavistock Institute of Human Relations in Britain is credited with coining the phrase and believed that technology influences but does not determine human behavior. The technical workflow may include human interactions through thoughtful selection (Fortunati and Sarrica 2010).

Traditional theories for journalism are limited, but a socio-technical systems approach can provide new insights into human actors, audiences, and nonhuman actors in cross-media news production. This method acknowledges the increasing influence of technology tools and techniques on journalism (Lewis and Westlund 2014). Hence, the actor-network theory (ANT) is a valuable framework for exploring the socio-technical dimensions of journalism. As journalism is constantly evolving and impacted by technology, ANT is introduced to examine new actors in journalism and broaden the sociological perspective by including technology. It advocates for a shift in viewpoint that brings attention to technological innovations and integration in journalism, in contrast to human-centric perspectives that prevailed in journalism studies (Stalph 2019). According to Anderson and Kreiss (2013), ANT offers the conceptual framework and analytical tools to investigate how the social and technical domains are intricately intertwined and create complex socio-technical realities that influence power dynamics, practices, and comprehension in domains such as journalism and politics.

Similarly, the four primary tenets of the socio-technical perspective are open systems, dynamic stability, technical and social function optimization, and boundary control. The power dynamics between journalists, publishers, editors, and audiences are then examined using these analytical approaches (Fortunati and Sarrica 2010). Each component, the Four A's (actors, actants, audiences, and activities), within the framework of cross-media news reporting, emphasizes editorial, business, and technology as equally important areas to examine the organizational forces influencing journalism. As a comprehensive framework for understanding and researching the whole spectrum of players, actors, and viewers involved in cross-media news work activities, it advocates for developing a socio-technical emphasis for studying institutional news creation (Lewis and Westlund 2014).

Actors, objects, materials, relations, and mediation processes all interact to shape journalism's identity and potential. Journalism and other businesses have ever-changing infrastructures, and at times of change, infrastructural imaginaries are essential (Young and Hermida 2024). The evolving nature of human actors, nonhuman technological actors, and various audience representations—as well as the news production, distribution, and interpretation processes that involve the interrelationships of actors, nonhuman technological actors, and audiences—needs to be better conceptualized in modern journalism (Lewis and Westlund 2014). The collection, creation, and distribution of news in the modern day are all part of intricate socio-technical systems in which journalism and technology are closely related. Various computational artifacts and systems assist professionals like journalists and editors (Nishal and Diakopoulos 2025).

According to Schmidt and Lawrence (2020), taking into consideration the interaction between people and technology as well as the interaction between editorial, business, and technology in news organizations, Lewis and Westlund's socio-technical systems provide a framework for examining how journalism is changing as it adapts to such technologies. The socio-technical systems for newswork are shaped by domain-specific values. The designers may present their work to the public, media, and technology companies and weigh the particular value tensions that each partnership provides (Nishal and Diakopoulos 2025). Thus, by co-developing information goods and services for many platforms, technologists are mediating increasing cross-awareness and cooperation between the editorial and commercial sides. The socio-technical emphasis would also acknowledge this approach (Lewis and Westlund 2014).

In this study, socio-technical systems theory examines the interplay between social and technical elements within systems. It explores how technological advancements and social dynamics shape journalistic practices in this broader media landscape. It provides a holistic understanding of the complexities in this field. With evolving technology, collaboration, and innovation integrated in news media, this approach outlines the continuous adaptation to technological changes and audience expectations. Nonetheless, this framework points to the power dynamics in the media ecosystem and sheds light on the influence of various stakeholders on journalistic practices.

2.2 DESTINY Strategy

The DESTINY strategy provides a structured approach for digital engagement, storytelling, time, innovation, network, and yield. The DESTINY strategy has been proposed in the paper by Lim et al. (2025) and employed to fill in knowledge gaps in marketing theory and practice. This study applies this existing strategy drawn from marketing that can be extended to media research. This approach in journalism examines the impact and distribution of journalistic content.

Digital platforms use narrative and creativity, emphasizing increasing reach, engaging more deeply, creating meaningful relationships, and highlighting the shift from return on investment (ROI) to return on value (ROV). This well-coordinated approach seeks to apply academic knowledge in real-world contexts, encouraging teamwork that produces tangible results (Lim et al. 2025). The DESTINY approach provides a thorough framework that can be modified for journalism to enhance digital storytelling, engagement, creativity, and network development, eventually increasing the significance and influence of journalistic content.

It is contended that factors connected to the medium-specific legacy influence media adaptation more than structural distinctions between national media systems, because news organizations in a changing and uncertain environment try to replicate the strategies used by their competitors. To connect new audiences and create alternate revenue sources, traditional players frequently endure due to their reluctance to change—combining cost-cutting with investigating new digital news business models and funding a range of projects (Cornia et al. 2018). Nonetheless, this study draws upon the DESTINY approach to explore how news media can interact with audiences using creative and emotive storytelling, scheduling content, and establishing networks. Together, these elements can improve journalism's significance and efficacy in the digital era (Table 1).

Table 1. DESTINY strategy

Digital	• Digital formats • Digital platforms • Leveraging for speed, dynamic updates, and interaction
Engagement	• Interactive content • Participation mechanisms • Use of social media and comment sections
Storytelling	• Tailored content • Emotional connection • Relatable and impactful
Time	• Timing the release of content • Strategic communication intervals • Scheduling posts
Innovation	• Use multimedia elements (audio, video, interactive graphics, images) • New business models (paywall, personalized content) • Use of technology and AI tools
Network	• Include diverse stakeholders • Collaboration with academia, government, industry, and society
Yield	• Shift focus from ROI to ROV • Prioritize audience satisfaction and loyalty

3 Research Method

The two research questions are:

RQ1: How are legacy print organizations attempting to bridge the gap with their audiences through hybrid strategies?

RQ2: What innovations have been adopted in reconnecting print media with existing and disengaged audiences?

This exploratory study is based on 19 semi-structured and in-depth interviews conducted between December 2024 and June 2025 with journalists, editors, and the digital content team from eight Indian newspaper organizations. All the news professionals are from legacy print media and have over 10 years of experience. In-depth, semi-structured interviews allow participants to explore important issues. Researchers often use these interviews as a standalone method or in conjunction with other methods to investigate complex behaviors, opinions, and emotions and collect diverse experiences (Longhurst 2009). Although there is flexibility to modify the interview to follow the participant's direction, these interviews follow a predetermined list of topics and include prewritten questions and prompts (Thille et al. 2021).

All the traditional newspapers, both national and regional, have large readership bases and are long-established publishing houses contributing to the media landscape for decades. These organizations are often characterized by their print-first approach and have gradually transitioned into digital formats. The sample included six national-level news organizations and two regional-language newspapers. All the news organizations are print media. Out of the 19 interviewees, there are journalists (n = 8), editors (n = 7), and technologists (n = 4). In qualitative research, saturation is a key idea that denotes the point at which no new information or themes are revealed after the data collection has been explored. It guarantees results and makes the most of the data, accomplishing the study's goal (Naeem et al. 2024; Hennink et al. 2017). The saturation level was reached at 12 interviews, and further information was not provided that the researcher sought in this study.

The identity of the respondents was protected because of the non-disclosure contracts they signed with their organization. The respondents participated in the interview willingly and were not paid for it. The interviewees are all full-time employees of the newspapers. This study used a purposive sampling method that allowed us to select the interviewees based on their experience. The purposive technique relies heavily on the researcher's expertise, judgment, and intelligence and allows them more opportunities to perform and extract the best information from the samples (Oliver and Jupp 2006). The interviews were conducted in English in person, through Zoom meetings, or by telephone. The duration of the interviews ranged from 35 min to 1 h. It was recorded and transcribed verbatim.

Based on the research questions, an interview guide was employed to ensure consistency (Brewster et al. 2015). This discussion guide was developed after a thorough literature review, theoretical framework selection, and research question formulation. It mainly focused on how they plan stories for audience-centric storytelling, balance editorial judgement with engagement tendencies or analytics, use of analytics dashboards or audience metrics in decision-making, face challenges in adapting to audiences and mobile-first demands, use of AI-powered tools or automation in the storytelling process and their job role, editorial guidelines for mobile formats, and use cases that led to higher engagement or reach. This paper adopts a deductive approach design, which assesses theories that start with a well-established theory or generalization and look for evidence that the theory applies to a particular situation (Hyde 2000; Haque 2022). It aims to test theory-based notions and connections with empirical data (Haque 2022; Bucher 2021).

Data analysis is qualitative research's most challenging and important component (Basit 2003). In this study, three steps are involved in data analysis, as Pearse (2019) outlined. The codebook is used to analyze the gathered data. The codes have been updated and verified. Coding is essential to qualitative research (Parameswaran et al. 2019) and enables the researcher to interact and connect with the data to understand the emerging phenomena better and develop a theory based on the data (Basit 2003). The identification of themes was done next. Finding patterns in the data and relating the codes to one another yielded themes. A theme is a level of patterned response or meaning within a dataset (Braun and Clarke 2006). The dataset was compared with the competing frameworks using pattern matching at this stage. The themes are developed from the need to bridge the human, technological, and organizational dimensions of the newsroom, with the focus area on the gap in expectation and engagement with the audience. The emerging themes include: the organizational structure and culture, technological infrastructure and integration, audience expectation and engagement gap, content strategy and platformization, and labor processes and skills. Finally, the results are analyzed and documented.

4 Findings

Socio-technical systems theory perceives the disconnect between legacy print newsrooms and their audiences. This disparity is evident in this evolving media landscape because it conceptualizes organizations as complex systems composed of interdependent social (people, culture, processes) and technical (technology, tools, infrastructure) subsystems. Socio-technical systems posit that a misalignment or lack of integration between social and technical subsystems can lead to reduced organizational effectiveness and audience disconnect. This transition has profound implications for the print industry, affecting revenue streams, business models, and user involvement.

The various factors that lead to this gap are quite evident in the media landscape. Firstly, legacy print media grapples with the constant change among audiences rapidly moving to digital platforms and engaging with interactive, real-time, and multimedia content. Secondly, traditional newsrooms have organizational hierarchies and rigid structures that slow them to adapt to digital audience expectations. Thirdly, the audience shifts to digital as they find legacy brands less responsive to their needs and consumption patterns.

Accordingly, there has been a paradigm shift from the traditional approach to digital in the Indian newsroom. The Reuters Institute Digital News Report 2025 study reported that 39% of Indians obtained their news from print media, whilst 76% did so online, including social media. Despite the increasing popularity of online platforms, legacy news media in India continue to play a significant role. The audience continues to have a high degree of trust in legacy news sources. Their online editions rank among the top news websites, demonstrating how these traditional organizations have adapted to digital formats (Newman 2025a). The focus is heavily on audio and digital formats to reach the Gen Z audience. The evolving audiences have altered traditional journalistic roles (Tandoc and Thomas 2014). Actors in Indian digital newsrooms have profoundly transformed roles and workflows to connect with the digital-first and younger audiences in this evolving media landscape. The younger audiences are a crucial segment for Indian news media, as the population of India is among the youngest in the world. Nearly one in two Indians, comprising over 600 million people, are under 25 (Farcis 2025). This younger generation increasingly consumes news through mobile, video, and social media platforms. Thus, the implication is witnessed in the designing and developing for small-screen devices, visual-first and snackable news, distribution on messaging apps and social feeds, and engagement through instant polls, emoji reactions, and swipe features.

Hence, this study analyzes how various actors in Indian news media are adapting to this transition and opting for a user-focused approach. Newsrooms are adopting innovative technology and AI tools to reach out to audiences in this media ecosystem, which is more algorithmic and audience-informed gatekeeping. The journalistic actors work with non-journalistic actors, where the various news departments have blurred. The focus is creating experiences rather than merely pushing information with these creative technologies to enhance journalism. As a result of integrating social and technical elements, news organizations are navigating the challenges of the digital age and leveraging new technologies to improve their operations and audience engagement. In the following section, the DESTINY strategy, which focuses on organizational change and innovation approaches, outlines how newsroom actors adapt to this change, catering to audiences, especially mobile-first cultures, implications, and associated challenges.

4.1 Digital: Navigating the Digital Turn

It is no longer the linear flow of news (Kristensen 2021) in this digital media landscape. Digital formats enhance the impact and reach of journalism by addressing various barriers and leveraging modern tools and techniques. News media use liquid news designed to flow across multiple platforms, formats, and devices, adapting to audience behavior and contextual needs (Karlsson 2012). In India, people prefer to watch (40%) over reading (38%), followed by 23% who like to listen (Newman 2025a). Hence, most print media have a digital presence with e-papers, podcasts, YouTube summaries, and Instagram explainers. The respondents highlighted that the focus has shifted from physical formats to digital-first storytelling. Audiences now consume news on mobile, on iPad, through voice assistants, and in visually engaging formats. They prefer videos, podcast snippets, or carousel posts on Instagram.

Hence, news organizations have shifted to modify their operational frameworks and embrace multiplatform models due to the transformation of news consumption and content creation brought about by digitalization and new technologies. News organizations must adjust to new platforms to offer content in various ways (Vázquez-Herrero et al. 2020). Newsrooms create content in different formats for multiple channels—online, print, social media, YouTube, and podcasts. The Reuters Institute Digital News Report 2025 indicates that video-based platforms are still stronger and that consumption is becoming more fragmented. Facebook and YouTube were the only networks with a 10% or more weekly news reach ten years ago, compared to six current networks (Newman 2025a). Journalists' conceptions of their duties are influenced by their perceptions of what audiences want from them (Hanusch and Tandoc 2017). Aligning with this view, a data journalist with more than 11 years of experience with print media commented:

> We have Chartbeat, a real-time analytics platform that helps us understand how the audience engages with the content and what headlines drive the traffic. Accordingly, we can churn out and push for stories in different formats. We also have our SEO team to give us trending topics.

In the case of an article, most mobile readers like to interact with surveys, view videos, browse through headlines, and react to push notifications. The fact that many people never open the article suggests they were looking for something outside the conventional format. Some of these mobile-first formats that engage better than articles are threads, short vertical videos, annotated cards, Q&A explainers, visual timelines, community threads, live feeds, swipeable galleries, interactive polls, and push notification series (Scherer 2025).

4.2 Engagement: Redefining Audience Engagement

The feedback from the audience plays a significant role in the news media. Audience feedback tools, like reader comments, social media, and online analytics, make conveying such expectations to journalists simple and common practice (Hanusch and Tandoc 2017). The respondents underlined that the audiences want more than just news; they want to be more involved, interact, and engage in the digital ecosystem. Consequently, news media cater to two-way communication through comment sections, social polls, reader letters, citizen reporters, or live and text-based Q&A sessions.

Journalists deliver real-time news through messages, participate in real-time discussions, and respond live to major events. In addition to using other channels, media outlets have begun to offer news through WhatsApp. Consumers increasingly use smartphone messaging apps like WhatsApp for news (Boczek and Koppers 2019). In the Reuters Digital News Report 2025, the survey revealed that Indians are heavy users of multiple social networks. More likely to use YouTube (55%), WhatsApp (46%), and Instagram (37%) for news than many other countries. The heavy sharing culture of news is often via WhatsApp (69%) (Newman 2025a).

The subject of audience metrics in media organizations has advanced rapidly over the years. Technological advancements have enabled modern media organizations and journalists to comprehend media selection behaviors in novel and sophisticated ways, depending on exposure metrics like readership and circulation. As a result, while choosing and ranking journalistic information, journalists are frequently aggressively urged to consider the audience's needs. To improve news content, editors, analysts, and journalists at legacy media businesses often utilize analytics tools in their digital newsrooms. In addition, liquid news enables several user engagement features that can influence the settings and content of news items. Interactivity and user involvement in news production are another sub-feature of liquid news (Kristensen 2021). This is evident with breaking a single story into tweets, reels, carousels, or videos. The idea is to cater to audiences that support different platforms. A senior editor with more than 18 years of experience in both broadcast newsrooms and print media indicated that:

> We have to spend much time in case of a single story. As it is no longer linear storytelling, we use images, interactive elements, and multimedia elements in different formats for various platforms.

Engaged journalism techniques make meaningful audience involvement possible (Schmidt and Lawrence 2020). Looking at the latest trends, with news from various social networks, games, and entertainment applications vying for users' attention, competition on the lock screen is fiercer. For instance, one of the regional Indian newspaper organizations has developed a phygital product incorporating custom-built games in the print version. News organizations employ notifications even more strategically in this high-choice world to keep users interested without driving them to unsubscribe. In addition to wanting more relevant and personalized information, audiences don't want to lose out on significant local, national, and worldwide news (Newman 2025b). This is evident in the following comment by one of the respondents, who is a metro editor with more than 23 years of experience and has worked in multiple media organisations:

> Our organization has mobile applications that give highly personalized experiences to the audience. It delivers stories and appears at the top as the main headline related to the locality one resides in. As readers are more interested in local news.

The use of metrics can help to understand how the stories are received, but raises concern about the degree to which metrics should determine newsworthiness (Chua and Westlund 2019). In addition, the algorithmic feedback loop in the news media can impact user behavior, news consumption, and societal polarization by using social media as a platform for political information (Shmargad and Klar 2020). This can amplify certain types of content, potentially creating echo chambers (Khritankov 2023) and filter bubbles, keeping consumers intellectually isolated in their own informational bubble and restricting their exposure to other points of view (Song et al. 2016). An award-winning journalist and author, associated with print media for more than two decades, commented:

> Digital news stories are measured with pageviews and the number of likes. Thus, entertainment, crime, and trending stories top the chart. On the other hand, civic issues, policy and governance, development reporting, or farming community articles get fewer spontaneous clicks. It is a serious concern, as over-reliance on them can distort editorial priorities.

4.3 Storytelling: Narratives that Click

Television and print still play a significant role with older groups in India. Television and print remain much more important in India than in most other countries, according to the Digital News Report 2025. However, those under 45 years prefer social media and video networks, podcasts, and online news sites. Digital access points are growing for social media, video networks, and podcasts (Newman 2025a). Hence, Indian print media are working on narrative journalism involving characters, conflict, and emotional storytelling. There is no takeaway for dry news in the age of algorithmic content.

Journalists create immersive stories incorporating a narrative format, drawing users and increasing human connection with the story. Pulitzer Prize-winning stories examined from 1995 to 2011 reveal that the results of emotional storytelling are a significant component of the examined stories. Journalists outsource emotional work by reporting other people's feelings and using sources to discuss them (Wahl-Jorgensen 2012). The respondents in this study shared that they are experimenting with different formats to enhance engagement and storytelling that creates a more connected and satisfied audience. The multidisciplinary field of interactive digital storytelling (IDS) uses digital media to expand on traditional storytelling conventions and approaches. Adding interactive multimedia elements to conventional linear news stories has been the main emphasis of creating digital journalism, a significant storytelling field (Sizemore and Zhu 2011).

Digital technology has undoubtedly influenced journalism in various ways. Meanwhile, most of these initiatives incorporate multimedia content—such as pictures, animation, and video—as an adjunct to text. Text, the foundation of journalism, has essentially not altered (Sizemore and Zhu 2011). Journalists in this study have emphasized the challenge of working on a story in different formats as they are creating liquid content that is easily adaptable and can be shared across multiple platforms—print, web, mobile, social media, video, and podcasts. Reinforcing this point, an assistant editor with more than 15 years of experience in the news industry commented:

> Now you need to keep adding value and work on a particular story. For instance, first it goes as a headline push notification, followed by sending it online as a Twitter thread, reworking it for a social media post, having a short video reel, including it in a podcast segment, and for print media.

In this digital space, information consumption is becoming less formal and more vocal due to a generation of social media influencers. Traditional news media are losing influence and reach to alternative ecosystems, including YouTubers and podcasters. The recent Reuters Digital News Report 2025 stated that people are paying more attention to social and video platforms for political commentary, chat, and satire. Some of the news personalities who are quite popular include Dhruv Rathee (29 million followers), Ravish Kumar (14 million followers), Ranveer Allahbadia (11 million followers), and Akash Banerjee (5.7 million followers). Politicians are also building direct connections with huge followers, like Prime Minister of India Narendra Modi with 24 million followers on YouTube and technology entrepreneur Elon Musk with 220 million on X. This is the trend in India because of the growth of online video, and part of it is driven by less friction and lower bandwidth costs (Newman 2025a).

It was observed that the actors of the newsroom are aware that the audience is active and wants to interact and be more involved in specific social and environmental issues. A respondent reiterated that the users are more informed because of their active grassroots involvement and documents through the Right to Information (RTI) in some cases. Their quotes are given prominence in news stories. On similar lines, a senior executive with more than 18 years of experience in both audio-visual and print media noted (Table 2):

> The monopoly on controlling the information that journalists or newsrooms used to enjoy a few years ago no longer exists. Audiences are active and want to be more involved and engage with local incidents or issues. We cannot ignore the voices of audiences in our content.

Table 2. Liquid content conversion table

Content type	Potential repurposed formats	Suitable platforms
Breaking news	Video explainer, audio bulletin, Instagram carousel	Twitter/X, Instagram, YouTube Shorts
Long-form article	Podcast episode, YouTube explainer, infographic series	Website, LinkedIn, YouTube, Spotify,
Data story	Interactive visualization, scrollytelling, quiz/poll	Website, Instagram Stories, Interactive Apps
Video report	Short clip, GIF/meme, OTT mini-series	YouTube, Instagram Reels, OTT Platforms
Podcast	Article summary, video snippet, quote cards	Spotify, YouTube, Website
Social media post	Meme, news explainer reel, fact-check thread	Instagram, WhatsApp, Twitter/X
Infographic	Explainer video, web story, tweet thread	Instagram, Website, Twitter/X
Live event coverage	Highlight reel, podcast recap, newsletter	YouTube Live, Instagram Live, Email

4.4 Time: Timeliness and Tempo

In the digital media ecosystem, real-time reporting can add news value to a story and engage with the audience. In the study, the respondents have experimented with various ways, like live blogs, breaking news alerts, and push notifications, to make them more relevant and deliver them promptly to capture audience interest. In addition to wanting more relatable and personalized information, audiences do not want to lose out on significant local, national, and worldwide news. While some users are content to get alerts on lighter or more specialized news, others want breaking news (Newman 2025b).

For instance, an Indian national print media delivers political analysis on weekends. For another, it is data-driven infographics, op-eds, and podcasts on the weekend. Other newspapers publish real-time alerts on mobile apps and social platforms and include short clips, photo galleries, and opinion pieces throughout the day in timed intervals. The fast notification topics will include budgets, elections, or important incidents, followed by video explainers, expert columns, and WhatsApp summaries, are included in their coverage. On the other hand, regional newspapers cover more localized news stories and schedule print and digital media follow-ups. It updates tier-2 and tier-3 areas with real-time WhatsApp and app alerts. WhatsApp delivers important updates in local languages, followed by photo essays. The most critical component is the selection of stories, rethinking publication timing, and delivering content at the right time through various platforms. A senior journalist with more than 17 years of experience and associated with print media mentioned:

> Our coverage of important events or incidents gets published the next day. Our audience will not read the same content and have higher expectations from the organization. We add value and analysis that provides informed opinion about a particular issue, which you will not find on social media or television, as they are always in a hurry to report. In many newspapers, you will find the first cut of the story on the web and on their social media. The core aspect is that the publishing time of the newsroom must correspond with the real-world actions of users on digital platforms.

However, the responders in this study are conscious that user overload can cause notification fatigue, but it can also mislead the audience by being unclear and inaccurate (Guo et al. 2024). There is more news than ever before, delivered faster, in more formats, on more devices, and reaching more people because the internet has transformed news creation and consumption. But there are no set guidelines for creating alerts (Lugo-Ortiz and Rodríguez Sánchez 2022). News overload has detrimental cognitive and attitudinal effects on news. News curation services provide consumers suffering from an overabundance of news with filtered and arranged news content (Song et al. 2016). Notifications can benefit consumers but can be disruptive due to appearance, alert type, sender-recipient relationship, and job complexity. Even helpful or significant notifications can cause disruption (Mehrotra et al. 2016). The rise in smartphone usage has led to a surge in alerts, impacting consumers and producers of digital content, potentially causing reduced productivity, attention, and alert fatigue (Rizk et al. 2020).

4.5 Innovation: Journalistic Innovation in Tools, Formats, and Workflows

Quantifiable journalistic output and technological feasibility within the selected digital infrastructure are key factors in negotiations of news value, with newsworthiness in the digital newsroom being influenced by macro-level digital infrastructure (Kristensen 2021). The Indian newsroom is experimenting with AI tools and technology that can be integrated to streamline the journalistic work. Several AI tools are adopted for research, updates, personalized content, translation, fact-checking, and summarization of news stories. A chief technology officer with more than 12 years of experience in the field of journalism, and associated with the digital team of a newspaper, commented:

> Several print media organizations are using AI tools to summarize the stories. In our organization, we keep 80–100 words of copy that give the gist of the story. It targets readers who can quickly glance through the news updates.

The Reuters Digital News Report 2025 reported that the most significant interest shown by news media is in translating into different languages, summarizing articles, or turning them into audio or video. Audiences in India are increasingly using various formats to access news, including AI chatbots. Sometimes, consumers are not aware that they are consuming generative AI. This survey reported that 15% of India use a chatbot for news weekly, mainly educated and English-speaking audiences. According to users in India, there is a strong sense that AI can make the news more straightforward to understand and more trustworthy and accurate (Newman 2025a). Journalists and editors are considering stories and distribution tactics to access intermediary platforms. Expected reception encompasses algorithmic operations, audience behavior, and audience experience. News must be enjoyable, draw people to websites and social media, and promote subscriptions (Kristensen 2021). On AI tools integrated in the newsroom, a principal correspondent with 16 years of experience in both digital and print media noted:

> The use of AI tools has helped us understand the audience better. The feedback from the audience plays a significant role in the newsroom. Accordingly, the content is created, the adjustments related to the word limit are made, and the use of keywords is incorporated. It does not have much to do with commercial interest, but the fact is, as journalists, you should write what people want to read.

Automation in the newsroom brings along opportunities as well as constraints. The interview subjects are mindful of the potential pitfalls and strategic trade-offs in adopting AI in the newsroom. Automation integration in news production faces challenges, particularly in maintaining human judgment. Strong monitoring procedures are needed to sustain editorial authority while allowing journalists to manage algorithmic results. The emergence of generative AI complicates this process, as it is used in various media modalities (Nishal and Diakopoulos 2025). The news automation process is complex and sometimes difficult for news consumers to access, despite the numerous benefits for news organizations in creating creative news content. It undermines the fundamental journalistic ethic of transparency (Cools and Koliska 2024).

A few journalists expressed skepticism about artificial intelligence replacing jobs in the future due to the routine nature of journalism. To maintain professional authority, journalism must reinforce professional ideals through new algorithmic practices, reassess education and knowledge, and reclaim specialized work practice tasks (Møller et al. 2024). Beyond conventional job and labor precarities, the deskilling of journalism results in a new kind of uncertainty of practice that impacts journalistic quality (Quintanilha 2023). The interviews strongly suggest technological advancements are needed to overcome the various constraints in the newsroom, but ethical guidelines should be in place.

4.6 Network: Collaboration, Distribution, and Influence

Several print media outlets in India have collaborated with various stakeholders on projects that span social campaigns and educational partnerships. The partnership with society, NGOs, schools, municipalities, and industry has led to civic engagement and public service. This partnership has led to co-creating and amplifying the media content.

One such use case is print media's partnership with schools, NGOs, and corporate volunteers to teach underprivileged children. It motivated the educated public to volunteer for this campaign. It has been a successful campaign since 2008, reaching over 90,000 learners and mobilizing over 4500 teachers nationwide. Similarly, a regional newspaper undertook an initiative to support the central government's sanitation mission. It mobilized communities and created awareness through workshops and published success stories. It covered around 500 villages across four districts in the year 2015. Likewise, another national daily newspaper embarked on a program to enhance student awareness of current affairs and get them into reading habits in 2013. They partnered with the school and educational boards to distribute educational content that was especially curated for the school. It incorporated workshops and quizzes that were participated in by around 1200 schools across 11 cities. The other projects from traditional new media focus on areas like environment, water conservation, civic engagement, and funding for education.

This is a global issue of connecting with local communities and influencing initiatives. Journalism must be embedded in community conversations and is not isolated. The local news coverage crisis prompts policymakers and community activists to analyze socioeconomic and media factors that impact community definition and create new mechanisms to promote local news ecosystems (Weber and Mathews 2022).

4.7 Yield: Impact, Revenue, and Reach

Yield in print media is another crucial component that evaluates the impact, revenue generation, and reach in the digital age. However, the critical question arises on how to measure these factors and who will oversee them. In a market where intermediary players monetize, media organizations must declare their goal to negotiate the best audience measurement method and approach (Kristensen 2021). Despite the decline in advertising and subscriptions, news professionals still place a high value on the financial significance of their print products and consider that journalists need to understand companies' economic plans and explore new monetization strategies like paywalls and analytics for local journalism to survive (Jenkins and Nielsen 2020). Likewise, the Indian newsroom is thinking out of the box to increase traffic for subscribers and readers, boost revenue generation, and have a social presence. Several newsrooms have installed a paywall, integrated AI tools to speed up generating stories and assisting journalists, and made transitions in the business model. News professionals realize that the long-established business model does not work. However, they should also comprehend business strategies and the demands of local newsrooms to sustain themselves in the market and recognize the need for new monetization methods (Jenkins and Nielsen 2020). Newspapers invest in digital news to create successful operations and transform the industry (Cornia et al. 2018).

The respondents in this study highlighted that the print media is investing and focusing on digital transformation and community-driven news. The priority has shifted to digital content through different formats and channels. Revenue diversification has integrated launching events and conclaves, education portals, and branded content studios to diversify revenue beyond traditional advertising. News organizations are reassessing journalistic ideals and striking a balance between traditional and modern journalism. Organizations are pressured to define editorial ideals and goals when using analytics tactics. For example, they must decide if article clicks should determine news selection and ranking. Market-driven journalism is not always the result of audience measurement, even if it might be considered a step in that direction (Kristensen 2021).

Technological actors like algorithmic customization, behavioral monitoring, and authentication are essential in creating, disseminating, and consuming content. According to Lewis and Westlund (2014), positions in journalism concentrate on search engine optimization (SEO) and social media optimization (SMO), business metrics that gather large amounts of data to enhance return on investment (ROI), and interactive applications that change the audience's perspective from one of recipient to one of participant (Lewis and Westlund 2014). Apart from generating online content, the focus is on local stories or commentary and monetizing them as their unique selling proposition (USP). Local news can be pitched as a niche product to set itself apart in a competitive digital media landscape (Jenkins and Nielsen 2020). In much the same way, a deputy editor with 26 years of experience in the publishing industry remarked (Table 3):

> The native language media have a future for many years, as they have a loyal audience and can generate revenue compared to national media.

Table 3. Structural and strategic challenges of legacy print media

New actors in journalism	Audience-driven	Digital innovation
Alternative media, digital start-ups, and content marketers	News avoidance	AI tools integration and AI chatbots
News influencers and bloggers	Trust deficit	Technology in the newsroom
News podcasters and YouTubers	Polarization and misinformation	Automation concerns
Social media companies, social media, and video platforms	Notification fatigue Algorithmic feedback loop	Metrics-driven focus

5 Conclusion

The key finding of this study using the socio-technical systems framework reveals a disconnect between the legacy print media and its audience in India. The traditional news media strive to adapt to digital transformation and stay relevant in the digital era. The challenges lie in the legacy newsrooms' rigid structures and print-focused mindset, which make it complicated to shift to the changing expectations of digital audiences. Several newsrooms are taking a step ahead to work on their editorial strategies, prioritizing user orientation to boost engagement, widen their reach among the audience, and strengthen long-term viability. Our findings suggest that integrating AI summaries and algorithmic filters is not enough to report news stories; how they are narrated and shared plays a significant role. The user needs differ for different platforms; adapting to user-first strategies will give the news industry a deeper understanding of the audience. Adding to the previous research in this field, this study extends it further and addresses the disconnect between traditional news media and its user by introducing the DESTINY strategy that provides a strategic roadmap to adapt to a user-centric approach. This strategy examines the evolving media-audience relationship to improve relevance and user engagement. It is observed that the younger and more tech-savvy audiences choose the immediacy and interactivity of digital forms. In contrast, older generations and those with lower levels of digital literacy continue to rely on print media in India.

The relationship between newsrooms and digital platforms has significantly transformed the media landscape, affecting power dynamics at multiple levels. In line with Lasorsa et al. (2012), our study reveals that the news media actors adapt to fit into their preexisting routines, acquire skills, and negotiate with the established conventions. It further indicates that the future seems uncertain, raising the question of the sustainability and survival of traditional media houses in parallel with digital platforms. Similar to the findings of Negreira-Rey et al. (2024), this study emphasizes delivering hyperlocal news narratives and building a deeper relationship with communities. Local media have been expanding in smaller regions, and their presence is crucial for democratic, social, and participatory communication within the communities. Hence, it is critical to reemphasize the importance of community while resisting the financial drive (Tandoc and Thomas 2014). However, concerns arise when metrics are used solely to monitor engagement measures for business and transactional goals and not to establish community connections. In line with Vázquez-Herrero et al. (2020), Chua and Westlund (2019), and Schmidt and Lawrence (2020), this study underlines both the opportunities and threats related to integrating metrics in the newsroom. Online news sources have been adjusting to the shifting news convergence, which has led to integrating metrics in newsrooms and creating new roles and functions. This has resulted in engaging audiences on various platforms, defining newsworthiness, monetizing subscriptions and advertising, and relying on metrics for multimedia storytelling.

This study highlights several impediments to the Indian newsroom in the digital age. The platformized news environments challenge media function and transition in the media ecosystem. From a socio-technical viewpoint, a legacy newsroom integrating AI tools explores whether AI enhances journalism, depending on how journalists use technology, how the workflow is restructured, what values are upheld, and how management supports the transition. Similar to the earlier study by Nishal and Diakopoulos (2025), our findings indicate a need for balance in journalistic tools, public needs, and interactions between designers, technology providers, and platforms to ensure their decisions align with normative frameworks of journalism. It is imperative to have a mix of legal framework, ethical guidelines, and technological advancement. Traditional media can enhance its position in the news landscape by considering audience consumption patterns, adapting workflows, responsible use of AI, and fostering a supportive newsroom culture.

Funding and Acknowledgement. The authors did not receive any funding for this article's research, writing, and publishing.

Declaration of Interests. The authors declare no competing interests.

References

Anderson, C.W., Kreiss, D.: Black boxes as capacities for and constraints on action: electoral politics. J. Dev. Represent. Qual. Sociol. **36**(4), 365–382 (2013). https://doi.org/10.1007/s11133-013-9258-4

Basit, T.: Manual or electronic? The role of coding in qualitative data analysis. Educ. Res. **45**(2), 143–154 (2003). https://doi.org/10.1080/0013188032000133548

Boczek, K., Koppers, L.: What's new about Whatsapp for news? A mixed-method study on news outlets' strategies for using WhatsApp. Dig. J. **8**(1), 126–144 (2019). https://doi.org/10.1080/21670811.2019.1692685

Braun, V., Clarke, V.: Using thematic analysis in psychology. Qual. Res. Psychol. **3**(2), 77–101 (2006). https://doi.org/10.1191/1478088706qp063oa

Brewster, A.L., et al.: Integrating new practices: a qualitative study of how hospital innovations become routine. Implement. Sci. **10**(1), 357 (2015). https://doi.org/10.1186/s13012-015-0357-3

Bucher, J.: Inductive reasoning. Encycl. Res. Methods Criminol. Crim. Just. **12**, 200–204 (2021). https://doi.org/10.1002/9781119111931.ch36

Chua, S., Westlund, O.: Audience-centric engagement, collaboration culture and platform counterbalancing: a longitudinal study of ongoing sensemaking of emerging technologies. Media Commun. **7**(1), 153 (2019)

Cools, H., Koliska, M.: News automation and algorithmic transparency in the newsroom: the case of the Washington Post. J. Stud. **25**(6), 662–680 (2024). https://doi.org/10.1080/1461670x.2024.2326636

Cornia, A., et al.: Comparing legacy media responses to the changing business of news: cross-national similarities and differences across media types. Int. Commun. Gazette **15**, 174804851880864 (2018). https://doi.org/10.1177/1748048518808641

Farcis, S.: India's Youth: Hit Hard by the Pandemic (2025). https://unesdoc.unesco.org/ark:/48223/pf0000376731_eng

Fortunati, L., Sarrica, M.: The future of the press: insights from the sociotechnical approach. Inform. Soc. **26**(4), 247–255 (2010). https://doi.org/10.1080/01972243.2010.489500

Guo, Z., et al.: Push, overload, and exhaustion. Int. J. Cyber Behav. Psychol. Learn. **14**(1), 1–17 (2024). https://doi.org/10.4018/ijcbpl.362809

Hanusch, F., Banjac, S.: Studying role conceptions in the digital age. Routledge Handbook Develop. Dig. J. Stud. **16**, 28–39 (2018). https://doi.org/10.4324/9781315270449-3

Hanusch, F., Tandoc, E.C.: Comments, analytics, and social media: the impact of audience feedback on journalists' market orientation. Journalism **20**(6), 695–713 (2017). https://doi.org/10.1177/1464884917720305

Haque, M.S.: Inductive and/or deductive research designs. Princip. Soc. Res. Methodol. **1**(1), 59–71 (2022). https://doi.org/10.1007/978-981-19-5441-2_5

Hennink, M.M., et al.: Code saturation versus meaning saturation: how many interviews are enough? Qualit. Health Res. **27**(4), 591–608 (2017). https://doi.org/10.1177/1049732316665344

Hyde, K.F.: Recognising deductive processes in qualitative research. Qualit. Market Res. Int. J. **3**(2), 82–90 (2000). https://doi.org/10.1108/13522750010322089

Ihlebæk, K.A., Figenschou, T.U.: Journalism as a strategic action field: how to study contestations and power dynamics between professional journalism and its challengers. Dig. J. **16**, 1–18 (2023). https://doi.org/10.1080/21670811.2023.2214901

Jenkins, J., Nielsen, R.K.: Preservation and evolution: local newspapers as ambidextrous organizations. Journalism **15**, 146488491988642 (2020). https://doi.org/10.1177/1464884919886421

Karlsson, M.: Charting the liquidity of online news. Int. Commun. Gazette **74**(4), 385–402 (2012). https://doi.org/10.1177/1748048512439823

Khritankov, A.: Positive feedback loops lead to concept drift in machine learning systems. Appl. Intell. **53**(19), 22648–22666 (2023). https://doi.org/10.1007/s10489-023-04615-3

Kristensen, L.M.: Audience metrics: operationalizing news value for the digital newsroom. J. Pract. **16**, 1–18 (2021). https://doi.org/10.1080/17512786.2021.1954058

Lasorsa, D.L., et al.: Normalizing Twitter: journalism practice in an emerging communication space. J. Stud. **13**(1), 19–36 (2012). https://doi.org/10.1080/1461670x.2011.571825

Lewis, S.C., Westlund, O.: Actors, actants, audiences, and activities in cross-media news work. Dig. J. **3**(1), 19–37 (2014). https://doi.org/10.1080/21670811.2014.927986

Lim, W.M., et al.: How to bridge the communication gap between and within marketing theory and practice? The digital, engagement, storytelling, time, innovation, network, and yield (DESTINY) strategy. J. Glob. Market. **54**, 1–11 (2025). https://doi.org/10.1080/08911762.2025.2507483

Longhurst, R.: Interviews: in-depth, semi-structured. Int. Encycl. Hum. Geogr. **44**, 580–584 (2009). https://doi.org/10.1016/b978-008044910-4.00458-2

Loosen, W., et al.: What journalists want and what they ought to do (in)congruences between journalists' role conceptions and audiences' expectations. J. Stud. **21**(12), 1–31 (2020). https://doi.org/10.1080/1461670x.2020.1790026

Lugo-Ortiz, L., Rodríguez Sánchez, I.: Push-notifications as journalistic micro-narratives: language and professional practices. Anàlisi **66**, 25–44 (2022). https://doi.org/10.5565/rev/analisi.3465

McQuail, D.: Journalism and society. SAGE **16**, 21 (2013)

Mehrotra, A., et al.: My phone and me. In: Proceedings of the 2016 CHI Conference on Human Factors in Computing Systems (2016). https://doi.org/10.1145/2858036.2858566

Møller, L.A., et al.: Reinforce, readjust, reclaim: how artificial intelligence impacts journalism's professional claim. Journalism **26**, 1373–1390 (2024). https://doi.org/10.1177/14648849241269300

Naeem, M., et al.: Demystification and actualisation of data saturation in qualitative research through thematic analysis. Int. J. Qualit. Methods **23**, 23 (2024). https://doi.org/10.1177/16094069241229777

Negreira-Rey, M.-C., et al.: Studies in Big Data (2024). https://link.springer.com/bookseries/11970. Accessed 20 Sept 2024

Newman, N.: Overview and Key Findings of the 2025 Digital News Report (2025a). https://reutersinstitute.politics.ox.ac.uk/digital-news-report/2025/dnr-executive-summary

Newman, N.: Walking the Notification Tightrope: How to Engage Audiences While Avoiding Overload (2025b). https://reutersinstitute.politics.ox.ac.uk/digital-news-report/2025/walking-notification-tightrope-how-engage-audiences-while-avoiding. Accessed 01 June 2025

Nishal, S., Diakopoulos, N.: Values as problems, principles, and tensions in sociotechnical system design for journalism. In: Proceedings of the 2025 ACM Designing Interactive System Conference, pp. 2975–2991 (2025). https://doi.org/10.1145/3715336.3735717

Oliver, P., Jupp, V.: Purposive Sampling. Sage (2006)

Parameswaran, U.D., et al.: To live (code) or to not: a new method for coding in qualitative research. Qualit. Soc. Work **19**(4), 147332501984039 (2019). https://doi.org/10.1177/1473325019840394

Pearse, N.: An illustration of deductive analysis in qualitative research. Academic Conferences International Limited (2019). https://doi.org/10.34190/rm.19.006

Quintanilha, T.L.: Uma Nova Forma de Precariedade (da Prática)? A Descompetencialização Profissional no Centro do Sequestro da Qualidade no Jornalismo. Comunicação e sociedade **44**, e023019 (2023). https://doi.org/10.17231/comsoc.44(2023).4622

Rizk, Y., et al.: A Snooze-less User-Aware Notification System for Proactive Conversational Agents. Cornell University (2020). https://doi.org/10.48550/arxiv.2003.02097

Rodríguez-Vázquez, A.-I., et al.: Audiences first: professional profiles, tools and strategies of digital newsrooms to connect with the public. Stud. Big Data **14**, 211–226 (2022). https://doi.org/10.1007/978-3-030-88028-6_16

Scherer, H.: Formats that outperform the article on news apps. The Audiencers (2025). https://theaudiencers.com/when-the-article-is-no-longer-enough-formats-that-outperform-the-article-on-news-apps/#1-threads. Accessed 03 Aug 2025

Schmidt, T.R., Lawrence, R.G.: Engaged journalism and news work: a sociotechnical analysis of organizational dynamics and professional challenges. J. Pract. **14**(5), 518–536 (2020). https://doi.org/10.1080/17512786.2020.1731319

Shmargad, Y., Klar, S.: Sorting the news: how ranking by popularity polarizes our politics. Polit. Commun. **37**(3), 423–446 (2020). https://doi.org/10.1080/10584609.2020.1713267

Sizemore, J.H., Zhu, J.: Interactive non-fiction: towards a new approach for storytelling in digital journalism. Interact. Storytell. **24**, 313–316 (2011). https://doi.org/10.1007/978-3-642-25289-1_37

Song, H., et al.: Perceived news overload and its cognitive and attitudinal consequences for news usage in South Korea. J. Mass Commun. Quart. **94**(4), 1172–1190 (2016). https://doi.org/10.1177/1077699016679975

Stalph, F.: Hybrids, materiality, and black boxes: concepts of actor-network theory in data journalism research. Sociol. Compass **13**, 11 (2019). https://doi.org/10.1111/soc4.12738

Tandoc, E.C., Thomas, R.J.: The ethics of web analytics. Dig. J. **3**(2), 243–258 (2014). https://doi.org/10.1080/21670811.2014.909122

Thille, P.H., et al.: More than words: methods to elicit talk in interviews. Family Pract. **38**(4), 545–547 (2021). https://doi.org/10.1093/fampra/cmab043

Vázquez-Herrero, J., et al.: Journalistic Metamorphosis. Springer, Berlin (2020)

Wahl-Jorgensen, K.: The strategic ritual of emotionality: a case study of Pulitzer Prize-winning articles. J. Theory Pract. Crit. **14**(1), 129–145 (2012). https://doi.org/10.1177/1464884912448918

Weber, M.S., Mathews, N.: Explicating local: an audience-based framing of local community and local news. Dig. J. **16**, 1–20 (2022). https://doi.org/10.1080/21670811.2022.2142629

Young, M.L., Hermida, A.: Why infrastructure studies for journalism? Dig. J. **67**, 1–17 (2024). https://doi.org/10.1080/21670811.2024.2396551

Wearable Technology Digital Transformation: Analyzing Smartwatch Utilization for People in Indonesia

Jonathan William Widjaja(✉) and Christian

Bina Nusantara University, Jakarta, Indonesia
jonathanw7f@gmail.com

Abstract. The rapid growth of wearable technology has brought tremendous advances especially in smartwatch where people use them as health monitoring, productivity, and entertainment. Despite those rapid enhancements in smartwatch, there are still few research that covers the barriers and benefits of the utilization of smartwatch in developing countries like Indonesia. In this study, a quantitative approach was employed, with 209 respondents to examine the influence of 7 valuable factors which is timeliness, sufficiency, relevance, user satisfaction, perceived usefulness, perceived ease of use, and flow experience. The study's result reveals that five of these factors which is timeliness, sufficiency, relevance, flow experience, and perceived usefulness have significant impact on the utilization of smartwatch. However, perceived ease of use and user satisfaction doesn't have significant impact on the utilization of smartwatch. This is may be due to difficulty endured by the users on operating smartwatch. Also users are not satisfied with the data accuracy, comfort, and features of smartwatch.

Keywords: Digital transformation · Wearable technology · Smartwatch · TAM · Content richness · User satisfaction

1 Introduction

Digital Transformation (DX) is about adopting disruptive technologies to increase productivity, value creation, and the social welfare [1]. This means that the integration of digital technology is to improve procedures, efficiency, and customer experiences is known as digital transformation. This shift in technology has grown a lot as the result of the increase in internet smartphone usage, and many other factors which promotes digital technology. As a result various industries including software technology, healthcare, and many more are using digital technology to promote accessibility and growth from all over the world. One of the countries that was affected by digital transformation is Indonesia.

Because of those advances, wearable technology is one of many advances affected by digital transformation. Wearable technology itself is an electronic gadget designed to be used on the body [2]. Watches, bracelets, accessories, and glasses are a few of the

A. Elbanna et al. (Eds.): TDIT 2025, IFIP AICT 778, pp. 305–317, 2026.
https://doi.org/10.1007/978-3-032-16775-0_19

many designed wearable technologies. This technology itself can analyze, gather, and store data on the user's activity. The purpose of wearable technology is to increase user experience, provide convenience, and help users to organize various aspects of their lives [3].

Knowing the information above, the smartwatch is one of the wearable technologies that has recently been used in Indonesia. As many brands has arrived such as Apple, Samsung, Xiaomi, Huawei and many more. Smartwatch is a gadget that allows the users to access smartphone without touching it [4]. Smartwatch itself has gained popularity as many people use it on a daily basis because of the features that it provides. Those features itself is widely used by people for health monitoring, entertainment, and productivity.

As many research still focuses on developed countries like the United States, France, China, and South America few studies focus on developing countries these studies, most of those research is done in a country with high digital literacy, advanced digital infrastructure, and equitable access to technology [5]. However, the conditions are different for developing countries like Indonesia, where digital transformation are currently still growing, and there are still gaps in technology access and user's readiness to adopt technologies. This difference shows how important to explore how users in developing countries like Indonesia use wearable technology, because the way they use and accept technology is likely to be different from developed countries.

Therefore, although smartwatch popularity has increased in recent years, only a few studies that explored the challenges and obstacles faced by smartwatch users in Indonesia. As one of the highest digital-economic growth in Southeast Asia, Indonesia has a unique and under-researched context to understand wearable technology adoption. From this gap, this study aims to analyze the utilization of smartwatches in Indonesia.

2 Literature Review

2.1 Content Richness

Content richness has 3 main points which is sufficiency, timeliness, and relevance [6]. Sufficiency or adequacy in content richness reflects to the diverse information that's given to the users. Timeliness is crucial since outdated information loses its value [7, 8]. That being so, technology information is viewed as time-critical [9]. Relevance of the information shown plays an important role, as content richness itself is considered suitable when the information provided fulfills the user's needs [10]. Some previous studies has explored that there are relationships between PU and content richness [11, 12]. Technology itself is considered to have high quality content when it successfully fulfils the user's needs.

2.2 User Satisfaction

In general, satisfaction is the mind state in which the user's emotion is connected with their expectation regarding to past experiences. The level of technology used positively or negatively decides how satisfied the users are. Technology triggers both extrinsic or intrinsic motivation in users find it easily used (ease to use), beneficial, and productive.

From there, the user's expectations are set on their own confidence and inventiveness [13–15]. This implies that the expectations of the users are met, because they are satisfied. Not only that, but another key factor in the adoption of a service is user satisfaction. Researchers suggest that one of the key factors that influence technology's long-term use is linked between the user's satisfaction and ongoing intention to use the technology [14, 16, 17]. When talking about wearable technology, especially smartwatches, user satisfaction is made by overall usability, the perceived ease of use, and the ability to meet personal expectations [18]. So, from there the positive user experience will result in powerful engagement and trust, which will strengthen the continuation into daily life.

2.3 TAM Model

TAM model a verifiable model used to foresee and understand the adoption of new information technologies. The TAM model is used universally by numerous studies to explore technology's adoption [19, 20]. For this study, the TAM model will be used regarding smartwatches. There are two variables which is perceived usefulness and ease of use. Perceived usefulness implies to the view point of user when they find the technology useful. As for ease of use, it is to know what level of comfort that the technology offer in the user's standpoint [21, 22]. So, from there when applying TAM Model, it helps this research to understand how user satisfaction influences the sustained utilization of smartwatches in Indonesia.

2.4 Flow Theory

Lately, IT Systems like Flow is indicated by a feeling of judgement, enjoyment, and control. Users is expected to use technology in a daily basis when they have realize and believe that technology has the most enjoyment. So from there, a variation of positive elements results in one experience of technology flow of technology through the engagement of behavioral repertoire, thoughts and attention [23–25]. As a result of time passes quickly in a form of flow, users can feel inspired. This means that the insolvent experiences, engaging, and pleasurable contribute continuously to interaction which creates an online steady flow [26, 27].

Some research has shown that the internet itself, e-learning, and online entertainment have started using flow experience. From there, it could be expressed in unself-conscious ways that technology is applicable [28]. Also based on recent research, flow experience can predict the technology's adoption. Recent studies also found out that ease of use and perceived enjoyment crucially impact smartwatch adoption. This means that it has aligned with the flow theory. So from there, making sure that the user experience is crucial when it comes to increasing the satisfaction and maximizing the long-term use of smartwatches in Indonesia.

2.5 User's Utilization of Smartwatch

User's utilization of smartwatch includes a variety of behaviours and interactions that's related to wearable technologies. Usage of smartwatch generally are receiving notifications, communicating with other people, recording data, and receiving advice during daily activities. User's typically use smartwatch to track fitness and fitness, extension from their smartphone, and fast information access [29]. Factors that influences the continuation of smartwatch adoption is driven by content richness, TAM, user satisfaction, and flow experience [30].

3 Methodology

3.1 Research Model

Based on the research model, this study proposes the following hypotheses (Fig. 1):

H1: Sufficiency (SUF) positively influences Perceived usefulness (PEU) in Utilization of Smartwatch (USW).

H2: Timeliness (TML) positively influences Perceived usefulness (PEU) in USW.

H3: Relevance (RLV) positively influences Perceived usefulness (PEU) in USW.

H4: User satisfaction (UST) positively influences in USW.

H5: Perceived usefulness (PEU) positively influences USW.

H6: Perceived ease of use (PUS) positively influences USW.

H7: Flow Experience (FEX) positively influences USW.

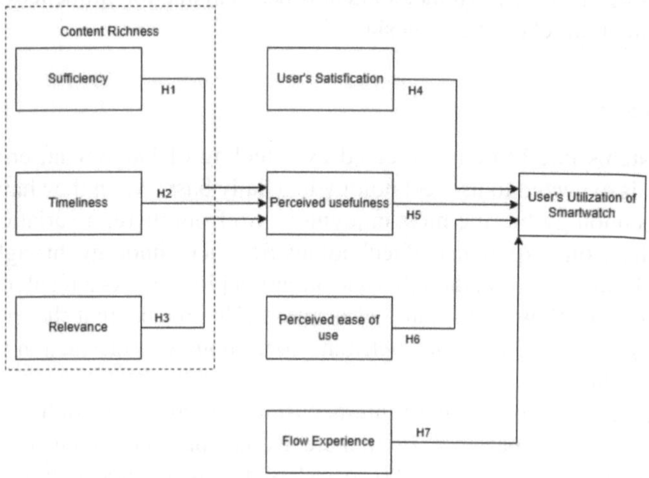

Fig. 1. Research model

3.2 Data Collection

This study collected data through an online questionnaire distributed via internet and social media platforms (Instagram, Line, WhatsApp, and TikTok) in Indonesia using Google Forms. The questionnaire was divided into two sections: the respondent's profile and the variables developed for the study (SUF, TML, RLV, UST, PEU, PUS, and FEX). Each variable was measured using a five-point Likert scale ranging from 1 (Strongly Disagree) to 5 (Strongly Agree).

3.3 Sampling Technique

The sampling method applied was random sampling. The questionnaire was distributed between March 11, 2025, and March 26, 2025. A total of 209 responses were collected from individuals who use smartwatches and reside in Indonesia. After data collection, the responses were validated using Smart PLS 4 software. Prior to conducting Structural Equation Modeling (SEM), the data underwent factor analysis, validity assessment, and quality proficiency testing to ensure the reliability and validity of the model.

4 Data Analysis and Result

4.1 Sample Demographic

Out of the total respondents, 86.6% reported using a smartwatch, while 13.4% indicated otherwise. The most commonly used smartwatch brands were Xiaomi Watch (27.5%), Apple Watch (26.9%), and Huawei Band (17%), followed by Imoo Watch Phone, Garmin Fenix, Realme Watch, and others.

Regarding the duration of smartwatch usage, the majority had been using a device for over 1 year (29.1%), followed by periods of 6 months to 1 year (23.6%) and 3–6 months (23.1%).

In terms of usage frequency, 42.9% of respondents used their smartwatch daily, with 33% using it two to five times per week.

As for usage objectives, the primary reasons included monitoring health and fitness (59.3%), using clock functions (54.4%), improving productivity and time management (45.6%), and receiving notifications (45.6%).

The demographic characteristics of the respondents, including Age, Gender, Education Background, and Domicile, are presented in Table 1.

From the total of 181 respondents (86.6%) that has used smartwatch, the number of valid respondents was trimmed to 124 because of issues on the convergent and discriminant validity. This trimming process was necessary because some of the items failed to fulfil the threshold value especially in the outer loadings. By excluding these responses, the final dataset guarantees a more accurate analysis that lines up with the Structural Equation Modelling(SEM) requirements.

Table 1. Sample demographic

Variables	Categories	Frequency	Percentage (%)
Age	21–25	115	63.2
	17–20	52	28.6
	>25	13	7.1
	<17	2	1.1
Gender	Male	88	48.4
	Female	94	51.6

(*continued*)

Table 1. (*continued*)

Variables	Categories	Frequency	Percentage (%)
Education background	Sarjana S1	125	68.7
	SMA	40	22
	SMK	11	6
	Diploma	4	2.2
	Sarjana S2	2	1.1
Domisile	Tangerang	50	27.5
	Jakarta	47	25.8
	Bekasi	18	9.9
	Bogor	17	9.3
	Others	50	27.5

4.2 Convergent Validity

Table 2 above presents 4 key measurements to evaluate the data which is the Outer Loading, Cronbach alpha, Composite Reliability, and AVE. First, Outer loading lies between 0.711 and 0.930 which is >0.7 suggesting that the reliability is good and exceeds the threshold [31]. Second, the Cronbach Alpha lies between 0.830 and 0.912 which exceeds the threshold of 0.7 [32]. Third, the composite reliability lies between 0.887 and 0.938 which exceeds the threshold of 0.7 [31]. Fourth, the AVE lies between 0.665 and 0.790 which exceeds the threshold of 0.5 [32].

Table 2. Convergent validity

Construct	Item	Outer loading	Cronbach alpha	Composite reliability (C)	AVE
Timeliness	TML1	0.895	0.894	0.926	0.758
	TML2	0.865			
	TML3	0.895			
	TML4	0.826			
Sufficiency	SUF1	0.930	0.885	0.921	0.745
	SUF2	0.840			
	SUF3	0.884			
	SUF4	0.794			
Relevance	RLV1	0.887	0.883	0.920	0.741
	RLV2	0.807			

(*continued*)

Table 2. (*continued*)

Construct	Item	Outer loading	Cronbach alpha	Composite reliability (C)	AVE
	RLV3	0.901			
	RLV4	0.846			
User satisfaction	UST1	0.771	0.886	0.922	0.747
	UST2	0.894			
	UST3	0.856			
	UST4	0.929			
Perceived usefulness	PEU1	0.910	0.912	0.938	0.790
	PEU2	0.825			
	PEU3	0.890			
	PEU4	0.770			
Perceived ease of use	PUS1	0.910	0.871	0.912	0.723
	PUS2	0.878			
	PUS3	0.900			
	PUS4	0.867			
Flow experience	FEX1	0.918	0.872	0.913	0.724
	FEX2	0.807			
	FEX3	0.837			
	FEX4	0.837			
User's utilization of smartwatch	USW1	0.891	0.830	0.887	0.665
	USW2	0.809			
	USW3	0.839			
	USW4	0.711			

The Outer Loading, Cronbach alpha, and Composite reliability results from the Table 2 shows that they exceeds the threshold value. This implies that the constructs are reliable and error free. Hence, the AVE also exceeds the threshold value. Which suggests that all of the constructs in this study pleased the convergent validity.

4.3 Discriminant Validity

Table 3 above presents the discriminant validity which measures the degree of variation between one of the research model components and others. To confirm that each model construct had a greater variance with its measurements than the variance between a specific construct and the other latent constructs in the research model, AVE was calculated as part of the study. The square root of all construct AVE has to be more that the threshold value which is 0.5 [33]. Hence, they also has to be more greater than the variance between construct and the residue of the mode construct. When an AVE of a construct exceeds 0.5, then at least the minimum of 50% of the measurement variance is described by the construct. The discriminate score was calculated using the PLS-SEM. Table 3 shows the cross loading and loading. The result shows that the cross loading and loading of the measured items has a higher loading bellow their latent constructs with other constructs [34].

Table 3. Discriminant validity

	FEX	PEU	PUS	RLV	SUF	TML	UST	USW
FEX1	**0.918**	0.843	0.731	0.807	0.788	0.785	0.815	0.771
FEX2	**0.807**	0.592	0.485	0.607	0.607	0.583	0.600	0.653
FEX3	**0.837**	0.760	0.752	0.732	0.738	0.755	0.747	0.679
FEX4	**0.837**	0.636	0.517	0.610	0.580	0.616	0.618	0.641
PEU1	0.746	**0.910**	0.703	0.846	0.849	0.797	0.796	0.784
PEU2	0.691	**0.825**	0.531	0.702	0.690	0.676	0.688	0.699
PEU3	0.764	**0.890**	0.761	0.772	0.801	0.803	0.811	0.770
PEU4	0.644	**0.770**	0.535	0.615	0.613	0.634	0.685	0.630
PUS1	0.696	0.747	**0.910**	0.697	0.729	0.763	0.782	0.666
PUS2	0.601	0.620	**0.878**	0.581	0.631	0.641	0.727	0.597
PUS3	0.676	0.703	**0.900**	0.671	0.740	0.716	0.734	0.630
PUS4	0.639	0.580	**0.867**	0.562	0.619	0.624	0.649	0.520
RLV1	0.749	0.803	0.634	**0.887**	0.823	0.825	0.772	0.758
RLV2	0.620	0.688	0.572	**0.807**	0.705	0.673	0.662	0.611
RLV3	0.763	0.787	0.640	**0.901**	0.788	0.779	0.772	0.725
RLV4	0.665	0.707	0.599	**0.846**	0.716	0.686	0.696	0.649
SUF1	0.753	0.835	0.744	0.840	**0.930**	0.852	0.837	0.773
SUF2	0.621	0.675	0.657	0.700	**0.840**	0.702	0.713	0.672
SUF3	0.727	0.838	0.735	0.811	**0.884**	0.787	0.756	0.738
SUF4	0.660	0.646	0.485	0.678	**0.794**	0.632	0.617	0.676
TML1	0.763	0.795	0.706	0.793	0.814	**0.895**	0.796	0.759
TML2	0.676	0.748	0.643	0.721	0.765	**0.865**	0.786	0.693
TML3	0.771	0.777	0.727	0.784	0.758	**0.895**	0.784	0.701
TML4	0.595	0.666	0.621	0.706	0.678	**0.826**	0.707	0.602
UST1	0.583	0.633	0.598	0.581	0.596	0.635	**0.771**	0.544
UST2	0.782	0.798	0.768	0.763	0.796	0.803	**0.894**	0.742
UST3	0.671	0.743	0.640	0.720	0.699	0.746	**0.856**	0.667
UST4	0.781	0.840	0.795	0.827	0.825	0.847	**0.929**	0.802
USW1	0.724	0.798	0.612	0.764	0.766	0.723	0.730	**0.891**

(continued)

Table 3. (*continued*)

	FEX	PEU	PUS	RLV	SUF	TML	UST	USW
USW2	0.645	0.627	0.474	0.561	0.587	0.566	0.603	**0.809**
USW3	0.677	0.762	0.637	0.746	0.777	0.721	0.697	**0.839**
USW4	0.584	0.558	0.488	0.498	0.545	0.556	0.589	**0.711**

4.4 Path Analysis

Table 4 and Fig. 2 above presents the result of the hypothesis testing. The T-Statistic evaluates if the path coefficient notably different than zero. Also, the *p*-Value shows the probability that the result that was observed happens only by chance [31]. Generally, the threshold of the *p*-value is below 0.05. Where the hypothesis with *p*-value below 0.05 is considerably accepted, and *p*-value above or equal to 0.05 is considerably rejected [31]. Figure 3 shows that H1, H2, H3, H5 and H7 are accepted because it's *p*-value is below 0.05 and H4 and H6 are rejected because the *p*-value is above 0.05. These findings shows that H1, H2, H3, H5 and H7 has statistically significant associations among the constructs. Hence, the findings above shows beneficial evidence that supports the theoretical structure that increases the comprehension about the relationship within the models.

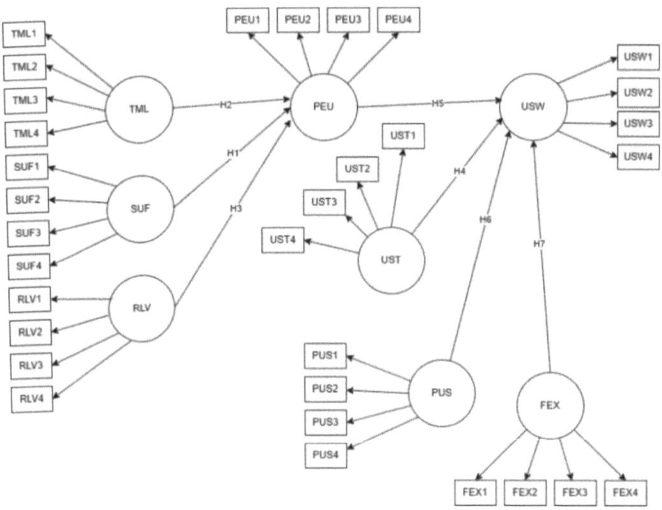

Fig. 2. Conceptual model

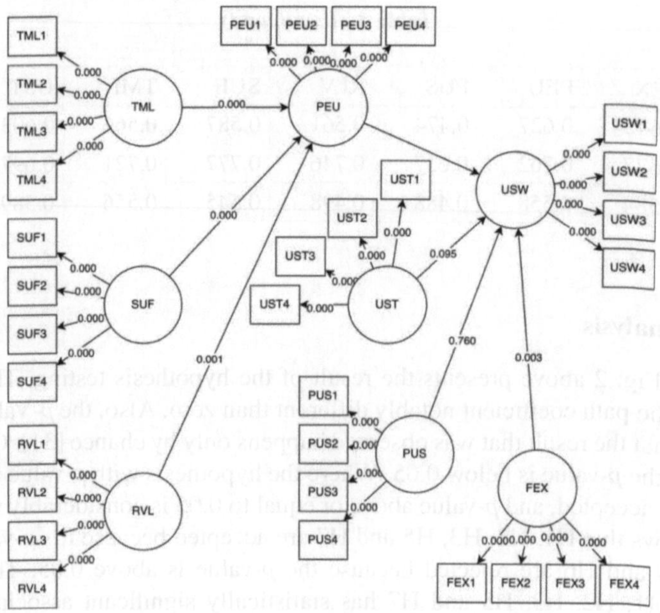

Fig. 3. Path analysis

Table 4. Path analysis table

	Path	Mean	ST-dev	T-statistic	*p*-value	Decision
H1	SUF > PEU	0.367	0.084	4.225	0.000	Accepted
H2	TML > PEU	0.276	0.072	3.912	0.000	Accepted
H3	RLV > PEU	0.306	0.090	3.464	0.001	Accepted
H4	UST > USW	0.175	0.104	1.669	0.095	Rejected
H5	PEU > USW	0,482	0.111	4.348	0.000	Accepted
H6	PUS > USW	0,029	0.100	0.306	0.760	Rejected
H7	FEX > USW	0.283	0.095	2.992	0.003	Accepted

5 Conclusion

Based on the research findings, it can be concluded that the key factors that influences the utilization of smartwatches are Timeliness, Sufficiency, Relevance, Flow Experience, and Perceived Usefulness. These factors significantly affect users when utilizing smartwatches in a positive way. Also, these factors align with the initial hypothesis given in this research. Timeliness assesses timely accuracy and advanced feature that smartwatch offers, whereas sufficiency makes sure that the information and function that's given fulfills the user needs comprehensively. Relevance shows that the various feature is in accordance with the hope and expectation of people in Indonesia. Flow experience measures the degree of involvement and users' emotional satisfaction when using smartwatch. Perceived usefulness shows how much practical usefulness that the user feels when using smartwatch. These 5 variables give a comprehensive representation in digital transformation of wearable technology in Indonesia.

However, the initial hypothesis in Perceived Ease of Use and User Satisfaction didn't affect significantly on the utilization of smartwatch. The reason why Perceived Ease of Use didn't affect significantly with Utilization of Smartwatch is because smartwatch users may feel that smartwatches are hard to use. In other words, smartwatch users needs effort to understand how to understand how to operate smartwatches. As for why User Satisfaction didn't affect significantly on Utilization of Smartwatch, it may be because smartwatch users are not satisfied with the data accuracy, feature, and comfort offered by the device. This dissatisfaction reduces the users motivation to use smartwatch regularly in their daily activities.

6 Limitation and Further Study

This study has several limitations that should be acknowledged. First, the sample size was small with 209 respondents which may limit the universality of findings. A larger sample size would provide stronger statistical power. Hence, it would reduce biases when interpreting data. Second, the demographic skew, as most respondents came from a specific geographic region, the lack of diversity may influence the result making the result less representative in a broader population.

Future studies should consider on increasing the sample size to improve the validity and reliability of the findings. Hence, a more balanced and diverse demographic representation is recommended to explore the cultural, age-related factors, and economic difference.

Acknowledgments. This study utilized Generative AI(GenAI) to improve the language throughout the text. This includes improving sentence clarity and formal writing. To ensure accuracy and academic integrity, all content that was generated from GenAI are carefully examined and edited. Data analysis, result interpretation and conclusions did not make use of GenAI. This research utilized these data [Respondent Data] that has been anonymized to protect respondents privacy and comply with research ethics. In terms of author contributions in this research, second author provides supervision as he gives reliable feedback and continuous guidance throughout this research process. This ensures that this study aligned with it's goals. As for first author, he was responsible on drafting every part of the manuscript ensuring the research stayed clear and consistent.

Disclosure of Interests. The authors have no competing interests to declare that are relevant to the content of this article.

References

1. Wang, L.: Digital transformation and total factor productivity. Financ. Res. Lett. **58**, 104338 (2023). https://doi.org/10.1016/j.frl.2023.104338
2. Kurniawati, E., Idris, I., Handayati, P., Osman, S.: Digital transformation of MSMEs in Indonesia during the pandemic. Entrep. Sustain. **9**, 316–331 (2021). https://doi.org/10.9770/jesi.2021.9.2(21)
3. Kibuuka, R., Extension, K.P.: The impact of wearable technology on health monitoring. Res. Invent. J. Public Health Pharm. **3**, 5–8 (2024)
4. Cheng, Q., et al.: Enhancing mobile interaction: practical insights from smartphone and smartwatch integration. In: Adjunct Proceedings of the 26th International Conference on Mobile Human-Computer Interaction, in MobileHCI '24 Adjunct. Association for Computing Machinery, New York (2024). https://doi.org/10.1145/3640471.3680451
5. Baudier, P., Ammi, C., Fosso-Wamba, S.: Differing perceptions of the smartwatch by users within developed countries. J. Glob. Inform. Manag. **28**, 101 (2020). https://doi.org/10.4018/JGIM.2020100101
6. Al-Maroof, R., Alhumaid, K., Alhamad, A.Q., Aburayya, A., Salloum, S.: User acceptance of smart watch for medical purposes: an empirical study. Fut. Internet **13**, 127 (2021). https://doi.org/10.3390/fi13050127
7. Suwarno, B., Dhewanto, W., Fajarindra-Belgiawan, P.: Evaluating service quality dimensions in social commerce: a semi-systematic literature review. Int. J. Appl. Bus. Res. **2024**(1), 21–47 (2024)
8. Desmal, A.J., Othman, M.K., Hamid, S., Zolait, A.: Exploring the information quality of mobile government services: a literature review. PeerJ Comput. Sci. **8**, e1028 (2022). https://doi.org/10.7717/peerj-cs.1028
9. Beierle, F., Dhakal, U., Cohrdes, C., Eicher, S., Pryss, R.: Public perception of the German COVID-19 contact-tracing app corona-warn-app. In: Proceedings of the 2021 IEEE 34th International Symposium on Computer-Based Medical Systems (CBMS), pp. 342–347 (2021). https://doi.org/10.1109/CBMS52027.2021.00031
10. Wardat, S., Akour, M.: Adoption of smart watches as wearable technology in TESOL education among university students. Smart Learn. Environ. **11**(1), 35 (2024). https://doi.org/10.1186/s40561-024-00323-8
11. Chidiac, D., Bowden, J.: When media matters: the role of media richness and naturalness on purchase intentions within influencer marketing. J. Strat. Market. **31**, 1–21 (2022). https://doi.org/10.1080/0965254X.2022.2062037
12. Suziana, A., Akbar, L.A.: Pengaruh content richness, perceived value dan social influence Terhadap Minat Berlangganan (Survey pada Pengguna Aplikasi Vidio di Kota Padang). Jurnal Ekonomika Dan Bisnis (JEBS) **4**(1), 79–93 (2024)
13. Gute, D., Schlögl, S., Groth, A.: Keep on running! An analysis of running tracking application features and their potential impact on recreational runner's intrinsic motivation. In: Kurosu, M. (ed.) Human-Computer Interaction. User Experience and Behavior, pp. 359–373. Springer, Cham (2022)
14. Al-Oraini, B.: Self-determination and intention to adopt massive open online courses (MOOC) for professional development. E-Learn. Dig. Media **21**, 20427530241256336 (2024). https://doi.org/10.1177/20427530241256338
15. Al-Zouba, A., Samikon, S.: The user motivation factors impact on immersive technology acceptance. Revista de Gestão Social e Ambiental **18**, e07072 (2024)
16. Sharabati, A.-A.A., Al-Haddad, S., Al-Khasawneh, M., Nababteh, N., Mohammad, M., Abu-Ghoush, Q.: The impact of TikTok user satisfaction on continuous intention to use the application. J. Open Innov. Technol. Market Compl. **8**(3), 125 (2022). https://doi.org/10.3390/joitmc8030125

17. Uzir, M.U.H., et al.: Applied artificial intelligence: acceptance-intention-purchase and satisfaction on smartwatch usage in a Ghanaian context. Heliyon **9**(8), e18666 (2023). https://doi.org/10.1016/j.heliyon.2023.e18666
18. Sahi, G., Shastri, L.B.: Fusing technology, style, and health: investigating factors driving continued use of smartwatches (2024)
19. Al-Maroof, R.A., Arpaci, I., Al-Emran, M., Salloum, S.A., Shaalan, K.: Examining the Acceptance of WhatsApp Stickers Through Machine Learning Algorithms. In: Al-Emran, M., Shaalan, K., Hassanien, A.E. (eds.) Recent Advances in Intelligent Systems and Smart Applications. SSDC, vol. 295, pp. 209–221. Springer, Cham (2021). https://doi.org/10.1007/978-3-030-47411-9_12
20. Al-Maroof, R.S., Salloum, S.A.: An integrated model of continuous intention to use of Google classroom. In: Al-Emran, M., Shaalan, K., Hassanien, A.E. (eds.) Recent Advances in Intelligent Systems and Smart Applications, pp. 311–335. Springer, Cham (2021)
21. Gündüz, N., Zaim, S., Erzurumlu, Y.: Investigating impact of health belief and trust on technology acceptance in smartwatch usage: Turkish senior adults case. Int. J. Pharm. Healthc. Mark. **18**, 102 (2024). https://doi.org/10.1108/IJPHM-11-2022-0102
22. Wang, Z., et al.: "Consumer acceptance of sports wearables: the role of products attributes. SAGE Open **13**, 653 (2023). https://doi.org/10.1177/21582440231182653
23. Chen, X., Wu, L., Jia, L., AlGerafi, M.: Flow experience and innovative behavior of university teachers: model development and empirical testing. Behav. Sci. **15**, 363 (2025). https://doi.org/10.3390/bs15030363
24. Arghashi, V., Yuksel, C.A.: Interactivity, inspiration, and perceived usefulness! How retailers' AR-apps improve consumer engagement through flow. J. Retail. Consum. Serv. **64**, 102756 (2022). https://doi.org/10.1016/j.jretconser.2021.102756
25. Chellappa, V.: Exploring students' intention to use a mobile application for learning construction ergonomics. Educ. Inf. Technol. **25**, 453 (2025). https://doi.org/10.1007/s10639-025-13453-4
26. Paschmann, J.W., Bruno, H.A., van Heerde, H.J., Völckner, F., Klein, K.: Driving mobile app user engagement through gamification. J. Market. Res. **62**(2), 249–273 (2024). https://doi.org/10.1177/00222437241275927
27. Zhao, H., Khan, A.: The students' flow experience with the continuous intention of using online English platforms. Front. Psychol. **12**, 7084 (2022). https://doi.org/10.3389/fpsyg.2021.807084
28. Liu, R., Yang, J., Yao, J.: How smartwatch use drives user reciprocity: the mediating effects of self-expansion and self-extension. Front. Psychol. **13**, 15274 (2022). https://doi.org/10.3389/fpsyg.2022.1041527
29. Oliveira, W., et al.: The effects of personalized gamification on students' flow experience, motivation, and enjoyment. Smart Learn. Environ. **9**(1), 16 (2022). https://doi.org/10.1186/s40561-022-00194-x
30. Almarzouqi, A., Aburayya, A., Salloum, S.A.: Determinants of intention to use medical smartwatch-based dual-stage SEM-ANN analysis. Inform. Med. Unlock. **28**, 100859 (2022). https://doi.org/10.1016/j.imu.2022.100859
31. Hair, J., Hult, G.T.M., Ringle, C., Sarstedt, M.: A Primer on Partial Least Squares Structural Equation Modeling (PLS-SEM) (2022)
32. Hair, J., Hollingsworth, C., Randolph, A., Chong, A.: An updated and expanded assessment of PLS-SEM in information systems research. Ind. Manag. Data Syst. **117**, 442–458 (2017). https://doi.org/10.1108/IMDS-04-2016-0130
33. Fornell, C., Larcker, D.F.: Evaluating structural equation models with unobservable variables and measurement error. J. Market. Res. **18**(1), 39–50 (1981). https://doi.org/10.2307/3151312
34. Cheng, T., Chen, C.: The impact of e-learning on workplace on-the-job training. Int. J. e-Educ. e-Bus. e-Manag. e-Learn. **12**, 212–228 (2015)

Author Index

Published by Springer Nature Switzerland AG 2026
A. Elbanna et al. (Eds.): TDIT 2025, IFIP AICT 778, pp. 319–320, 2026.
https://doi.org/10.1007/978-3-032-16775-0

MIX
Papier aus verantwortungsvollen Quellen
Paper from responsible sources
FSC® C105338

If you have any concerns about our products,
you can contact us on
ProductSafety@springernature.com

In case Publisher is established outside the EU,
the EU authorized representative is:
Springer Nature Customer Service Center GmbH
Europaplatz 3, 69115 Heidelberg, Germany

Printed by Libri Plureos GmbH
in Hamburg, Germany